Study Guide

for

Berk

Infants, Children, and Adolescents

Seventh Edition

prepared by

Amelia G. Benner

Kimberly Michaud

Laura E. Berk
Illinois State University

Allyn & Bacon

Boston Columbus Indianapolis New York San Francisco Upper Saddle River
Amsterdam Cape Town Dubai London Madrid Milan Munich Paris Montreal Toronto
Delhi Mexico City Sao Paulo Sydney Hong Kong Seoul Singapore Taipei Tokyo

10 9 8 7 6 5 4 3 2 1 14 13 12 11 10

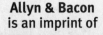

Allyn & Bacon
is an imprint of

PEARSON

www.pearsonhighered.com

ISBN-10: 0-205-01051-2
ISBN-13: 978-0-205-01051-6

CONTENTS

PREFACE

As you embark on the fascinating journey of studying human development, it is our hope that this Study Guide will help you master the material in your text, *Infants, Children, and Adolescents,* Seventh Edition, by Laura E. Berk. Our intention in preparing the Study Guide is to provide you with active practice in learning the content in your textbook and thought-provoking questions that help you clarify your own thinking. Each chapter in the Study Guide is organized into the following seven sections:

BRIEF CHAPTER SUMMARY

We begin with a brief summary of the material, mentioning major topics covered and general principles emphasized in text discussion. Each text chapter includes two additional summaries: an informal one at the beginning of the chapter, and a structured summary at the end of the chapter. Thus, the summary in the Study Guide will be your third review of the information covered in each chapter. It is intended to remind you of major points in the text before you embark on the remaining activities in the Study Guide.

LEARNING OBJECTIVES

We have organized the main points in each chapter into a series of objectives that indicate what you should be able to do once you have mastered the material. We suggest that you look over these objectives before you read each chapter. You may find it useful to take notes on information pertaining to the objectives as you read. When you finish a chapter, try to answer the objectives in a few sentences or a short paragraph. Then check your answers against the text and revise your responses accordingly. Once you have completed this exercise, you will have generated your own review of chapter content. Because it is written in your own words, it should serve as an especially useful chapter overview that can be referred to when you prepare for examinations.

STUDY QUESTIONS

The main body of each chapter consists of study questions, organized according to major headings in the textbook, that assist you in identifying main points and grasping concepts and principles. Text pages on which answers can be found are indicated next to each entry. The study questions section can be used in a number of different ways. You may find it helpful to answer each question as you read the chapter. Alternatively, try reading one or more sections and then testing yourself by answering the relevant study questions. Finally, use the study questions section as a device to review for examinations. If you work through it methodically, your retention of chapter material will be greatly enhanced.

ASK YOURSELF

In each chapter of the textbook, critical-thinking questions appear at the end of each major section. Four types of questions are included: Review questions, which assist with recall and comprehension of information in the text; Apply questions, which encourage application of your knowledge to controversial issues and problems; Connect questions, which help you to integrate what you have learned across age periods and aspects of development; and Reflect questions, which help make the study of child development personally meaningful by encouraging you to relate theory and research to your own life. In each chapter of the Study Guide, you will be asked to log in to the text's MyDevelopmentLab to access the Ask Yourself questions. Answering the questions will help you analyze important theoretical concepts and research findings. On the MyDevelopmentLab website, each question is page-referenced to chapter material that will help you formulate a response. Model answers are also provided.

SUGGESTED READINGS

A list of three to four suggested readings complements each text chapter. The readings have been carefully selected for their interest value and readability; the majority are recently published. A brief description of the content of each suggested reading is provided.

CROSSWORD PUZZLES

To help you master the central vocabulary of the field, we have provided crossword puzzles that test your knowledge of important terms and concepts. Answers can be found at the back of the Study Guide. If you cannot think of the term that matches a clue in the puzzles, your knowledge of information related to the term may be insecure. Reread the material in the text chapter related to each item that you miss. Also, try a more demanding approach to term mastery: After you have completed each puzzle, cover the clues and write your own definitions of each term.

PRACTICE TESTS

Once you have thoroughly studied each chapter, find out how well you know the material by taking the two multiple-choice practice tests. Then check your answers using the key at the back of the Study Guide. Each item is page-referenced to chapter content so you can look up answers to questions that you missed. If you answered more than a few items incorrectly, spend extra time rereading the chapter, writing responses to chapter objectives, and reviewing the study questions in this Study Guide.

Now that you understand how the Study Guide is organized, you are ready to begin using it to master *Infants, Children, and Adolescents.*

We wish you a rewarding and enjoyable course of study.

Amelia G. Benner
Kimberly Michaud
Laura E. Berk

STUDENT REGISTRATION & LOGIN

MyDevelopmentLab & MyDevelopmentLab CourseCompass

MyDevelopmentLab is a state-of-the-art, interactive, and instructive online solution for child and lifespan development. MyDevelopmentLab combines multimedia, tutorials, videos, simulations, animations, and tests to make teaching and learning fun. Below you will find instructions to register and access MyDevelopmentLab and MyDevelopmentLab CourseCompass. If you are not sure which access you will need, check with your instructor.

STUDENT REGISTRATION & LOGIN: MyDevelopmentLab
Refer to the following page for registration information for MyDevelopmentLab CourseCompass.

Before You Begin
To complete your registration and access MyDevelopmentLab, you will need:

- ☑ Your school zip code
- ☑ A MyDevelopmentLab student access code (packaged with your text or available for purchase at www.mydevelopmentlab.com)
- ☑ A valid email address
- ☑ Course ID (available from your instructor)

Registration

1. Enter **www.mydevelopmentlab.com** in your Web browser.
2. Under "Register or Buy Access," click **Students.**
3. Click the **MyDevelopmentLab** link.
4. If you have an access code, click **I already have an access code.**
   Click **It came with my textbook** or **I bought it separately from my textbook.**
   If you need to purchase access, click **I need to buy access.**
   Select **I want to buy MyDevelopmentLab WITH an E-book of my textbook** or **I want to buy MyDevelopmentLab WITHOUT E-book of my textbook.**
5. Select *Infants, Children, and Adolescents,* Seventh Edition (the title of your text).
6. After reading through the License Agreement and Privacy Policy, click "I Accept."
7. Do you have a Pearson Education account?
   a. If **Yes**—fill in your username and password.
   b. If **No**—Create a username and password per the guidelines provided.
   c. If **Not Sure**—Enter your email address and click **Search.**
8. Check or enter required information in the appropriate fields.

If successful, you will receive a **Confirmation Screen** with your information (this screen is also emailed to you).

Login and Accessing the Ask Yourself Questions

1. Enter **www.mydevelopmentlab.com** in your Web browser.
2. Under "Log In," click **MyDevelopmentLab.**
3. Select *Infants, Children, and Adolescents,* Seventh Edition (the title of your text).
4. Enter the **Login Name** and **Password** you created and click **Login.**
5. From the Table of Contents page, select the **Chapter** you wish to view.
6. Under **Chapter Topics,** select the **Topic** you wish to view. This **opens the E-Book** for that topic.
7. Next to the **Ask Yourself** box, select the **Explore** icon.
8. Complete questions and choose **Submit Answers for grading** or Clear answers to start over.

STUDENT REGISTRATION & LOGIN: MyDevelopmentLab CourseCompass

Before You Begin

To register for MyDevelopmentLab CourseCompass you will need:

- ☑ Course ID (available from your instructor)
- ☑ Your school zip code
- ☑ A MyDevelopmentLab CourseCompass student access code (packaged with your text)
- ☑ A valid email address

Registration

1. Enter **www.mydevelopmentlab.com** in your Web browser.
2. Under "Register or Buy Access," click **Students.**
3. Click the **MyDevelopmentLab CourseCompass** link.
4. Confirm that you have everything you need to register, then click **Next.**
5. Enter your **Course ID,** then click **Find Course.**
6. If you have a code, select the **Access Code** button. If you need to purchase access, click **Buy Now.**
7. After reading through the License Agreement and Privacy Policy, click "I Accept."
8. Do you have a Pearson Education account?
    - **a.** If **Yes**—fill in your username and password.
    - **b.** If **No**—Create a username and password per the guidelines provided.
    - **c.** If **Not Sure**—Enter your email address and click **Search.**
9. Check or enter required information in the appropriate fields.

If successful, you will receive a **Confirmation Screen** with your information (this screen is also emailed to you).

Login and Accessing the Ask Yourself Questions

1. Enter **www.mydevelopmentlab.com** in your Web browser.
2. Under "Log In," click **MyDevelopmentLab CourseCompass.**
3. Enter the **Login Name** and **Password** you created and click **Login.**
4. You will see your **Course** listed under **Courses.**
5. Click on this Course and select the **Chapter Contents** from the left navigation menu.
6. From the Table of Contents page, select your **chapter.**
7. Under **Chapter Topics,** select the Topic you wish to view. This opens the **E-Book** for that topic.
8. Next to the Ask Yourself box, select the **Explore** icon.
9. Complete questions and choose **Submit Answers for grading** or Clear answers to start over.

CHAPTER 1
HISTORY, THEORY, AND RESEARCH STRATEGIES

BRIEF CHAPTER SUMMARY

Child development is an area of study devoted to understanding constancy and change, from conception through adolescence. It is part of a larger, interdisciplinary field, developmental science, which looks at all changes throughout the lifespan. Research on child development has been stimulated both by scientific curiosity and by social pressures to improve children's lives. Researchers often divide development into three broad domains—physical, cognitive, and emotional and social. However, these domains are not really distinct; rather, they combine in an integrated, holistic fashion. Further, researchers usually divide the first two decades of life into five age periods. In addition, researchers identify the transition from adolescence to adulthood as a distinct period: emerging adulthood.

Theories are orderly, integrated ideas, based on scientific verification, that guide and give meaning to our observations and give us a basis for practical action. This chapter provides an overview of philosophical and theoretical approaches to child study, from medieval to modern times. It also reviews major research strategies used to study child behavior and development.

All major theories of child development take a stand on three basic issues: (1) Is development a continuous process, or is it discontinuous, following a series of distinct stages? (2) Does one general course of development characterize all children, or are there many possible courses, influenced by the distinct contexts in which children grow up? (3) Are genetic or environmental factors (nature or nurture) more important in development, and are individual differences stable or characterized by substantial plasticity? Recent theories take a balanced stand on these issues. Contemporary researchers realize that answers may vary across domains of development and even, as research on resilience illustrates, across individuals.

Research methods commonly used to study children include systematic observation; self-reports; the clinical, or case study, method; and ethnography. Investigators of child development may use a correlational research design, which shows a relationship but does not allow inferences about cause and effect. They may also use an experimental design, which permits cause-and-effect inferences. To study how participants change over time, investigators use special developmental research strategies, including longitudinal, cross-sectional, sequential, and microgenetic designs. Each method and each design has both strengths and limitations.

Conducting research with children poses special ethical dilemmas. Guidelines have been developed that can be used to determine if the benefits of research outweigh the risks, and to ensure that children's rights are protected.

LEARNING OBJECTIVES

After reading this chapter, you should be able to:

1.1 Explain the importance of the terms *applied* and *interdisciplinary* as they help to define the field of child development. (p. 4)

1.2 List the age periods researchers use to study child development, and cite the three domains in which development is often divided. (pp. 5–6)

1.3 Explain the role of theories in understanding child development, describe the three basic issues on which major theories take a stand, and explain the concepts of *plasticity* and *stability* in development. (pp. 7–9)

1.4 Trace historical influences on modern theories of child development, from medieval times through the early twentieth century. (pp. 11–14)

1.5 Describe the theoretical perspectives that influenced child development research in the mid-twentieth century, and cite the contributions and limitations of each. (pp. 14–21)

1.6 Summarize six recent theoretical perspectives of child development, noting the contributions of major theorists. (pp. 21–29)

1.7 Identify the stand that each modern theory takes on the three basic issues of child development presented earlier in this chapter. (pp. 29–30)

1.8 Describe the methods commonly used to study children, and cite the strengths and limitations of each. (pp. 30–35)

1.9 Contrast correlational and experimental research designs, and cite the strengths and limitations of each. (pp. 35, 37–39)

1.10 Describe research designs used to study development, noting the strengths and limitations of each. (pp. 40–43)

1.11 Discuss children's research rights, explain why research involving children raises special ethical concerns, describe how the concept of *informed consent* applies to child participants, and discuss the use of deception in research with children. (pp. 43, 45–46)

STUDY QUESTIONS

The Field of Child Development

1. True or False: Research on *child development* has been stimulated by both scientific curiosity and social pressures to better children's lives. (p. 4)

2. Child development is an interdisciplinary field. Explain what this means. (p. 4)

____

____

____

Domains of Development

1. List the three broad domains in which development is often divided. (p. 5)

   A. ______________________________

   B. ______________________________

   C. ______________________________

Periods of Development

1. List the six age periods used to segment the first two-and-a-half decades of life. (p. 6)

   A. ____________________ Age span: ____________________

   B. ____________________ Age span: ____________________

   C. ____________________ Age span: ____________________

   D. ____________________ Age span: ____________________

   E. ____________________ Age span: ____________________

   F. ____________________ Age span: ____________________

Basic Issues

1. What are the three elements of a good *theory*? (p. 7)

   A. ______________________________

   B. ______________________________

   C. ______________________________

2. Cite two reasons that theories are important to the study of child development. (p. 7)

   A. ______________________________

   B. ______________________________

3. Explain how theories differ from opinions. (p. 7)

   ____

   ____

   ____

Continuous or Discontinuous Development?

1. Describe the two views used to explain the course of development. (pp. 7–8)

   A. ______________________________

   ____

   B. ______________________________

   ____

2. The (*continuous* / *discontinuous*) perspective maintains the belief that development occurs in stages. Explain what this means. (p. 8)

   ____

   ____

One Course of Development or Many?

1. Explain how distinct *contexts* can influence child development. (p. 8)

   ____

   ____

   ____

2. Give an example of one personal and one environmental factor that shape the context of a child's development. (pp. 8–9)

   Personal: ______________________________

   ____

   Environmental: ______________________________

   ____

Relative Influence of Nature and Nurture?

1. Briefly discuss how nature and nurture can be used to explain the underlying causes of development. (p. 9)

   Nature: ______________________________

   ____

   Nurture: ______________________________

   ____

2. Describe how a theory's position on nature and nurture affects whether there is an emphasis on stability or change. (p. 9)

3. True or False: A theorist who stresses the plasticity of development would probably consider environment more influential than heredity. (p. 9)

A Balanced Point of View

1. True or False: Theorists today regard heredity and environment as interwoven, each affecting the potential of the other to modify the child's traits and capacities. (p. 9)

Biology and Environment: Resilient Children

1. Define *resilience,* and explain why researchers are increasingly interested in this concept. (p. 10)

   A.

   B.

2. List and briefly describe the four broad factors that appear to offer protection from the damaging effects of stressful life events. (pp. 10–11)

   A.

   B.

   C.

   D.

Historical Foundations

Medieval Times

1. In medieval times, childhood (was / was not) regarded as a distinct developmental period. Cite evidence to support your response. (pp. 11–12)

The Reformation

1. True or False: Puritan doctrine stressed the innate goodness of all children. Briefly explain your response. (p. 12)

2. True or False: The Puritans placed a high value on the development of reasoning in children. (p. 12)

Philosophies of the Enlightenment

1. During the Enlightenment, the British philosopher John Locke regarded the child as a *tabula rasa,* which means ________________________________. Explain his view. (p. 12)

____

____

____

2. Briefly summarize Locke's stance on each of the three basic issues of human development. (p. 12)

   Continuous or discontinuous development?

   ____

   ____

   One course of development or many?

   ____

   ____

   Relative influence of nature or nurture?

   ____

   ____

3. Explain Jean-Jacques Rousseau's view of children as noble savages. (p. 13)

____

____

____

4. In what ways did the theories of John Locke and Jean-Jacques Rousseau differ? (p. 13)

____

____

____

5. Cite two concepts included in Rousseau's theory that remain important to modern theories of child development. (p. 13)

   A. ____

   B. ____

Scientific Beginnings

1. Briefly describe the two principles emphasized in Darwin's theory of evolution. (p. 13)

   A. ____

   ____

   B. ____

   ____

2. Who is generally regarded as the founder of the child study movement? (p. 13)

____

3. The ________________________ *approach* to child development uses age-related averages to represent typical development. (p. 13)

4. Who constructed the first successful intelligence test, and what was it used for? (p. 14)

   A. ____

   B. ____

5. A translated version of this test was developed for use with English-speaking children. What is the name of this instrument? (p. 14)

   ____

Mid-Twentieth-Century Theories

The Psychoanalytic Perspective

1. Summarize the basic concepts of the *psychoanalytic perspective.* (p. 15)

   ____

   ____

   ____

2. Freud's ________________________ *theory* emphasized that how parents manage their child's sexual and aggressive drives in the first few years of life is crucial for healthy personality development. (p. 15)

3. Name and briefly describe the three components of personality outlined in Freud's theory. (p. 15)

   A. ____

   ____

   B. ____

   ____

   C. ____

   ____

4. Match each of the following stages of psychosexual development with the appropriate description. (p. 16)

_____	Stage in which sexual instincts die down	A. Oral
_____	Stage in which the infant desires sucking activities	B. Anal
_____	Stage in which the Oedipal and Electra conflicts take place	C. Phallic
_____	Stage marked by mature sexuality	D. Latency
_____	Stage in which toilet training becomes a major issue between parent and child	E. Genital

5. Cite one contribution and three limitations of Freud's theory. (p. 15)

   Contribution: ____

   ____

   Limitation: ____

   ____

   Limitation: ____

   ____

   Limitation: ____

   ____

6. In what ways did Erikson build upon and improve Freud's theory? (pp. 15–16)

____

____

____

____

7. Match each of Erikson's stages with the appropriate description. (p. 16)

_____ Successful resolution of this stage depends on the adult's success at caring for other people or productive work.
_____ The primary task of this stage is the development of a sense of self and a sense of one's place in society.
_____ Successful resolution of this stage depends on a warm, loving relationship with the caregiver.
_____ In this stage, children experiment with adult roles through make-believe play.
_____ Successful resolution of this stage depends on parents granting the child reasonable opportunities for free choice.
_____ Successful resolution of this stage involves reflecting on life's accomplishments.
_____ The development of close relationships with others helps ensure successful resolution of this stage.
_____ Children who develop the capacity for cooperation and productive work will successfully resolve this stage.

A. Basic trust vs. mistrust
B. Autonomy vs. shame and doubt
C. Initiative vs. guilt
D. Industry vs. inferiority
E. Identity vs. role confusion
F. Intimacy vs. isolation
G. Generativity vs. stagnation
H. Integrity vs. despair

8. Cite two contributions of psychoanalytic theory. (p. 16)

A. ____

B. ____

9. Discuss two reasons why psychoanalytic theory is no longer in the mainstream of child development research. (p. 17)

A. ____

____

B. ____

____

Behaviorism and Social Learning Theory

1. What two directly observable events are the focus of *behaviorism*? (p. 17)

A. ____

B. ____

2. True or False: Watson's study of little Albert, an 11-month-old baby who was taught to fear a white rat by associating it with a loud noise, supported Pavlov's concept of classical conditioning. (p. 17)

3. Summarize B. F. Skinner's operant conditioning theory. (p. 17)

____

____

____

4. Describe the concept of modeling, also known as imitation or observational learning, as emphasized in Bandura's *social learning theory.* (p. 18)

____

____

____

5. Summarize Bandura's revisions to his social learning theory, which stress the importance of cognition in the learning process. (p. 18)

____

____

____

6. Behaviorism and social learning theory have had a major applied impact on the field of child development through the introduction of *behavior modification.* Explain this technique. (p. 18)

____

____

____

7. Discuss two limitations of behaviorism and social learning theory. (pp. 18–19)

   A. ______________________________

   ____

   B. ______________________________

   ____

Piaget's Cognitive-Developmental Theory

1. True or False: Both Piaget's *cognitive-developmental theory* and behaviorism maintain that knowledge is imparted to children through the use of reinforcement. Briefly explain your response. (p. 19)

____

____

2. Describe Piaget's notions of adaptation and equilibrium. (p. 19)

   Adaptation: ______________________________

   ____

   Equilibrium: ______________________________

   ____

3. Match each of Piaget's stages with the appropriate description. (pp. 19–20)

_____ During this stage, thought becomes more complex, and children develop the capacity for abstract reasoning.
_____ This stage is characterized by the use of eyes, ears, hands, and mouth to explore the environment.
_____ During this stage, children use symbols and engage in make-believe play.
_____ This stage is marked by the development of logical, organized reasoning skills.

A. Sensorimotor
B. Preoperational
C. Concrete operational
D. Formal operational

4. What did Piaget use as his chief method for studying child and adolescent thought? (p. 20)

____

5. Discuss three lasting contributions of Piaget's theory. (p. 20)

   A. ______

   B. ______

   C. ______

6. Cite three recent challenges to Piaget's theory. (pp. 20–21)

   A. ______

   B. ______

   C. ______

Recent Theoretical Perspectives

Information Processing

1. Briefly describe the *information-processing* view of child development. (p. 21)

2. How are flowcharts used by information-processing researchers? (pp. 21–22)

3. In what basic way are information processing and Piaget's theory alike? In what basic way are they different? (p. 22)

   Alike: ______

   Different: ______

4. Cite one strength and two limitations of the information-processing approach. (pp. 22–23)

   Strength: ______

   Limitation: ______

   Limitation: ______

5. Briefly describe a new area of investigation, called *developmental cognitive neuroscience.* (p. 23)

6. List three areas in which developmental cognitive neuroscientists are making rapid progress in the field of child development. (p. 23)

   A.

   B.

   C.

Ethology and Evolutionary Developmental Psychology

1. What is the study of *ethology*? (p. 23)

2. Contrast the notion of a critical period with that of a *sensitive period.* (pp. 23–24)

   Critical period:

   Sensitive period:

3. Explain how John Bowlby used the principles of ethology to understand the infant–caregiver relationship. (p. 24)

4. Briefly explain the primary focus of *evolutionary developmental psychology.* (p. 24)

Vygotsky's Sociocultural Theory

1. Explain the importance of social interaction in Vygotsky's *sociocultural theory.* (pp. 24–25)

2. For each of the following statements, indicate whether it pertains to Piaget's theory (P), Vygotsky's theory (V) or both (B). (pp. 19–21, 24–25)
    _____ Adults and more expert peers help children to acquire the ways of thinking and behaving that make up a community's culture.
    _____ Children are active, constructive beings.
    _____ Cognitive development arises out of children's independent efforts to make sense of their world.
    _____ Biology strongly contributes to development.
    _____ Cognitive development is a socially mediated process.
    _____ Children undergo stagewise changes.
    _____ Children in every culture develop unique strengths.

3. Vygotsky's emphasis on culture and social experience led him to neglect ______________________________ contributions to development. (p. 25)

Ecological Systems Theory

1. Explain how Bronfenbrenner's *ecological systems theory* views development. (pp. 25–26)

    ____

    ____

2. To explain the contribution of both biological and environmental influences on development, Bronfenbrenner characterized his perspective as a(n) ______________________________ model. (p. 26)

3. Match each level of ecological systems theory with the appropriate description or example. (pp. 26–27)
    _____ Relationship between the child's home and school — A. *Microsystem*
    _____ The influence of cultural values — B. *Mesosystem*
    _____ The parent's workplace — C. *Exosystem*
    _____ The child's interaction with parents — D. *Macrosystem*

4. Provide examples of factors in each system that can enhance development. (pp. 26–27)

    Microsystem: ____

    Mesosystem: ____

    Exosystem: ____

    Macrosystem: ____

5. Bronfenbrenner's ______________________ refers to temporal changes that affect development, such as the timing of the birth of a sibling. (p. 27)

6. In ecological systems theory, development is controlled by (environmental circumstances / inner dispositions / the interaction of environmental circumstances and inner dispositions). (p. 27)

New Directions: Development as a Dynamic System

1. Describe the *dynamic systems perspective.* (p. 28)

    ____

    ____

    ____

2. Based on the dynamic systems perspective, explain how individuals develop both universal traits and individual abilities. (p. 28)

    Universal traits: ____

    ____

    Individual abilities: ____

    ____

Comparing Child Development Theories

1. Identify the stances that the following modern theories take on the three basic issues of childhood and child development: (p. 30)

Theory	Continuous or Discontinuous Development?	One Course of Development or Many?	Nature or Nurture as More Important?
Psychoanalytic perspective	______	______	______
Behaviorism and social learning theory	______	______	______
Piaget's cognitive-developmental theory	______	______	______
Information processing	______	______	______
Ethology and evolutionary developmental psychology	______	______	______
Vygotsky's sociocultural theory	______	______	______
Ecological systems theory	______	______	______
Dynamic systems perspective	______	______	______

Studying the Child

1. Research usually begins with a(n) ______________________, or a prediction about behavior drawn from a theory. (p. 30)

Common Research Methods

1. Compare and contrast *naturalistic* and *structured observation* techniques, noting one strength and one limitation of each approach. (pp. 31–33)

Naturalistic: ____

____

Strength: ____

____

Limitation: ____

____

Structured: ____

____

Strength: ____

____

Limitation: ____

____

2. Explain how *clinical interviews* differ from structured interviews, and note the benefits and limitations of each technique. (p. 33)

   Clinical: ______________________________

   ____

   Benefits: ______________________________

   ____

   Limitations: ______________________________

   ____

   Structured: ______________________________

   ____

   Benefits: ______________________________

   ____

   Limitations: ______________________________

   ____

3. Cite the primary aim of the *clinical,* or *case study, method,* and note the procedures often used to achieve this goal. (p. 34)

   Aim: ______________________________

   ____

   Procedures: ______________________________

   ____

4. What are the drawbacks of using the clinical method? (p. 34)

   ____

   ____

5. ______________________ is a research method aimed at understanding a culture or distinct social group. This goal is achieved through ______________________, a technique in which the researcher lives with the cultural community and participates in all aspects of daily life. (pp. 34–35)

6. Cite two limitations of the ethnographic method. (p. 35)

   A. ______________________________

   B. ______________________________

Cultural Influences: Immigrant Youths: Adapting to a New Land

1. True or False: Students who are first-generation (foreign-born) and second-generation (American- or Canadian-born, with immigrant parents) achieve in school as well as or better than students of native-born parents. (p. 36)

2. On average, adolescents from immigrant families are (more / less) likely to commit delinquent and violent acts, to use drugs and alcohol, or to have early sex. (p. 36)

3. Discuss two ways in which family and ethnic community influence the academic achievement of adolescents from immigrant families. (p. 36)

   A. ______________________________

   ____

   B. ______________________________

   ____

General Research Designs

1. Explain the basic features of the *correlational design.* (p. 37)

   ____

   ____

2. True or False: The correlational design is preferred by researchers because it allows them to infer cause and effect. Explain your response. (p. 37)

   ____

   ____

   ____

3. A *correlation coefficient* can range from ________ to ________. The magnitude of the number shows the (strength / direction) of the relationship between the two variables, whereas the sign indicates the (strength / direction) of the relationship. (p. 37)

4. For a correlation coefficient, a positive sign means that as one variable increases, the other (increases / decreases), while a negative sign indicates that as one variable increases, the other (increases / decreases). (p. 37)

5. A researcher determines that the correlation between warm, consistent parenting and child delinquency is –.80. Explain what this indicates about the relationship between these two variables. (p. 37)

   ____

   ____

   ____

6. If the same researcher had found a correlation of +.45, what would this have indicated about the relationship between warm, consistent parenting and child delinquency? (p. 37)

   ____

   ____

   ____

7. What is the primary distinction between a correlational design and an *experimental design*? (pp. 37–38)

   ____

8. Describe the difference between an *independent* and a *dependent variable.* (p. 37)

   Independent: ______________________________

   ____

   Dependent: ______________________________

   ____

9. What is the feature of an experimental design that enables researchers to infer a cause-and-effect relationship between the variables? (pp. 37–38)

____

____

10. Researchers engage in ________________ of participants to treatment conditions. Why is this important in experimental studies? (p. 38)

____

____

11. In ________________ experiments, researchers randomly assign people to treatment conditions in natural settings. (p. 38)

12. True or False: Natural experiments differ from correlational research in that groups of participants are carefully chosen to ensure that their characteristics are as much alike as possible. (p. 39)

Designs for Studying Development

1. In a(n) ________________ *design,* participants are studied repeatedly at different ages, and changes are noted as the participants get older. What are two advantages of this type of research design? (p. 40)

   A. ____

   ____

   B. ____

   ____

2. Identify three problems in conducting longitudinal research. (pp. 40–41)

   A. ____

   B. ____

   C. ____

3. In what way do *cohort effects* threaten the accuracy of longitudinal research findings? (p. 41)

____

____

____

4. Describe the *cross-sectional design.* (p. 41)

____

____

____

5. In cross-sectional designs, researchers (do / do not) need to worry about participant dropout and practice effects. (p. 41)

6. Summarize two drawbacks of the cross-sectional design. (pp. 41–42)

   A. ____

   ____

   B. ____

   ____

7. In ______________________________ *designs,* researchers conduct several similar cross-sectional or longitudinal studies at varying times. List three advantages of this design. (p. 42)

   A. ______________________________

   B. ______________________________

   C. ______________________________

8. In a(n) ______________________________, researchers present children with a novel task and follow their mastery over a series of closely spaced sessions. (p. 43)

9. The *microgenetic design* is especially useful for studying (physical / cognitive / emotional and social) development. (p. 43)

10. List three reasons why microgenetic studies are difficult to carry out. (p. 43)

    A. ______________________________

    ____

    B. ______________________________

    ____

    C. ______________________________

    ____

Social Issues: Education: Can Musical Experiences Enhance Intelligence?

1. True or False: The "Mozart effect" has a long-lasting influence on intelligence. (p. 44)

2. Describe the two features interventions must have to produce lasting gains in mental test scores. (p. 44)

   A. ______________________________

   ____

   B. ______________________________

   ____

3. Explain how enrichment activities, such as music or chess lessons, can aid a child's developing intelligence. (p. 44)

   ____

   ____

   ____

Ethics in Research on Children

1. Why are ethical concerns especially complex when children participate in research? (p. 43)

   ____

   ____

   ____

2. Briefly describe the following children's research rights. (p. 45)

   Protection from harm: ______________________________

   ____

   Informed consent: ______________________________

   ____

   Privacy: ______________________________

   ____

   Knowledge of results: ______________________________

   ____

   Beneficial treatments: ______________________________

   ____

3. For children _____ years and older, their own informed consent should be obtained in addition to parental consent prior to participation in research. (p. 45)

4. What is debriefing, and why does it rarely work well with children? (p. 46)

   A. ______________________________

   ____

   B. ______________________________

   ____

ASK YOURSELF . . .

For *Ask Yourself* questions for this chapter, along with feedback on the accuracy of your answers, please log on to MyDevelopmentLab (for registration and access, please visit mydevelopmentlab.com or follow the instructions on page ix).

(1) Select the Multimedia Library.

(2) Choose the explore option.

(3) Find your chapter from the drop down box.

(4) Click find now.

(5) Complete questions and choose "Submit answers for grading" or "Clear answers" to start over.

SUGGESTED READINGS

Cabeza, R., Nyberg, L., & Park, D. (2009). *Cognitive neuroscience of aging: Linking cognitive and cerebral aging*. New York: Oxford University Press. Examines a new scientific discipline, known as the cognitive neuroscience of aging. Topics include noninvasive measures of cerebral aging; the effects of cerebral aging on cognitive functions like perception, memory, and attention; and applications of brain research.

Coll, C. G., & Marks, K. (2009). *Immigrant stories: Ethnicity and academics in middle childhood.* New York: Oxford University Press. A longitudinal study of first- and second-generation immigrant youths, this book examines the unique challenges and strengths of these children and their families. Topics include cultural attitudes and identity development, academic achievement, the importance of community resources, and the importance of public policies for immigrant families.

Freeman, M., & Mathison, S. (2008). *Researching children's experiences.* New York: Guilford. Presents an extensive overview of research methods commonly used to study children and adolescents. The authors also present information on recruiting minors for research, the roles and responsibilities of researchers, the importance of understanding the child's developmental level, and ethical considerations and challenges.

CROSSWORD PUZZLE 1.1

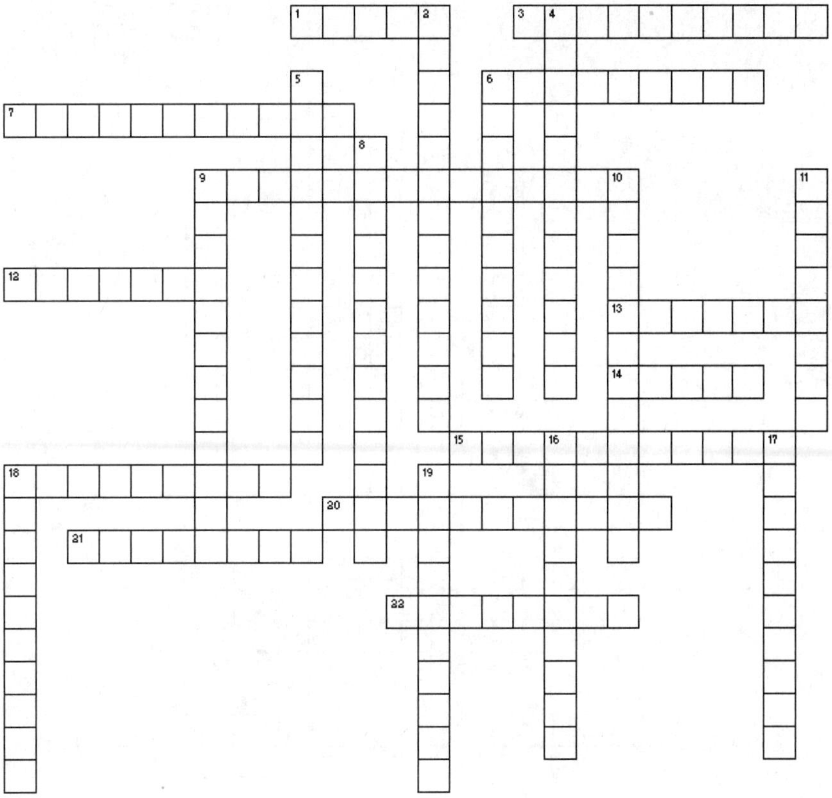

Across

1. _____________ development: field of study devoted to understanding constancy and change from conception through adolescence and emerging adulthood
3. In ecological systems theory, connections between the child's immediate settings
6. In ecological systems theory, social settings that do not contain the child but that affect his or her experiences in immediate settings
7. Emphasizes the study of directly observable events
9. Theory that emphasizes the unique developmental history of each child
12. _____________ systems perspective: the child's mind, body, and physical and social worlds form an integrated system
13. Nature-___________ controversy
14. Qualitative change characterizing a particular time period of development
15. In ecological systems theory, activities and interaction patterns in the child's immediate surroundings
18. Piaget's _________-developmental theory suggests that children actively construct knowledge as they manipulate and explore their world.
20. In ecological systems theory, cultural values, laws, customs, and resources that influence experiences and interactions at inner levels of the environment
21. Theory concerned with the adaptive value of behavior
22. Social ____________ theory: emphasizes the role of observational learning in the development of behavior

Down

2. Development as a process in which new ways of understanding and responding to the world emerge at specific times
4. ___________ developmental psychology seeks to understand the adaptive value of species-wide cognitive, emotional, and social competencies as those competencies change with age
5. Freud's theory focusing on early sexual and aggressive drives
6. ___________ systems theory: view of the child as developing within a complex system of relationships
8. Theory that focuses on how social interaction contributes to development
9. Erikson's stage theory of development entailing resolution of psychological conflicts
10. In ecological systems theory, temporal changes in a child's environment
11. Unique combinations of personal and environmental circumstances that can result in different paths of change
16. Ability to adapt effectively in the face of threats to development
17. Genetically determined, naturally unfolding course of growth
18. Development as gradually adding more of the same types of skills that were there to begin with
19. Information-________________ approach: views the human mind as a symbol-manipulating machine

CROSSWORD PUZZLE 1.2

Across

3. ____________ effects refer to the impact of cultural historical change on the accuracy of findings.
8. Describes, explains, and predicts behavior
9. The clinical method, or ______________ study method
11. Design in which researchers present children with a novel task and follow their mastery over a series of closely spaced sessions
13. Behavior ____________: procedures that combine conditioning and modeling to eliminate undesirable behaviors and increase desirable responses.
15. ____________ observation: observing a behavior of interest in the natural environment.
16. Developmental cognitive ___________ is the study of relationships between changes in the brain and the developing child's cognitive processes and behavior.
18. Design that permits inferences about cause and effect
19. In a ___________________ interview, the researcher uses a flexible, conversational style to probe for a participant's point of view.
20. Design in which the same participants are studied repeatedly, at different ages
22. Variable expected to be influenced by the experimental manipulations

Down

1. ______________ period: a time that is optimal for certain capacities to emerge.
2. Structured _______________: the researcher sets up a situation that evokes a behavior of interest and observes that behavior in a laboratory setting.
3. A number describing how two variables are related is called a correlation.
4. ______________ designs allow researchers to conduct several similar cross-sectional or longitudinal studies at varying times.
5. Variable manipulated by the researcher
6. ________________ assignment helps researchers control characteristics of participants that could reduce the accuracy of their findings.
7. _____________ interview: each participant is asked the same questions in the same way.
10. Approach that uses age-related averages to represent typical development
12. Design in which groups of people differing in age are studied at the same point in time (two words, hyph.)
14. Design in which researchers gather information without altering the participants' experience
17. Developmental ______________: an interdisciplinary field that includes all changes throughout the lifespan.

PRACTICE TEST #1

1. Child development is an area of study devoted to understanding __________ (p. 4)
   a. how to best educate and rear typically developing children.
   b. constancy and change from conception to adolescence.
   c. abnormal development from birth to adolescence.
   d. the transition between childhood and adolescence.

2. The field of child development __________ (p. 4)
   a. has grown through the combined efforts of people from many fields.
   b. is of scientific, rather than applied, importance.
   c. primarily focuses on infants and toddlers.
   d. is part of a larger, interdisciplinary field known as neuroscience.

3. The broad domains of child development are __________ (p. 5)
   a. physical, emotional, and cultural.
   b. emotional, cultural, and cognitive.
   c. physical, cognitive, and emotional and social.
   d. physical, cognitive, and cultural.

4. The early childhood period is from __________ (p. 6)
   a. conception to 6 years.
   b. birth to 6 years.
   c. 1 to 5 years.
   d. 2 to 6 years.

5. During middle childhood, children __________ (p. 6)
   a. first establish ties with peers.
   b. begin to master academic skills.
   c. begin to establish autonomy from the family.
   d. define their personal values and goals.

6. Emerging adulthood __________ (p. 6)
   a. is limited to developing nations.
   b. first became apparent during the past few decades.
   c. rarely appears in industrialized nations.
   d. spans ages 14 to 22.

7. A theory's continued existence depends on __________ (p. 7)
   a. scientific verification.
   b. ultimate truth.
   c. interdisciplinary usefulness.
   d. its cultural value.

8. Theories that regard development as taking place in stages __________ (p. 8)
   a. accept the continuous perspective.
   b. emphasize nature over nurture.
   c. accept the discontinuous perspective.
   d. emphasize nurture over nature.

9. The most consistent asset of resilient children is __________ (p. 11)
   a. a strong bond to a competent, caring adult.
   b. high intelligence.
   c. socially valued talents.
   d. access to good schools.

10. During which time period was childhood first regarded as a distinct development period? (pp. 11–12)
    a. medieval times
    b. the sixteenth century
    c. the seventeenth century
    d. the eighteenth century

11. Alfred Benet and Theodore Simon are best known for __________ (p. 14)
    a. viewing the child as a tabula rasa.
    b. launching the normative approach.
    c. developing the principles of natural selection and survival of the fittest.
    d. constructing the first successful intelligence test.

12. Freud's psychosexual theory emphasizes __________ (p. 15)
    a. that in addition to mediating between id impulses and superego demands, the ego makes a positive contribution to development.
    b. that how parents manage their child's sexual and aggressive drives in the first few years is crucial for healthy development.
    c. that adolescence is the most crucial time period for healthy sexual and psychological development.
    d. modeling, also known as imitation or observational learning, as a powerful source of development.

13. Erik Erikson was one of the first theorists to __________ (p. 15)
    a. view a child's soul as tainted by original sin.
    b. study imprinting.
    c. recognize the lifespan nature of development.
    d. view children as blank slates who can be molded by adults.

14. The teenager who wears the same clothes and hairstyle as his friends is displaying __________ learning. (p. 18)
    a. observational
    b. naturalistic
    c. experimental
    d. normative

15. __________ researchers often use flowcharts to map the precise steps individuals use to solve problems and complete tasks. (p. 21)
    a. Piagetian
    b. Information-processing
    c. Social learning
    d. Ethological

16. Vygotsky's theory focuses on __________ (pp. 24–25)
    a. the adaptive value of species-wide competencies as those competencies change with age.
    b. the relationship between changes in the brain and the developing child's behavior patterns.
    c. the development of a child within a complex system of relationships affected by multiple levels of the environment.
    d. how the values, beliefs, customs, and skills of a social group are transmitted to the next generation.

17. Both behaviorism and social learning theory __________ (p. 27)
    a. view development as discontinuous.
    b. emphasize later experiences over earlier ones.
    c. view development as continuous.
    d. focus on evolution and heredity.

18. Dynamic systems theory __________ (p. 28)
    a. views early experience as unrelated to later development.
    b. emphasizes how culture is transmitted to the next generation.
    c. focuses on one course of development.
    d. emphasizes that change in the system is always ongoing.

19. Professor Dagan believes that development takes place in stages. Professor Dagan's belief is consistent with __________ (p. 30)
    a. behaviorism.
    b. ecological systems theory.
    c. Piaget's cognitive-development theory.
    d. Vygotsky's sociocultural theory.

20. A limitation of naturalistic observation is that __________ (p. 31)
    a. it may not yield observations typical of participants' behavior in everyday life.
    b. it does not distinguish between human and animal behavior.
    c. it relies too heavily on self-reports.
    d. researchers cannot control conditions under which participants are observed.

21. A strength of the clinical method is that __________ (p. 34)
    a. it permits study of behaviors rarely seen in everyday life.
    b. researchers can apply the results to many individuals.
    c. it provides rich, descriptive insights into processes of development.
    d. each participant has an equal opportunity to display the behavior of interest.

22. Research reveals that children of immigrant parents __________ (p. 36)
    a. do not achieve in school as well as students of native-born parents.
    b. are less likely than children of native-born parents to have early sex.
    c. are more likely than children of native-born parents to commit violent acts.
    d. have lower self-esteem than children of native-born parents.

23. A major limitation of correlational studies is that __________ (p. 37)
    a. researchers cannot infer cause and effect.
    b. results may be distorted by cohort effects.
    c. participants may become "test-wise."
    d. ethical standards are difficult to maintain.

24. A limitation of the __________ design is that it requires intensive study of participants' moment-by-moment behaviors. (p. 39)
    a. longitudinal
    b. cross-sectional
    c. sequential
    d. microgenetic

25. Microgenetic studies are difficult to conduct because __________ (p. 39)
    a. the time required for children to change their behavior is hard to anticipate.
    b. age differences may be distorted because of cohort effects.
    c. researchers cannot control the conditions under which participants are observed.
    d. researchers must control numerous independent variables.

26. The most widely discussed threat to the accuracy of longitudinal findings is __________ (p. 41)
    a. selective attrition.
    b. cohort effects.
    c. practice effects.
    d. biased sampling.

27. Sequential designs combine __________ (p. 42)
    a. naturalistic and structured observations.
    b. correlational and experimental strategies.
    c. cross-sectional and longitudinal strategies.
    d. observational and sociocultural learning.

28. Gains in intellectual performance, widely publicized as the "Mozart effect," __________ (p. 44)
    a. typically last only a few years.
    b. are difficult to replicate.
    c. appear only in infants and toddlers.
    d. have only been replicated in adults, not children.

29. The ethical principle of informed consent requires __________ (p. 45)
    a. special interpretation when applied to research on children.
    b. concealment of children's identities on all information collected in the course of research.
    c. children in control groups to have the right to alternative beneficial treatments.
    d. investigators to inform children of the results of research.

30. Which of the following statements about ethics in research on children is true? (p. 45)
    a. For children age 10 and older, parents are not required to give informed consent.
    b. When working with special populations, such as abused children, ethical guidelines are often violated.
    c. The ultimate responsibility for the ethical integrity of research lies with the investigator.
    d. Because of limited cognitive understanding, children under the age of 7 rarely participate in research.

PRACTICE TEST #2

1. The field of child development __________ (p. 4)
   a. is interdisciplinary.
   b. primarily focuses on abnormal development.
   c. primarily consists of psychologists and physicians.
   d. is still in its infancy.

2. The domains of development __________ (p. 5)
   a. are separate and distinct.
   b. combine in an integrated fashion.
   c. represent continuous stages.
   d. vary with age.

3. The prenatal period __________ (p. 6)
   a. does not represent a distinct period of development.
   b. begins when a fetus is viable.
   c. is the most rapid time of change.
   d. involves the physical, but not the cognitive, domain.

4. Thought becomes abstract and idealistic during __________ (p. 6)
   a. early childhood.
   b. middle childhood.
   c. adolescence.
   d. emerging adulthood.

5. A theory's continued existence depends on __________ (p. 7)
   a. scientific verification.
   b. funding for research.
   c. public acceptance.
   d. its overall appeal.

6. Contexts __________ (p. 8)
   a. involve qualitative changes in behaving that characterize specific periods of development.
   b. are processes in which new ways of understanding and responding to the world emerge at specific times.
   c. are the complex forces of the physical and social world that influence our biological makeup.
   d. foster different cognitive capacities, social skills, and feelings about the self and others.

7. Personal characteristics that contribute to resilience in childhood include __________ (pp. 10–11)
   a. high intelligence and high emotional reactivity.
   b. a sociable disposition and musical talent.
   c. moderate intelligence and a humorous disposition.
   d. athletic ability and high emotional reactivity.

8. The Puritans viewed children as __________ (p. 12)
   a. noble savages.
   b. blank slates.
   c. born evil and stubborn.
   d. angelic and kind.

9. John Locke regarded development as __________ (p. 12)
   a. continuous.
   b. stable.
   c. discontinuous.
   d. highly influenced by heredity.

10. G. Stanley Hall and Arnold Gesell __________ (p. 13)
    a. applied imprinting and natural selection to human development.
    b. developed the concept of maturation to explain child development.
    c. regarded development as a genetically determined process that unfolds much like a flower.
    d. sought a way to identify children with learning problems who needed to be placed in special classes.

11. According to the psychoanalytic perspective, children __________ (p. 15)
    a. begin as nothing at all; their characters are shaped entirely by experience with adult members of society.
    b. are noble savages, naturally endowed with a sense of right and wrong and an innate plan for orderly, healthy growth.
    c. are naturally knowledgeable about their needs because the timetable of development is the product of millions of years of evolution.
    d. move through a series of stages in which they confront conflicts between biological drives and social expectations.

12. During Erik Erikson's industry versus inferiority psychosocial stage, individuals __________ (p. 16)
    a. gain a sense of trust that the world is good.
    b. learn to work and cooperate with others.
    c. form personal identities.
    d. explore values and vocational goals.

13. According to behaviorism, __________ (p. 17)
    a. the human mind can be viewed as a symbol-manipulating system.
    b. directly observable events are the appropriate focus of study.
    c. observational learning is a powerful source of development.
    d. children actively work to maintain equilibrium.

14. Which of the following perspectives studies the relationship between changes in the brain and the developing child's cognitive processing and behavior patterns? (p. 23)
    a. the normative approach
    b. behaviorism
    c. developmental cognitive neuroscience
    d. the information-processing approach

15. Which of the following perspectives seeks to understand the adaptive value of species-wide cognitive, emotional, and social competencies as those competencies change with age? (p. 24)
    a. developmental cognitive neuroscience
    b. behaviorism
    c. sociocultural theory
    d. evolutionary developmental psychology

16. Connections between microsystems fall within Bronfenbrenner's __________ (p. 26)
    a. mesosystem.
    b. exosystem.
    c. macrosystem.
    d. chronosystem.

17. Many courses of development are possible, according to __________ (p. 30)
    a. the psychoanalytic perspective.
    b. behaviorism.
    c. the information-processing perspective.
    d. the ethological perspective.

18. Early experiences set the course of later development, according to __________ theory. (p. 30)
    a. social learning
    b. sociocultural
    c. ecological systems
    d. psychoanalytic

19. Heredity, brain growth, and dialogues with more expert members of society jointly contribute to development, according to __________ (p. 30)
    a. Piaget's cognitive-development theory.
    b. the ethological perspective.
    c. Vygotsky's sociocultural theory.
    d. Freud's psychosexual theory.

20. Researchers observe behavior in a laboratory using __________ (pp. 31–32)
    a. naturalistic observation.
    b. structured observation.
    c. correlational observation.
    d. case studies.

21. Researchers employ a flexible, conversational style when they conduct __________ interviews. (p. 33)
    a. ethnographic
    b. structured
    c. clinical
    d. microgenetic

22. Ethnographies reveal that immigrant parents __________ (p. 36)
    a. view education as the surest way to improve life chances.
    b. view financial independence as the surest way to improve life chances.
    c. stress individual goals over allegiance to family.
    d. encourage complete assimilation into the majority culture.

23. Researchers gather information on individuals, generally in natural life circumstances, and make no effort to alter their experiences in a(n) __________ (p. 37)
    a. correlational design.
    b. experimental design.
    c. cross-sectional study.
    d. longitudinal study.

24. A strength of the cross-sectional design is that it __________ (p. 39)
    a. allows for cause-and-effect inferences.
    b. reveals cohort effects.
    c. is more efficient than the longitudinal design.
    d. offers insights into the process of individual development.

25. A disadvantage of the microgenetic design is that __________ (p. 39)
    a. age-related changes are often distorted by cohort effects.
    b. it requires intensive study of participants' moment-by-moment behaviors.
    c. it offers few insights into the process of development.
    d. it does not permit the study of individual development.

26. Cohort effects __________ (p. 41)
    a. always operate broadly on an entire generation.
    b. occur when specific experiences influence some children but not others in the same generation.
    c. are a limitation of the sequential, longitudinal, and microgenetic designs.
    d. can be controlled or eliminated through random assignment.

27. Research suggests that __________ can lead to small increases in intelligence. (p. 44)
    a. drama lessons
    b. playing competitive sports
    c. sustained musical experiences
    d. reading Shakespeare

28. Children's research rights include the right to __________ (p. 45)
    a. parental involvement in the research design.
    b. beneficial treatments.
    c. financial compensation.
    d. refute the results.

29. When harm to child participants seems possible, investigators should __________ (p. 45)
    a. provide the children with informed consent forms.
    b. find other means for obtaining the information or abandon the research.
    c. offer an alternative beneficial treatment, if one is available.
    d. ask parents to intervene on behalf of the child.

30. Researchers should use deception tactics in studies involving children __________ (p. 46)
    a. as long as the parents are debriefed following the session.
    b. as long as the children are not debriefed following the session.
    c. only if the risk of harm is minimal.
    d. only if the study is conducted from behind one-way mirrors.

CHAPTER 2
GENETIC AND ENVIRONMENTAL FOUNDATIONS

BRIEF CHAPTER SUMMARY

This chapter examines the foundations of development: heredity and environment. The principles of genetic transmission determine the characteristics that make us human and contribute to individual differences in appearance and behavior. Inheritance of harmful recessive genes and abnormalities of the chromosomes are major causes of serious developmental problems. Genetic counseling and prenatal diagnosis help people at risk for transmitting hereditary disorders assess their chances of giving birth to a healthy baby.

Environmental factors also affect development. The family has an especially powerful impact, operating as a complex, dynamic social system in which members exert direct, indirect, and third-party effects on one another. Socioeconomic status influences child-rearing practices: Poverty and homelessness undermine effective family functioning and children's well-being, while affluence may lead to overscheduling and lack of emotional closeness, which also have negative consequences. The quality of community life, from neighborhoods and schools to small towns and cities, also contributes to children's development. Cultural values—for example, the degree to which a society emphasizes collectivism versus individualism—combine with public policies, laws, and government programs to shape experiences in all of these contexts.

Some child development specialists believe that it is useful and possible to determine "how much" heredity and environment contribute to individual differences. Others think that the effects of heredity and environment cannot be clearly separated. Instead, they want to discover "how" these two major determinants of development work together in a complex, dynamic interplay.

LEARNING OBJECTIVES

After reading this chapter, you should be able to:

2.1 Distinguish between genotypes and phenotypes. (p. 51)

2.2 Describe the structure and function of chromosomes and DNA molecules. (p. 52)

2.3 Explain the process of mitosis. (p. 53)

2.4 Describe the process of meiosis, and explain how it leads to genetic variability. (pp. 53–54)

2.5 Describe the genetic events that determine the sex of the new organism. (pp. 54–55)

2.6 Identify two types of twins, and explain how each is created. (p. 55)

2.7 Explain how alleles influence the inheritance of traits, such as through dominant–recessive inheritance, incomplete dominance, X-linked inheritance, genomic imprinting, mutation, and polygenic inheritance. (pp. 56–60)

2.8 Describe major chromosomal abnormalities, and explain how they occur. (pp. 60–62)

2.9 Discuss reproductive choices available to prospective parents, noting the pros and cons of reproductive technologies, and the alternative of adoption. (pp. 63–68)

2.10 Describe family functioning from the ecological systems perspective, citing direct and indirect family influences and explaining the view of the family as a dynamic, changing system. (pp. 69–71)

2.11 Discuss the impact of socioeconomic status, including affluence and poverty, on family functioning. (pp. 71–75)

2.12 Summarize the role of neighborhoods and schools in the lives of children, including contributions of social support as an outgrowth of family–neighborhood ties. (pp. 75–77)

2.13 Discuss how cultural values and public policies influence the well-being of children. (pp. 77–81)

2.14 Explain the various ways heredity and environment may combine to influence complex human traits, and discuss epigenesis. (pp. 82–88)

STUDY QUESTIONS

1. ______________ are directly observable characteristics that depend in part on the ______________, the complex blend of genetic information that determines our species and also influences all of our unique characteristics. (p. 51)

Genetic Foundations

1. Rodlike structures in the nuclei of cells that store and transmit genetic information are called ______________. (p. 52)
2. Humans have (23 / 46) pairs of *chromosomes* in each cell. (p. 52)

The Genetic Code

1. Chromosomes are made up of a chemical substance called ______________. It looks like a twisted ladder and is composed of segments called ______________. (p. 52)
2. The process through which DNA duplicates itself so that each new body cell contains the same number of chromosomes is called ______________. (p. 53)

The Sex Cells

1. Sex cells, or ______________, are formed through the process of (*mitosis* / *meiosis*). (p. 53)
2. True or False: Sex cells contain only half the number of chromosomes normally present in body cells. (p. 53)
3. When the sperm and ova unite at conception, the cell that results is called a(n) ______________. (p. 53)
4. During meiosis, the process of ______________, in which chromosomes next to each other break at one or more points and exchange segments, creates new hereditary combinations unique to the individual. (p. 53)
5. Explain why the genetic variability produced by meiosis is important in an evolutionary sense. (p. 54)

   ____

   ____

Boy or Girl?

1. The 22 matching pairs of chromosomes are called ______________. (p. 54)
2. The twenty-third pair of chromosomes, also called the *sex chromosomes,* determines the sex of the child. In females, this pair is called ______________, whereas in males it is called ______________. (p. 54)

Multiple Births

1. Match each of the following terms with the appropriate description. (p. 55)

   _____ This type of twinning may result from environmental influences like temperature changes, variations in oxygen levels, or late fertilization of the ovum.
   _____ This is the most common type of multiple birth.
   _____ Older maternal age, use of fertility drugs, and in vitro fertilization are major causes of this type of twinning.
   _____ These twins are genetically no more alike than ordinary siblings.
   _____ These twins share the same genetic makeup.

   A. *Fraternal*, or *dizygotic, twins*
   B. *Identical*, or *monozygotic, twins*

2. True or False: During the early years of life, children of single births are often healthier and develop more rapidly than twins. (p. 55)

Patterns of Genetic Inheritance

1. Each of two forms of a gene located at the same place on the *autosome* is called a(n) ______________. (p. 56)
2. If the *alleles* from both parents are alike, the child is ______________ and will display the inherited trait. If the alleles inherited from the mother and father are different, then the child is ______________, and relationships between the alleles determine the trait, or phenotype. (p. 56)
3. Describe *dominant–recessive inheritance.* (p. 56)

   ____

   ____

4. For each of the following characteristics, indicate whether it is dominant (D) or recessive (R). (p. 56)

_____ Blond hair	_____ Pattern baldness	_____ Dark hair	_____ Curly hair
_____ Red hair	_____ Facial dimples	_____ Farsightedness	_____ Nearsightedness
_____ Albinism	_____ Double-jointedness	_____ Type A blood	_____ Type O blood

5. One of the most common recessive disorders is ______________, which affects the way the body breaks down proteins contained in many foods. (p. 56)
6. ___________ *genes* enhance or dilute the effects of other genes. (p. 57)
7. True or False: Serious diseases typically result from dominant alleles. Explain your answer. (p. 57)

   ____

   ____

8. Describe *incomplete dominance,* and name one condition that results from this pattern of inheritance. (p. 57)

   A. ____

   ____

   B. ____

9. (Males / Females) are more likely to be affected by *X-linked inheritance.* Explain why. (p. 57)

   ____

   ____

10. Name one X-linked disorder. (pp. 57, 59)

    ____

11. In recent decades, the proportion of male births has declined in many industrialized countries. Briefly explain why. (p. 59)

    ____

    ____

12. ______________ occurs when alleles are chemically marked in such a way that one pair member is activated, regardless of its makeup. (p. 59)
13. List three conditions or diseases that are caused by *genomic imprinting.* (p. 59)

    A. ____

    B. ____

    C. ____

14. Explain how harmful genes are created. (p. 60)

____

____

15. Describe *polygenic inheritance,* and give an example of a trait that is determined by this pattern of inheritance. (p. 60)

A. ____

____

B. ____

Chromosomal Abnormalities

1. Most chromosomal defects are the result of mistakes during ______________, when the ovum and sperm are formed. (p. 60)

2. ______________________, the most common chromosomal abnormality, often results from a failure of the twenty-first pair of chromosomes to separate during meiosis. For this reason, the disorder is sometimes called *trisomy 21.* (pp. 60–61)

3. List the physical and behavioral characteristics of *Down syndrome.* (p. 61)

   Physical: ____

   ____

   Behavioral: ____

   ____

4. True or False: The risk of Down syndrome rises with maternal age. (p. 61)

5. Disorders of the sex chromosomes result in (more / less) serious consequences than disorders of the autosomes. (p. 61)

6. Identify whether the following claims about individuals with sex chromosome disorders are true (T) or false (F). (p. 62)

   (T/F) Males with XYY syndrome are more aggressive and antisocial than XY males.

   (T/F) Most children with sex chromosome disorders suffer from mental retardation.

   (T/F) Girls with Turner syndrome have trouble with spatial relationships, such as drawing pictures and noticing changes in facial expressions.

   (T/F) Children with sex chromosome disorders have intellectual problems that are usually very specific.

Reproductive Choices

Genetic Counseling

1. What is the purpose of *genetic counseling,* and who is most likely to seek this service? (p. 63)

   A. ____

   ____

   B. ____

   ____

Social Issues: Health: The Pros and Cons of Reproductive Technologies

1. For each of the following descriptions, indicate whether it applies to donor insemination (D), in vitro fertilization (IV), or surrogate motherhood (S). (pp. 66–67)
   _____ Among babies conceived this way, the rate of low birth weight is nearly three times as high as in the general population.
   _____ This procedure is one of the most controversial forms of medically assisted conception.
   _____ A "sex sorter" method helps ensure that couples who carry X-linked diseases have a daughter.
   _____ Sperm is injected from an anonymous man into a woman.
   _____ This procedure is often used to treat women whose fallopian tubes are permanently damaged.
   _____ May promote exploitation of financially needy women.
   _____ This procedure is 70 to 80 percent successful.
   _____ Each year, about 40,000 U.S. babies are conceived through this technique.

2. Briefly describe new reproductive options being explored by researchers, as well as the ethical debates surrounding them. (p. 67)

   Techniques: ______________________________

   ____

   Ethical concerns: ______________________________

   ____

Prenatal Diagnosis and Fetal Medicine

1. _______________ are medical procedures that permit detection of developmental problems before birth. (p. 63)
2. List six types of *prenatal diagnostic methods.* (p. 64)

   A. ______________________________

   B. ______________________________

   C. ______________________________

   D. ______________________________

   E. ______________________________

   F. ______________________________

3. True or False: The techniques used in fetal medicine generally cause no harm to the developing fetus. (p. 64)
4. Summarize the goals of the Human Genome Project, and explain why this program offers hope for correcting hereditary defects. (pp. 64–65)

   A. ______________________________

   ____

   B. ______________________________

   ____

5. Describe three steps that prospective parents can take before conception to increase their chances of having a healthy baby. (p. 68)

   A. ______________________________

   B. ______________________________

   C. ______________________________

The Alternative of Adoption

1. Adopted children and adolescents have (fewer / more) learning and emotional difficulties than other children. Cite three possible reasons for this trend. (pp. 65–66)

   A. ____________________

   B. ____________________

   C. ____________________

2. Discuss research findings on international adoptees' development in comparison to birth siblings or agemates who stay behind. (pp. 67–68)

   ____

3. True or False: Adoptees usually begin the search for their birth parents during early adolescence. Explain your answer. (p. 68)

   ____

Environmental Contexts for Development

The Family

1. Distinguish between direct and indirect familial influences. (pp. 70–71)

   Direct: ____________________

   Indirect: ____________________

2. Describe the practice of *coparenting,* and explain how this technique benefits children. (pp. 70–71)

   A. ____________________

   B. ____________________

3. Discuss some ways in which the family system must adapt over time. (p. 71)

   ____

Socioeconomic Status and Family Functioning

1. List the three variables that determine a family's *socioeconomic status (SES).* (p. 71)

   A. ____________________ B. ____________________

   C. ____________________

2. Compare child characteristics emphasized in lower-SES families with those emphasized in higher-SES families. (pp. 71–72)

   Lower-SES: ____

   ____

   Higher-SES: ____

   ____

3. Describe the influence of SES on parenting practices and parent–child interaction. (p. 72)

   ____

   ____

   ____

4. Briefly summarize several factors that explain SES differences in family interaction. (p. 72)

   ____

   ____

   ____

5. True or False: Higher-SES children show more advances in cognitive development and tend to perform better in school than their lower-SES peers. (p. 72)

Social Issues: Education: Worldwide Education of Girls: Transforming Current and Future Generations

1. Cite two ways that educating girls benefits the welfare of families, societies, and future generations. (p. 73)

   A. ____

   ____

   B. ____

   ____

2. How does education influence family health? (p. 73)

   ____

   ____

   ____

3. True or False: The empowerment that education provides women is associated with more equitable husband–wife relationships and a reduction in harsh disciplining of children. (p. 73)

Affluence

1. Identify two factors that contribute to poor adjustment in affluent youths. (pp. 72, 74)

   A. ____

   ____

   B. ____

   ____

2. What simple routine is associated with a reduction in adjustment difficulties for both affluent and low-SES youths? (p. 74)

   ____

Poverty

1. What four subgroups of the population are hardest hit by poverty? (p. 74)

   A. ______________________ B. ______________________

   C. ______________________ D. ______________________

2. The poverty rate is (higher / lower) among children than any other age group. Explain your answer. (p. 74)

3. Cite some of the long-term consequences of childhood poverty. (pp. 74–75)

4. Describe how the constant stressors that accompany poverty gradually weaken the family system. (p. 75)

5. Why has the number of homeless children risen in the past 30 years? Briefly summarize the challenges that these children face. (p. 75)

   A. ______________________

   B. ______________________

Beyond the Family: Neighborhoods and Schools

1. Neighborhood resources have a greater impact on children growing up in (disadvantaged / well-to-do) areas. Explain your answer. (p. 76)

2. Briefly explain four ways in which family–neighborhood ties can promote positive development. (p. 76)

   A. ______________________

   B. ______________________

   C. ______________________

   D. ______________________

3. List four broad features of the school environment that affect students' developmental outcomes. (p. 77)

   A. ______________________________

   B. ______________________________

   C. ______________________________

   D. ______________________________

4. Why are higher-SES parents more likely to have regular contact with teachers than lower-SES parents? (p. 77)

   ____

   ____

The Cultural Context

1. What are *subcultures*? (p. 78)

   ____

   ____

2. The African-American ______________ *household,* in which one or more adult relatives live with the parent–child nuclear family unit, is a vital feature of black family life. (p. 78)

3. Distinguish the characteristics of *collectivist* versus *individualistic societies.* (p. 78)

   Collectivist: ______________________________

   ____

   Individualistic: ______________________________

   ____

4. What are *public policies*? (pp. 78–79)

   ____

5. List some of the indicators of children's well-being in which the United States lags behind other nations. (pp. 79–80)

   ____

   ____

   ____

6. Cite three reasons why attempts to help children and youths in the United States have been difficult to realize. (p. 80)

   A. ______________________________

   B. ______________________________

   C. ______________________________

7. The ______________________________ is a legal agreement that commits each cooperating country to work toward guaranteeing environments that foster children's development, protect them from harm, and enhance their community participation and self-determination. The United States (is / is not) one of the two countries in the world that has not yet ratified this agreement. (p. 81)

Cultural Influences: The African-American Extended Family

1. Cite characteristics of the African-American extended family that help reduce the stress of poverty and single parenthood. (p. 79)

____

____

2. How does the African-American extended family help transmit cultural values? (p. 79)

____

____

____

Understanding the Relationship Between Heredity and Environment

1. _______________ is a field devoted to uncovering the contributions of nature and nurture as they relate to individual differences in human traits and abilities. (p. 82)

The Question, "How Much?"

1. Name the two methods used by behavioral geneticists to infer the role of heredity in complex human characteristics. (p. 82)

   A. _______________ B. _______________

2. What are *heritability estimates*? (p. 82)

____

____

____

3. Heritability estimates are obtained from _______________ *studies,* which compare characteristics of family members. (p. 82)

4. True or False: Heritability estimates for intelligence and personality are approximately .50, indicating that genetic makeup can explain half of the variance in these traits. (p. 83)

5. Discuss three limitations of heritability estimates. (pp. 83–84)

   A. _______________

   ____

   B. _______________

   ____

   C. _______________

   ____

The Question, "How?"

1. In *range of reaction,* heredity (limits / increases) responsiveness to varying environments. In *canalization,* heredity (restricts / expands) the development of certain behaviors. (p. 84)

2. Range of reaction highlights two important points. List them. (p. 84)

   A. _______________

   B. _______________

3. Provide an example of a strongly canalized behavior. (p. 84)

____

4. Match each type of *genetic–environmental correlation* with its appropriate description. (p. 85)

_____ Children increasingly seek out environments that fit their genetic tendencies (*niche-picking*).

_____ A child's style of responding influences other's responses, which then strengthens the child's original style.

_____ Parents provide an environment consistent with their own heredity.

A. Passive correlation
B. Evocative correlation
C. Active correlation

5. The tendency to choose environments that complement our heredity is called ______________. (p. 85)

6. __________ means development resulting from ongoing, bidirectional exchanges between heredity and all levels of the environment. Researchers call this view of the relationship between heredity and the environment the _____________ framework. (p. 86)

7. Provide an example of *epigenesis.* (p. 86)

____

____

Biology and Environment: A Case of Epigenesis: Smoking During Pregnancy Alters Gene Expression

1. Maternal smoking during pregnancy is among the risk factors for _______________, one of the most common disorders of childhood. (p. 87)

2. What does animal research reveal about environmental influences associated with ADHD? (p. 87)

____

____

____

3. True or False: Because the DD genotype is rare, the effects of prenatal nicotine exposure are limited in the general population. (p. 87)

ASK YOURSELF . . .

For *Ask Yourself* questions for this chapter, along with feedback on the accuracy of your answers, please log on to MyDevelopmentLab (for registration and access, please visit mydevelopmentlab.com or follow the instructions on page ix).

(1) Select the Multimedia Library.

(2) Choose the explore option.

(3) Find your chapter from the drop down box.

(4) Click find now.

(5) Complete questions and choose "Submit answers for grading" or "Clear answers" to start over.

SUGGESTED READINGS

Lindsey, D. (2008). *Future of children: Wealth, poverty, and opportunity in America.* New York: Oxford University Press. Presents an overview of child and family poverty in the United States, including historical trends, racial and ethnic differences, and the role of public policy in child development.

Mundy, L. (2008). *Everything conceivable: How assisted reproduction is changing men, women, and the world.* New York: Knopf. A compelling look at reproductive technologies, this book examines current research, as well as controversies, surrounding assisted reproduction. The author also includes personal narratives, myths, and the social consequences of assisted reproduction.

Segal, N. L. (2007). *Indivisible by two: Lives of extraordinary twins.* Cambridge, MA: Harvard University Press. A fascinating look into the lives of multiples, this book follows 12 sets of twins, triplets, and quadruplets. The author not only describes the unique experiences of multiples, but she also highlights the many challenges faced by the parents, friends, and spouses of these extraordinary individuals.

CROSSWORD PUZZLE 2.1

Across

5. Genes that enhance or dilute the effects of other genes
8. A heterozygous individual who can pass a recessive trait to his or her children
12. ____________ inheritance: many genes determine a characteristic.
16. Having two different alleles at the same place on a pair of chromosomes
19. The genetic makeup of an individual
20. The 22 matching chromosomes pairs in each human cell
22. Dominant-____________ inheritance: in heterozygous pairings, only one allele affects the child's traits
23. Directly observable characteristics
24. ____________ chromosomes: the 23rd pair of chromosomes; XX in females, XY in males

Down

1. ____________ inheritance: the recessive gene is carried on the X chromosome
2. The process of cell duplication
3. Each of two forms of a gene located at the same place on the autosomes
4. Genomic ____________: alleles are chemically marked in such a way that one pair member is activated, regardless of its makeup.
6. A segment of a DNA molecule that contains hereditary instructions
7. An exchange of genes between chromosomes next to each other during meiosis (2 words)
9. Fraternal, or ____________, twins
10. ____________ dominance: a pattern of inheritance in which both alleles are expressed in the phenotype.
11. A sudden but permanent change in a segment of DNA
13. Human sperm and ova
14. Rodlike structures in the cell nucleus that store and transmit genetic information
15. Having two identical alleles at the same place on a pair of chromosomes
17. Cell formed by the union of the sperm and the ovum at conception
18. Long, double-stranded molecules that make up chromosomes (abbr.)
21. The process of cell division

CROSSWORD PUZZLE 2.2

Across

4. Development resulting from ongoing, bidirectional exchanges between heredity and environment
8. Group of people with beliefs and customs that differ from those of the larger culture
9. _____________-environmental correlation: the notion that heredity influences the environments to which an individual is exposed
12. In _________________ societies, people think of themselves as separate entities and are largely concerned with their own personal needs.
13. ___________ diagnosis methods: medical procedures that permit detection of problems before birth
15. A measure of a family's social position and economic well-being (abbr.)
16. In ____________-family households, parent and child live with one or more adult relatives.
17. __________ studies: comparison of the characteristics of family members to obtain heritability estimates

Down

1. _____________ policies: laws and government programs designed to improve the condition of children and families
2. Tendency for individuals to actively choose environments that complement their heredity (2 words; hyph.)
3. Tendency of heredity to restrict the development of some characteristics to just one or a few outcomes
5. ____________ genetics: field devoted to uncovering the contributions of nature and nurture to individual differences in human traits and abilities
6. ____________ estimate: the extent to which individual differences in complex traits in a specific population are due to genetic factors
7. In ______________ societies, people define themselves as part of a group and stress group over individual goals.
10. Genetic _________________ is designed to help couples assess their chances of giving birth to a baby with a hereditary disorder.
11. _____________: mutually supporting each other's parenting behaviors
14. Range of ____________: a person's genetically determined response to a range of environmental conditions

PRACTICE TEST #1

1. Eye color is an example of a __________ (p. 51)
   a. phenotype.
   b. genotype.
   c. chromosome.
   d. gamete.

2. Human chromosomes come in __________ pairs. (p. 52)
   a. 23 heterogeneous
   b. 23 matching
   c. 46 heterogeneous
   d. 46 matching

3. Genes __________ (p. 52)
   a. are all the same length.
   b. are made up of 100 to several thousand cells.
   c. are segments of DNA along the length of the chromosome.
   d. contain rodlike structures called chromosomes.

4. DNA duplicates itself through __________ (p. 53)
   a. fraternal twinning.
   b. mitosis.
   c. meiosis.
   d. fertilization.

5. During mitosis, genes send instructions to the cytoplasm for making __________ (p. 53)
   a. gametes.
   b. proteins.
   c. chromosomes.
   d. karotypes.

6. Gametes are formed during __________ (p. 53)
   a. crossing over.
   b. meiosis.
   c. canalization.
   d. mitosis.

7. In the male, __________ sperm is/are produced when meiosis is complete. (p. 54)
   a. one
   b. four
   c. hundreds of
   d. millions of

8. In a human, 22 pairs of chromosomes are __________ (p. 54)
   a. sex chromosomes.
   b. nonmatching.
   c. autosomes.
   d. karotypes.

9. The most common type of multiple birth results from __________ (p. 55)
   a. the release and fertilization of two ova.
   b. in vitro fertilization.
   c. the separation of a zygote into two clusters.
   d. the fertilization of one ovum by two sperm.

10. Monozygotic twins __________ (p. 55)
    a. result from the release and fertilization of two ova.
    b. are no more alike genetically than ordinary siblings.
    c. have the same genetic makeup.
    d. are more frequent in developing countries than in industrialized ones.

11. If the alleles from both parents are alike, the child __________ (p. 56)
    a. is heterozygous.
    b. will inherit a dominant genetic disease.
    c. will inherit a recessive genetic disease.
    d. is homozygous.

12. __________ is/are an example of a recessive characteristic. (p. 56)
    a. Blond hair
    b. Facial dimples
    c. Curly hair
    d. Type A blood

13. In 95 percent of cases, Down syndrome results from __________ (pp. 60–61)
    a. failure of the autosomes to separate.
    b. an error during the early stages of mitosis.
    c. the body's inability to break down proteins.
    d. a failure of the twenty-first pair of chromosomes to separate during meiosis.

14. Josh has Klinefelter syndrome. He probably has trouble __________ (p. 62)
    a. drawing pictures.
    b. telling right from left.
    c. reading.
    d. noticing changes in facial expressions.

15. __________ is the most widely used prenatal diagnostic technique. (p. 64)
    a. Chorionic villus sampling
    b. Amniocentesis
    c. Maternal blood analysis
    d. Fetoscopy

16. Most parents who have used in vitro fertilization __________ (p. 66)
    a. eventually tell their children about their origins.
    b. also have biological children.
    c. do not tell their children about their origins.
    d. have a strong desire for twins or triplets.

17. Children adopted after infancy __________ (p. 66)
    a. fare as well as children adopted during infancy.
    b. fare much better in development than children who are raised by their biological parents.
    c. often live with their extended family.
    d. often have a preadoptive history of abuse and neglect.

18. Marq and Val have a warm and considerate marital relationship, whereas Quinn and Anna have a tense and hostile relationship. Which of the following statements about their parenting is likely true? (p. 70)
    a. Marq and Val are more likely than Quinn and Anna to emphasize external characteristics like obedience, neatness, and cleanliness.
    b. Both sets of parents are likely to engage in coparenting, particularly as their children enter adolescence.
    c. Marq and Eva are more likely than Quinn and Anna to engage in coparenting.
    d. Quinn and Anna are more likely than Marq and Eva to emphasize traits like curiosity, self-direction, and social maturity.

19. Mary Beth can directly promote her granddaughter's development by __________ (p. 71)
    a. responding warmly to her.
    b. providing her parents with child-rearing advice.
    c. providing financial assistance to her parents.
    d. modeling child-rearing skills for her parents.

20. People who work in professional occupations tend to __________ than people who work in skilled occupations. (p. 71)
    a. marry earlier
    b. have children earlier
    c. give birth to more children
    d. give birth to fewer children

21. Affluent youths __________ (p. 72)
    a. usually have parents who engage in regular family interaction.
    b. are more likely than low-SES youths to engage in drug use.
    c. are less likely than high-SES youths to be diagnosed with depression.
    d. are less likely than low-SES youths to engage in drug use.

22. According to a United Nations report, the most effective means of combating poverty is __________ (p. 73)
    a. educating girls.
    b. delaying age of first marriage.
    c. limiting family size.
    d. spending more money on health care.

23. Parent–teacher contact is more frequent in __________ (p. 77)
    a. small towns.
    b. large school districts.
    c. low-SES families.
    d. high school than in elementary school.

24. Caucasian-American parents __________ than African-American parents. (p. 78)
    a. live closer to their relatives
    b. see more relatives during the week
    c. more often establish family-like relationships with friends
    d. live in fewer extended-family homes

25. In individualistic societies, people __________ (p. 78)
    a. define themselves as part of a group.
    b. are largely concerned with their own personal needs.
    c. stress group over individual goals.
    d. often reside in extended-family homes.

26. The United States __________ (p. 79)
    a. has more public policies safeguarding children than most industrialized nations.
    b. has a smaller childhood poverty rate than the Czech Republic and Germany.
    c. does not rank well on any key measure of children's health and well-being.
    d. ranks ninth among 28 industrialized nations in the teenage pregnancy rate.

27. Heritability estimates measure __________ (p. 82)
    a. the extent to which individual differences in complex traits in a specific population are due to genetic factors.
    b. each person's unique, genetically determined response to the environment.
    c. the extent to which our genes influence the environments to which we are exposed.
    d. the tendency to actively choose environments that complement our heredity.

28. Parents who are musically talented take their children to instrumental and vocal lessons. This is an example of a(n) __________ genetic–environmental correlation. (p. 85)
    a. passive
    b. evocative
    c. dynamic
    d. active

29. The concept of epigenesis can help researchers __________ (p. 86)
    a. make sense of how internal stimulation triggers gene activity.
    b. to extend an individual's range of reaction.
    c. trace the effects of evocative correlation.
    d. understand development as a series of complex changes between nature and nurture.

30. Maternal smoking during pregnancy is among the risk factors for __________ (p. 87)
    a. ADHD.
    b. mental retardation.
    c. childhood obesity.
    d. autism.

PRACTICE TEST #2

1. An individual's __________ is the complex blend of genetic information that determines our species and influences all our unique characteristics. (p. 51)
   a. phenotype
   b. karotype
   c. genotype
   d. gamete

2. __________ store and transmit genetic information. (p. 52)
   a. Phenotypes
   b. Chromosomes
   c. Genotypes
   d. Gametes

3. Each rung of a DNA ladder consists of __________ (p. 52)
   a. a pair of chemical substances called bases.
   b. 23 matching pairs of chromosomes.
   c. a single gene.
   d. a gamete and an autosome.

4. Chromosomes copy themselves during __________ (p. 53)
   a. fertilization.
   b. meiosis.
   c. monozygotic twinning.
   d. mitosis.

5. At the microscopic level, biological events are the result of __________ (p. 53)
   a. fertilization.
   b. incomplete dominance.
   c. both genetic and nongenetic forces.
   d. neither genetic nor nongenetic forces.

6. New individuals are created when __________ combine. (p. 53)
   a. gametes
   b. zygotes
   c. autosomes
   d. phenotypes

7. In the female, meiosis results in __________ ovum/ova. (p. 54)
   a. one
   b. four
   c. hundreds of
   d. millions of

8. The Y chromosome __________ (pp. 54–55)
   a. carries a large amount of genetic material.
   b. is relatively large.
   c. is short.
   d. stores genetic information.

9. Fraternal twins __________ (p. 55)
   a. result from the separation of a zygote into two clusters.
   b. are the most common type of multiple birth.
   c. have the same genetic makeup.
   d. are genetically more alike than ordinary siblings.

10. Dizygotic twinning is more likely in __________ than in __________ (p. 55)
    a. younger women; older women.
    b. slightly built women; overweight women.
    c. Asian women; African-American women.
    d. later births; first births.

11. __________ is an example of an X-linked disorder. (p. 57)
    a. Hemophilia
    b. PKU
    c. Cystic fibrosis
    d. Triple X syndrome

12. In genomic imprinting, alleles are __________ (p. 59)
    a. separated.
    b. chemically marked.
    c. divided.
    d. mutated.

13. __________ is an established cause of mutation. (p. 60)
    a. Ionizing radiation
    b. Incomplete dominance
    c. Genomic imprinting
    d. Polygenic inheritance

14. __________ mothers bear the majority of babies with genetic defects. (p. 61)
    a. Older
    b. Younger
    c. Affluent
    d. Middle-income

15. __________ is the only prenatal diagnostic method that is safe enough to use routinely. (p. 63)
    a. Amniocentesis
    b. Ultrasound
    c. Fetoscopy
    d. Maternal blood analysis

16. Using __________, researchers have corrected genetic abnormalities by delivering DNA carrying a functional gene to the cells. (p. 64)
    a. genomic imprinting
    b. gene therapy
    c. proteomics
    d. canalization

17. The success rate of __________ is about 70 to 80 percent. (p. 66)
    a. assisted reproductive technologies
    b. in vitro fertilization
    c. donor insemination
    d. the "sex sorter" method

18. Contemporary researchers view the family as a __________ (p. 70)
    a. network of interdependent relationships.
    b. unidirectional influence on child development.
    c. part of the chronosystem.
    d. series of mesosystems.

19. Which of the following has led to smaller family size in industrialized nations? (p. 71)
    a. rising infant mortality rates
    b. expansion of women's roles
    c. declining divorce rates
    d. access to free or low-cost birth control

20. When asked about the personal qualities they desire for their children, lower-SES parents emphasize __________ and higher-SES parents emphasize __________ (p. 72)
    a. psychological traits; external characteristics.
    b. psychological traits; intellectual abilities.
    c. intellectual abilities; psychological traits.
    d. external characteristics; psychological traits.

21. The diverse benefits of girls' schooling largely accrue through enhanced verbal skills and __________ (p. 73)
    a. empowerment.
    b. enhanced mathematical skills.
    c. enhanced physical skills.
    d. enhanced global understanding.

22. For both affluent and low-SES children, regularly __________ is associated with a reduction in adjustment difficulties. (p. 74)
    a. attending scouting programs
    b. eating dinner with parents
    c. eating breakfast in the morning
    d. participating in competitive sports

23. An estimated 23 percent of the homeless in the United States are __________ (p. 75)
    a. mentally ill.
    b. substance abusers.
    c. families with children.
    d. adolescents.

24. Studies show that impoverished children whose families moved into low-poverty neighborhoods __________ (p. 76)
    a. had trouble adjusting to their new surroundings.
    b. showed little change in their behavior.
    c. improved more in social skills than in academics.
    d. showed substantially better health and school achievement.

25. Higher-SES parents tend to interact frequently with their children's teachers because __________ (p. 77)
    a. they generally live in smaller towns.
    b. their backgrounds and values are often similar.
    c. their children often socialize with their teacher's children.
    d. they have more daily stressors than low-SES parents and need more encouragement.

26. In collectivist societies, people __________ (p. 78)
    a. value an interdependent self.
    b. think of themselves as separate entities.
    c. encourage assimilation into the majority culture.
    d. limit child-oriented public policies.

27. __________ is/are especially common among African Americans. (p. 79)
    a. Individualistic values
    b. Use of reproductive technologies
    c. Family reunions
    d. Nuclear-family households

28. __________ is an example of strongly canalized skill. (p. 84)
    a. Reading
    b. Steering a bike
    c. Walking
    d. Writing

29. Missy, an active, friendly baby, receives more patient, sensitive interactions from adults than her twin, Melanie, a passive, quiet infant. This is an example of a(n) __________ genetic–environmental correlation. (p. 85)
    a. passive
    b. evocative
    c. dynamic
    d. active

30. In one study, 5-year-olds with both prenatal nicotine exposure and the DD genetic makeup __________ (p. 87)
    a. demonstrated symptoms consistent with autism.
    b. scored high in impulsivity, overactivity, and oppositional behaviors.
    c. were at high risk for overweight and obesity.
    d. developed juvenile diabetes.

CHAPTER 3
PRENATAL DEVELOPMENT

BRIEF CHAPTER SUMMARY

This chapter begins with a discussion of motivations for parenthood and current changes in birth patterns. Today, men and women are more likely to weigh the pros and cons of having children than they were in previous generations. The American family has declined in size over time, and births to women over age 30 have increased. Although reproductive capacity declines with age, adults who delay childbearing until their education is complete, their careers are established, and they are emotionally more mature may be better able to invest in parenting.

At no other time is change as rapid as it is before birth. Prenatal development takes place in three phases: (1) the period of the zygote, during which the newly fertilized ovum travels down the fallopian tube and attaches itself to the uterine wall; (2) the period of the embryo, during which the groundwork for all body structures is laid down; and (3) the period of the fetus, the "growth and finishing" phase.

The prenatal period is a vulnerable time. The developing organism can be endangered by teratogens, including drugs, cigarettes, alcohol, radiation, and environmental pollution, as well as infectious disease, inadequate exercise and nutrition, maternal stress, Rh blood incompatibility, and maternal age. Prenatal health care is vitally important to ensure the health of mother and baby.

For most expectant parents, however, the prenatal period is not a time of medical hazard. Rather, it is a time of major life change in which mothers and fathers prepare for parenthood.

LEARNING OBJECTIVES

After reading this chapter, you should be able to:

3.1 Cite advantages and disadvantages of parenthood mentioned by contemporary American couples. (pp. 92–93)

3.2 Review current trends in family size, parenting quality, and childbearing age, and discuss their impact on child development. (pp. 93–95)

3.3 List the three phases of prenatal development, and describe the major milestones of each. (pp. 95–102)

3.4 Define the term *teratogen,* and summarize the factors that affect their impact. (pp. 102–104)

3.5 List agents known to be or suspected of being teratogens, and discuss evidence supporting the harmful effects of each. (pp. 105–112)

3.6 Discuss the impact of other maternal factors on prenatal development. (pp. 112–116)

3.7 Discuss the importance of prenatal health care, and cite some of the barriers to seeking such care. (pp. 116–119)

3.8 Describe factors that contribute to personal adjustment as expectant mothers and fathers prepare for parenthood. (pp. 120–122)

STUDY QUESTIONS

Motivations for Parenthood

Why Have Children?

1. List five advantages and five disadvantages of parenthood mentioned by American couples. (pp. 92–93)

   Advantages:

   A. ______________________________

   B. ______________________________

   C. ______________________________

   D. ______________________________

   E. ______________________________

   Disadvantages:

   A. ______________________________

   B. ______________________________

   C. ______________________________

   D. ______________________________

   E. ______________________________

How Large a Family?

1. List two major reasons that family size has declined in industrialized nations. (p. 93)

   A. ______________________________

   B. ______________________________

2. Describe the benefits of growing up in a small family. (p. 93)

   ____

   ____

   ____

3. True or False: Children's mental test performance tends to decline with later birth order. (pp. 93–94)

4. Describe factors that contribute to lower intelligence scores for children in large families. (p. 94)

   ____

   ____

   ____

5. True or False: As new children are born, parents reallocate their energies to accommodate the needs of both older and younger children. (p. 94)

Is There a Best Time During Adulthood to Have a Child?

1. Cite reasons why many modern couples are delaying childbearing into their thirties and beyond. (p. 95)

   ____

   ____

2. True or False: Both males and females experience a decline in reproductive capacity with age. (p. 95)

Prenatal Development

Conception

1. Approximately once every 28 days, an ovum is released from one of a woman's two ___________________, and it travels through one of the two _________________________, which are long, thin structures that lead to the uterus. (p. 96)
2. The male produces vast numbers of sperm in the _________________________, two glands located in the scrotum. (p. 96)
3. True or False: Sperm live for up to 10 days and can lie in wait for the ovum, which survives for 3 days after being released in the fallopian tube. (p. 96)

Period of the Zygote

1. The period of the zygote lasts about _____________ weeks, from fertilization until the tiny mass of cells drifts down and out of the fallopian tube and attaches itself to the wall of the uterus. (p. 97)
2. Match each term with the appropriate definition. (pp. 97–98)

   _____ Will become the structures that provide protective covering and nourishment to the new organism
   _____ Hollow, fluid-filled ball that is formed by a tiny mass of cells four days after fertilization
   _____ Will become the new organism

   A. *Blastocyst*
   B. *Embryonic disk*
   C. *Trophoblast*
3. List two functions of the *amniotic fluid.* (p. 98)

   A. ______________________________

   B. ______________________________
4. True or False: As many as 30 percent of zygotes do not make it through the first two weeks. (p. 98)
5. The ____________________________ permits food and oxygen to reach the developing organism and waste products to be carried away. (p. 98)
6. The *placenta* is connected to the developing organism by the ______________________________. (p. 98)

Period of the Embryo

1. The period of the *embryo* lasts from implantation through the ________________ week of pregnancy. (p. 99)
2. True or False: The most rapid prenatal changes take place during the period of the embryo. (p. 99)
3. List the organs and structures that will be formed from each of the three layers of the embryonic disk. (p. 99)

   Ectoderm: ______________________________

   Mesoderm: ______________________________

   Endoderm: ______________________________
4. Briefly summarize prenatal growth during the second month of pregnancy. (p. 99)

   ____

   ____

   ____

Period of the Fetus

1. True or False: The sex of the developing *fetus* can be determined, via ultrasound, starting in the third month of pregnancy. (p. 100)
2. Prenatal development is divided into ____________________, or three equal time periods. (p. 100)
3. The white, cheeselike substance that protects the skin from chapping in the amniotic fluid is called ____________. (p. 100)
4. ____________ is a white, downy hair that covers the entire body of the fetus. (p. 100)
5. The age at which the baby can first survive if born early is called the *age of* ____________________. When does this typically occur? (p. 100)

   ____

6. How does the enlargement of the cerebral cortex impact the developing fetus? (pp. 100–101)

   ____

   ____

   ____

7. List changes in fetal behavior during each of the following time periods. (p. 101)

   20 weeks: ______________________________

   28 weeks: ______________________________

   30–34 weeks: ______________________________

   End of pregnancy: ______________________________

8. During the third trimester, fetuses (can / cannot) distinguish the tone and rhythm of different voices and sounds. (p. 101)
9. Describe major changes in the fetus during the final three months of pregnancy. (p. 101)

   ____

   ____

   ____

Prenatal Environmental Influences

Teratogens

1. Define the term *teratogen,* and describe four factors that affect the impact of *teratogens* on the developing organism. (pp. 102–103)

   Teratogen: ______________________________

   ____

   A. ______________________________

   B. ______________________________

   C. ______________________________

   D. ______________________________

2. A(n) ____________________ period is a limited time span in which a part of the body or a behavior is biologically prepared to develop rapidly and is especially sensitive to its surroundings. (p. 103)
3. True or False: The period of the zygote is the time when teratogens are most likely to cause serious defects. (p. 104)

4. ______________, or isotretinoin, is a commonly used prescription acne medication that causes widespread abnormalities in the developing fetus. (p. 106)

5. True or False: Heavy caffeine intake during pregnancy is associated with low birth weight and increased risk of miscarriage. (p. 106)

6. Describe the difficulties faced by babies who are prenatally exposed to cocaine, heroine, or methadone. (pp. 106–107)

____

____

____

7. Explain why it is difficult to isolate the precise damage caused by prenatal drug exposure. (p. 107)

____

____

____

8. Place a check mark next to each potential consequence of prenatal exposure to tobacco. (p. 107)

_____ Low birth weight	_____ High birth weight	_____ High fetal activity	_____ Miscarriage
_____ Prematurity	_____ Impaired heart rate	_____ Short eyelid openings	_____ Poor sleep
_____ Rapid weight gain	_____ Piercing cry	_____ Bone deformities	_____ Thin upper lip
_____ Short attention span	_____ Low mental test scores	_____ Neural tube defects	_____ Impulsivity

9. True or False: If the mother stops smoking at any time during her pregnancy, even during the last trimester, she reduces the chances that her baby will be negatively impacted. (p. 107)

10. Explain the mechanisms through which smoking harms the fetus. (p. 107)

____

____

____

11. What is "passive smoking," and how does it affect the developing organism? (p. 108)

A. ____

B. ____

12. Infants who have a range of physical and behavioral abnormalities and whose mothers drank heavily throughout most or all of pregnancy are said to have ______________________________. (p. 108)

13. Match the following characteristics with the proper diagnosis. (pp. 108–109)

_____ At least three areas of mental functioning are impaired, despite typical physical growth and absence of facial abnormalities
_____ Characterized by two of the three facial abnormalities and brain injury
_____ Distinguished by slow physical growth, a pattern of three facial abnormalities, and brain injury

A. *Fetal alcohol syndrome (FAS)*
B. *Partial fetal alcohol syndrome (p-FAS)*
C. *Alcohol-related neurodevelopmental disorder (ARND)*

14. Describe physical and mental impairments associated with fetal alcohol spectrum disorders that persist from the preschool years through early adulthood. (p. 109)

    Preschool and school years: ____

    ____

    Adolescence and early adulthood: ____

    ____

15. Describe two ways in which alcohol produces its devastating effects. (p. 109)

    A. ____

    ____

    B. ____

    ____

16. True or False: Mild drinking, less than one alcoholic drink per day, is associated with poor outcomes for the child. Therefore, no amount of alcohol is safe to drink during pregnancy. (p. 109)

17. True or False: Low doses of radiation exposure, such as through medical X-rays, are believed to be safe for the developing fetus and have not been linked to any negative outcomes. (p. 110)

18. Match each of the following environmental pollutants with its effect on development. (pp. 110–111)

    _____ This teratogen, commonly found in paint chippings from old buildings and other industrial materials, is related to low birth weight, prematurity, brain damage, and physical defects.

    _____ In the 1950s, children prenatally exposed to this teratogen in a Japanese community displayed mental retardation, abnormal speech, and uncoordinated movements.

    _____ Women who ate fish contaminated with this substance gave birth to babies with slightly reduced birth weights, smaller heads, persisting attention and memory difficulties, and lower intelligence test scores in childhood.

    A. Mercury
    B. PCBs
    C. Lead

19. List the outcomes associated with embryonic and fetal exposure to rubella. (pp. 111–112)

    Embryonic: ____

    ____

    ____

    Fetal: ____

    ____

20. When women carrying the AIDS virus become pregnant, they pass on the disease to their baby approximately ____ to ____ percent of the time. (p. 112)

21. True or False: There is no known drug that can reduce the risk of prenatal AIDS transmission. (p. 112)

22. Pregnant women can become infected with __________________________, a parasitic disease found in many animals, from eating raw or undercooked meat or from contact with the feces of infected cats. (p. 112)

Biology and Environment: The Prenatal Environment and Health in Later Life

1. List four health problems in adults that have been associated with low birth weight. (p. 104)
   A. ______
   B. ______
   C. ______
   D. ______
2. True or False: Low-birth-weight babies often remain underweight in childhood and throughout their lives. (p. 105)
3. According to research, why does a high birth weight lead to an increased risk of breast cancer later in life? (p. 105)
   ______
   ______

Other Maternal Factors

1. Regular, moderate exercise during pregnancy is associated with (increased / decreased) birth weight and an (increased / decreased) risk of maternal diabetes and high blood pressure. (p. 113)
2. Summarize the behavioral and health problems of prenatally malnourished babies. (p. 113)
   ______
   ______
3. List the vitamin and mineral supplements that have been found to reduce prenatal complications and birth defects. (p. 114)
   A. ______ B. ______
   C. ______ D. ______
   E. ______ F. ______
4. True or False: Prenatal malnutrition is currently limited to developing countries, and it has been entirely eradicated in the United States through government programs for low-income pregnant women. (p. 114)
5. Describe the mechanisms through which maternal stress affects the developing organism, and note outcomes associated with severe emotional stress during pregnancy. (pp. 114–115)
   Mechanisms: ______
   ______
   ______
   Outcomes: ______
   ______
   ______
6. Under what conditions can *Rh factor incompatibility* cause problems for the developing fetus? (p. 115)
   ______
   ______
   ______
7. Problems resulting from the Rh factor are more likely to affect (firstborn /later-born) children. (p. 115)

8. True or False: Healthy women in their thirties experience far more prenatal difficulties than women in their twenties. (p. 115)

9. The physical immaturity of teenage mothers (does /does not) usually lead to pregnancy complications. (p. 116)

Social Issues: Health: The Nurse–Family Partnership: Reducing Maternal Stress and Enhancing Child Development Through Social Support

1. How does the Nurse–Family Partnership seek to improve quality of life for expectant mothers and their children? (p. 116)

____

____

2. How did mothers and children benefit from the Nurse–Family Partnership? (p. 116)

   Mothers: ____

   ____

   Children: ____

   ____

3. (Professional nurses / Trained paraprofessionals) were most effective in preventing poor outcomes associated with prenatal stress. (p. 116)

The Importance of Prenatal Health Care

1. Describe two potential complications that can arise during pregnancy. (p. 117)

   A. ____

   ____

   B. ____

   ____

2. Name two groups of women who often do not receive adequate prenatal care, and note the consequences for their babies. (p. 117)

   A. ______________________ B. ______________________

   Consequences: ____

   ____

3. Discuss some of the barriers to obtaining prenatal health care. (p. 117)

____

____

____

Biology and Environment: Prenatal Iron Deficiency and Memory Impairments in Infants of Diabetic Mothers

1. True or False: Low-income ethnic minority adults are twice as likely as white adults to suffer from diabetes. (p. 118)

2. Today, about ____ percent of pregnant mothers are diabetic. (p. 118)

3. List the consequences of the mother's high blood glucose levels on the developing fetus. (p. 118)

____

____

4. How might the lower intelligence test scores and memory abilities of children of diabetic mothers be caused by prenatal damage to the hippocampus? (p. 118)

____

____

Preparing for Parenthood

1. More than _____ percent of pregnancies in industrialized nations result in healthy newborn babies. (p. 120)

Seeking Information

1. Pregnant mothers regard ______________________ as an extremely valuable source of information, second in importance only to their doctors. (p. 120)

The Baby Becomes a Reality

1. What changes and experiences help expectant parents come to view the baby as a reality? (pp. 120–121)

____

____

____

Models of Effective Parenthood

1. True or False: Men and women who have had good relationships with their own parents are more likely to develop positive images of themselves as parents during pregnancy. (p. 121)
2. Cite three benefits of participating in special intervention programs for expectant mothers and fathers. (p. 121)

   A. ____

   B. ____

   C. ____

The Parental Relationship

1. True or False: Having a baby typically improves a troubled marital relationship. (p. 121)

ASK YOURSELF . . .

For *Ask Yourself* questions for this chapter, along with feedback on the accuracy of your answers, please log on to MyDevelopmentLab (for registration and access, please visit mydevelopmentlab.com or follow the instructions on page ix).

(1) Select the Multimedia Library.

(2) Choose the explore option.

(3) Find your chapter from the drop down box.

(4) Click find now.

(5) Complete questions and choose "Submit answers for grading" or "Clear answers" to start over.

SUGGESTED READINGS

Curtis, G. B., & Schuler, J. (2009). *Your pregnancy for the father-to-be.* New York: Perseus Publishing. Written for a general audience, this book provides information to expectant fathers about physical changes during pregnancy, medical tests and procedures, and the importance of providing the mother with social support during pregnancy and after the baby arrives. Other topics include costs of having a baby, child-care expenses, planning for the future, and the impact of pregnancy on a couple's relationship.

Dombrowski, S. C., & Martin, R. P. (2008). *Prenatal exposures: Psychological and educational consequences for children.* New York: Springer. A compelling look at prenatal development, this book examines the effects of teratogens on the developing organism. The authors also present research on environmental factors, such as social support, that contribute to development outcomes in prenatally exposed babies.

Simkin, P., Bolding, A., Durham, J., & McGinnis, M. (Eds.). (2010). *Pregnancy, childbirth, and the newborn.* New York: Meadowbrook Press. Presents up-to-date research on pregnancy, childbirth, and the transition to parenthood. Topics include what to expect during pregnancy, the importance of nutrition and exercise, the dangers of drugs and alcohol, prenatal care, myths and facts about childbirth, and frequently asked questions.

CROSSWORD PUZZLE 3.1

Across

4. Age of __________________: age at which the fetus can first survive if born early
7. The _____________ cord connects the prenatal organism to the placenta.
8. _____________ tube: primitive spinal cord
10. Zygote four days after fertilization, when it forms a hollow, fluid-filled ball
11. Membrane that encloses the developing organism in amniotic fluid
12. Ring of cells which will become the structures that provide protective covering and nourishment to the new organism
15. ____________ fluid: keeps the temperature in the womb constant and provides a cushion against jolts

Down

1. White, cheeselike substance that covers the fetus and prevents chapping
2. Outer membrane that forms a protective covering and sends out villi from which the placenta emerges
3. The prenatal organism from two to eight weeks after conception
5. The blastocyst burrows deep into the uterine lining during _____________.
6. The prenatal organism from the ninth week to the end of pregnancy
9. White, downy hair that covers the fetus
13. Separates the mother's bloodstream from that of the fetus while permitting the exchange of nutrients and waste products
14. Embryonic _____________: cluster of cells inside the blastocyst which will become the new organism

CROSSWORD PUZZLE 3.2

Across

1. Fetal alcohol _____________: mental retardation, slow growth, and facial abnormalities resulting from maternal alcohol consumption during pregnancy
3. Environmental agent that causes damage during the prenatal period
4. _________ _______ incompatibility: may cause the mother to build up antibodies that destroy the fetus's red blood cells (2 words)
5. Fetal alcohol _____________ disorder: a range of physical, mental, and behavioral outcomes caused by prenatal alcohol exposure
6. Three equal periods of time in prenatal development
7. ___________ fetal alcohol syndrome: a form of fetal alcohol spectrum disorder characterized by facial abnormalities and brain injury, but less severe than fetal alcohol syndrome, usually seen in children whose mothers drank alcohol in smaller quantities during pregnancy

Down

2. Alcohol-related _____________ disorder: the least severe form of fetal alcohol spectrum disorders; involves brain injury, but with typical physical growth and absence of facial abnormalities

PRACTICE TEST #1

1. When Americans are asked about their reasons for having children, they most often list __________ as an important factor. (p. 92)
   a. being accepted as a responsible and mature member of the community
   b. having someone to carry on after their death
   c. the warm, affectionate relationship that children provide
   d. gaining a sense of accomplishment

2. When Americans are asked about the disadvantages of parenthood, they cite __________ most often. (p. 92)
   a. financial strain
   b. loss of freedom
   c. loss of privacy
   d. family–work conflict

3. Which of the following is true about family size and intelligence? (p. 94)
   a. Large families have less intelligent children than small families.
   b. Children's mental test performance declines with later birth order.
   c. Only children are more intelligent than children with siblings.
   d. There is a strong trend for mothers who are low in intelligence to give birth to more children.

4. Only children are __________ children with siblings. (p. 94)
   a. as well-adjusted as
   b. more independent than
   c. more selfish than
   d. smarter than

5. Fertilization usually takes place in the __________ (p. 96)
   a. cervix.
   b. fallopian tube.
   c. corpus luteum.
   d. uterus.

6. The period of the zygote lasts about _____ weeks. (p. 97)
   a. 2
   b. 3
   c. 4
   d. 5

7. The trophoblast __________ (p. 98)
   a. will become the developing organism.
   b. multiplies fast and forms the amnion.
   c. is the thick inner ring of cells inside the blastocyst.
   d. produces the neural tube and vernix.

8. The most rapid prenatal changes take place during the __________ (p. 99)
   a. third trimester.
   b. second trimester.
   c. period of the embryo.
   d. period of the zygote.

9. The period of the fetus __________ (p. 100)
   a. is the longest prenatal period.
   b. lasts about six weeks.
   c. is the most sensitive period for teratogens.
   d. is divided into three trimesters.

10. During the fetal period, teratogenic damage __________ (p. 104)
    a. primarily affects the liver and kidneys.
    b. is likely to be severe.
    c. is most likely to occur.
    d. is usually minor.

11. The effects of teratogens __________ (p. 104)
    a. are immediate.
    b. are obvious.
    c. go beyond physical damage.
    d. are short-term.

12. High birth weight is associated with __________ in adulthood. (p. 105)
    a. heart disease
    b. breast cancer
    c. stroke
    d. diabetes

13. Children of women who took DES, widely prescribed between 1945 and 1970 to prevent miscarriages, showed __________ (pp. 105–106)
    a. an increased risk of genital abnormalities.
    b. gross deformities of the arms and legs.
    c. below average intelligence.
    d. immune system abnormalities.

14. Drinking more than one cup of coffee per day during pregnancy is __________ (p. 106)
    a. safe.
    b. linked to respiratory distress.
    c. linked to low birth weight.
    d. linked to high blood pressure in infancy.

15. Several researchers have linked prenatal marijuana exposure to __________ (p. 107)
    a. brain hemorrhages.
    b. depression in childhood.
    c. urinary tract deformities.
    d. eye deformities.

16. The more cigarettes a mother smokes during pregnancy, the __________ (p. 107)
    a. higher the baby's birth weight.
    b. higher the chances of bone deformities.
    c. higher the chances of facial abnormalities.
    d. greater the chances that her baby will be affected.

17. Mental impairment associated with all three FASD diagnoses is __________ (p. 109)
    a. permanent.
    b. temporary.
    c. mild.
    d. delayed.

18. Ionizing radiation during pregnancy __________ (p. 110)
    a. is safe in low doses.
    b. is safe if it is infrequent.
    c. can cause high blood pressure in the mother.
    d. can cause mutation.

19. Pregnant women are wise to avoid eating long-lived predatory fish to decrease the risk of __________ contamination. (p. 110)
    a. PCB
    b. mercury
    c. lead
    d. dioxin

20. Having mumps during pregnancy increases the risk of __________ (p. 111)
    a. miscarriage.
    b. mental retardation.
    c. low birth weight.
    d. prematurity.

21. __________ is recommended for healthy women during pregnancy. (p. 113)
    a. A 4,000 calorie a day diet
    b. A weekly prenatal visit
    c. Vigorous exercise
    d. Moderate exercise

22. Folic acid intake during the last 10 weeks of pregnancy __________ (p. 114)
    a. increases the risk of premature delivery.
    b. reduces the risk of low birth weight.
    c. is no longer necessary.
    d. increases the risk of spina bifada.

23. Cretinism has been virtually eradicated in the United States because __________ (p. 114)
    a. table salt is fortified with iodine.
    b. bread is fortified with folic acid.
    c. cereal is fortified with calcium.
    d. pasta is fortified with magnesium.

24. The risk of prenatal and birth complications increases after age __________ (p. 115)
    a. 30.
    b. 35.
    c. 40.
    d. 45.

25. The Nurse–Family Partnership __________ (p. 116)
    a. combines group prenatal care with educational classes.
    b. strives to reduce pregnancy and birth complications.
    c. provides nursing services in developing countries.
    d. pairs trained paraprofessionals with high-stressed pregnant moms with young children.

26. Symptoms of preeclampsia include __________ (p. 117)
    a. spotting or bleeding.
    b. a sharp increase in maternal blood pressure.
    c. a drastic decrease in maternal blood sugar.
    d. cramping, fever, and rash.

27. Which of the following is true about adolescent mothers? (p. 117)
    a. They are just as likely as older mothers to receive prenatal care.
    b. Their bodies are not yet mature enough to maintain a healthy pregnancy.
    c. Their infants are three times as likely to be born underweight.
    d. They are more likely than older mothers to have medically-induced labors.

28. Infants born to mothers with inadequate prenatal care are _____ times as likely to die as are babies of mothers who receive early medical attention. (p. 117)
   a. two
   b. three
   c. four
   d. five

29. Research shows that children born to diabetic mothers have memory impairments caused by damage to the __________ (p. 118)
   a. frontal lobe.
   b. cerebral cortex.
   c. hippocampus.
   d. cerebellum.

30. Expectant mothers rank __________ as second in importance, after their doctors, for providing valuable information about pregnancy and childbirth. (p. 120)
   a. reading books
   b. watching videos
   c. consulting with their mothers
   d. attending prenatal classes

PRACTICE TEST #2

1. Today, in Western industrialized nations, the decision to have children is a __________ (p. 92)
   a. biological given.
   b. true individual choice.
   c. compelling social expectation.
   d. practical matter.

2. In the United States today, __________ percent of married couples do not have children. (p. 92)
   a. 15
   b. 20
   c. 25
   d. 30

3. The average number of children per North American couple today is __________ (p. 93)
   a. 3.1.
   b. 2.8.
   c. 1.8.
   d. 1.3.

4. About once every 28 days, an ovum is drawn into the __________ (p. 96)
   a. fallopian tubes.
   b. ovaries.
   c. corpus luteum.
   d. uterus.

5. Between the seventh and ninth days after conception, __________ occurs. (p. 98)
   a. fertilization
   b. the formation of the spinal cord
   c. rapid brain growth
   d. implantation

6. The __________ permits food and oxygen to reach the developing organism and waste products to be carried away. (p. 98)
   a. placenta
   b. yolk sac
   c. amniotic fluid
   d. umbilical cord

7. The period of the embryo lasts _____ weeks. (p. 99)
   a. 2
   b. 4
   c. 6
   d. 12

8. The __________ will develop the muscles, skeleton, circulatory system, and other internal organs. (p. 99)
   a. ectoderm
   b. mesoderm
   c. endoderm
   d. neural tube

9. The developing organism responds to touch in the __________ month. (p. 99)
   a. first
   b. second
   c. third
   d. fourth

10. During the period of the fetus, the __________ (p. 100)
    a. most rapid prenatal changes take place.
    b. nervous system develops.
    c. embryonic disk forms three layers of cells.
    d. developing organism increases rapidly in size.

11. Kristal, who is in her second trimester of pregnancy, wonders how her developing baby is protected in the amniotic fluid. You should tell her that __________ protects the skin from chapping. (p. 100)
    a. lanugo
    b. the villi
    c. vernix
    d. the yolk sac

12. The age of viability occurs between _____ and _____ weeks. (p. 100)
    a. 16; 18
    b. 20; 22
    c. 22; 26
    d. 28; 30

13. __________ predicts a more active infant in the first month of life. (p. 101)
    a. Rapid weight gain
    b. Higher fetal activity
    c. Irregular fetal activity
    d. Maternal exercise

14. In the period of the zygote, teratogens __________ (p. 104)
    a. rarely have any impact.
    b. affect the ears, eyes, and teeth.
    c. cause the most serious defects.
    d. cannot cause miscarriages.

15. According to research on the prenatal environment and health in later life, which of the following babies is most at-risk for high blood pressure in middle adulthood? (p. 104)
    a. Dante, who weighed 4 pounds, 9 ounces at birth
    b. Lola, who weighed 8 pounds, 7 ounces at birth
    c. Barron, whose mother took aspirin during her pregnancy
    d. Shayla, whose mother rarely exercised in her third trimester

16. When taken by expectant mothers four to six weeks after conception, thalidomide produced __________ (p. 105)
    a. gross deformities of the embryo's developing arms and legs.
    b. high rates of vaginal cancer.
    c. infertility in female offspring.
    d. immune system abnormalities.

17. Smoking during pregnancy is associated with __________ (p. 107)
    a. facial abnormalities.
    b. mental retardation.
    c. low birth weight.
    d. a flattened philtrum.

18. The more alcohol a woman consumes during pregnancy, the __________ (p. 109)
    a. greater the child's birth weight.
    b. higher the mother's blood pressure.
    c. poorer the child's motor coordination.
    d. greater the chances of gross deformities of the arms and legs.

19. Low-level exposure to polychlorinated biphenyls (PCBs) is __________ (p. 110)
    a. associated with smaller head size.
    b. safe as long as it is not consumed.
    c. related to high birth weight.
    d. a danger associated with paint flaking off the walls of old buildings.

20. Even tiny amounts of __________ in the paternal bloodstream cause a dramatic change in sex ratio of offspring. (p. 111)
    a. lead
    b. dioxin
    c. mercury
    d. PCBs

21. In the mid-1960s, a worldwide epidemic of __________ led to the birth of more than 20,000 American babies with serious defects and to 13,000 fetal and newborn deaths. (p. 111)
    a. cytomegalovirus
    b. mumps
    c. rubella
    d. chickenpox

22. Expectant mothers can avoid the risk of toxoplasmosis by __________ (p. 112)
    a. turning over litter box care to other family members.
    b. avoiding exposure to X-rays.
    c. not eating albacore tuna.
    d. making sure the meat they eat is not overcooked.

23. For pregnant women with a history of miscarriages, exercise __________ (p. 113)
    a. is fine in moderation.
    b. is just as safe as for mothers with no miscarriage history.
    c. can endanger the pregnancy.
    d. should include a 30-minute workout four to five times a week.

24. Prenatal malnutrition __________ (p. 114)
    a. is not limited to developing countries.
    b. is highest in industrialized nations.
    c. does not have a sensitive period.
    d. has been eradicated in most Western nations.

25. Intense maternal anxiety during the first two trimesters is associated with __________ (p. 114)
    a. limb deformities.
    b. heart disease.
    c. prematurity.
    d. diabetes.

26. Rh incompatibility is associated with __________ (p. 115)
    a. prematurity.
    b. low birth weight.
    c. diabetes.
    d. mental retardation.

27. Infants born to teenagers have a higher rate of problems because __________ (p. 116)
    a. many come from low-income backgrounds where health problems are common.
    b. many of their mothers have genetic disorders that are passed on to offspring.
    c. of their mother's young maternal age.
    d. their fathers often have genetic disorders that are passed on to offspring.

28. Research on the Nurse-Family Partnership showed that home-visited mothers __________ (p. 116)
    a. had longer intervals between their first and second births.
    b. were more willing to accept help from their extended family.
    c. had less frequent contact with their child's father but had other forms of support.
    d. had higher incomes and more stable employment prior to becoming pregnant.

29. In a study comparing the newborns of diabetic mothers with typically developing newborns, researchers found that __________ (p. 118)
    a. both groups of babies preferred their mother's voice over that of a stranger.
    b. the newborns of diabetic mothers preferred a stranger's voice to that of their mother.
    c. typically developing newborns preferred the stranger's voice to that of their mother.
    d. the newborns of diabetic mothers did not distinguish between their mother's voice and that of a stranger.

30. Research suggests that in a troubled marriage, __________ (p. 121)
    a. the parental relationship lessens family conflict.
    b. pregnancy adds to family conflict.
    c. the excitement of pregnancy brings the spouses closer together.
    d. expectant mothers are unlikely to seek or receive prenatal care.

CHAPTER 4
BIRTH AND THE NEWBORN BABY

BRIEF CHAPTER SUMMARY

Childbirth takes place in three stages: (1) dilation and effacement of the cervix, (2) birth of the baby, and (3) delivery of the placenta. Production of stress hormones helps the infant withstand the trauma of childbirth. The Apgar Scale is used to assess the baby's physical condition at birth.

In natural, or prepared, childbirth, the expectant mother and a companion typically attend classes, master relaxation and breathing techniques to counteract pain, and prepare for coaching during childbirth. Some women choose home birth as a noninstitutional option. Social support during labor and delivery reduces pain and use of medication. However, various medical interventions are commonly a part of childbirth in the United States. These procedures help save the lives of many babies but can introduce new problems when used routinely.

Although most births proceed normally, serious complications sometimes occur. The most common complications result from oxygen deprivation and prematurity. Fortunately, many babies who experience severe birth trauma recover with the help of favorable child-rearing environments, which can be supported by high-quality intervention. The high rate of underweight babies in the United States—one of the worst in the industrialized world—could be greatly reduced by improving health and social conditions.

Infants begin life with a remarkable set of skills for relating to the surrounding world. Newborns display a wide variety of reflexes—automatic responses to specific forms of stimulation. In the early weeks, babies move in and out of different states of arousal (degrees of sleep and wakefulness) frequently but spend the most time in either rapid-eye-movement (REM) sleep, during which the brain stimulates itself, and non-REM (NREM) sleep.

Crying is the first way that babies communicate their needs. Newborns' senses of touch, taste, smell, and sound are well-developed. Vision is the least mature sensory capacity. Tests such as the Neonatal Behavioral Assessment Scale (NBAS) have been developed to assess the newborn's reflexes, state changes, responsiveness to stimuli, and other reactions.

The baby's arrival brings profound changes to the family system, which does not significantly strain a happy marriage but may cause distress in a troubled marriage. Special interventions exist to ease the transition to parenthood. Couples who support each other in their new roles typically adjust well.

LEARNING OBJECTIVES

After reading this chapter, you should be able to:

4.1 Describe the events leading up to childbirth and the three stages of labor. (pp. 126–128)

4.2 Discuss the baby's adaptation to labor and delivery, and describe the newborn baby's appearance. (p. 128)

4.3 Explain the purpose and main features of the Apgar Scale. (pp. 128–129)

4.4 Discuss the concept of natural childbirth, noting the typical features of a natural childbirth program, the benefits of the natural childbirth experience, the contributions of doula support, and the importance of social support. (pp. 129–131)

4.5 Discuss the benefits and concerns associated with home delivery. (pp. 131–132)

4.6 List common medical interventions used during childbirth, circumstances that justify their use, and any dangers associated with each. (pp. 132–134)

4.7 Discuss the risks of oxygen deprivation, preterm birth, and low birth weight, and summarize factors that can help infants survive a traumatic birth. (pp. 135–138)

4.8 Describe interventions for preterm infants, including infant stimulation and parent training. (pp. 138–141)

4.9 Discuss birth complications, parenting, and resilience, and summarize the findings from the Kauai Study regarding the long-term consequences of birth complications. (pp. 141–142)

4.10 Discuss parents' feelings and involvement with their newborn babies, noting research on bonding and rooming in. (pp. 142–143)

4.11 Name and describe major newborn reflexes, noting the functions served by each, and discuss the importance of assessing newborn reflexes. (pp. 143–145)

4.12 Describe the newborn baby's states of arousal, including sleep characteristics and ways to soothe a crying baby. (pp. 145–149)

4.13 Describe the newborn baby's responsiveness to touch, taste, smell, sound, and visual stimulation, including techniques for reducing infant stress to painful medical procedures. (pp. 149–152)

4.14 Describe Brazelton's Neonatal Behavioral Assessment Scale (NBAS), and explain its usefulness. (pp. 152–153)

4.15 Describe typical changes in the family system after the birth of a new baby, along with interventions that foster the transition to parenthood, and cite factors that affect adjustment to new parenthood. (pp. 154–157)

STUDY QUESTIONS

The Stages of Childbirth

1. Describe three signs that indicate that labor is near. (p. 126)

   A. ____________________

   B. ____________________

   C. ____________________

2. For each of the following statements, indicate whether it pertains to Stage 1, Stage 2, or Stage 3 of childbirth. (pp. 126–128)

   _____ Lasts about 50 minutes for a first baby.
   _____ The climax of this phase is called *transition*.
   _____ The placenta separates from the wall of the uterus.
   _____ Lasts 12 to 14 hours with a first birth.
   _____ The mother feels a natural urge to squeeze and push with her abdominal muscles.
   _____ The baby's head crowns.
   _____ Brings labor to an end.
   _____ Contractions cause the cervix to open and dilate.
   _____ The baby is born.
   _____ The placenta is delivered.

The Newborn Baby's Appearance

1. The average newborn baby is _________ inches long and weighs ________ pounds. (p. 128)

2. Explain why the newborn's head is large in comparison to the trunk and legs. (p. 128)

   ____

   ____

Assessing the Newborn's Physical Condition: The Apgar Scale

1. List the five characteristics assessed by the *Apgar Scale.* (pp. 128–129)

   A. ______________________________

   B. ______________________________

   C. ______________________________

   D. ______________________________

   E. ______________________________

2. On the Apgar Scale, a score of ________ or better indicates that the infant is in good physical condition; a score between ________ and ________ indicates that the baby requires special assistance; a score of ________ or below indicates a dire emergency. (p. 128)

Approaches to Childbirth

1. True or False: In many village and tribal cultures, expectant mothers know very little about the childbirth process. (p. 129)
2. Explain how childbirth practices have changed over time in Western societies. (pp. 129–130)

   ____

   ____

Natural, or Prepared, Childbirth

1. What is the goal of *natural childbirth*? (p. 130)

   ____

2. List and briefly describe three features of a typical natural childbirth program. (p. 130)

   A. ______________________________

   ____

   B. ______________________________

   ____

   C. ______________________________

   ____

3. Mothers who go through natural childbirth have (more / less) favorable attitudes toward the childbirth experience than those who do not. (p. 130)
4. Summarize the benefits of social support during childbirth. (pp. 130–131)

   ____

   ____

   ____

5. Name the childbirth position favored by research findings, and cite the benefits of using this position. (p. 131)

   Position: ______________________________

   Benefits: ______________________________

   ____

6. True or False: Most doctors discourage the water birth method, as it increases the risk of anoxia. (p. 131)

Home Delivery

1. True or False: More than 10 percent of American women choose to give birth at home. (p. 131)
2. Home births are typically handled by certified _______________, who have degrees in nursing and additional training in childbirth management. (pp. 131–132)

Medical Interventions

Fetal Monitoring

1. Explain the purpose of *fetal monitors.* (p. 132)

____

____

2. Cite four reasons why fetal monitoring is a controversial procedure. (pp. 132–133)

   A. ____

   B. ____

   C. ____

   D. ____

Labor and Delivery Medication

1. True or False: Some form of medication is used in more than 80 percent of U.S. births. (p. 133)
2. ___________________ are drugs given in mild doses to relieve pain during labor, while ___________________ are a stronger type of painkiller that blocks sensation. (p. 133)
3. The most common approach to controlling pain during labor is ___________________, in which a regional pain-relieving drug is delivered continuously through a catheter into a small space in the lower spine. (p. 133)
4. Cite two problems associated with routine use of labor and delivery medication. (p. 133)

   A. ____

   B. ____

Instrument Delivery

1. In what circumstance is delivery with forceps or a vacuum extractor appropriate? (p. 133)

____

____

2. Summarize the risks associated with instrument delivery using forceps and vacuum extraction. (pp. 133–134)

   Forceps: ____

   ____

   Vacuum extractor: ____

   ____

Induced Labor

1. Briefly describe an *induced labor.* (p. 134)

   ____

   ____

2. Describe two ways that an induced labor differs from a naturally occurring labor. (p. 134)

   A. ____

   ____

   B. ____

   ____

Cesarean Delivery

1. What is a *cesarean delivery*? (p. 134)

   ____

   ____

2. In what circumstances is a cesarean delivery warranted? (p. 134)

   ____

   ____

3. A natural labor after a cesarean is associated with slightly (decreased / increased) rates of rupture of the uterus and infant death. (p. 134)

4. ______________________ is largely responsible for the rise in cesarean deliveries worldwide. (p. 134)

Birth Complications

Oxygen Deprivation

1. Describe the physical difficulties associated with cerebral palsy. (p. 135)

   ____

   ____

2. ____________ refers to inadequate oxygen supply during the birth process. (p. 135)

3. Placenta ____________ refers to a premature separation of the placenta, whereas placenta ____________ refers to a detachment of the placenta resulting from implantation of the blastocyst so low in the uterus that the placenta covers the cervical opening. (p. 135)

4. True or False: The vast majority of children who experience *anoxia* display lifelong impairments in cognitive and linguistic skills. (p. 136)

5. Infants born more than six weeks early are at risk for ______________________, a condition in which the baby's lungs are so poorly developed that the air sacs collapse, causing serious breathing difficulties. (p. 136)

Preterm and Low-Birth-Weight Infants

1. Babies are considered premature if they are born ________ weeks or more before the end of a full 38-week pregnancy or if they weigh less than ________ pounds. (p. 136)

2. True or False: Birth weight is the best available predictor of infant survival and healthy development. (p. 136)

3. List the problems associated with low birth weight that persist through childhood and adolescence and into adulthood. (p. 137)

____

____

____

____

4. The rate of premature birth is highest among ______________________. Explain why. (p. 137)

____

____

5. Distinguish between *preterm* and *small-for-date infants.* (p. 137)

Preterm: ____

____

Small-for-date: ____

____

6. Of the two types of babies, (preterm / small-for-date) infants usually have more serious problems. (p. 137)

7. Describe the characteristics of preterm infants, and explain how those characteristics may influence the behavior of parents. (pp. 137–138)

A. ____

____

B. ____

____

8. Discuss several interventions for preterm infants. (pp. 138–139)

____

____

____

____

9. Briefly describe the concept of kangaroo care, and discuss the benefits associated with this type of infant stimulation. (pp. 138–139)

A. ____

____

B. ____

____

10. True or False: Research suggests that all preterm children, regardless of family characteristics, require continuous, high-quality interventions well into the school years in order to maintain developmental gains. (p. 139)

Social Issues: Health: A Cross-National Perspective on Health Care and Other Policies for Parents and Newborn Babies

1. ______________________ refers to the number of deaths in the first year of life per 1,000 live births. (p. 140)

2. True or False: African-American and Native-American infants are more than twice as likely as white infants to die in the first year of life. (p. 140)

3. ____________________, the rate of death in the first month of life, accounts for 67 percent of the infant death rate in the United States. (p. 140)

4. List the two leading causes of *neonatal mortality.* (p. 140)

   A. ____________________

   B. ____________________

5. Discuss the factors largely responsible for the relatively high rates of *infant mortality* in the United States. (p. 140)

   ____

   ____

   ____

6. Discuss factors linked to lower infant mortality rates. (p. 141)

   ____

   ____

   ____

Birth Complications, Parenting, and Resilience

1. In the Kauai longitudinal study, what factors predicted long-term difficulties following birth trauma? What factors predicted favorable outcomes? (p. 142)

   A. ____________________

   ____

   B. ____________________

   ____

2. True or False: The Kauai study tells us that as long as birth injuries are not overwhelming, a supportive home can restore children's growth. (p. 142)

Precious Moments After Birth

1. True or False: Fathers provide their infants with as much stimulation and affection as mothers do. (p. 142)

2. True or False: The parent–infant relationship requires close physical contact in the hours immediately following birth. (p. 143)

3. ____________________ is an arrangement in which the infant stays in the mother's hospital room all or most of the time. (p. 143)

The Newborn Baby's Capacities

Reflexes

1. What is a *reflex*? (p. 143)

   ____

2. Match each reflex with the appropriate response or function. (p. 144)

_____ Spontaneous grasp of adult's finger
_____ When the sole of the foot is stroked, the toes fan out and curl
_____ Helps infant find the nipple
_____ Prepares infant for voluntary walking
_____ Permits feeding
_____ Infant lies in a "fencing position"
_____ Protects infant from strong stimulation
_____ In our evolutionary past, may have helped infant cling to mother
_____ Helps infants survive if dropped into water

A. Eye blink
B. Rooting
C. Sucking
D. Swimming
E. Moro
F. Palmar grasp
G. Tonic neck
H. Stepping
I. Babinski

3. Briefly explain the adaptive value of three newborn reflexes. (pp. 143–144)

A. ____

B. ____

C. ____

4. Explain how some reflexes form the basis for complex motor skills that will develop later. (pp. 144–145)

____

____

____

____

5. When do most newborn reflexes disappear? (p. 145)

____

6. Explain the importance of assessing newborn reflexes. (p. 145)

____

____

____

States

1. Match each of the following *states of arousal* with its correct description. (p. 146)

_____ Regular, or *NREM, sleep*
_____ Irregular, or *REM, sleep*
_____ Drowsiness
_____ Quiet alertness
_____ Waking activity and crying

A. The infant's body is relatively inactive, with eyes open and attentive. Breathing is even.
B. The infant is either falling asleep or waking up. The eyes open and close; when open, they have a glazed look.
C. The infant is at full rest and shows little or no body activity. The eyelids are closed, no eye movements occur, the face is relaxed, and breathing is slow and regular.
D. Gentle limb movements, occasional stirring, and facial grimacing occurs. Breathing is irregular.
E. The infant shows bursts of uncoordinated body activity. Face may be relaxed or tense and wrinkled. Crying may occur.

2. Why do infants spend so much time in REM sleep? (p. 146)

____

____

3. What is the most effective way to soothe a crying baby when feeding and diaper changing do not work? (p. 148)

___

4. How do the cries of brain-damaged babies and those who have experienced prenatal and birth complications differ from those of healthy infants, and how might this difference affect parental responding? (p. 149)

   A. ___

   ___

   B. ___

   ___

5. Persistent crying, or __________, is a fairly common problem in newborns characterized by intense crying and difficulty calming down, which generally subsides between ___ to ___ months of age. Describe an intervention aimed at reducing this condition. (p. 149)

___

___

Social Issues: Health: The Mysterious Tragedy of Sudden Infant Death Syndrome

1. What is *sudden infant death syndrome (SIDS)*? (p. 147)

___

___

2. True or False: In industrialized countries, SIDS is the leading cause of infant mortality between 1 week and 12 months of age. (p. 147)

3. Place a checkmark by each risk factor associated with SIDS. (p. 147)

_____ Prematurity
_____ Home birth
_____ Being an active fetus
_____ Maternal cigarette smoking
_____ Parent–infant cosleeping
_____ Sleeping on the back
_____ Sleeping on the stomach
_____ Pacifier use
_____ Poor Apgar scores
_____ Cesarean delivery
_____ Respiratory infection
_____ High birth weight
_____ Impaired brain functioning
_____ Prenatal drug abuse
_____ Being wrapped very warmly
_____ Living in poverty

4. List three ways to reduce the incidence of SIDS. (p. 147)

   A. ___

   B. ___

   C. ___

Sensory Capacities

1. True or False: Infants are born with a poorly developed sense of touch and, consequently, they are not sensitive to pain. (p. 149)

2. True or False: Infants not only have taste preferences, but they are also capable of communicating these preferences to adults through facial expressions. (p. 150)

3. True or False: Certain odor preferences are innate. (p. 150)

4. Explain the survival value of a newborn's sense of smell. (p. 150)

5. At birth, infants prefer (pure tones / complex sounds). (p. 151)

6. True or False: Infants can discriminate almost all of the speech sounds of any human language. (p. 151)

7. Cite the characteristics of human speech preferred by infants. (p. 151)

8. Vision is the (most / least) mature of the newborn baby's senses. (p. 151)

9. Describe the newborn baby's *visual acuity*. (pp. 151–152)

10. True or False: Infants have well-developed color vision at birth, and they are immediately capable of discriminating colors. (p. 152)

Neonatal Behavioral Assessment

1. Which types of behavior does the *Neonatal Behavioral Assessment Scale (NBAS)* evaluate? (p. 152)

2. What is the Neonatal Intensive Care Unit Network Neurobehavioral Scale (NNNS) specifically designed to evaluate? (p. 152)

3. Since the NBAS is given to infants all around the world, researchers have been able to learn a great deal about individual and cultural differences in newborn behavior and the ways in which various child-rearing practices affect infant behavior. Briefly discuss these findings. (p. 152)

4. Why is a single NBAS score not a good predictor of later development, and what should be used in place of a single score? (p. 153)

   A. ______

   B. ______

5. How are NBAS interventions beneficial for the early parent–infant relationship? (p. 153)

The Transition to Parenthood

1. Discuss several changes in the family system following the birth of a new baby. (p. 154)

Changes in the Family System

1. True or False: For most new parents, the arrival of a baby causes significant marital strain. (p. 154)
2. Describe changes in the division of labor in the home following childbirth. (p. 154)
3. In what ways does postponing childbearing until the late twenties or thirties ease the transition to parenthood? (p. 154)
4. Explain how a second birth affects the family system. (p. 156)

Biology and Environment: Parental Depression and Child Development

1. Describe how the mother's depressed mood affects her newborn infant in the first months of life. (p. 155)
2. Describe parenting practices associated with persistent maternal depression, and note how these parenting behaviors impact the development of the child. (p. 155)

   Parenting practices:

   Impact on child:

3. True or False: Persistent paternal depression is a strong predictor of child behavior problems. (p. 155)

4. Briefly summarize interventions for postpartum depression. (p. 155)

____

____

Single-Mother Families

1. True or False: Planned births and adoptions by single 30- to 45-year-old women are increasing. (p. 156)
2. The majority of nonmarital births are (planned / unplanned) and to women in their _____. (p. 156)
3. Describe common stressors associated with being a single mother. (pp. 156–157)

____

____

____

Parent Interventions

1. Discuss how interventions for low-risk parents differ from interventions for high-risk parents. (p. 157)

   Low-risk: ____

   ____

   ____

   High-risk: ____

   ____

   ____

2. What additional support(s) may be necessary to help low-income single parents adjust favorably? (p. 157)

____

____

ASK YOURSELF . . .

For *Ask Yourself* questions for this chapter, along with feedback on the accuracy of your answers, please log on to MyDevelopmentLab (for registration and access, please visit mydevelopmentlab.com or follow the instructions on page ix).

(1) Select the Multimedia Library.

(2) Choose the explore option.

(3) Find your chapter from the drop down box.

(4) Click find now.

(5) Complete questions and choose "Submit answers for grading" or "Clear answers" to start over.

SUGGESTED READINGS

Caplan, A. L., Blank, R. H., & Merrick, J. C. (Eds.). (2010). *Compelled compassion.* New York: Springer-Verlag. A compelling look at medical interventions for severely premature or ill newborns, including consequences for caregiving, the importance of public policies, legal implications, and commentary from parents and heath-care workers.

Fox, B. (2009). *When couples become parents: The creation of gender in the transition to parenthood.* Toronto: University of Toronto Press. Examines the many surprises and challenges of negotiating the transition to parenthood, with an emphasis on how gender roles often change during the first year. Other topics include the importance of family support, combining work and family, and strategies new parents can use to cope with the challenges of parenthood.

Simonds, W., Rothman, B. K., & Norman, B. M. (2007). *Laboring on: Birth in transition.* New York: Taylor & Francis. The book examines a variety of issues concerning pregnancy and labor, including approaches to childbirth, medical interventions, debates over midwifery, and women's health-care reform.

CROSSWORD PUZZLE 4.1

Across

3. ____________ labor: a labor started artificially by breaking the amnion and giving the mother a hormone that stimulates contractions
5. Inadequate oxygen supply
6. ____________ monitors: electronic instruments that track the baby's heart rate during labor
7. Climax of the first stage of labor; the frequency and strength of contractions peak and the cervix opens completely
8. A mild pain-relieving drug
9. ____________ delivery: a surgical delivery in which the doctor makes an incision in the mother's abdomen and lifts the baby out of the uterus
11. Natural, or ______________, childbirth: approach designed to overcome the idea that birth is a painful ordeal requiring extensive medical intervention

Down

1. Positioning of the baby in the uterus such that the buttocks or feet would be delivered first
2. Infants whose birth weight is below normal when length of pregnancy is taken into account (3 words)
4. ____________ and effacement of the cervix: widening and thinning of the cervix during the first stage of labor
10. The ___________ Scale is used to assess the newborn immediately after birth.

CROSSWORD PUZZLE 4.2

Across

1. An inborn, automatic response to a particular form of stimulation
2. A "regular" sleep state in which the heart rate, breathing, and brain wave activity are slow and regular (abbr.)
3. _____________ mortality: the number of deaths in the first year of life per 1,000 live births
8. Arrangement in which the baby stays in the mother's hospital room all or most of the time (2 words)
10. Visual ___________: fineness of visual discrimination

Down

1. An "irregular" sleep state in which brain wave activity is similar to that of the waking state (abbr.)
2. Test developed to assess the behavior of the infant during the newborn period (abbr.)
4. __________ mortality: the number of deaths in the first month of life per 1,000 live births
5. States of ______________: different degrees of sleep and wakefulness
6. Parents' feelings of affection and concern for the newborn baby
7. Infants born several weeks or months before their due date
9. The unexpected death of an infant younger than 1 year of age that remains unexplained after thorough investigation (abbr.)

PRACTICE TEST #1

1. The frequency and strength of contractions are at their peak during __________ (p. 127)
   a. transition.
   b. lightening.
   c. crowning.
   d. the third stage of labor.

2. The average newborn baby is _____ inches long and _____ pounds in weight. (p. 128)
   a. 19; 7
   b. 19; 8
   c. 20; 7.5
   d. 21; 6.5

3. Which of the following is a typical feature of a newborn baby's appearance? (p. 128)
   a. small head
   b. bowed legs
   c. small eyes
   d. curly hair

4. Two Apgar ratings are given because __________ (p. 128)
   a. some babies have trouble adjusting at first but do quite well after a few minutes.
   b. one is given by the parents and one is given by the attending nurse or doctor.
   c. one score is for appearance, pulse, and grimace, and the other is for activity and respiration.
   d. one score is given immediately after birth, and the other score is given when the pediatrician first visits.

5. An Apgar score of 2 for heart rate indicates __________ (p. 129)
   a. no heartbeat.
   b. a heartbeat of 1–50 beats per minute.
   c. a heartbeat of 51–99 beats per minute.
   d. a heartbeat of 100–140 beats per minute.

6. Marla is a trained lay attendant who provides support to mothers during labor. Marla is a __________ (p. 130)
   a. midwife.
   b. physician's assistant.
   c. doula.
   d. labor coach.

7. Research favors the __________ position for delivery. (p. 131)
   a. fetal
   b. sitting
   c. sideways
   d. lying

8. Most home births are handled by __________ (pp. 131–132)
   a. doctors.
   b. doulas.
   c. certified nurse-midwives.
   d. family members.

9. It is just as safe to give birth at home as in a hospital for __________ (p. 132)
   a. mothers with a nursing background.
   b. second-time mothers assisted by their partners.
   c. mothers of any age who have a labor coach present.
   d. healthy mothers assisted by trained professionals.

10. Fetal monitoring __________ (p. 132)
    a. is a safe medical procedure that has saved many lives.
    b. poses significant risks to the baby and mother.
    c. is not used routinely in the United States.
    d. increases the mother's use of pain medication during delivery.

11. In the United States, the most common approach to controlling pain during labor is __________ (p. 133)
    a. Lamaze breathing.
    b. a spinal block.
    c. epidural analgesia.
    d. oxytocin.

12. Infant anoxia is associated with __________ (p. 135)
    a. cerebral palsy.
    b. high blood pressure.
    c. cancer.
    d. epidural analgesia.

13. Tobacco and cocaine use during pregnancy can cause __________ (p. 135)
    a. placenta previa.
    b. toxoplasmosis.
    c. placenta abruptio.
    d. toxemia.

14. The best available predictor of infant survival is __________ (p. 136)
    a. teratogen exposure.
    b. birth weight.
    c. quality of prenatal care.
    d. birth length.

15. Small-for-date infants are born __________ (p. 137)
    a. several weeks or more before their due date.
    b. above their estimated arrival weight.
    c. below their expected weight considering length of the pregnancy.
    d. with fewer problems than most preterm babies.

16. Kangaroo care __________ (pp. 138–139)
    a. keeps preterm babies in an isolette.
    b. is found in almost 50 percent of U.S. hospitals.
    c. fosters improved alertness and sleep in preterm babies.
    d. is not possible in developing countries without hospital intensive care units.

17. In the United States, the federal government mandates _____ weeks of __________ maternity leave for employees in companies with at least 50 workers. (p. 141)
    a. 6; unpaid
    b. 6; paid
    c. 12; unpaid
    d. 12; paid

18. The Kauai study tells us that __________ (p. 142)
    a. children with serious birth complications rarely overcome them, regardless of home environment.
    b. as long as birth injuries are not overwhelming, a supportive home can restore children's growth.
    c. even minor birth complications often lead to long-term learning and behavioral difficulties.
    d. birth complications are usually caused by medical errors during labor and/or delivery.

19. Toward the end of pregnancy, higher levels of oxytocin __________ (p. 143)
    a. can interfere with milk production.
    b. heighten responsiveness to the baby.
    c. can interfere with bonding.
    d. reduce the chances of birth complications.

20. The human parent–infant relationship __________ (p. 143)
    a. must be established soon after birth or attachment difficulties may occur.
    b. cannot be helped or harmed by contact with the baby after birth.
    c. does not depend on a precise, early period of togetherness.
    d. takes several months to fully develop.

21. When you stroke a newborn's cheek near the corner of his mouth, he __________ (p. 144)
    a. displays the Moro reflex.
    b. displays the tonic neck reflex.
    c. fans his toes out and curls them.
    d. turns his head toward the source of stimulation.

22. The __________ reflex may prepare an infant for voluntary reaching. (p. 144)
    a. tonic neck
    b. rooting
    c. palmar grasp
    d. Babinski

23. An infant whose eyes open and close and have a glazed look is probably displaying __________ (p. 146)
    a. NREM sleep.
    b. drowsiness.
    c. quiet alertness.
    d. waking activity.

24. An infant in quiet alertness is __________ (p. 146)
    a. at full rest and shows little or no body activity.
    b. either falling asleep or waking up.
    c. relatively inactive, with eyes open and attentive.
    d. breathing very irregularly.

25. SIDS is most likely to occur between _____ and _____ months. (p. 147)
    a. 1; 3
    b. 2; 4
    c. 3; 6
    d. 8; 10

26. Brain imaging research suggests that because of nervous system immaturity, __________ (p. 150)
    a. newborns do not feel most types of pain, unless it is intense.
    b. newborns often confuse minor discomfort with intense pain.
    c. preterm babies have poorly developed pain receptors, and, therefore, feel little pain.
    d. preterm babies feel the pain of a medical injection especially intensely.

27. Babies purse their lips when a taste is __________ (p. 150)
    a. sour.
    b. sweet.
    c. bitter.
    d. salty.

28. __________ is the least developed of the newborn baby's senses. (p. 151)
    a. Touch
    b. Smell
    c. Vision
    d. Hearing

29. In one study, infants born to mothers who were depressed during pregnancy were __________ as babies of nondepressed mothers. (p. 155)
    a. four times as likely to have engaged in violent antisocial behavior by age 16
    b. three times as likely to die of SIDS in the first year of life
    c. eight times as likely to become teenage parents
    d. twice as likely to be diagnosed with mental retardation or autism

30. The majority of nonmarital births are __________ (p. 156)
    a. to adolescent girls.
    b. unplanned.
    c. to women in their thirties.
    d. to ethnic minority women.

PRACTICE TEST #2

1. The first stage of labor lasts an average of __________ with a first birth. (p. 126)
   a. 50 minutes
   b. 4 to 6 hours
   c. 5 to 7 hours
   d. 12 to 14 hours

2. The third stage of labor lasts an average of __________ (p. 128)
   a. 5 to 10 minutes.
   b. 20 to 50 minutes.
   c. 2 to 3 hours.
   d. 4 to 6 hours.

3. During childbirth, the force of the contractions __________ (p. 128)
   a. often causes physical harm to the baby.
   b. intensifies the baby's production of stress hormones.
   c. cuts off the air supply to the baby.
   d. causes the baby to be tired and lethargic.

4. Which of the following statements about the newborn baby's appearance is true? (p. 128)
   a. The head is small in comparison to the trunk and legs.
   b. Boys and girls tend to be similar in length and weight.
   c. Boys tend to be slightly longer and heavier than girls.
   d. The average newborn is 22 inches long and 8 pounds in weight.

5. On the Apgar scale, a baby with irregular, shallow breathing and strong reflexive response should be rated 1 in __________ and 2 in __________ (p. 129)
   a. activity; appearance.
   b. respiration; heart rate.
   c. muscle tone; respiration.
   d. respiration; grimace.

6. Among the Mayans of the Yucatán, the mother leans against the body of a woman called the __________, who supports her weight and breathes with her during each contraction. (p. 129)
   a. doula
   b. labor coach
   c. midwife
   d. head helper

7. Mothers who are supported during labor __________ than mothers were are not supported. (p. 131)
   a. less often have cesarean deliveries
   b. produce higher levels of oxytocin
   c. remember less about the experience
   d. have babies with lower Apgar scores

8. Home birth is __________ (p. 132)
   a. more popular in the U.S. than in other industrialized nations.
   b. chosen by about 5 percent of American mothers.
   c. just as safe as hospital delivery for some mothers.
   d. almost always a risky option.

9. Fetal monitoring is linked to __________ (pp. 132–133)
   a. increased use of epidural analgesia.
   b. low Apgar scores in infants.
   c. higher rates of infant death.
   d. an increase in the number of cesarean deliveries.

10. __________ may be given in mild doses during labor to help a mother relax. (p. 133)
    a. Anesthetics
    b. Analgesics
    c. Anxiety medication
    d. Oxytocin

11. Epidural analgesia __________ (p. 133)
    a. does not cross the placenta.
    b. shortens labor for most women.
    c. weakens uterine contractions.
    d. numbs the lower half of the body.

12. Forceps __________ (p. 133)
    a. have been banned from most U.S. hospitals.
    b. often damage the birth canal, leading to infertility.
    c. pull the baby through most or all of the birth canal.
    d. can increase the risk of brain damage.

13. About 10 percent of American children experienced __________ during labor and delivery. (p. 135)
    a. anoxia
    b. cerebral palsy
    c. placenta abruption
    d. a breech delivery

14. Infants born more than six weeks early __________ (p. 136)
    a. commonly have respiratory distress syndrome.
    b. commonly have cerebral palsy.
    c. are small-for-date babies.
    d. cannot benefit from kangaroo care.

15. About 60 percent of twins __________ (p. 137)
    a. are small-for-date.
    b. are normal birth weight.
    c. are premature.
    d. have hyaline membrane disease.

16. Stimulating preterm infants __________ (p. 138)
    a. is harmful because they are so fragile.
    b. is not possible because they are cared for in isolettes.
    c. promotes faster weight gain and greater alertness.
    d. impedes physical and cognitive growth.

17. After serious physical defects, __________ is the second leading cause of neonatal mortality. (p. 140)
    a. accidental injury
    b. birth trauma
    c. low birth weight
    d. sudden infant death syndrome

18. Many hospitals offer __________ to promote early parental engagement with the newborn. (p. 143)
    a. doulas
    b. rooming in
    c. relaxation classes
    d. labor coaches

19. The __________ reflex is permanent. (p. 144)
   a. swimming
   b. sucking
   c. eye blink
   d. tonic neck

20. The __________ reflex helps an infant find a nipple. (p. 144)
   a. sucking
   b. rooting
   c. Moro
   d. Babinski

21. An infant displaying the Babinski reflex will respond to certain foot stimulation by __________ (p. 144)
   a. paddling and kicking.
   b. lifting one foot and then the other.
   c. fanning out and curling her toes as her foot twists in.
   d. lying in a "fencing" position.

22. The most fleeting state of arousal is __________ (p. 145)
   a. quiet alertness.
   b. drowsiness.
   c. REM sleep.
   d. crying.

23. During __________, brain-wave activity is remarkably similar to that of the waking state. (p. 146)
   a. NREM sleep
   b. quiet alertness
   c. REM sleep
   d. drowsiness

24. __________ increases the risk of SIDS as much as fifteenfold. (p. 147)
   a. Sleeping on the back
   b. Exposure to cigarette smoke after birth
   c. Hard bedding
   d. Prenatal drug abuse

25. Crying typically peaks at about __________ and then declines. (p. 148)
   a. 2 to 3 weeks
   b. 6 weeks
   c. 2 to 3 months
   d. 6 months

26. When parents practice proximal care, __________ (p. 149)
   a. the risk of colic increases.
   b. crying does not peak until after 6 months.
   c. the amount of crying in the early months is reduced.
   d. babies learn independence and self-soothing.

27. Newborns who __________ are susceptible to colic. (p. 149)
   a. have hearing or visual impairments
   b. react especially strongly to unpleasant stimuli
   c. weigh over 8 pounds at birth
   d. sleep alone most of the time

28. At birth, newborns prefer __________ (p. 151)
    a. pure tones to voices.
    b. complex sounds to pure tones.
    c. nonspeech sounds to speech.
    d. foreign languages to their own language.

29. About __________ percent of fathers report paternal depression after the birth of a child. (p. 155)
    a. 1 to 2
    b. 3 to 5
    c. 7 to 9
    d. 10 to 15

30. Planned births and adoptions by __________ are increasing. (p. 156)
    a. married 25- to 35-year-old couples
    b. married 40- to 50-year-old couples
    c. single 30- to 45-year-old women
    d. single 30- to 45-year-old men

CHAPTER 5
PHYSICAL DEVELOPMENT IN INFANCY AND TODDLERHOOD

BRIEF CHAPTER SUMMARY

During the first two years, body size increases dramatically, following organized patterns of growth. The skull also grows rapidly, accommodating large increases in brain size. Neurons in the brain form an elaborate communication system. Myelination improves the efficiency of message transfer. Neurophysiological methods of brain functioning allow researchers to identify relationships between the brain and psychological development.

The cerebral cortex is the largest and most complex brain structure. Each hemisphere specializes in different functions, but brain plasticity allows some recovery of abilities lost to damage in one hemisphere. Stimulation of the brain is essential during sensitive periods—periods in which the brain is developing most rapidly.

Various factors affect early physical growth. Heredity contributes to height, weight, and rate of physical maturation. Nutrition is crucial: Rapidly growing babies need extra calories to keep their developing organs functioning properly. Breast milk, which is ideally suited to meet infants' needs, is especially important in promoting survival and health in poverty-stricken regions. Rapid weight gain in infancy appears to be related to later overweight and obesity; malnutrition in the early years can lead to permanent stunting of physical growth and of brain development. Parental affection is essential for normal physical growth.

Babies are born with built-in learning capacities that allow them to benefit from experience immediately. Infants are capable of classical and operant conditioning. They also learn through their natural preference for novel stimulation and through imitation.

Motor development, like physical growth, follows an organized sequence, with large individual differences in rate of motor progress. According to dynamic systems theory, each new motor skill is a joint product of central nervous system development, the body's movement possibilities, the child's goals, and environmental supports for the skill. Cultural variations in infant-rearing practices also influence motor development. Reaching plays a vital role in infant cognitive development because it opens up a new way of exploring the environment. Reaching improves as depth perception advances and infants gain control of body movements.

Hearing and vision undergo major advances in the first year. Babies begin to organize sounds into complex patterns, detecting regularities that facilitate later language learning. Newborns prefer human speech to nonspeech sounds, and infants have a remarkable ability to extract regularities from complex, continuous speech, which prepares them to utter their first words around age 12 months. Visual development is supported by maturation of the eye and visual centers in the cerebral cortex. Depth perception develops gradually, helping infants to avoid falling. Pattern perception begins at birth; newborns prefer to look at patterned rather than plain stimuli. Babies' tendency to look for structure in a pattern stimulus also applies to face perception; they quickly learn to prefer their mother's face to that of an unfamiliar woman. Size constancy and object constancy also begin in the first week of life. Through intermodal perception, babies perceive input from different sensory systems in a unified way. Perception is guided by the discovery of affordances—the action possibilities that a situation allows.

LEARNING OBJECTIVES

After reading this chapter, you should be able to:

5.1 Describe changes in body size, proportions, muscle–fat makeup, and skeletal growth over the first two years. (pp. 162–164)

5.2 Describe brain development during infancy and toddlerhood at the microscopic level of individual brain cells. (pp. 164–166)

5.3 Discuss current neurophysiological methods of measuring brain functioning, and identify which measure is most appropriate during infancy and toddlerhood. (pp. 166–167)

5.4 Describe brain development during infancy and toddlerhood at the larger level of the cerebral cortex, including research on brain lateralization and plasticity. (pp. 167–169)

5.5 Describe research findings related to the existence of sensitive periods in brain development, and note evidence of brain growth spurts and the need for appropriate stimulation. (pp. 169, 171–172)

5.6 Explain how the organization of sleep and wakefulness changes over the first two years. (pp. 172, 174)

5.7 Discuss the impact of heredity on early physical growth. (p. 174)

5.8 Discuss the nutritional needs of infants and toddlers, the advantages of breastfeeding, and the extent to which chubby babies are at risk for later overweight and obesity. (pp. 174–176)

5.9 Discuss the impact of severe malnutrition on the development of infants and toddlers, and cite two dietary diseases associated with this condition. (pp. 176–178)

5.10 Describe growth faltering, noting common symptoms and family circumstances surrounding the disorder. (p. 178)

5.11 Explain how infants learn through classical conditioning, operant conditioning, habituation and recovery, and imitation. (pp. 179–183)

5.12 Describe the general course of motor development during the first two years, along with factors that influence it. (pp. 183–184)

5.13 Explain the dynamic systems theory of motor development, highlighting cultural variations in motor development. (pp. 184–186)

5.14 Describe the development of reaching and grasping, and explain how early experiences affect these skills. (pp. 187–188)

5.15 Describe the development of bowel and bladder control. (pp. 188–189)

5.16 Summarize the development of hearing in infancy, giving special attention to speech perception. (pp. 189–190)

5.17 Summarize the development of vision in infancy, with particular attention to depth perception and pattern perception. (pp. 190, 191–193, 195–196)

5.18 Discuss the development of object perception during the first year of life. (pp. 196–197)

5.19 Explain the concept of intermodal perception. (pp. 197–198)

5.20 Explain the Gibsons' differentiation theory of perceptual development. (pp. 198–199)

STUDY QUESTIONS

Body Growth

Changes in Body Size and Muscle–Fat Makeup

1. Infant and toddler growth is marked by (steady gains / little spurts). (p. 162)
2. "Baby fat" helps the infant ____. (p. 162)

3. Describe sex and ethnic differences in body size and muscle–fat makeup during infancy. (p. 162)

   Sex differences: ____

   ____

   Ethnic differences: ____

   ____

Changes in Body Proportions

1. According to the two patterns of body growth, the (*cephalocaudal* / *proximodistal*) *trend* refers to growth from "head to tail," while the (*cephalocaudal* / *proximodistal*) *trend* refers to growth from the center of the body outward. (p. 162)

Skeletal Growth

1. The best way of estimating a child's physical maturity is to use ______________________, a measure of development of the bones of the body. Explain how this estimate is obtained. (p. 163)

   ____

   ____

2. True or False: African-American children tend to be slightly behind Caucasian-American children in skeletal age. (p. 164)

3. Cite three possible consequences of girls' greater physical maturity during infancy and childhood. (p. 164)

   A. ____

   B. ____

   C. ____

4. At birth, the bones of the skull are separated by six gaps, or soft spots, called ______________. Explain their function. (p. 164)

   ____

   ____

Brain Development

Development of Neurons

1. The human brain has 100 to 200 billion ____________, or nerve cells, that store and transmit information by releasing chemicals called ______________________ across tiny gaps called ______________. (p. 164)

2. Explain the process of *synaptic pruning.* (p. 165)

   ____

   ____

3. About half the brain's volume is made up of ____________, which are responsible for ________________, the coating of neural fibers with an insulating fatty sheath that improves the efficiency of message transfer. (p. 165)

Neurophysiological Methods

1. Match each of the following methods of measuring brain functioning to the appropriate description. (p. 166)

_____ Electroencephalogram (EEG)
_____ Event-related potentials (ERPs)
_____ Functional magnetic resonance imaging (fMRI)
_____ Positron emission tomography (PET)
_____ Near-infrared spectroscopy (NIRS)

A. Thin, flexible optical fibers are attached to the scalp and infrared light is beamed at the brain. Absorption by areas of the cerebral cortex varies with changes in blood flow and oxygen metabolism.
B. Frequency and amplitude of brain waves in response to particular stimuli are recorded in specific areas of the cerebral cortex.
C. Electrodes are taped to the scalp to record the stability and organization of electrical brain-wave activity in the brain's outer layers—the cerebral cortex.
D. After injection or inhalation of a radioactive substance, the individual lies inside a tunnel-shaped apparatus with a scanner that emits fine streams of X-rays, which detect increased blood flow and oxygen metabolism in the brain as the person processes particular stimuli.
E. A scanner magnetically detects increased blood flow and oxygen metabolism in areas of the brain as the individual processes particular stimuli. The result is a computerized moving picture of activity anywhere in the brain.

2. True or False: Near-infrared spectroscopy (NIRS) works well in infancy and early childhood because the child can sit on the parent's lap and move during testing, unlike other methods of measuring brain functioning. (p. 166)

Development of the Cerebral Cortex

1. The ______________________ is the largest, most complex brain structure, accounting for 85 percent of the brain's weight and containing the greatest number of neurons and synapses. (p. 167)

2. The cortical region known as the ______________________ is responsible for thought, including consciousness, memory, reasoning, and problem solving. (p. 168)

3. Indicate which of the following functions are usually controlled by the left hemisphere (L) and which are controlled by the right hemisphere (R). (p. 168)

_____ Spoken language
_____ Anger
_____ Written language
_____ Reading maps
_____ Recognizing geometric shapes
_____ Joy

4. How do *lateralization* and *brain plasticity* help the brain learn and adapt? (pp. 168–169)

Lateralization: ____

____

Brain plasticity: ____

____

5. The brain is (more / less) plastic during the first few years than at any later time in life. (p. 169)

Biology and Environment: Brain Plasticity: Insights from Research on Brain-Damaged Children and Adults

1. Adults who suffered brain injuries in infancy and early childhood show (fewer / more) cognitive impairments than adults with later-occurring injuries. (p. 170)
2. Describe the impact of brain injury on childhood language development and spatial skills, noting how this relates to brain plasticity. (p. 170)

   Language: ______________________________

   ____

   Spatial skills: ______________________________

   ____

3. True or False: Recovery after early brain injury is greater for language than for spatial skills. (p. 170)
4. Describe the negative consequences of high brain plasticity. (p. 170)

   ____

   ____

5. True or False: Brain plasticity is restricted to early childhood and is no longer evident by the time individuals reach adulthood. Explain your response. (p. 170)

   ____

   ____

Sensitive Periods in Brain Development

1. Extreme ______________________ results in permanent brain damage, confirming the existence of sensitive periods in brain development. (p. 169)
2. What does research on orphanage children reveal about cognitive catch-up? (pp. 169, 171)

   ____

   ____

   ____

   ____

3. True or False: Good parenting can protect the young brain from the potentially damaging effects of both excessive and inadequate stress-hormone exposure. (p. 171)
4. Distinguish between *experience-expectant* and *experience-dependent brain growth,* and provide an example of each. (p. 172)

   Experience-expectant: ______________________________

   ____

   Experience-dependent: ______________________________

   ____

5. Evidence (does / does not) exist for a sensitive period in the first few years of life for mastering skills that depend on extensive training, such as musical performance or gymnastics. (p. 172)

Changing States of Arousal

1. In general, newborn babies sleep a total of ___ to ___ hours per day. The total sleep time of an infant declines (quickly / slowly); the average 2-year-old sleeps ___ to ___ hours per day. (p. 172)
2. The brain hormone that promotes drowsiness is called ____________________. (p. 171)

Cultural Influences: Cultural Variations in Infant Sleeping Arrangements

1. For each of the following statements about parent–infant cosleeping, indicate if it is true (T) or false (F). (p. 173)
   _____ Ninety percent of North American parents cosleep with their babies.
   _____ Among the Maya, mother–infant cosleeping is interrupted only by the birth of a new baby.
   _____ Compared to Caucasian-American families, African-American families are more likely to cosleep with their children.
   _____ Parent–child cosleeping is more common in collectivist than individualistic societies.
   _____ Over the past two decades, cosleeping has decreased in Western nations.
   _____ During the night, cosleeping babies breastfeed three times longer than infants who sleep alone.
   _____ Parent–child cosleeping is a significant risk factor for SIDS.
   _____ Cosleeping reduces mothers' total sleep time.
   _____ Research consistently shows that cosleeping children are significantly more likely than their peers to have emotional problems
2. List two groups of parents who should probably not cosleep with their babies. (p. 173)
   A. ____________________
   B. ____________________

Influences on Early Physical Growth

Heredity

1. True or False: When diet and health are adequate, height and rate of physical growth are largely determined by heredity. (p. 174)
2. Under what circumstances are children and adolescents who suffer from illness or poor nutrition likely to show catch-up growth? (p. 174)
   ____

Nutrition

1. List four nutritional and health benefits of breast milk. (p. 175)
   A. ____________________
   B. ____________________
   C. ____________________
   D. ____________________
2. List two ways that breastfeeding can benefit mothers and infants in poverty-stricken regions of the world. (pp. 175–176)
   A. ____________________
   B. ____________________
3. Rapid weight gain in infancy (is / is not) related to obesity at older ages. (p. 176)

4. Cite three ways in which parents can prevent infants and toddlers from becoming overweight at later ages. (p. 176)

   A. ______________________________

   B. ______________________________

   C. ______________________________

Malnutrition

1. For each of the following statements, indicate whether it describes *marasmus* (M) or *kwashiorkor* (K). (p. 177)

   _____ Caused by an unbalanced diet very low in protein
   _____ Usually appears in the first year of life
   _____ Causes a swollen abdomen
   _____ Caused by a diet low in all essential nutrients
   _____ Usually strikes after weaning
   _____ Causes the body to become painfully thin

2. Indicate which of the following are consequences of extreme malnutrition. (p. 177)

   _____ Low basal metabolism rate
   _____ Rapid catch-up growth
   _____ Permanent loss in brain weight
   _____ Heart disease
   _____ Poor gross-motor skills
   _____ Difficulty paying attention
   _____ Decreased stress response
   _____ Withdrawal and listlessness

3. True or False: Inadequate nutrition is largely confined to developing countries, and recent surveys indicate that it is almost nonexistent in the United States and Canada. (p. 178)

4. What is food insecurity, and in what two populations is food insecurity especially high? (p. 178)

   A. ______________________________

   B. ______________________________ C. ______________________________

Emotional Well-Being

1. What are the signs of *growth faltering*? (p. 178)

   ____

   ____

2. Discuss the family circumstances that often surround growth faltering. (p. 178)

   ____

   ____

   ____

Learning Capacities

1. Define learning, and identify two basic forms of learning in which infants are equipped. (pp. 178–179)

   A. ______________________________

   B. ______________________________ C. ______________________________

Classical Conditioning

1. In *classical conditioning,* a(n) ______________________________ is paired with a stimulus that leads to a(n) ______________________________. (p. 179)

2. Why is classical conditioning of great value to infants? (p. 179)

____

____

3. Match each of the following terms to the correct definition. (p. 179)

_____ A neutral stimulus that leads to a new response once learning has occurred (UCR)
_____ A learned response exhibited toward a previously neutral stimulus
_____ A reflexive response
_____ A stimulus that automatically leads to a reflexive response

A. *Unconditioned stimulus (UCS)*
B. *Unconditioned response*
C. *Conditioned stimulus (CS)*
D. *Conditioned response (CR)*

4. In classical conditioning, if the CS is presented alone enough times, without being paired with the UCS, the CR will no longer occur. This is referred to as ______________________. (p. 180)

5. Some responses, such as ______________, are very difficult to classically condition in young babies. Explain why. (p. 180)

____

____

Operant Conditioning

1. Briefly explain how learning takes place through *operant conditioning.* (p. 180)

____

2. Define the terms *reinforcer* and *punishment* as they relate to operant conditioning. (p. 180)

Reinforcer: ____

____

Punishment: ____

____

3. Describe how operant conditioning contributes to the development of social relationships. (p. 180)

____

____

Habituation

1. Define the terms *habituation* and *recovery.* (pp. 180–181)

Habituation: ____

____

Recovery: ____

____

2. As infants get older, they habituate to stimuli more (slowly / quickly). What does this indicate about their cognitive development? (p. 181)

____

____

Imitation

1. Define *imitation,* and indicate how it contributes to early learning. (p. 181)

   A. ____________________

   B. ____________________

   ____

2. Explain the role of *mirror neurons* in relation to imitation and learning. (p. 182)

   ____

   ____

Motor Development

The Sequence of Motor Development

1. Distinguish between gross- and fine-motor development. (p. 183)

   Gross: ____________________

   ____

   Fine: ____________________

   ____

2. For each of the following, indicate whether it is a gross-motor skill (G) or fine-motor skill (F). (p. 184)

   _____ Crawling
   _____ Reaching for objects
   _____ Grasping
   _____ Sitting upright
   _____ Walking
   _____ Scribbling with crayons

3. True or False: Although the sequence of motor development is fairly uniform, large individual differences exist in the rate of development. (p. 184)

Motor Skills as Dynamic Systems

1. According to the *dynamic systems theory of motor development,* mastery of motor skills involves acquisition of increasingly complex systems of action. Explain what this means. (pp. 184–185)

   ____

   ____

2. List four factors that contribute to the development of each new motor skill. (p. 185)

   A. ____________________

   B. ____________________

   C. ____________________

   D. ____________________

3. True or False: Dynamic systems theory regards motor development as a genetically determined process. Briefly explain your response. (p. 185)

   ____

   ____

Dynamic Motor Systems in Action

1. What did Galloway and Thelen's microgenetic studies reveal about infant motor development? (pp. 185–186)

____

____

Cultural Variations in Motor Development

1. In Wayne Dennis's orphanage research, what effects did lying on their backs have on babies' motor development? (p. 186)

____

____

2. Give at least one example of how cultural variations in infant-rearing practices affect motor development. (p. 186)

____

____

Fine-Motor Development: Reaching and Grasping

1. Match each of the following terms to the appropriate definition. (pp. 187–188)

_____ A well-coordinated movement in which infants use the thumb and index finger opposably	A. *Prereaching*
_____ Poorly coordinated swipes or swings toward an object	B. *Ulnar grasp*
_____ A clumsy motion in which the fingers close against the palm	C. *Pincer grasp*

2. Explain how reaching and depth perception are related. (p. 188)

____

____

3. Does heavy enrichment lead to advanced motor development in infancy? Explain. (p. 188)

____

____

Bowel and Bladder Control

1. At what age should parents begin toilet training their children? Why is this an appropriate age for most children? (p. 188)

   Age: ____

   Reason: ____

   ____

2. Name three effective toilet training techniques. (p. 189)

   A. ____

   B. ____

   C. ____

Perceptual Development

Hearing

1. What is the greatest change in hearing that takes place over the first year of life? (p. 189)

2. Describe the changes in auditory perception over the first year of life that prepare infants for language acquisition. (pp. 189–190)

   Around 5 months:

   6–8 months:

   7–9 months:

3. Research shows that infants are impressive statistical analyzers of sound patterns. Explain what this means. (p. 190)

Biology and Environment: "Tuning in" to Familiar Speech, Faces, and Music: A Sensitive Period for Culture-Specific Learning

1. Describe changes in the ability to perceive familiar speech and familiar faces over the first year of life. (p. 191)

   Familiar speech:

   Familiar faces:

2. How do research findings on musical rhythm perception support the notion of a sensitive period for culture-specific learning? (p. 191)

Vision

1. What is depth perception, and why is it important in infant development? (p. 192)

   A.

   B.

2. Describe Gibson and Walk's visual cliff, and explain what their studies reveal about infant depth perception. (p. 192)

   A.

   B.

3. Name and briefly describe the three cues for depth. (p. 192)

   A. ____

   ____

   B. ____

   ____

   C. ____

   ____

4. Explain what infants learn from crawling that promotes sensitivity to depth information. (pp. 192–193)

   ____

   ____

5. The principle of ____________________, which accounts for early pattern preferences, states that if infants can detect a difference in contrast between two or more patterns, they will prefer the one with more contrast. (p. 193)

6. True or False: By the end of the first year, a suggestive image of a pattern is all that babies need to recognize a familiar form. (p. 195)

7. Summarize the development of face perception across the first year of life. (p. 195)

   Birth–1 month: ____

   ____

   2–4 months: ____

   ____

   5–12 months: ____

   ____

Social Issues: Education: Development of Infants with Severe Visual Impairments

1. True or False: Children with severe visual impairments show delays in motor, cognitive, and social development. (p. 194)

2. Give two reasons why children with visual impairments reach motor milestones later than their sighted counterparts. (p. 194)

   A. ____

   ____

   B. ____

   ____

3. How do severe visual impairments affect the caregiver–infant relationship? (p. 194)

   ____

   ____

4. Cite five intervention techniques that can help infants with severe visual impairments become aware of their physical and social surroundings. (p. 194)

   A. ______________________________

   B. ______________________________

   C. ______________________________

   D. ______________________________

   E. ______________________________

Object Perception

1. True or False: *Size* and *shape constancy* emerge gradually over time as infants acquire more advanced knowledge of objects in the environment. (p. 196)
2. True or False: When two objects are touching, whether moving in unison or standing still, infants younger than 4 months of age do not perceive the boundary between the two objects, and therefore, cannot distinguish them. (pp. 196–197)

Intermodal Perception

1. What is *intermodal perception*? (p. 197)

   ____

2. What are *amodal sensory properties*? (p. 197)

   ____

3. True or False: From birth, infants are capable of combining information from multiple sensory systems. Cite research to support your answer. (pp. 197–198)

   ____

   ____

4. Explain how intermodal perception helps broaden the infant's social world. (p. 198)

   ____

   ____

5. True or False: Exposure to concurrent sights, sounds, and touches is often too overwhelming for infants, hindering cognitive development. Explain your answer. (p. 198)

   ____

   ____

Understanding Perceptual Development

1. Explain the Gibsons' *differentiation theory.* (p. 198)

   ____

   ____

2. According to differentiation theory, perception is guided by the discovery of ______________________, or the action possibilities that a situation offers an organism with certain motor capabilities. (p. 199)

ASK YOURSELF . . .

For *Ask Yourself* questions for this chapter, along with feedback on the accuracy of your answers, please log on to MyDevelopmentLab (for registration and access, please visit mydevelopmentlab.com or follow the instructions on page ix).

(1) Select the Multimedia Library.

(2) Choose the explore option.

(3) Find your chapter from the drop down box.

(4) Click find now.

(5) Complete questions and choose "Submit answers for grading" or "Clear answers" to start over.

SUGGESTED READINGS

Dykes, F., & Hall-Moran, V. (Eds.). (2009). *Infant and young child feeding.* Hoboken, NJ: Wiley. Examines the importance of nutrition in infancy and early childhood, with an emphasis on preventing overweight and obesity, as well as preventing chronic conditions like cardiovascular disease and cancer in adulthood. The authors also discuss cultural and SES differences in infant feeding practices.

Marcus, C., Loughlin, G. M., Donnelly, D., & Carroll, J. L. (Eds.). (2008). *Sleep in children.* Boca Raton, FL: CRC Press. Explores developmental changes in sleep from infancy to adolescence. Topics include normal and abnormal sleep; maturational changes in sleep; and the relationship between sleep, growth, and neurocognitive development.

Woodward, A., & Needham, A. (2009). *Learning and the infant mind.* New York: Oxford University Press. A compelling look at infant cognition, this book presents research on early learning, including knowledge of objects, categorization, and the relationship between locomotion and cognitive development.

CROSSWORD PUZZLE 5.1

Across

4. The largest, most complex brain structure is the ___________ cortex.
7. Cells that serve the function of myelination
8. _______________ conditioning: form of learning in which spontaneous behavior is followed by a stimulus that changes the probability that the behavior will occur again
9. Experience-______________ brain growth: early organization of the brain that depends on ordinary experiences with the environment
12. _____________ conditioning: form of learning that involves associating a neutral stimulus with a stimulus that leads to a reflexive response
13. Process in which neural fibers are coated with an insulating fatty sheath that improves the efficiency of message transfer
14. Brain ________________: ability of other parts of the brain to take over functions of damaged regions
15. In operant conditioning, a stimulus that increases the occurrence of a response
16. In classical conditioning, a stimulus that leads to a reflective response (abbr.)
19. Growth centers in the bones
20. In operant conditioning, a stimulus that decreases the occurrence of a response
22. In classical conditioning, an originally reflexive response that is produced by a CS after learning has occurred (abbr.)
23. The gaps between neurons across which messages are sent

Down

1. An increase in responsiveness to a new stimulus following habituation
2. _______________ cortex: part of the brain responsible for thought
3. Soft spots that separate the bones of the skull at birth
5. Experience-______________ brain growth: growth and refinement of brain structures result from specific learning experiences.
6. Synaptic ________________: loss of connective fibers by seldom-stimulated neurons
10. In classical conditioning, a neutral stimulus that through pairing with a UCS leads to a new response (abbr.)
11. Specialization of functions of the two hemispheres of the cerebral cortex
17. ____________ age: an estimate of physical maturity based on development of the bones of the body
18. Nerve cells that store and transmit information
21. In classical conditioning, a reflexive response that is produced by a UCS (abbr.)

CROSSWORD PUZZLE 5.2

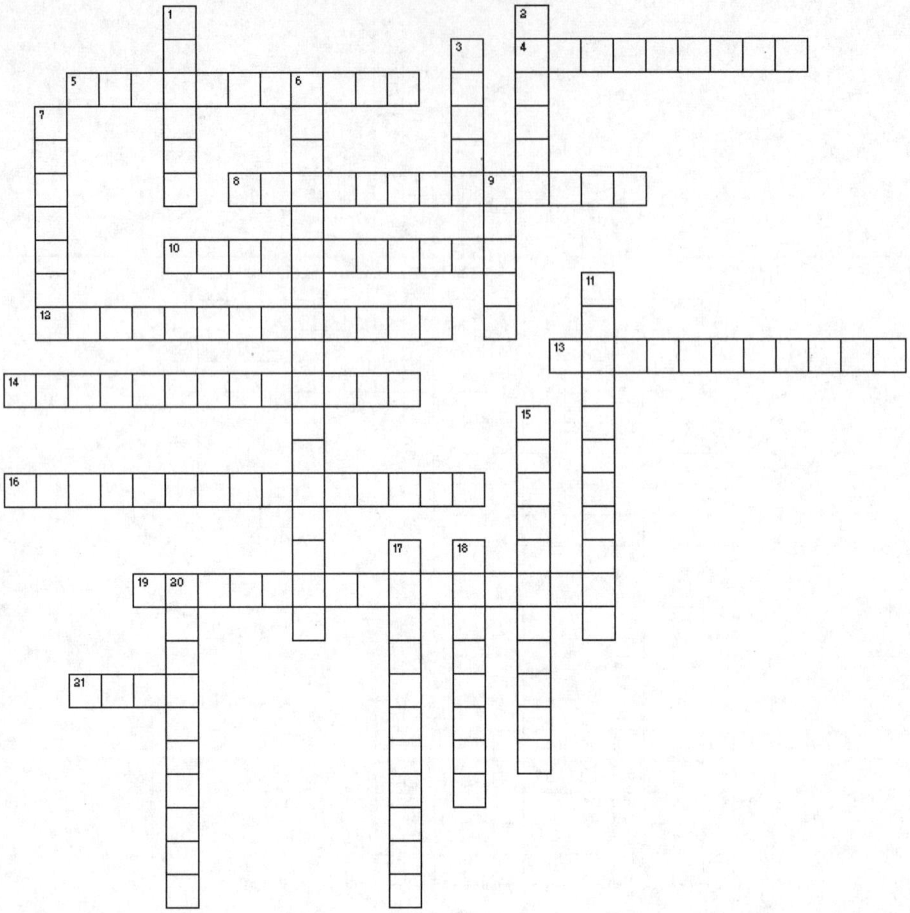

Across

4. Learning by copying another person
5. The action possibilities that a situation offers an organism with certain motor capabilities
8. Specialized cells in many areas of the cerebral cortex; believed to be the biological basis for imitation (2 words)
10. A gradual reduction in the strength of a response as a result of a repeated stimulation
12. ____________ trend: during the prenatal period, the head develops more rapidly than the lower part of the body.
13. Contrast ____________: if babies can detect a difference in contrast between two or more patterns, they will prefer the one with more contrast.
14. ____________ trend: growth proceeds from the center of the body outward.
16. Growth disorder caused by a lack of affection and stimulation (2 words)
19. ____________ theory: view that perceptual development involves detection of increasingly fine-grained, invariant features of the environment
21. ____________ constancy: perception of an object's dimensions as the same, despite changes in the size of its retinal image

Down

1. ____________ sensory properties: information that overlaps two or more sensory systems, resulting in perception of such input as an integrated whole
2. Well-formed grasp involving thumb and forefinger opposition
3. ____________ constancy: perception of an object's shape as the same, despite changes in the shape projected on the retina
6. Chemicals released by neurons that cross the synapses to send messages to other neurons
7. ____________ systems theory of motor development: views new motor skills as a reorganization of previously mastered skills that lead to more effective ways of exploring and controlling the environment.
9. Clumsy grasp in which the fingers close against the palm
11. The poorly coordinated, primitive reaching movements of newborn infants
15. A disease usually appearing between 1 and 3 years of age that is caused by a diet low in protein
17. ____________ capacity: by analyzing the speech stream for patterns, infants acquire a stock of speech structures for which they will later learn meanings.
18. A disease usually appearing in the first year of life that is caused by a diet low in all essential nutrients
20. ____________ perception combines information from more than one sensory system.

PRACTICE TEST #1

1. By the end of the first year, a typical infant's height is about _____ inches. (p. 162)
   a. 24
   b. 28
   c. 32
   d. 36

2. Skeletal age can be measured by __________ (p. 163)
   a. X-raying the bones.
   b. weighing the body.
   c. adding the months from conception forward.
   d. measuring the skull.

3. At birth, the __________ is nearer to its adult size than any other physical structure. (p. 164)
   a. skull
   b. brain
   c. heart
   d. liver

4. Neurons that are seldom stimulated __________ (p. 165)
   a. accumulate in the right hemisphere of the brain.
   b. are responsible for myelination.
   c. are responsible for brain plasticity.
   d. lose their synapses in synaptic pruning.

5. A neuroimaging technique that works well with infants and young children is __________ because the child can move within limited range during testing. (p. 166)
   a. electroencephalogram
   b. functional magnetic resonance imaging
   c. near-infrared spectroscopy
   d. position emission tomography

6. For most people, the right side of the brain handles __________ (p. 168)
   a. reading.
   b. spatial abilities.
   c. spoken language.
   d. positive emotion.

7. If a 1-month-old kitten is deprived of light for just three or four days, __________ (p. 169)
   a. damage to the brain's visual centers is severe.
   b. the brain's visual centers develop normally.
   c. the visual centers of the brain degenerate.
   d. damage to the brain's visual centers is permanent.

8. Research on brain plasticity reveals that after an early brain injury, __________ (p. 170)
   a. spatial skills are more impaired than vocabulary skills.
   b. grammatical skills are more impaired than spatial skills.
   c. children catch up in spatial skills by age 5.
   d. delays in language development persist beyond age 5.

9. The newborn baby takes round-the-clock naps that total about _____ to _____ hours. (p. 172)
   a. 9; 11
   b. 12; 15
   c. 16; 18
   d. 19; 21

10. Which of the following statements about parent–infant cosleeping is true? (p. 173)
    a. About 60 percent of American parents currently cosleep with their babies.
    b. Most experts advise against cosleeping, as it greatly increases the risk of infant injury.
    c. The practice helps infants sleep and makes breastfeeding more convenient.
    d. The practice often leads to bedtime struggles and interferes with the development of autonomy.

11. When diet and health are adequate, __________ (p. 174)
    a. height and weight are largely determined by the environment.
    b. weight and rate of physical growth are largely determined by the environment.
    c. height, but not weight, is largely determined by the environment.
    d. height and rate of physical growth are largely determined by heredity.

12. The World Health Organization recommends breastfeeding until __________ of age. (p. 175)
    a. 6 months
    b. 12 months
    c. 18 months
    d. 2 years

13. __________ is caused by a diet low in all essential nutrients. (p. 177)
    a. Kwashiorkor
    b. Growth faltering
    c. Marasmus
    d. Food insecurity

14. In as many as half of cases, a disturbed parent–infant relationship contributes to __________ (p. 178)
    a. kwashiorkor.
    b. growth faltering.
    c. marasmus.
    d. food insecurity.

15. In classical conditioning, a(n) __________ is paired with stimulus that leads to a(n) __________ (p. 179)
    a. conditioned stimulus; unconditioned stimulus.
    b. unconditioned stimulus; neutral response.
    c. conditioned stimulus; neutral stimulus.
    d. neutral stimulus; reflexive response.

16. In classical conditioning, if learning occurs, the neutral stimulus becomes a(n) __________ (p. 179)
    a. conditioned stimulus.
    b. unconditioned stimulus.
    c. unconditioned response.
    d. conditioned response.

17. Which of the following motor skills is most likely to develop first? (p. 184)
    a. jumping in place
    b. building a tower of two cubes
    c. scribbling vigorously
    d. playing pat-a-cake

18. By the end of the first year, infants use the thumb and index finger in a well-coordinated __________ (p. 187)
    a. ulnar grasp.
    b. voluntary reach.
    c. pincer grasp.
    d. prereach.

19. Toilet training is best delayed until _____ months. (p. 188)
    a. 12
    b. 18
    c. 22
    d. 27

20. Seven-month-old infants __________ (p. 190)
    a. cannot detect regular syllable-stress patterns.
    b. can detect simple word-order rules.
    c. can detect words that start with weak syllables.
    d. cannot generalize speech rules to nonspeech sounds.

21. Which of the following statements is true about research involving discrimination of human and monkey faces? (p. 191)
    a. By 9 months, babies can distinguish both human and monkey faces.
    b. Six-month-olds look longer at novel human faces, but not novel monkey faces.
    c. Six-month-olds look longer at monkey faces, but not novel human faces.
    d. By 9 months, babies lose their ability to distinguish monkey faces.

22. The well-known visual cliff test shows that crawling babies have __________ abilities. (p. 192)
    a. pattern perception
    b. face perception
    c. depth perception
    d. shape constancy

23. Very young babies prefer to look at __________ (p. 193)
    a. large, bold checkerboards.
    b. detailed patterns.
    c. patterns with less contrast.
    d. plain stimuli.

24. Infants with severe visual impairments must rely on __________ to identify the whereabouts of objects. (p. 194)
    a. touch
    b. instinct
    c. previous experience
    d. sound

25. Habituation research reveals that size constancy is present __________ (p. 196)
    a. within the first week of life.
    b. by 1 month of age.
    c. by 3 months of age.
    d. by 5 months of age.

26. Habituation research, in which a ball moves back and forth behind a screen, reveals that at age 4 months, infants __________ (p. 197)
    a. can monitor a curvilinear course at varying speeds.
    b. first perceive the ball's path as continuous.
    c. first perceive the ball's path as discontinuous.
    d. rely on adult input to detect the identity of the object.

27. In intermodal perception, babies make sense of simultaneous input from more than one sensory system by __________ (p. 197)
    a. perceiving them as integrated wholes.
    b. attending to individual modalities.
    c. being more sensitive to variant features.
    d. pairing it with an unconditioned stimulus.

28. Research on perceptual development indicates that babies seek out __________ relationships. (p. 198)
    a. unstable
    b. dynamic
    c. invariant
    d. novel

29. Differentiation theorists view perceptual development as a built-in tendency to seek __________ (p. 198)
    a. conflicting cues.
    b. consistency.
    c. novel stimuli.
    d. variation.

30. A baby's sensitivity to affordances makes his or her exploratory actions __________ (p. 199)
    a. future oriented and largely successful.
    b. less likely to be overwhelmed by complex intermodal stimuli.
    c. more sensitive to invariant features.
    d. reactive and blundering until around age 18 months.

PRACTICE TEST #2

1. In the proximodistal growth trend, __________ (p. 162)
   a. growth proceeds from head to tail.
   b. the head develops more rapidly than the lower part of the body.
   c. the arms and the legs grow first, and then the chest and the trunk.
   d. growth proceeds from the center of the body outward.

2. At birth, the bones of the skull are __________ (p. 164)
   a. pliable, like cartilage.
   b. separated by fontanels.
   c. overlapping.
   d. sutured or seamed together.

3. The human brain has about __________ to __________ neurons. (p. 164)
   a. 100; 200 thousand
   b. 100; 200 million
   c. 10; 20 billion
   d. 100; 200 billion

4. About half of the brain's volume is made up of __________ (p. 165)
   a. water.
   b. glial cells.
   c. ERPs.
   d. unstimulated neurons.

5. In __________, after injection or inhalation of a radioactive substance, a person lies on an apparatus with a scanner than emits fine streams of X-rays. (p. 166)
   a. an EEG
   b. fMRI
   c. PET
   d. NIRS

6. For most people, the left side of the brain is responsible for __________ (p. 168)
   a. verbal abilities.
   b. judging distances.
   c. reading maps.
   d. negative emotion.

7. Research on brain plasticity reveals that __________ (p. 170)
   a. plasticity is greatest during synaptic pruning.
   b. the adult brain can produce a small number of new neurons.
   c. brain plasticity is restricted to early childhood.
   d. language processing is more lateralized at birth than spatial processing.

8. Adoption studies reveal that the longer children spend in institutions, the __________ (p. 171)
   a. higher their oxytocin levels.
   b. faster their cognitive catch-up.
   c. higher their cortisol levels.
   d. greater the metabolic activity in the prefrontal cortex.

9. By about _____ months, children generally need only one nap. (p. 172)
   a. 9
   b. 12
   c. 15
   d. 18

10. Brock and Rhea are expecting their first baby and have some concerns parent–infant cosleeping. You should tell Brock and Rhea that __________ (p. 173)
    a. their concerns are valid, as cosleeping is a dangerous practice.
    b. their sleep will be greatly disrupted if they choose to cosleep.
    c. the practice provides valuable bonding time.
    d. cosleeping is linked to long-term adjustment problems in children.

11. Twin studies reveal that __________ contributes considerably to __________ (p. 174)
    a. the environment; height.
    b. genetic makeup; body weight.
    c. the environment; rate of growth.
    d. birth weight; adult weight.

12. The U.S. Department of Health and Human Services advises exclusive breastfeeding for the first _____ months. (p. 175)
    a. 4
    b. 6
    c. 9
    d. 12

13. __________ is caused by an unbalanced diet very low in protein. (p. 177)
    a. Kwashiorkor
    b. Growth faltering
    c. Marasmus
    d. Food insecurity

14. Baby Sam is withdrawn and apathetic. His weight, height, and head circumference are substantially below age-related growth norms. Sam displays signs of __________ (p. 178)
    a. kwashiorkor
    b. growth faltering.
    c. marasmus.
    d. food insecurity.

15. In classical conditioning, if learning occurs, the conditioned stimulus elicits a(n) __________ (p. 179)
    a. neutral stimulus.
    b. neutral response.
    c. unconditioned stimulus.
    d. conditioned response.

16. In operant conditioning, a stimulus that increases the occurrence of a response is a(n) __________ (p. 180)
    a. neutral stimulus.
    b. punishment.
    c. reinforcer.
    d. unconditioned stimulus.

17. Which of the following motor skills is most likely to develop the latest? (p. 184)
    a. crawling
    b. sitting alone
    c. grasping a cube
    d. building tower of two cubes

18. Three-month-old J.T's newborn grasp reflex has now been replaced by __________, a clumsy motion in which the young infant's fingers close against the palm. (p. 187)
    a. prereaching
    b. the ulnar grasp
    c. voluntary reaching
    d. the pincer grasp

19. A toddler who __________ shows signs of toilet training readiness. (p. 188)
    a. is learning to walk
    b. sleeps through the night
    c. stays dry for an hour at a time
    d. stops playing during urination

20. Between 4 and 7 months, infants __________ (p. 189)
    a. can distinguish musical tunes on the basis of variations in rhythmic patterns.
    b. prefer music with pauses between phrases to those with awkward breaks.
    c. recognize the same melody when it is played in different keys.
    d. detect sound regularities that will facilitate later language learning.

21. Research reveals that infants __________ (p. 190)
    a. have an impressive statistical learning capacity.
    b. make slow progress in perceiving the structure of speech.
    c. are not capable of screening out sounds not used in their own language.
    d. listen longer to speech with no clause and phrase boundaries.

22. Artists use __________ to make a painting look three-dimensional. (p. 192)
    a. size constancy
    b. binocular depth cues
    c. shape constancy
    d. pictorial depth cues

23. One-year-old Lola was born with a severe visual impairment. How can Lola's parents help compensate for her visual loss? (p. 194)
    a. To protect her from injury, Lola should be discouraged from independent exploration.
    b. Lola's parents should heighten sensory input by combining sound and touch.
    c. Lola's parents should avoid overstimulation by focusing on one sensory modality at a time.
    d. Without surgery, little can be done to compensate for early visual loss.

24. Newborns prefer to look at drawings of faces with __________ features. (p. 195)
    a. upside down
    b. sideways
    c. upright
    d. complex

25. Habituation research reveals that shape constancy is present __________ (p. 196)
    a. within the first week of life.
    b. by 1 month.
    c. by 3 months.
    d. by 5 months.

26. Which of the following statements is true about infants' perception of object identity? (p. 197)
    a. As infants become familiar with many types of objects, they rely more on motion and spatial arrangement to identify them.
    b. When two objects are touching and stand still, babies younger than 4 months cannot distinguish them.
    c. Until at least 2 years, babies think that a moving rod whose center is hidden behind a box is two rod pieces.
    d. Perception of object identity is mastered quickly over the first weeks of life.

27. At 3 to 4 months, infants' intermodal perception is such that they can __________ (p. 197)
    a. make sense of complex amodal relationships.
    b. discriminate positive from negative emotion in each sensory modality.
    c. perceive and remember the unique face–voice pairings of unfamiliar adults.
    d. match faces with voices on the basis of lip–voice synchrony.

28. Intermodal sensitivity is crucial for _________ development. (p. 198)
    a. fine-motor
    b. gross-motor
    c. perceptual
    d. emotional

29. When 6-month-old Veronica gazes at an adult's face, she will probably require _________ input to distinguish positive from negative emotional expressions. (p. 198)
    a. both vocal and visual
    b. only vocal
    c. only visual
    d. both visual and sensory

30. According to the Gibsons' differentiation theory, perception is guided by the discovery of _________ (p. 199)
    a. amodal properties.
    b. affordances.
    c. coherent wholes.
    d. dynamic features.

CHAPTER 6
COGNITIVE DEVELOPMENT IN INFANCY AND TODDLERHOOD

BRIEF CHAPTER SUMMARY

According to Piaget, from earliest infancy, children actively build psychological structures, or schemes, as they manipulate and explore their world. The vast changes that take place in Piaget's sensorimotor stage are divided into six substages. By acting on the world, infants make strides in intentional behavior, mastery of object permanence, and problem solving. In the final substage, mental representations, internal depictions of information that the mind can manipulate, appear.

Alternative explanations for babies' amazing cognitive accomplishments include the core knowledge perspective, which holds that babies are born with a set of innate knowledge systems, or core domains of thought, that support early, rapid cognitive development. Despite ongoing challenges from critics, core knowledge research has sharpened the field's focus on clarifying the starting point for human cognition and on carefully tracking the changes that build on it.

Research findings have yielded broad agreement that many cognitive changes of infancy are gradual and continuous, rather than stagelike, and that various aspects of infant cognition change unevenly. These ideas form the basis for another major approach to cognitive development—information processing, which focuses on the development of mental strategies for storing and interpreting information. With age, infants' attention becomes more efficient and flexible, and memory improves and is supported by a capacity for mental representation. Infants group stimuli into increasingly complex categories. Babies' exploration of objects, expanding knowledge of the world, and advancing language skills foster categorization.

Vygotsky's sociocultural theory emphasizes that cognitive development is socially mediated as adults help infants and toddlers master challenging tasks. More specifically, skilled partners aid the child in carrying out tasks within his or her zone of proximal development.

A variety of infant intelligence tests have been devised to measure individual differences in early mental development. Most predict later performance poorly, but tests that focus on speed of habituation and recovery to visual stimuli and on object permanence are better predictors. Powerful influences on intellectual progress are the home environment, child care, and early intervention programs for at-risk infants and toddlers.

Behaviorist and nativist theories provide sharply contrasting accounts of language development. The interactionist view emphasizes that innate abilities and environmental influences combine to produce children's extraordinary language achievements. During the first year, infants prepare for language in many ways. First words appear around 12 months. Once toddlers produce about 200 words, they start to combine two words. Substantial individual differences exist in rate and style of early language progress. A rich social environment and parent–toddler conversation support infants' and toddlers' efforts to become competent speakers.

LEARNING OBJECTIVES

After reading this chapter, you should be able to:

6.1 Describe Piaget's view of development, noting how schemes change over the course of development. (pp. 204–205)

6.2 Describe the major cognitive achievements of Piaget's sensorimotor stage. (pp. 205–207)

6.3 Discuss follow-up research on the accuracy of Piaget's sensorimotor stage, including the concepts of object permanence, mental representation, problem solving, and symbolic understanding. (pp. 208–214)

6.4 Describe alternate views of cognitive development, including the core knowledge perspective. (pp. 214–216)

6.5 Describe the general structure of the information-processing system, explain how this approach differs from Piaget's perspective, and review the strengths and limitations of the information-processing theory of cognitive development. (pp. 217–218, 223–224)

6.6 Discuss changes in attention, memory, and categorization that take place over the first two years. (pp. 218–223)

6.7 Explain how Vygotsky's concept of the zone of proximal development expands our understanding of early cognitive development. (pp. 224–225)

6.8 Describe the mental testing approach, the meaning of intelligence test scores, and the extent to which infant tests predict later performance. (pp. 227–228)

6.9 Discuss environmental influences on early mental development, including home, child care, and early interventions for at-risk infants and toddlers. (pp. 228–232)

6.10 Describe three theories of language development, indicating the emphasis each places on innate and environmental influences. (pp. 233–236)

6.11 Summarize major milestones of language development in the first two years, individual differences, and ways adults can support infants' and toddlers' emerging capacities. (pp. 236–238)

6.12 Describe the characteristics of infants' first words and two-word phrases, and explain why language comprehension develops ahead of language production. (pp. 238–240)

6.13 Discuss individual and cultural differences in early language development, including factors that influence these differences. (pp. 240–241)

6.14 Explain how child-directed speech and conversation support early language development. (pp. 241–242)

STUDY QUESTIONS

Piaget's Cognitive-Developmental Theory

1. During Piaget's ________________________, which spans the first 2 years of life, infants and toddlers "think" with their eyes, ears, and hands. (p. 204)

Piaget's Ideas About Cognitive Change

1. According to Piaget, specific psychological structures—or organized ways of making sense of experience, called ______________________________—change with age. (p. 204)

2. Match the following terms with the appropriate description. (pp. 204–205)

_____ Creating new schemes or adjusting old ones to produce a better fit with the environment
_____ Taking new schemes, rearranging them, and linking them with other schemes to create an interconnected cognitive system
_____ Using current schemes to interpret the external world
_____ Building schemes through direct interaction with the environment

A. *Adaptation*
B. *Assimilation*
C. *Accommodation*
D. *Organization*

The Sensorimotor Stage

1. True or False: Piaget believed that infants already know a great deal about their world from the time they are born. (p. 205)

2. Match each of the following *sensorimotor* substages with its appropriate description. (p. 205)

_____ Infants' primary means of adapting to the environment is through reflexes.
_____ Infants engage in *goal-directed behavior* and begin to attain *object permanence.*
_____ Toddlers repeat behaviors with variation, producing new effects.
_____ Infants repeat chance behaviors largely motivated by basic needs.
_____ Babies try to repeat interesting events in the surrounding environment that are caused by their own actions.
_____ Toddlers create internal depictions of information that the mind can manipulate.

A. Reflexive schemes
B. Primary circular reactions
C. Secondary circular reactions
D. Coordination of secondary circular reactions
E. Tertiary circular reactions
F. *Mental representation*

3. Explain the differences between primary, secondary, and tertiary *circular reactions.* (pp. 205–206)

   Primary: ____

   ____

   Secondary: ____

   ____

   Tertiary: ____

   ____

4. The ability to coordinate schemes deliberately to solve simple problems is called ____________________, or ____________________, *behavior.* (p. 207)
5. The understanding that objects continue to exist when they are out of sight is called ____________________. (p. 207)
6. Describe the *A-not-B search error.* (p. 207)

   ____

   ____

7. Name the two most powerful mental representations. (p. 207)

   A. ____

   B. ____

8. Identify three new capacities that result from the ability to create mental representations. (p. 207)

   A. ____

   B. ____

   C. ____

Follow-Up Research on Infant Cognitive Development

1. Many studies show that infants understand concepts (earlier / later) than Piaget believed. (p. 208)
2. Explain the *violation-of-expectation method,* which is often used by researchers to identify infants' grasp of object permanence and other aspects of physical reasoning. (pp. 208–209)

   ____

   ____

   ____

   ____

3. Give two reasons why the violation-of-expectation method is controversial. (p. 208)

   A. ____

   B. ____

4. What did Renée Baillargeon conclude about object permanence, based on the tests she gave to infants? Why are these findings controversial? (p. 209)

   A. ____

   ____

   B. ____

   ____

5. True or False: Around 14 months, toddlers demonstrate a thorough understanding of hidden objects. (p. 209)

6. Mastery of object permanence is a (gradual / sudden) achievement. (p. 209)

7. True or False: Laboratory research on *deferred imitation* supports Piaget's conclusion that infants cannot mentally represent experience until about 18 months of age. Briefly explain your response. (pp. 210–211)

____

____

8. By 10 to 12 months of age, infants can solve problems by ______________, meaning that they apply a solution strategy from one problem to other relevant problems. (p. 211)

9. The symbolic capacity called ______________________ refers to the realization that words can be used to cue mental images of people and objects that are not physically present. (p. 211)

10. True or False: Infants regard pictures as symbols of objects. Briefly explain your response. (p. 212)

____

____

Social Issues: Education: Baby Learning from TV and Video: The Video Deficit Effect

1. How do infants initially respond to video images of people? Give specific examples. (p. 213)

____

____

2. What is the *video deficit effect*? What is one explanation for this phenomenon? (p. 213)

A. ____

____

B. ____

____

3. List several features that can be used to make video effective as a teaching tool for young children. (p. 213)

____

____

Evaluation of the Sensorimotor Stage

1. True or False: Recent research indicates that the cognitive attainments of infancy and toddlerhood do, in fact, develop together in the neat, stepwise fashion that Piaget postulated. (pp. 212, 213)

2. According to the ______________________________, babies are born with a set of innate knowledge systems, or core domains of thought. (p. 214)

3. Cite four domains of thought studied by *core knowledge* theorists. (p. 214)

A. ______________________ B. ______________________

C. ______________________ D. ______________________

4. True or False: Research on the core knowledge perspective is less controversial than violation-of-expectation results. (p. 215)

5. True or False: The core knowledge perspective acknowledges that experience is essential for children to extend their initial knowledge. (p. 215)

6. Follow-up research on Piaget's sensorimotor stage yields broad agreement on two issues. List them. (p. 216)

   A. ____________________

   B. ____________________

Information Processing

1. In what ways do information-processing researchers agree with Piaget's theory? (p. 217)

   ____

   ____

Structure of the Information-Processing System

1. Match each part of the information-processing system to the appropriate description. (pp. 217–218)

   _____ Area in which *mental strategies* are used to synthesize information
   _____ Area where sights and sounds are represented directly and briefly stored
   _____ The largest storage area, comprising the brain's permanent knowledge base

   A. *Sensory register*
   B. *Working,* or *short-term, memory*
   C. *Long-term memory*

2. Explain the role of the *central executive* in managing the complex activities of the working memory system. (p. 218)

   ____

   ____

3. Long-term memory has a(n) (limited / unlimited) capacity. (p. 218)

4. Information-processing researchers believe that the (structure / capacity) of the human mental system is similar throughout life. (p. 218)

5. What two factors do researchers believe are responsible for gains in information-processing capacity? (p. 218)

   A. ____________________

   B. ____________________

Attention

1. List three ways in which attention improves during infancy. (p. 218)

   A. ____________________

   B. ____________________

   C. ____________________

2. In toddlerhood, attention to novelty declines and ____________________ improves, increasing the capacity for goal-directed behavior. (p. 218)

3. Explain how adults can foster sustained attention during infancy and toddlerhood. (p. 219)

   ____

   ____

Memory

1. True or False: From the first few months of life, infant memory for operant responses is independent of context, meaning that infants apply learned responses to relevant new situations. (p. 219)

2. True or False: Habituation research confirms that infants need to be physically active to acquire new information. (pp. 219–220)

3. Distinguish between *recognition* and *recall* memory. (p. 220)

   Recognition: ______________________________

   ____

   Recall: ______________________________

   ____

4. Can infants engage in recall? Explain. (p. 220)

   ____

   ____

Biology and Environment: Infantile Amnesia

1. What is *infantile amnesia*? (p. 221)

   ____

   ____

2. Recall of personally meaningful one-time events from both the recent and the distant past is called ______________ *memory.* (p. 221)

3. Provide two explanations for infantile amnesia. (p. 221)

   A. ______________________________

   ____

   B. ______________________________

   ____

4. Explain how the phenomenon of infantile amnesia can be reconciled with infants' and toddlers' remarkable memory skills. (p. 221)

   ____

   ____

   ____

5. Research suggests that ______________________ and ______________________ contribute to the end of infantile amnesia. (p. 221)

Categorization

1. Explain how categorization helps infants make sense of experience. (p. 222)

   ____

   ____

2. True or False: Findings reveal that in the second half of the first year, as long as they have sufficient familiarity with category members, infants group objects into an impressive array of categories. (p. 222)

3. Briefly explain three views on how infants gain skill in categorization. (p. 223)

   A. ______________________________

   B. ______________________________

   C. ______________________________

4. True or False: Research has found that all infants, regardless of their culture or native language, sort objects in the same way. (p. 223)

Evaluation of Information-Processing Findings

1. Information-processing research underscores the (continuity / discontinuity) of human thinking from infancy into adulthood. (p. 223)

2. In what way does information-processing research challenge Piaget's view of early cognitive development? (p. 224)

   ____

   ____

3. What is the greatest drawback of the information-processing approach to cognitive development? (p. 224)

   ____

   ____

The Social Context of Early Cognitive Development

1. Vygotsky believed that ______________________________, such as voluntary attention, deliberate memory, categorization, and problem solving, have their origins in ______________________________. (p. 224)

2. Explain Vygotsky's concept of the *zone of proximal development,* and explain how adults use scaffolding to introduce children to new tasks. (p. 224)

   A. ______________________________

   ____

   B. ______________________________

   ____

Cultural Influences: Social Origins of Make-Believe Play

1. Briefly summarize Vygotsky's view of *make-believe play.* (p. 226)

   ____

   ____

2. Explain why adults' participation in toddlers' make-believe play is so important. (p. 226)

   ____

   ____

   ____

3. True or False: In some cultures, such as those of Indonesia and Mexico, make-believe play is more frequent and more complex with older siblings than with mothers. Briefly explain your response. (p. 226)

   ____

   ____

Individual Differences in Early Mental Development

1. Mental tests focus on ____________________________, measuring behaviors that reflect development and arriving at scores that predict future performance. (p. 227)

Infant Intelligence Tests

1. Briefly explain why it is difficult to measure babies' intelligence. (p. 227)

____

____

2. Most infant tests emphasize ___________________ and ____________________ responses. (p. 227)

3. One commonly used infant test is the _______________ Scales of Infant Development, designed for children between 1 month and 3½ years. (p. 227)

4. Intelligence tests are scored by computing a(n) __________________, which indicates the extent to which the raw score deviates from the typical performance of same-age individuals. (p. 227)

5. In constructing intelligence tests, designers engage in __________________, giving the tests to a large, representative sample and using the results as the standard for interpreting scores. (p. 227)

6. What is a *normal distribution*? (p. 228)

____

____

7. When intelligence tests are standardized, the mean IQ is set at _____. (p. 228)

8. True or False: Scores on infant intelligence tests are excellent predictors of later intelligence. Briefly explain your response. (p. 228)

____

____

____

9. Due to concerns that infant test scores do not tap the same dimensions of intelligence measured at older ages, they are labeled _____________________, or ____, rather than IQs. (p. 228)

10. For what purpose are infant intelligence tests largely used? (p. 228)

____

11. Why do habituation and recovery and Piagetian object-permanence tasks predict later IQ more effectively than traditional infant intelligence tests? (p. 228)

____

____

Early Environment and Mental Development

1. What is the *Home Observation for Measurement of the Environment (HOME)*? (p. 229)

____

____

2. Place an X next to each factor in the list that is evaluated by HOME. (p. 229)

_____ Parental acceptance of the child	_____ Opportunities for variety in daily stimulation
_____ Nutrition and opportunities for physical exercise	_____ Ethnicity and cultural background
_____ Emotional and verbal responsiveness of the parent	_____ Organization of the physical environment
_____ Socioeconomic status	_____ Strength of the parents' relationship
_____ Provision of appropriate play materials	_____ Parental involvement with the child

3. Regardless of SES and ethnicity, what aspects measured by HOME repeatedly predict better language and IQ scores in toddlerhood and early childhood? (p. 229)

____

____

____

4. Cite ways in which both heredity and home environment contribute to mental test scores. (p. 229)

   Heredity: ____

   ____

   Home environment: ____

   ____

5. Today, more than ______ percent of U.S. mothers with children under age 2 are employed. (p. 230)

6. List some of the consequences of low- versus high-quality child care for mental development. (p. 230)

   Low-quality: ____

   ____

   High-quality: ____

   ____

7. Describe the overall condition of child care for infants and toddlers in the United States. (p. 230)

____

____

____

8. In the United States, child-care settings that serve (low-SES / middle-SES) families tend to provide the worst care. Briefly explain your response. (p. 230)

____

____

9. List and briefly describe at least four signs of *developmentally appropriate practice* in infant and toddler child care. (p. 230)

   A. ______________________________

   B. ______________________________

   C. ______________________________

   D. ______________________________

Early Intervention for At-Risk Infants and Toddlers

1. Describe center- and home-based interventions for infants and toddlers. (p. 231)

   Center-based: ______________________________

   Home-based: ______________________________

2. Discuss the effectiveness of early intervention programs with regard to infant and toddler mental development. (p. 231)

   ____

3. Briefly describe the Carolina Abecedarian Project, and summarize the outcomes of this program. (pp. 231–232)

   A. ______________________________

   B. ______________________________

4. What is Early Head Start? Cite three services available through Early Head Start. (p. 232)

   A. ______________________________

   B. ______________________________

   C. ______________________________

   D. ______________________________

Language Development

1. On average, children say their first word at ______ months of age. (p. 233)

Three Theories of Language Development

1. According to the behaviorist perspective, what two processes account for early language acquisition, and how do they do so? (p. 233)

   A. ______________________________

   ____

   B. ______________________________

   ____

2. Why is the behaviorist perspective an incomplete explanation of early language development? (p. 233)

   ____

   ____

3. According to Chomsky's nativist perspective, all children have a(n) ______________________________, an innate system containing a universal grammar, or set of rules common to all languages, that enables them to understand and speak as soon as they pick up enough words. (p. 234)

4. Provide evidence supporting Chomsky's view that human infants are biologically primed to acquire language. (p. 234)

   ____

   ____

5. Name the two language-specific areas of the brain, and cite the function of each. (p. 234)

   A. ______________________________

   ____

   B. ______________________________

   ____

6. True or False: If the left-hemispheric region is injured in the early years, other regions of the brain take over its language functions. (p. 234)

7. True or False: Acquiring a second language is harder after a sensitive period has passed. Briefly explain your response. (p. 235)

   ____

   ____

8. True or False: Research supports the idea that there is a biologically-based sensitive period for optimum language development. (p. 235)

9. List two challenges to Chomsky's theory. (p. 235)

   A. ______________________________

   ____

   B. ______________________________

   ____

10. Name and summarize two views of the interactionist perspective of language development. (p. 236)

    A. ____

    ____

    B. ____

    ____

Getting Ready to Talk

1. At around 2 months of age, babies begin to make vowel-like noises, called ______________. At around 6 months of age, ______________ appears, in which infants repeat consonant–vowel combinations, often in long strings. (p. 236)

2. What does research on deaf-born infants reveal about an early sensitive period for language development? (pp. 236–237)

    ____

    ____

    ____

3. Describe *joint attention,* and indicate how it contributes to early language development. (p. 238)

    A. ____

    ____

    B. ____

    ____

4. Explain how caregivers can support conversational give-and-take in babies. (p. 238)

    ____

    ____

5. At the end of the first year, infants use ______________ gestures to direct adults' attention, to influence their behavior, and to convey helpful information. How do these gestures contribute to language development? (p. 238)

    ____

    ____

First Words

1. Briefly describe the nature of toddlers' first words (for example, to which subjects do these words commonly refer? (p. 238)

    ____

    ____

    ____

2. When young children learn new words, they tend to make two types of errors. Name and describe each error, and provide an example of each. (p. 239)

    A. ____

    ____

    B. ____

    ____

The Two-Word Utterance Phase

1. List three developments that support rapid vocabulary growth during toddlerhood. (p. 239)

   A. ______________________________

   B. ______________________________

   C. ______________________________

2. Explain the nature of *telegraphic speech.* (p. 239)

Comprehension versus Production

1. Distinguish between language *comprehension* and language *production.* (p. 240)

   Comprehension: ______________________________

   Production: ______________________________

2. (Comprehension / Production) requires that children recognize only the meaning of a word, but for (comprehension / production), children must recall not only the word but also the concept for which it stands. (p. 240)

Individual and Cultural Differences

1. True or False: Early vocabulary development proceeds at about the same rate for boys and girls. (p. 240)
2. Explain how a child's environment influences language development. (p. 240)

3. Distinguish between *referential style* and *expressive style* of early language learning. (p. 240)

   Referential: ______________________________

   Expressive: ______________________________

4. (Expressive / Referential) style is associated with faster vocabulary development. (p. 241)
5. Cite factors that influence the development of referential and expressive styles. (p. 241)

Supporting Early Language Development

1. Describe three ways in which caregivers can support early language learning. (p. 241)

   A. ______________________________

   B. ______________________________

   C. ______________________________

2. List five attributes of *child-directed speech.* (p. 241)

   A. ______________________________

   B. ______________________________

   C. ______________________________

   D. ______________________________

   E. ______________________________

3. True or False: Parent–toddler conversation strongly predicts early language development and academic success during the school years. Briefly explain your response. (p. 242)

   ____

   ____

Social Issues: Education: Parent–Child Interaction: Impact on Language and Cognitive Development of Deaf Children

1. True or False: Over 90 percent of deaf children have hearing parents who are fluent in sign language. (p. 243)

2. Describe outcomes for children who have hearing parents not fluent in sign language. (p. 243)

   ____

   ____

   ____

3. Discuss differences in parent–child communication experienced by deaf children of hearing parents and deaf children of deaf parents. (p. 243)

   Children of hearing parents: ______________________________

   ____

   Children of deaf parents: ______________________________

   ____

ASK YOURSELF . . .

For *Ask Yourself* questions for this chapter, along with feedback on the accuracy of your answers, please log on to MyDevelopmentLab (for registration and access, please visit mydevelopmentlab.com or follow the instructions on page ix).

(1) Select the Multimedia Library.

(2) Choose the explore option.

(3) Find your chapter from the drop down box.

(4) Click find now.

(5) Complete questions and choose "Submit answers for grading" or "Clear answers" to start over.

SUGGESTED READINGS

Columbo, J., McCardle, P., Freund, L. (Eds.). (2008). *Infant pathways to language.* New York: Psychology Press. Presents the latest research on early language development, including contemporary theories, genetic and environmental contributions, the importance of gestures, language disorders, and intervention strategies for young children with language delays.

Hallock, P. (2008). *One step forward, two steps back: Making change in Early Head Start.* Lanham, MD: University of America Press. Examines the experiences of economically at-risk families who participate in Early Head Start. The author provides an overview of Early Head Start services, emphasizes the importance of family involvement in early intervention, and discusses the unique challenges of working with poverty-stricken infants and toddlers.

Johnson, S. (2010). *Neoconstructivism: The new science of cognitive development.* New York: Oxford University Press. A compelling look at cognitive development in infants and young children, this book explores a diverse range of topics, including historical accounts of early learning, current theories, language acquisition, the importance of play, and the relationship between cognition and social understanding.

CROSSWORD PUZZLE 6.1

Across

2. In language development, the words and word combinations that children use
4. Style of early language learning in which toddlers use language mainly to label objects
7. Checklist for gathering information about the quality of children's home lives (abbr.)
8. ____________ quotient: a score that permits an individual's performance on an intelligence test to be compared to the performances of other same-age individuals
9. Innate system that permits children to speak in a rule-oriented fashion as soon as they learn enough words (abbr.)
13. Pleasant vowel-like noises made by infants
14. Style of early language learning in which toddlers use language mainly to label objects
16. _____________ memory: narrative accounts of significant, one-time events that are long-lasting because they are imbued with personal meaning
17. Early language error in which words are applied to a wider collection of objects and events than is appropriate
18. ____________ attention: the child attends to the same object or event as the caregiver, who offers verbal information.
19. Repetition of consonant–vowel combinations in long strings

Down

1. Zone of _______________ development: range of tasks that a child cannot yet handle independently but can accomplish with the help of more skilled partners
3. Early language error in which words are applied too narrowly
5. Form of speech marked by high-pitched, exaggerated expression, clear pronunciations, and distinct pauses between speech segments (2 words, hyph.)
6. _____________ speech: toddlers' two-word utterances that leave out smaller and less important words
10. Standards devised by NAEYC that specify program characteristics that meet the developmental and individual needs of young children are called _____________ appropriate practice.
11. In language development, the words and word combinations that children understand
12. ______________ quotient: a score on an infant intelligence test; based primarily on perceptual and motor responses
15. Type of play in which children pretend, acting out everyday and imaginary images

CROSSWORD PUZZLE 6.2

Across

4. ____________, or short-term, memory: conscious part of memory where we actively work on a limited amount of information.
5. ___________ effect: poorer performance after a video than a live demonstration (2 words)
7. Mental _______________: internal depictions of images the mind can manipulate
8. Piaget's first stage, during which infants and toddlers "think" with their eyes, ears, and hands
9. __________, or goal-directed, behavior is a sequence of actions in which schemes are deliberately combined to solve a problem.
10. New schemes are created and old ones adjusted to produce a better fit with the environment.
12. Mental _____________: procedures that operate on and transform information, thereby increasing the efficiency of thinking and the chances that information will be retained
13. The ability to remember and copy the behavior of a model who is not immediately present is known as ___________ imitation.
16. The practice of giving an intelligence test to a large, representative sample, which serves as the standard for interpreting individual scores.
17. Object _____________: understanding that objects still exist even when they are out of sight.
21. Type of memory that involves noticing whether a new experience is identical to or similar to a previous one
22. Type of memory that involves remembering something in the absence of perceptual support
23. The ______________ register part of the mental system holds sights and sounds until they decay or are transferred to short-term memory.
24. The internal arrangement and linking together of schemes so that they form a strongly interconnected cognitive system

Down

1. Process of building new schemes through direct contact with the environment
2. In Piaget's theory, a specific structure, or organized way of making sense of experience, that changes with age
3. __________ knowledge perspective: babies are born with a set of innate knowledge systems.
6. A special part of working memory that directs the flow of information (2 words)
7. Displaced ______________: realization that words can be used to cue mental images of things not physically present.
10. __-___-___ search error: if an object is moved from hiding place A to hiding place B, 8- to 12-month-old infants will search only in the first hiding place.
11. ___________ distribution: a bell-shaped distribution that results when individual differences are measured in large samples
14. ______-_______ memory: contains our permanent knowledge base (2 words, hyph.)
15. The external world is represented in terms of current schemes.
18. Violation-of-_____________ method: researchers habituate infants to an event and then determine whether they recover to a possible event or an impossible event.
19. Infantile ____________: the inability of most people to recall events that happened to them before age 3
20. When infants stumble onto a new experience caused by their own motor activity and then try to repeat the event again and again, they are exhibiting a __________ reaction.

PRACTICE TEST #1

1. According to Piaget, at times when children are not changing much, they __________ (pp. 204–205)
   a. accommodate more than they assimilate.
   b. assimilate more than they accommodate.
   c. shift from assimilation to accommodation.
   d. accommodate to disequilibrium.

2. According to Piaget, in the second year, the circular reaction __________ (p. 206)
   a. becomes an automatic reflex.
   b. centers around the child's body.
   c. disappears because it is no longer adaptive.
   d. becomes experimental and creative.

3. Some critics of the violation-of-expectation method believe that it __________ (p. 208)
   a. fails to consider environmental experiences.
   b. reveals babies' limited capacity to assimilate new experiences.
   c. indicates limited awareness of physical events.
   d. merely confirms the effects of deferred imitation.

4. According to Piaget, children cannot represent experience until about _____ months. (p. 209)
   a. 12
   b. 18
   c. 24
   d. 30

5. Recent studies of deferred imitation and problem solving reveal that __________ (p. 210)
   a. toddlers do not imitate rationally until about 18 months.
   b. deferred imitation is present as early as 6 weeks of age.
   c. infants are more likely to imitate accidental than purposeful behaviors.
   d. gains in recognition are accompanied by changes in brain-wave activity.

6. Before the age of __________, the American Academy of Pediatrics recommends against mass media exposure. (p. 213)
   a. 6 months
   b. 12 months
   c. 2½ years
   d. 3 years

7. In one study, after an adult on video announced where she had hid a toy, __________ (p. 213)
   a. most 18-month-olds retrieved the toy.
   b. few 2-year-olds searched.
   c. most 2-year-olds searched.
   d. few 3-year-olds retrieved the toy.

8. According to the core knowledge perspective, __________ (p. 214)
   a. babies are born with a set of innate knowledge systems.
   b. children make sense of the world by creating schemes.
   c. complex mental activities have their origins in social interaction.
   d. children's genetics have little effect on learning.

9. Follow-up studies of Piaget's sensorimotor stage have led researchers to __________ (p. 216)
   a. discard Piaget's observations as having any practical value to teachers and caregivers.
   b. agree that many cognitive changes in infancy are gradual and continuous.
   c. reject Piaget's description of the later sensorimotor substages.
   d. propose that various aspects of infant cognition develop simultaneously.

10. Sights and sounds are represented directly and stored briefly in __________ (p. 217)
    a. the sensory register.
    b. the central executive.
    c. working memory.
    d. autobiographical memory.

11. With the transition to toddlerhood, __________ (p. 219)
    a. attraction to novelty disappears.
    b. sustained attention improves.
    c. the primary circular reaction reappears.
    d. plans and activities become less complex.

12. Habituation research on infants' memory of actions confirms that __________ (p. 220)
    a. novelty preference is stronger than familiarity preference.
    b. Piaget's model of sensorimotor development is essentially correct.
    c. sensitivity to object appearance increases over the first half-year.
    d. infants need not be physically active to acquire new information.

13. __________ is the easiest form of memory. (p. 220)
    a. Recognition
    b. Recall
    c. Autobiographical memory
    d. Categorization

14. Pat cannot remember events that happened to her before the age of 3. Pat is experiencing __________ (p. 221)
    a. autobiographical memory.
    b. habituation and recovery.
    c. infantile amnesia.
    d. delayed working memory.

15. Vygotsky believed that complex mental activities, such as voluntary attention and deliberate memory, originate in __________ (p. 225)
    a. the frontal lobes.
    b. dynamic systems.
    c. social interaction.
    d. conceptual categories.

16. Research supports the idea that make-believe is the combined result of __________ and __________ (p. 226)
    a. children's readiness to engage in it; social experiences that promote it.
    b. advanced perspective-taking skills; adult involvement.
    c. cognitive maturity; access to play materials.
    d. children's independent efforts; access to a stimulating environment.

17. Infant intelligence tests __________ (p. 227)
    a. focus on how children's thinking changes with age.
    b. focus on the process of development.
    c. tap early language, cognition, and social behavior.
    d. precisely measure both IQ and DQ.

18. The Bayley III __________ and __________ Scales are good predictors of preschool mental test performance. (p. 228)
    a. Cognitive; Language
    b. Motor; Language
    c. Cognitive; Adaptive Behavior
    d. Adaptive Behavior; Social-Emotional

19. According to research findings, among the best infant predictors of IQ from early childhood into adolescence is __________ (p. 228)
    a. Piagetian object-permanence tasks and developmental quotients.
    b. habituation and recovery to novel visual stimuli.
    c. the rate at which the infant becomes fatigued during testing.
    d. the amount of fluctuation in IQ between infancy and toddlerhood.

20. Children who participate in center-based and home-based intervention programs __________ (p. 231)
    a. continue to lag behind agemates in both motor and cognitive development.
    b. tend to come from more organized homes than children who do not participate.
    c. have difficulty adjusting to highly structured preschool programs.
    d. score higher on mental tests by age 2 than children who do not participate.

21. According to the behaviorist perspective, children acquire language __________ (p. 233)
    a. through application of the universal grammar.
    b. by imitation and reinforcement.
    c. through the work of specialized language areas in the brain.
    d. at a sensitive period during childhood.

22. Information-processing theorists of language development argue that young children __________ (p. 236)
    a. cue their caregivers to provide appropriate language experiences.
    b. make sense of complex language environments by applying powerful cognitive capacities.
    c. master intricate grammatical structures with little experimentation.
    d. have difficulty learning more than one language at a time.

23. Marci's use of the word "car" only to refer to her own vehicle is an example of __________ (p. 239)
    a. telegraphic speech.
    b. underextension.
    c. joint attention.
    d. overextension.

24. Young children sometimes overextend words to groups of similar experiences because __________ (p. 239)
    a. they are still learning to assimilate adults' intermodal perceptual cues.
    b. their understanding of word meanings is too narrow.
    c. they have difficulty recalling, or have not acquired, a suitable word.
    d. emotion still influences their word learning more than cognitive achievements.

25. Two-year-old Luca's use of the words "more water" is an example of __________ (p. 239)
    a. underextension.
    b. referential style.
    c. overextension.
    d. telegraphic speech.

26. Language comprehension requires that children __________, whereas with language production, children __________ (p. 240)
    a. understand child-directed speech; must be able to combine multiple words.
    b. recognize the meaning of a word; must recall the word and its related concept.
    c. use preverbal gestures; must recognize the meaning of a word.
    d. overextend word meanings; must be capable of telegraphic speech.

27. The vocabularies of __________-style toddlers grow faster because all languages contain many more object labels than social terms. (p. 240)
    a. child-directed
    b. referential
    c. authoritative
    d. expressive

28. By __________ of age, children are more emotionally responsive to child-directed speech. (p. 241)
    a. 1 month
    b. 5 months
    c. 1 year
    d. 1½ years

29. Effective child-directed speech (CDS) can stimulate children's language development by __________ (p. 242)
    a. employing utterance length just ahead of the child's.
    b. urging the child to overextend and thus learn by error.
    c. moving the child beyond his or her zone of proximal development.
    d. discouraging joint attention while encouraging use of more complex sentences.

30. Over 90 percent of deaf children experience delayed language development and are deficient in social skills in toddlerhood through middle childhood because __________ (p. 243)
    a. their parents are not fluent in sign language.
    b. schools are not sensitive to their needs.
    c. they did not receive intervention until after the first year of life.
    d. caregivers tend to only communicate with them visually.

PRACTICE TEST #2

1. According to Piaget, infants __________ (p. 204)
   a. carry out many activities inside their heads.
   b. represent experience in play.
   c. "think" with their eyes and hands.
   d. cannot yet develop schemes.

2. According to Piaget, as babies enter Substage 2, they start to gain voluntary control over their actions through the __________ circular reaction. (p. 206)
   a. reflexive
   b. primary
   c. secondary
   d. tertiary

3. In Piaget's Substage 6, children __________ (p. 207)
   a. have limited anticipation of events.
   b. make the A-not-B search error.
   c. repeat chance behaviors again and again.
   d. create mental representations.

4. Research indicates that mastery of object permanence __________ (p. 209)
   a. typically occurs at Substage 3.
   b. is a spontaneous achievement.
   c. occurs through trial-and-error behavior.
   d. is a gradual achievement.

5. Recent studies of babies' problem solving __________ (p. 211)
   a. suggest that the primary circular reaction helps with trial-and-error experimentation.
   b. confirm that they are unable to solve problems by analogy until around 18 months.
   c. reveal that by 10 to 12 months, infants can solve problems by analogy.
   d. indicate that even 2-month-olds can solve problems by analogy.

6. When asked "Where is the doggy?" Baby Hannah gestures toward the dog bed where the dog usually sits. This is an example of __________ (p. 211)
   a. displaced reference.
   b. telegraphic speech.
   c. the A-not-B search error.
   d. inferred imitation.

7. Before age _____, the American Academy of Pediatrics recommends against mass media exposure. (p. 213)
   a. 2½
   b. 3
   c. 3½
   d. 4

8. Violation-of-expectation findings suggest that in the first few months, infants have some awareness of __________ (p. 214)
   a. object solidity and gravity, but not object permanence.
   b. object permanence, but not gravity or object solidity.
   c. object permanence and gravity, but not object solidity.
   d. object permanence, object solidity, and gravity.

9. Because the capacity of working memory is relatively restricted, __________ (p. 218)
   a. we must use mental strategies to increase our chances of retaining information.
   b. it can process only limited amounts of information from the sensory register.
   c. it cannot connect more than a few pieces of information.
   d. we cannot automatically use information gathered through it.

10. Habituation research reveals that preterm and newborn babies require __________ to habituate and recover to novel stimuli. (p. 220)
    a. 5 to 10 seconds
    b. 20 to 30 seconds
    c. 1 to 2 minutes
    d. 3 to 4 minutes

11. Nearly all studies of infantile amnesia agree that the acquisition of autobiographical memory depends on the child's __________ (p. 221)
    a. implicit memory.
    b. self-image.
    c. social experience.
    d. language development.

12. Babies' earliest categories are based on __________ (p. 222)
    a. prominent object parts.
    b. subtle sets of features.
    c. animate–inanimate distinctions.
    d. fine-grained perceptual features.

13. Language both builds on and fosters categorization by __________ (p. 223)
    a. increasing the efficiency of the sensory register.
    b. eliminating the need for context cues.
    c. calling infants' attention to commonalities among objects.
    d. expanding infants' recognition of familiar objects.

14. Cassie's dad helps her stack blocks. At first, he shows her how to place them together. Then, he helps her by straightening the blocks she places together. Eventually, he sits back, allowing Cassie to stack on her own. This is an example of __________ (p. 224)
    a. scaffolding.
    b. deferred imitation.
    c. dynamic instruction.
    d. operant conditioning.

15. Vygotsky's theory suggests that to promote children's make-believe play, parents and teachers should __________ (p. 226)
    a. provide children with elaborate plots and characters.
    b. provide a variety of toys and play materials.
    c. allow children to discover make-believe independently.
    d. play often with toddlers and guide them through such play.

16. Cognitive theories try to explain __________, while mental tests focus on __________ (p. 227)
    a. cognitive products; how children's thinking changes.
    b. children's future performance; the process of development.
    c. the process of development; cognitive products.
    d. cognitive products; predicting future performance.

17. Evan scored better than 50 percent of his agemates on an intelligence test. Evan has an IQ of _____ (p. 228)
    a. 60.
    b. 85.
    c. 100.
    d. 130.

18. In contrast to the United States, child care in most European countries and in Australia and New Zealand is __________ (p. 230)
    a. nationally regulated and funded.
    b. of substandard quality.
    c. free for most families.
    d. home-based or private.

19. The quality of child care in the United States is affected by a macrosystem of __________ (p. 230)
    a. high taxation and poor financial management.
    b. individualistic values and weak regulation.
    c. excessive government oversight.
    d. high cost and limited physical space.

20. B. F. Skinner proposed that language is acquired through __________ (p. 233)
    a. scaffolding.
    b. an innate language acquisition device.
    c. operant conditioning.
    d. social interaction.

21. Interactionist theories of language development emphasize interactions between __________ (p. 236)
    a. mental representations and brain development.
    b. imitation and reinforcement.
    c. social influences and age.
    d. inner capacities and environmental influences.

22. Babies transition from cooing to babbling when they __________ (p. 236)
    a. begin producing telegraphic speech.
    b. are consistently exposed to human speech.
    c. add consonants to vowels.
    d. comprehend commonly heard words.

23. Deaf infants exposed to sign language from birth __________ (pp. 236–237)
    a. stop babbling entirely.
    b. will coo, but not babble vocally.
    c. babble with their hands.
    d. often use confusing gestures.

24. By the end of the first year, infants use preverbal gestures to __________ (p. 238)
    a. replace verbal communication.
    b. influence adults' behavior.
    c. make greater sense of babbling.
    d. gain autonomy.

25. Tatiana applies the word "close" to closing a book, turning off the computer, and buttoning a sweater. This is an example of __________ (p. 239)
    a. underextension.
    b. overextension.
    c. telegraphic speech.
    d. child-directed speech.

26. Roger says "go car." This is an example of __________ (p. 239)
    a. underextension.
    b. overextension.
    c. telegraphic speech.
    d. child-directed speech.

27. When children's vocabulary permits telegraphic speech, they __________ (p. 239)
    a. focus on high-content words and omit smaller, less important ones.
    b. display a remarkable grasp of subtle grammatical rules.
    c. organize objects and events into simple categories.
    d. apply a word to a wider collection of objects and events than is appropriate.

28. Frieda's vocabulary consists of the words "dog," "cat," "ball," "mama," and "doll." Frieda's vocabulary is an example of __________ (p. 240)
    a. a referential style.
    b. an expressive style.
    c. telegraphic speech.
    d. child-directed speech.

29. From the end of the first year through early childhood, children who experience regular adult–child book reading __________ (p. 242)
    a. are substantially ahead of their agemates in language skills.
    b. tend to use more referential-style speech in their vocabularies.
    c. tend to use more expressive-style speech in their vocabularies.
    d. are substantially ahead of their agemates in using child-directed speech.

30. Compared to deaf parents of deaf children, hearing parents of deaf children are __________ (p. 243)
    a. more positive and more effective at achieving joint attention and turn-taking.
    b. more effective at combining preverbal gestures with sign language.
    c. less positive, less involved in play, and more directive and intrusive.
    d. less likely to seek intervention for their infants and toddlers.

CHAPTER 7
EMOTIONAL AND SOCIAL DEVELOPMENT IN INFANCY AND TODDLERHOOD

BRIEF CHAPTER SUMMARY

Erikson's psychosocial theory, which builds on Freud's psychoanalytic theory, provides an overview of the emotional and social tasks of infancy and toddlerhood. For Erikson, trust and autonomy grow out of warm, supportive parenting in the first year, followed by reasonable expectations for impulse control starting in the second year.

Emotions play an important role in the organization of relationships with caregivers, exploration of the environment, and discovery of the self. Infants' ability to express basic emotions, such as happiness, anger, sadness, and fear, and respond to the emotions of others expands over the first year. As toddlers become more self-aware, self-conscious emotions, such as shame, embarrassment, and pride, begin to emerge. Emotional self-regulation improves as a result of brain maturation, growth in representation and language, and sensitive child rearing.

Children's unique temperaments, or styles of emotional responding, are already apparent in early infancy. Heredity influences early temperament, but child-rearing and other experiences determine whether a child's temperament is sustained or modified over time. The goodness-of-fit model helps explain the bidirectional relationship between children's temperaments and parents' child-rearing styles.

Ethological theory is the most widely accepted view of the development of attachment—the strong affectionate tie that develops between infants and caregivers. According to this perspective, attachment evolved over the history of our species to promote survival. Research shows that responding promptly, consistently, and appropriately to infant signals supports secure attachment, whereas insensitive caregiving is linked to attachment insecurity. Because children and parents are embedded in larger contexts, family circumstances and cultural factors influence attachment patterns. Parents' internal working models—their view of their own attachment experiences—also play a role. Infants form attachment bonds not only with their mothers but also with other familiar people, including fathers and siblings. When grandparents serve as primary caregivers for children, strong attachment ties develop between them.

Though limited, peer sociability is already present in the first two years, and it is fostered by the early caregiver–child bond. Continuity of caregiving seems to play a role in the relationship between early attachment security or insecurity and later development.

Once self-awareness develops over the first and second year, it supports a diverse array of social and emotional achievements. Empathy, the ability to categorize the self, compliance, and self-control are all byproducts of toddlers' emerging sense of self.

LEARNING OBJECTIVES

After reading this chapter, you should be able to:

7.1 Discuss the first two stages of Erikson's psychosocial theory, noting the personality changes that take place during each stage. (pp. 248–249)

7.2 Describe the development of basic emotions, including happiness, anger, sadness, and fear, over the first year, noting the adaptive function of each. (pp. 250–252)

7.3 Summarize changes that occur during the first two years in understanding others' emotions. (pp. 252–253)

7.4 Discuss the nature of self-conscious emotions, explaining why they emerge during the second year and indicating their role in development. (pp. 253–254)

7.5 Trace the development of emotional self-regulation during the first two years. (pp. 254–255)

7.6 Discuss the three underlying components of temperament, and identify three types of children described by Thomas and Chess. (pp. 256–258)

7.7 Explain how temperament is measured. (p. 258)

7.8 Summarize the role of heredity and environment in the stability of temperament, including the goodness-of-fit model. (pp. 258–264)

7.9 Describe the unique features of ethological theory of attachment. (pp. 264–266)

7.10 Describe the Strange Situation and the Attachment Q-Sort procedures for measuring attachment, and cite the four patterns of attachment assessed by each. (pp. 266–267)

7.11 Discuss stability of attachment and the factors that affect attachment security. (pp. 268–274)

7.12 Discuss infants' formation of multiple attachments, and indicate how attachment paves the way for early peer sociability. (pp. 274–277)

7.13 Describe and interpret the relationship between secure attachment in infancy and cognitive, emotional, and social competence in childhood. (pp. 277–279)

7.14 Trace the emergence of self-awareness in infancy and toddlerhood, along with the emotional and social capacities it supports. (pp. 280–283)

STUDY QUESTIONS

Erikson's Theory of Infant and Toddler Personality

Basic Trust versus Mistrust

1. Expanding on Freud's views, Erikson emphasized the importance of the (quantity / quality) of caregiving in promoting successful development during infancy. (p. 248)

2. Based on Erikson's theory, summarize the psychological conflict of the first year, *basic trust versus mistrust,* and explain how it can be positively resolved. (p. 248)

   Conflict: ____

   ____

   Resolution: ____

   ____

Autonomy versus Shame and Doubt

1. In what way did Erikson expand upon Freud's view of development during toddlerhood? (p. 249)

   ____

   ____

2. Summarize the conflict of *autonomy versus shame and doubt,* and explain how it can be positively resolved. (p. 249)

   Conflict: ____

   ____

   Resolution: ____

   ____

Emotional Development

1. Because infants are unable to describe their feelings, ____________________ offer the most useful evidence of infant emotions. List two reasons why this evidence can still be unreliable. (pp. 249–250)

   A. ____________________

   B. ____________________

2. ____________________ vary with a person's developing capacities, goals, and context, meaning that researchers must interpret multiple cues in order to understand babies' emotions. (p. 250)

Development of Basic Emotions

1. Describe *basic emotions,* and list the seven examples cited in your text. (p. 250)

   Definition: ____________________

   Examples: ____________________

2. True or False: Infants come into the world with the ability to express all of the basic emotions. (p. 250)

3. How does the dynamic systems perspective help us understand how basic emotions become clear and well-organized? (p. 250)

4. Provide an example of how caregiver communication affects an infant's emotional development. (p. 250)

5. At approximately what age do infants' emotional expressions become well-organized? (p. 250)

6. Which interactions first evoke the *social smile,* and when does it develop? (p. 251)

   A. ____________________

   B. ____________________

7. Laughter, which appears around ____ to ____ months, reflects (faster / slower) processing of information than does smiling. (p. 251)

8. How do expressions of happiness change between early infancy and the end of the first year? (p. 251)

9. The frequency and intensity of infants' angry reactions (increase / decrease) with age. Why does this happen? (p. 251)

10. Provide an example of a situation in which an infant is likely to express sadness. (p. 251)

____

11. Fear reactions (increase / decrease) during the second half of the first year. (p. 252)

12. The most frequent expression of fear in infancy is to unfamiliar adults, a response called ____________________ *anxiety.* (p. 252)

13. Cite three factors that influence infants' and toddlers' reactions to strangers. (p. 252)

    A. ____

    B. ____

    C. ____

14. How does a *secure base* aid infants' exploration of the environment? (p. 252)

____

____

____

Understanding and Responding to the Emotions of Others

1. Some researchers believe that babies first respond to others' emotions through the automatic process of *emotional* ______________, in which they match the feeling tone of the caregiver in face-to-face communication; others, however, believe that infants gradually develop emotional responses through ____________________. (p. 252)

2. Briefly describe infants' emotional responsiveness at the following ages. (p. 253)

   3 to 4 months: ____

   ____

   4 to 5 months: ____

   ____

3. Explain how *social referencing* influences babies' interactions with caregivers and the environment. (p. 253)

____

____

____

Emergence of Self-Conscious Emotions

1. What are *self-conscious emotions?* Cite five examples. (p. 253)

   Definition: ____

   ____

   Examples: ____

2. Besides self-awareness, what ingredient is required for children to experience self-conscious emotions? (p. 254)

____

3. True or False: The situations in which adults encourage children's expressions of self-conscious emotions vary from culture to culture. (p. 254)

Beginnings of Emotional Self-Regulation

1. Define *emotional self-regulation.* (p. 254)

   ____

   ____

2. The voluntary, effortful management of emotions, called ____________________, develops gradually with the assistance of caregivers and the continued development of the prefrontal cortex. (p. 254)

3. Briefly explain how caregivers contribute to children's style of emotional self-regulation. (p. 255)

   ____

   ____

4. By the end of the second year, gains in representation and language lead to new ways of regulating emotion. Explain how this occurs. (p. 255)

   ____

   ____

   ____

5. True or False: Temper tantrums occur because toddlers cannot yet use language to manage their emotions and control their anger. (p. 255)

Temperament and Development

1. What is *temperament?* (p. 256)

   ____

   ____

2. ______________ refers to quickness and intensity of emotional arousal, attention, and motor activity, while ______________ refers to strategies that modify that reactivity. (p. 256)

3. Cite two important findings from the New York longitudinal study of temperament. (p. 256)

   A. ____

   ____

   B. ____

   ____

The Structure of Temperament

1. Match the three types of children identified by Thomas and Chess to their descriptions. (pp. 256–257)

   _____ Inactive; reacts mildly to environmental stimuli — A. *Easy child*
   _____ Quickly establishes regular routines in infancy; adapts to new experiences — B. *Difficult child*
   _____ Irregular in daily routines; reacts negatively and intensely — C. *Slow-to-warm-up child*

2. True or False: All children fit into one of the three temperament categories described above. (p. 257)

3. Of the three styles of temperament, the ______________ pattern places children at highest risk for adjustment problems. (p. 257)

4. Cite six dimensions of temperament identified by Mary Rothbart. (p. 257)

   A. ______________________________

   B. ______________________________

   C. ______________________________

   D. ______________________________

   E. ______________________________

   F. ______________________________

5. Define *effortful control,* and explain why it is important. (pp. 257–258)

   A. ______________________________

   ____

   B. ______________________________

   ____

Measuring Temperament

1. List the advantages and disadvantages of using parent reports to assess children's temperament. (p. 258)

   Advantages: ______________________________

   ____

   Disadvantages: ______________________________

   ____

2. Why can observations of temperament by researchers at home or in a laboratory be misleading? (p. 258)

   ____

   ____

3. Most physiological assessments of temperament have focused on ______________, or ______________ children, who react negatively to and withdraw from novel stimuli, and ______________, or ______________ children, who display positive emotion to and approach novel stimuli. (p. 258)

Biology and Environment: Development of Shyness and Sociability

1. True or False: Most children's dispositions become more extreme as they grow older because environmental factors have little effect on temperament. Explain your answer. (p. 259)

   ____

   ____

2. What area of the brain does Kagan believe contributes to individual differences in arousal? What is its purpose? (p. 259)

   ____

   ____

3. Cite four physiological correlates of approach–withdrawal behavior. (p. 259)

   A. ______________________________

   B. ______________________________

   C. ______________________________

   D. ______________________________

4. Heritability research indicates that genes contribute (modestly / substantially) to shyness and sociability. (p. 259)

5. Explain how child-rearing practices affect the chances that an emotionally reactive baby will become a fearful child. (p. 259)

____

____

____

Stability of Temperament

1. True or False: Temperamental stability from one age period to the next is generally low to moderate. (p. 258)
2. Long-term predictions about early temperament are best achieved after age ______, when styles of responding are better established. (p. 258)
3. True or False: Child rearing plays an important role in modifying biologically based temperamental traits. (p. 260)

Genetic Influences

1. Research shows that identical twins (are / are not) more similar than fraternal twins in temperament and personality. (p. 260)
2. Describe ethnic and sex differences in early temperament. (pp. 260–261)

   Ethnic: ____

   ____

   Sex: ____

   ____

Environmental Influences

1. True or False: Evidence confirms that the development of temperament is influenced by both genetic and environmental factors. (p. 261)
2. Provide one example each of how ethnic differences and sex differences affect parent–child interaction and, in turn, affect the development of temperament. (p. 261)

   Ethnic differences: ____

   ____

   Sex differences: ____

   ____

3. Explain how children reared in the same family develop distinct temperamental styles. (p. 262)

   ____

   ____

   ____

4. Both identical and fraternal twins tend to become (increasingly / decreasingly) similar from one another over time. Why does this occur? (p. 262)

   ____

   ____

Temperament and Child Rearing: The Goodness-of-Fit Model

1. Describe the *goodness-of-fit model.* (p. 262)

____

____

2. How does the goodness-of-fit model help to explain why children with difficult temperaments are at high risk for future adjustment problems? (p. 262)

____

____

____

3. True or False: Cultural values have little effect on the fit between parenting and child temperament. Provide an example that proves or disproves this statement. (p. 263)

____

____

Development of Attachment

1. Define *attachment.* (p. 264)

____

____

2. True or False: Both psychoanalytic and behaviorist theories emphasize feeding as an important context in which infants and caregivers build a close emotional bond. (p. 264)

3. How did research on rhesus monkeys challenge the idea that attachment depends on hunger satisfaction? (p. 264)

____

____

Bowlby's Ethological Theory

1. True or False: The *ethological theory of attachment,* which recognizes attachment as an evolved response that promotes survival, is the most widely accepted view of the infant's emotional tie to the caregiver. (p. 265)

2. Match each phase of attachment with the appropriate description. (p. 265)

_____ Attachment to the familiar caregiver is evident, and infants display *separation anxiety.*
_____ Infants are not yet attached to their mother and do not mind being left with an unfamiliar adult.
_____ Separation anxiety declines as children gain an understanding of the parent's comings and goings and can predict his or her return.
_____ Infants start to respond differently to a familiar caregiver than to a stranger.

A. Preattachment phase
B. "Attachment in the making" phase
C. "Clear-cut" attachment phase
D. Formation of a reciprocal relationship

3. What is an *internal working model,* and how does it relate to personality? (p. 266)

A. ____

____

B. ____

____

Measuring the Security of Attachment

1. The ______________________________, designed by Mary Ainsworth, is the most widely used laboratory technique for measuring the quality of attachment between 1 and 2 years of age. (p. 266)

2. Match each of the following attachment classifications with the appropriate description. (pp. 266–267)

_____	Before separation, these infants seek closeness to the parent and fail to explore. When she returns, they display angry behaviors, may continue to cry after being picked up, and cannot be easily comforted.	A. *Secure*
_____	Before separation, these infants use the parent as a base from which to explore. They are upset by the parent's absence, and they seek contact and are easily comforted when she returns.	B. *Avoidant*
_____	Before separation, these infants seem unresponsive to the parent. When she leaves, they react to the stranger in much the same way as to the parent. Upon her return, they are slow to greet her.	C. *Resistant*
_____	When the parent returns, these infants show confused, contradictory behaviors, such as looking away while being held.	D. *Disorganized/disoriented*

3. The ____________________ is an alternative to the *Strange Situation* for measuring attachment in children between 1 and 5 years of age. (p. 267)

Stability of Attachment

1. Describe the link between SES and children's attachment security. (p. 268)

____

____

____

2. (Securely / Insecurely) attached babies are more likely to maintain their attachment status. Cite one exception to this trend. (p. 268)

____

Cultural Variations

1. Cite two examples of how cultural variations in child rearing affect attachment security. (p. 268)

   A. ____

   ____

   B. ____

   ____

Factors That Affect Attachment Security

1. List four important factors that affect attachment security. (p. 269)

   A. ____

   B. ____

   C. ____

   D. ____

2. True or False: Adoption research shows that children can develop a first attachment bond as late as 4 to 6 years of age. (p. 269)

3. True or False: *Sensitive caregiving*—responding promptly, consistently, and appropriately to infants and holding them tenderly—is moderately related to attachment security in both biological and adoptive mother–infant pairs and in diverse cultures and SES groups. (p. 270)

4. Describe differences in caregiving experienced by securely attached and insecurely attached infants. (p. 270)

   Securely attached: ______________________________

   ____

   ____

   Insecurely attached: ______________________________

   ____

   ____

5. Describe *interactional synchrony.* (p. 270)

   ____

   ____

   ____

6. True or False: Moderate adult–infant coordination is a better predictor of attachment security than "tight" coordination, in which the adult responds to most infant cues. Briefly explain your response. (p. 270)

   ____

   ____

7. Among maltreated infants, ____________________ attachment is especially high. (p. 270)

8. Explain why children's characteristics do not show strong relationships with attachment. (p. 271)

   ____

   ____

   ____

9. Provide an example of how family circumstances can affect infant attachment. (p. 272)

   ____

   ____

10. True or False: Our early rearing experiences destine us to become sensitive or insensitive parents. Explain your answer. (p. 272)

   ____

   ____

Social Issues: Health: Does Child Care in Infancy Threaten Attachment Security and Later Adjustment?

1. True or False: American infants placed in full-time child care before 12 months of age are more likely than home-reared infants to display insecure attachments. (p. 273)

2. Identify three factors that influence the relationship between child care and attachment quality. (p. 273)

   A. ______________________________

   B. ______________________________

   C. ______________________________

3. Based on findings from the NICHD Study of Early Child Care, what factors contribute to higher rates of attachment insecurity? (p. 273)

   ____

   ____

4. List three ways child-care settings can foster attachment security. (p. 273)

   A. ______________________________

   B. ______________________________

   C. ______________________________

Multiple Attachments

1. Describe how mothers and fathers differ in the way they relate to and interact with babies, and discuss how these patterns are changing due to increasing maternal employment. (p. 274)

   Mothers: ______________________________

   ____

   Fathers: ______________________________

   ____

   Maternal employment: ______________________________

   ____

2. Explain how family attitudes and relationships affect fathers' caregiving and involvement with infants. (pp. 274–275)

   ____

   ____

3. What is a skipped-generation family? (p. 275)

   ____

   ____

4. In which ethnic groups are grandparents most likely to assume the parenting role? (p. 275)

   ____

5. Why can assuming the parenting role be stressful for grandparents? (p. 275)

   ____

   ____

   ____

6. When a new baby arrives, how is a preschool-age sibling likely to respond? Include both positive and negative reactions in your answer. (p. 276)

   Positive: ______________________________

   ____

   Negative: ______________________________

   ____

7. Cite four ways in which mothers can promote positive relationships between infants and their preschool-age siblings. (p. 277)

   A. ______________________________

   B. ______________________________

   C. ______________________________

   D. ______________________________

Cultural Influences: The Powerful Role of Paternal Warmth in Development

1. True or False: Fathers' warmth toward their children predicts later cognitive, emotional, and social competencies as strongly as mothers' warmth. (p. 276)

2. List two factors that promote paternal warmth. (p. 276)

   A. ______________________________

   B. ______________________________

From Attachment to Peer Sociability

1. How does peer interaction promote the development of verbal communication? (p. 278)

   ____

   ____

   ____

2. Explain the link between attachment to a sensitive caregiver and early peer relationships. (p. 278)

   ____

   ____

   ____

Attachment and Later Development

1. In a longitudinal study conducted by Sroufe and his collaborators, how did teachers rate preschoolers who were securely attached as babies? How did camp counselors rate their peer interactions at age 11? (p. 278)

   Preschool: ______________________________

   ____

   Age 11: ______________________________

   ____

2. Which attachment pattern is consistently related to fear, anxiety, anger, and aggression during the preschool and school years? (p. 278)

____

3. Some researchers have suggested that continuity of caregiving determines whether attachment is linked to later development. Briefly explain this relationship. (p. 279)

____

____

____

Self-Development

Self-Awareness

1. True or False: Over the first few months, an infant's self-awareness is limited and is expressed only in perception and action. Provide two examples that prove or disprove this statement. (p. 280)

   A. ____

   ____

   B. ____

   ____

2. Provide an example illustrating how, by age 2, self-recognition is well under way. (p. 280)

   ____

   ____

3. True or False: As early as 18 months, toddlers have an understanding of their own body dimensions and no longer make scale errors. (p. 281)

4. How does sensitive caregiving promote early self-development? (p. 281)

   ____

   ____

   ____

5. What is *empathy?* Describe how the growth of self-awareness leads to the development of empathy. (p. 282)

   A. ____

   ____

   B. ____

   ____

Categorizing the Self

1. List four categories that children can use to refer to themselves and others by the end of the second year. (p. 282)

   A. ____

   B. ____

   C. ____

   D. ____

2. Give an example of how toddlers use categories to organize their own behavior. (p. 282)

____

____

Self-Control

1. List three developmental milestones that are essential for the development of self-control. (p. 282)

   A. ____

   B. ____

   C. ____

2. Once toddlers become capable of *compliance,* do they always obey requests and demands? Explain. (p. 282)

____

____

3. True or False: Toddlers who experience parental warmth and gentle encouragement are more likely to be cooperative and advanced in self-control. (p. 283)

4. Children who are advanced in ________________ and ________________ are often better than their peers at *delaying gratification.* (p. 283)

5. List two ways adults can help toddlers develop compliance and self-control. (p. 283)

   A. ____

   B. ____

ASK YOURSELF . . .

For *Ask Yourself* questions for this chapter, along with feedback on the accuracy of your answers, please log on to MyDevelopmentLab (for registration and access, please visit mydevelopmentlab.com or follow the instructions on page ix).

(1) Select the Multimedia Library.

(2) Choose the explore option.

(3) Find your chapter from the drop down box.

(4) Click find now.

(5) Complete questions and choose “Submit answers for grading” or “Clear answers” to start over.

SUGGESTED READINGS

Kopp, C. B., & Brownell, C. A. (Eds.). (2007). *Socioemotional development in the toddler years: Transitions and transformations.* New York: Guilford. A comprehensive look at social/emotional development in toddlerhood, this book examines the importance of language, early social relationships, the emergence of self-regulation, and individual differences in emotional understanding.

Read, V. (2009). *Developing attachment in early years settings: Nurturing secure relationships from birth to five years.* New York: Taylor & Francis. Presents research-based strategies for fostering secure attachment in infants and young children. Topics include measuring attachment, individual differences in attachment, the importance of high-quality child care, and the relationship between attachment, emotional growth, and learning.

Strelau, J. (2008). *Temperament as a regulator of behavior: After fifty years of research.* New York: Percheron Press. Drawing on 50 years of research, this book examines the relationship between temperament and diverse aspects of behavior, including learning styles, physiological aspects of temperament, self-regulation, and the role of temperament in moderating the effects of stress. The author also provides an overview of assessment instruments used to measure temperament.

CROSSWORD PUZZLE 7.1

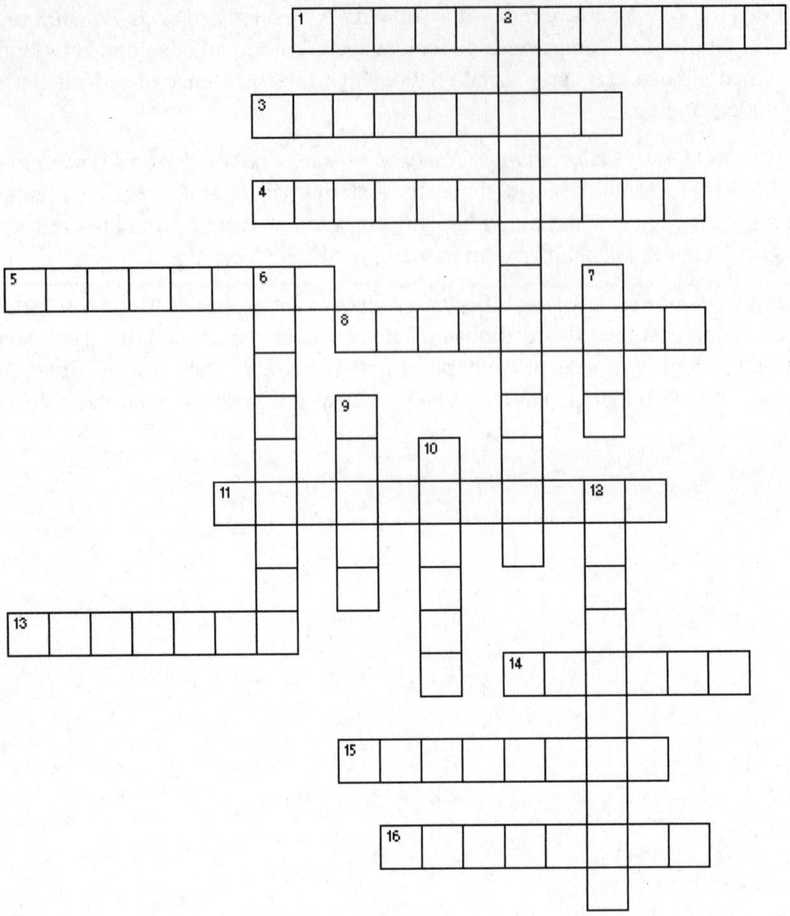

Across

1. Attachment style characterizing infants who respond in a confused, contradictory fashion when reunited with the parent
3. Interactional ____________: a sensitively tuned emotional dance, in which the caregiver responds to infant signals in a well-timed, appropriate fashion, and both partners match emotional states
4. Social __________: relying on a trusted person's emotional reaction to decide how to respond in an uncertain situation
5. Negative outcome of Erikson's psychological conflict of infancy
8. Attachment style characterizing infants who remain close to the parent prior to separation but display angry behavior upon reunion
11. The ____________ theory of attachment views the infant's emotional tie to the caregiver as an evolved response that promotes survival.
13. ___________ Situation: procedure involving brief separations from and reunions with the parent that assesses the quality of the attachment bond
14. Attachment style characterizing infants who are distressed at parental separation and are easily comforted upon parental return
15. Positive outcome of Erikson's psychological conflict of toddlerhood
16. ___________ working model: set of expectations derived from early caregiving experiences; guides all future close relationships

Down

2. Model of attachment in which an effective match between child-rearing practices and a child's temperament leads to favorable adjustment (3 words, hyph.)
6. _____________ caregiving involves prompt, consistent, and appropriate responses to infant signals.
7. Infants use the caregiver as a secure __________ from which to explore, returning for emotional support.
9. Attachment ___________: method for assessing the quality of the attachment bond in which a parent sorts a set of descriptors of attachment-related behaviors on the basis of how well they describe the child (hyph.)
10. The ____________ smile is evoked by the stimulus of the human face.
12. The strong, affectionate tie that humans feel toward special people in their lives

CROSSWORD PUZZLE 7.2

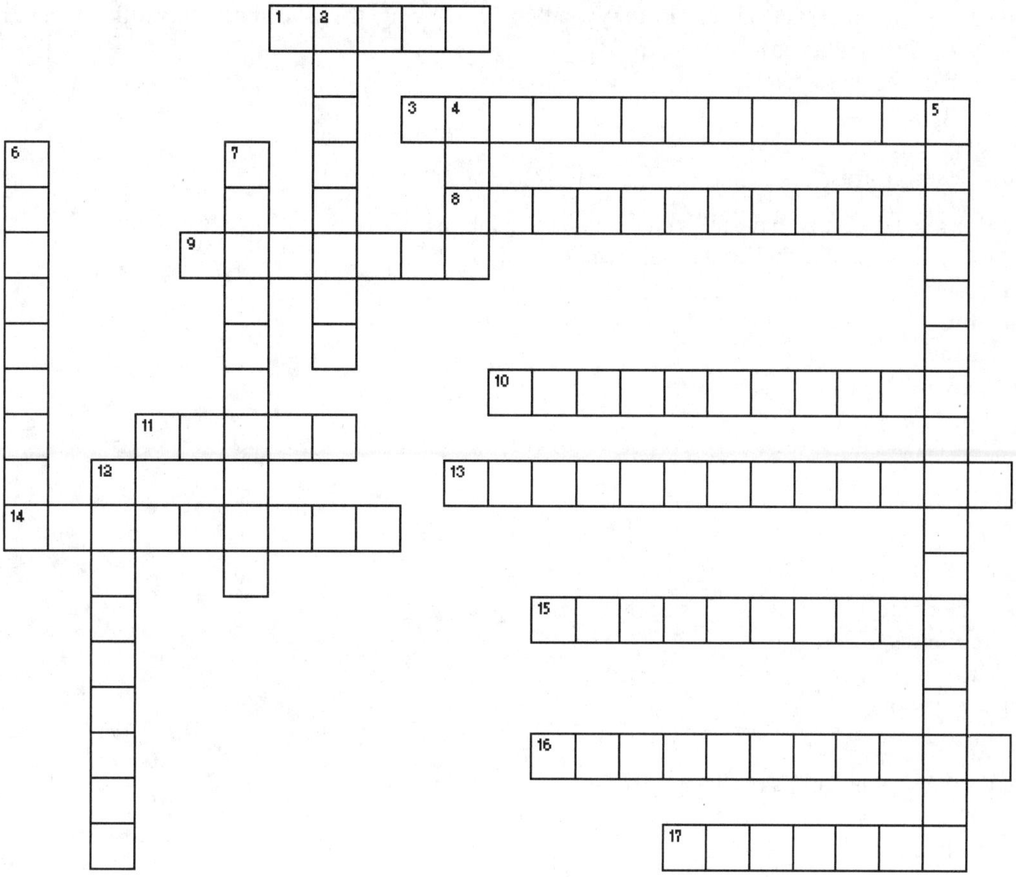

Across

1. _____________ emotions can be directly inferred from facial expressions.
3. Emotions involving injury or enhancement to the sense of self (2 words, hyph.)
8. Temperament style characterized by inactivity; mild, low-key reactions
9. The capacity to understand another's emotional state and to feel with that person
10. Early-appearing, stable individual differences in reactivity and self-regulation
11. __________ errors: attempting to do things that body size makes impossible
13. Delay of ______________: the ability to wait for an appropriate time and place to engage in a tempting act
14. Temperament style characterized by irregular daily routines, slow acceptance of new experiences, and negative, intense reactions
15. Emotional self-_____________: strategies for adjusting one's emotional state to a comfortable level of intensity
16. A child who reacts positively to and approaches novel stimuli
17. Stranger-______________: an infant's expression of fear in response to unfamiliar adults

Down

2. Attachment style characterizing infants who seem unresponsive to the parent when she is present and are not distressed when she leaves
4. Temperament style characterized by establishment of regular routines in infancy, general cheerfulness, and easy adaptation to new experiences
5. Babies become upset when their trusted caregiver leaves.
6. A child who reacts negatively to and withdraws from novel stimuli
7. Voluntary obedience to adult request and commands
12. The self-regulatory dimension of temperament, called ______________ control, involves voluntary suppression of a dominant, reactive response in order to plan and execute a more adaptive response.

PRACTICE TEST #1

1. According to Erikson, when the balance of care is sympathetic and loving, the psychological conflict of the first year—__________—is resolved on the positive side. (p. 248)
   a. autonomy versus shame and doubt
   b. initiative versus guilt
   c. industry versus inferiority
   d. basic trust versus mistrust

2. According to Erikson, adults who have difficulty establishing intimate ties may not have fully mastered the tasks of __________ and __________ during infancy and toddlerhood. (p. 248)
   a. shame; industry
   b. trust; initiative
   c. trust; autonomy
   d. autonomy; doubt

3. Laughter appears around __________ months of age. (p. 251)
   a. 3 or 4
   b. 5 or 6
   c. 7 or 8
   d. 9 or 10

4. As infants become capable of __________, anger increases. (p. 251)
   a. reflexive responses
   b. locomotion
   c. intentional behavior
   d. stranger anxiety

5. The most frequent expression of fear in infancy is to __________ (p. 252)
   a. novel events.
   b. unpleasant stimuli.
   c. animals.
   d. unfamiliar adults.

6. Around 3 to 4 months, infants become sensitive to __________ (p. 253)
   a. male versus female voices.
   b. the structure and timing of face-to-face interactions.
   c. positive and negative emotion in facial expressions.
   d. the pragmatic nature of language.

7. When infants engage in __________, they actively seek emotional information from a trusted person in an uncertain situation. (p. 253)
   a. social referencing
   b. effortful control
   c. self-regulation
   d. goodness of fit

8. Which of the following is an example of a self-conscious emotion? (p. 253)
   a. anger
   b. fear
   c. envy
   d. sadness

9. Toddlers show __________ by hanging their heads and hiding their eyes. (p. 254)
   a. shame
   b. anger
   c. envy
   d. pride

10. A toddler who does not cry until she gets into the car after a scary encounter with an animal is displaying __________ (p. 254)
    a. goodness of fit.
    b. effortful control.
    c. social referencing.
    d. interactional synchrony.

11. Babies who readily turn away from unpleasant events are __________ (p. 255)
    a. engaging in social referencing.
    b. displaying interactional synchrony.
    c. less motivated by basic emotions.
    d. less prone to distress.

12. Slow-to-warm-up children tend to __________ (p. 257)
    a. become increasingly difficult with age.
    b. show excessive fearfulness in the early years.
    c. be aggressive with peers.
    d. have overly permissive parents.

13. __________ children react negatively to and withdraw from novel stimuli. (p. 258)
    a. Uninhibited
    b. Highly sociable
    c. Shy
    d. Easy

14. One advantage of using laboratory research to measure temperament is __________ (p. 258)
    a. findings are usually subjective.
    b. children are generally less fearful than in other settings.
    c. researchers can better control children's experiences.
    d. it is convenient and objective.

15. Compared with sociable children, shy children show __________ (p. 259)
    a. greater pupil dilation.
    b. lower blood pressure.
    c. warming of the fingertips when faced with novelty.
    d. lower saliva concentrations of cortisol.

16. Parents of multiple children tend to __________ (p. 261)
    a. emphasize their similarities.
    b. emphasize each child's unique qualities.
    c. treat all the children the same, regardless of their temperament.
    d. have trouble applying goodness of fit.

17. During Bowlby's preattachment phase, infants __________ (p. 265)
    a. begin to develop a sense of trust.
    b. exhibit separation anxiety.
    c. do not mind being left with an unfamiliar adult.
    d. negotiate with caregivers.

18. Separation anxiety appears during Bowlby's __________ phase. (p. 265)
    a. preattachment
    b. formation of a reciprocal relationship
    c. attachment in the making
    d. clear-cut attachment

19. In response to the Strange Situation, resistant babies tend to __________ (p. 267)
    a. use the parent as a secure base and, when the parent returns after separation, actively seek contact.
    b. be unresponsive to the parent when she is present and show no distress when she leaves.
    c. seek closeness to the parent before separation and, after the parent returns, combine clinginess with anger.
    d. show confused, contradictory behaviors at reunion, such as approaching the parent with flat, depressed emotion.

20. In response to the Strange Situation, __________ babies tend to be unresponsive to the parent when she is present and show no distress when she leaves. (p. 267)
    a. secure
    b. avoidant
    c. resistant
    d. disoriented

21. Japanese infants rarely show __________ attachment. (p. 268)
    a. secure
    b. avoidant
    c. resistant
    d. disoriented

22. In studies of Western babies, __________ separated the experiences of secure from insecure babies. (p. 270)
    a. social referencing
    b. self-world differentiation
    c. compliance
    d. interactional synchrony

23. According to your text, which of the following Australian infants is most likely to have a high rate of secure attachment? (p. 273)
    a. Keith, who is enrolled in full-time government funded child care
    b. Lucia, who is cared for by a non-related babysitter
    c. Shane, who is cared for by his aunt
    d. Janette, who is cared for by family friends

24. Fathers tend to __________ than mothers. (p. 274)
    a. use more consistent discipline
    b. engage in more highly stimulating physical play
    c. talk to infants more
    d. devote more time to physical care

25. In a German study, fathers' __________ predicted children's secure internal working models of attachment during middle childhood and adolescence. (p. 274)
    a. play sensitivity
    b. physical caregiving
    c. physical proximity to their babies
    d. vocational satisfaction

26. Upon the arrival of a new sibling, __________ typically declines, especially for children over age 2. (p. 276)
    a. sensitive caregiving
    b. insecure attachment
    c. attachment security
    d. self-awareness

27. In an extensive longitudinal study by Alan Sroufe and his colleagues, securely attached babies were rated by their preschool teachers as __________ than their insecurely attached agemates. (p. 278)
    a. higher in behavioral problems
    b. lower in self-esteem
    c. lower in social skills
    d. higher in empathy

28. __________ attachment is consistently related to internalizing and externalizing problems. (p. 278)
    a. Resistant
    b. Disorganized/disoriented
    c. Avoidant
    d. Secure

29. A toddler's use of "I good girl" and "big, strong girl" shows that she is developing __________ (p. 282)
    a. independent thinking.
    b. a categorical self.
    c. compliance.
    d. resilience.

30. A toddler's use of consciencelike verbalizations (such as "No, can't!") to correct herself shows that she has become capable of __________ (pp. 282–283)
    a. independent thinking.
    b. self-awareness.
    c. compliance.
    d. resilience.

PRACTICE TEST #2

1. Erikson accepted Freud's emphasis on the importance of __________, but he expanded and enriched Freud's view. (p. 248)
   a. the parent–child relationship during feeding
   b. the triumph of the ego over the id
   c. strict discipline in early childhood
   d. the quality of caregiving

2. According to Erikson, the conflict of toddlerhood, __________, is resolved favorably when parents provide young children with suitable guidance and reasonable choices. (p. 249)
   a. autonomy versus shame and doubt
   b. initiative versus guilt
   c. industry versus inferiority
   d. basic trust versus mistrust

3. Determining exactly which emotions infants are experiencing is a challenge because they __________ (p. 249)
   a. display both basic and self-conscious emotions from birth.
   b. cannot describe their feelings.
   c. respond similarly to most emotional situations.
   d. do not display emotion with facial expressions.

4. Which of the following is a basic emotion? (p. 250)
   a. pride
   b. shame
   c. sadness
   d. embarrassment

5. Between 6 and 10 weeks, the __________ first appears. (p. 251)
   a. laugh
   b. reflexive smile
   c. social smile
   d. secure base

6. Baby Bella looks to her mom when she falls down. When her mom smiles, Bella tries to stand again. Bella is engaged in __________ (p. 253)
   a. effortful control.
   b. social referencing.
   c. self-soothing.
   d. interactional synchrony.

7. Which of the following is an example of a self-conscious emotion? (p. 253)
   a. embarrassment
   b. fear
   c. happiness
   d. anger

8. Self-conscious emotions require __________ (p. 254)
   a. social referencing.
   b. effortful control.
   c. delay of gratification.
   d. self-awareness.

9. When you remind yourself than an anxiety-provoking event will be over soon, you are engaging in __________ (p. 254)
   a. emotional self-regulation.
   b. delay of gratification.
   c. social referencing.
   d. interactional synchrony.

10. In collectivist cultures, like those of China and Japan, infants smile and cry less than American babies. One reason for this is __________ (p. 255)
    a. parents engage in fewer soothing behaviors, so infants learn to self-soothe.
    b. adults discourage the expression of strong emotion in babies.
    c. Chinese and Japanese infants are genetically less reactive than American infants.
    d. parents use classical conditioning to suppress emotional displays.

11. In Thomas and Chess's longitudinal study on temperament, 35 percent of the children __________ (p. 257)
    a. were identified as easy children.
    b. were identified as difficult children.
    c. were identified as slow-to-warm-up children.
    d. showed unique blends of temperamental characteristics.

12. The __________ temperament pattern has sparked the most interest because it places children at risk for adjustment problems. (p. 257)
    a. easy
    b. slow-to-warm-up
    c. difficult
    d. unidentifiable

13. The __________ child is inactive, negative in mood, and shows mild, low-key reactions to environmental stimuli. (p. 257)
    a. easy
    b. slow-to-warm-up
    c. difficult
    d. securely attached

14. A unique feature of Mary Rothbart's model of temperament is the inclusion of __________ (p. 257)
    a. parental temperament.
    b. both "fearful distress" and "irritable distress."
    c. reaction to regular routines.
    d. positive and negative affect.

15. A major reason that temperament is not more stable is that __________ (p. 258)
    a. temperament is not biologically based.
    b. children often change from one extreme to the other.
    c. temperament itself develops with age.
    d. measures for infant temperament are inconsistent.

16. From the first few weeks of life, the __________ of shy children are consistently __________ than those of sociable children. (p. 259)
    a. heart rates; lower
    b. coritsol levels; lower
    c. blood pressure; lower
    d. heart rates; higher

17. Compared to highly sociable children, shy children have __________ when faced with novelty. (p. 259)
    a. lower saliva concentrations of cortisol
    b. higher heart rates
    c. a slower rise in blood pressure
    d. warmer fingertips

18. Research on sex differences in temperament indicates that parents __________ (p. 261)
    a. encourage their young daughters to be assertive and their sons to seek physical closeness.
    b. rate daughters as more alert and more awkward than sons from birth.
    c. rate sons as better coordinated and more alert than girls from birth.
    d. have similar expectations for their sons and daughters.

19. According to Bowlby, children in the preattachment phase __________ (p. 265)
    a. exhibit stranger anxiety when their own mother leaves for a time.
    b. recognize their own mother's smell, voice, and face, but do not mind when she leaves for a time.
    c. exhibit separation anxiety when their own mother leaves for a time.
    d. have learned that their own actions affect the behavior of others.

20. According to Bowlby, during the "attachment in the making" phase, __________ (p. 265)
    a. infants respond differently to a familiar caregiver than to a stranger.
    b. built-in signals help bring newborn babies into close contact with other humans, who comfort them.
    c. babies display clear-cut separation anxiety when their mothers leave them.
    d. rapid growth in representation and language enables toddlers to understand and predict a caregiver's behavior.

21. According to Bowlby, attachment to the familiar caregiver is first evident in the __________ phase. (p. 265)
    a. attachment in the making
    b. preattachment
    c. formation of reciprocal relationship
    d. clear-cut attachment

22. In the Strange Situation, infants who seem unresponsive to the parent when she is present and do not protest when she leaves display __________ attachment. (p. 267)
    a. secure
    b. avoidant
    c. resistant
    d. disorganized/disoriented

23. In the Strange Situation, infants who show confused, contradictory behaviors at reunion and a dazed facial expression display __________ attachment. (p. 267)
    a. secure
    b. avoidant
    c. resistant
    d. disorganized/disoriented

24. Which pattern of attachment reflects the greatest insecurity? (p. 267)
    a. slow-to-warm-up
    b. avoidant
    c. resistant
    d. disorganized/disoriented

25. __________ attachment is as stable as attachment security. (p. 268)
    a. Disorganized/disoriented
    b. Avoidant
    c. Resistant
    d. Clear-cut

26. German babies show considerably more __________ attachment than American babies do. (p. 268)
    a. secure
    b. avoidant
    c. resistant
    d. disorganized/disoriented

27. Infants in Israeli kibbutzim frequently show __________ attachment. (p. 269)
    a. secure
    b. avoidant
    c. resistant
    d. disorganized/disoriented

28. __________ is best described as a sensitively tuned "emotional dance." (p. 270)
    a. Social referencing
    b. Self-awareness
    c. Interactional synchrony
    d. Compliance

29. Research suggests that infants placed in __________ child care before 12 months of age are __________ likely than infants who remain home to display insecure attachment. (p. 273)
    a. part-time; less
    b. full-time; less
    c. full-time; more
    d. extremely infrequent; more

30. Research on the Aka of Central Africa reveals that the strong father–infant relationship is due in great part to __________ (p. 276)
    a. an exceptionally cooperative and intimate marital relationship.
    b. the lack of respect for women within the tribe.
    c. the strong division of male and female duties in the tribe.
    d. the lack of respect for men within the tribe.

CHAPTER 8
PHYSICAL DEVELOPMENT IN EARLY CHILDHOOD

BRIEF CHAPTER SUMMARY

During early childhood, the rapid increase in body size tapers off and the child's shape becomes more streamlined, leading to improvements in posture and balance. In various parts of the skeleton, new epiphyses emerge, where cartilage hardens into bone. At the end of this period, children start to lose their primary teeth.

Between ages 2 and 6, the brain increases from 70 percent of its adult weight to 90 percent. The cerebral cortex, especially, shows gains in myelination and formation of synapses, followed by synaptic pruning. Prefrontal-cortical areas devoted to inhibition, attention, working memory, and planning show rapid growth from early to middle childhood. Hand preference strengthens, a sign of greater brain lateralization. In addition, connections between different parts of the brain increase. These changes support improvements in a wide variety of physical and cognitive skills.

Both heredity and environmental factors continue to influence physical growth and health in early childhood. Heredity influences physical growth by controlling production and release of two vital hormones from the pituitary gland. Emotional well-being continues to influence body growth and health. Although total sleep needs decline, substantial variability exists. Appetite declines, reflecting a slower rate of physical growth. With reduced caloric intake, preschoolers need a high-quality diet. Infectious disease interacts with malnutrition to seriously undermine children's growth, an effect that is especially common in developing countries. Although widespread immunization has led to dramatic declines in childhood diseases in the industrialized world, many children in the United States are not fully immunized.

Unintentional injuries are the leading cause of childhood death in industrialized nations. Preventive efforts are necessary at several levels, including laws that promote safety, improvement of community environments, and efforts to change parents' and children's behavior.

During the preschool years, children continue to integrate motor skills into dynamic systems. Gross-motor skills, such as running, jumping, and throwing appear and become better coordinated. Gains in fine-motor development can be seen in preschoolers' ability to dress themselves, draw representational pictures, and print letters of the alphabet. As in other areas, heredity and environment combine to influence early childhood motor development.

LEARNING OBJECTIVES

After reading this chapter, you should be able to:

8.1 Describe changes in body size, proportions, and skeletal maturity during early childhood. (pp. 290–291)

8.2 Discuss brain development in early childhood, including synaptic growth and pruning, lateralization and handedness, and other advances that help to establish links between various parts of the brain. (pp. 291–295)

8.3 Summarize the effects of heredity and hormones on physical growth and health in early childhood. (p. 297)

8.4 Describe the effects of emotional well-being on physical growth and health in early childhood. (p. 297)

8.5 Describe the effects of restful sleep on physical growth and health in early childhood. (pp. 298–299)

8.6 Discuss the impact of nutrition on early childhood physical growth and health. (pp. 299–300)

8.7 Explain how infectious disease and immunizations impact early physical growth and health in early childhood. (pp. 301–304)

8.8 Summarize individual, family, community, and societal factors related to early childhood injuries, and describe ways to prevent them. (pp. 304–307)

8.9 Cite major milestones of gross- and fine-motor development in early childhood. (pp. 308–312)

8.10 Discuss individual differences in preschoolers' motor skills, and cite ways to enhance early motor development. (pp. 312–314)

STUDY QUESTIONS

Body Growth

1. True or False: In contrast to the rapid increases in body size seen during infancy, early childhood is marked by a slower pattern of growth. (p. 290)
2. On average, children add ____ to ____ inches in height and about ____ pounds in weight each year. (p. 290)
3. True or False: Growth norms and trends in body size are consistent across cultures. (p. 290)

Skeletal Growth

1. Between ages 2 and 6, approximately 45 new ________________________, or growth centers in which cartilage hardens into bone, emerge in various parts of the skeleton. (p. 290)
2. Explain how both genetics and environment influence the age at which children lose their primary, or "baby," teeth. (p. 290)

   Genetics: ____

   ____

   Environment: ____

   ____

3. True or False: Care of primary teeth is essential because diseased baby teeth can affect the health of permanent teeth. (p. 290)

Brain Development

1. List at least five skills that are supported by brain development between the ages of 2 and 6. (p. 291)

   ____

2. True or False: By 4 years of age, the child's brain has produced an overabundance of synaptic connections, contributing to the plasticity of the young brain. (p. 292)
3. For most children, the (right / left) hemisphere is especially active between 3 and 6 years of age and then levels off. In contrast, activity in the (right / left) hemisphere increases steadily throughout early and middle childhood. (p. 293)
4. Handedness reflects the greater capacity of one side of the brain, or the ________________________ *cerebral hemisphere,* to carry out skilled motor action. (p. 293)
5. For left-handed individuals, language is occasionally located in the right hemisphere or, more often, language is shared between the brain hemispheres. This indicates that brains of left-handers tend to be (less / more) strongly lateralized than those of right-handers. (p. 293)
6. List three theories that attempt to explain the origins of handedness. (p. 293)

   A. ____

   B. ____

   C. ____

7. True or False: Many left-handers have serious developmental problems. Explain your answer. (p. 294)

____

____

8. For each of the following statements, indicate whether it describes the cerebellum (C), reticular formation (RF), hippocampus (H), amygdala (A), or corpus collosum (CC). (pp. 294–295)

_____ Development of this structure contributes to improvements in sustained, controlled attention.
_____ An inner brain structure that plays a central role in processing emotional information.
_____ This structure supports smooth coordination of movements on both sides of the body and integration of many aspects of thinking, including perception, attention, memory, language, and problem solving.
_____ A structure that aids in the balance and control of body movement.
_____ Changes in this brain structure contributes to the preschool-age child's ability to play hopscotch, throw a ball with well-coordinated movements, and print letters of the alphabet.
_____ In socially anxious children, this brain structure is overly reactive to threatening situations.
_____ An inner brain structure that plays a vital role in memory and in images of space that help us find our way.
_____ A structure in the brain stem that maintains alertness and consciousness.
_____ Changes in this structure contribute to the dramatic gains in memory and spatial understanding in early and middle childhood.
_____ A large bundle of fibers connecting the two cerebral hemispheres.

Influences on Physical Growth and Health

Biology and Environment: Low-Level Lead Exposure and Children's Development

1. What two factors have led to a sharp decline in children's lead levels from 1980 to today? (p. 296)

   A. ____

   B. ____

2. Describe the developmental consequences associated with high levels of lead exposure. (p. 296)

____

____

____

3. Although the overall impact of low-level lead exposure on all developmental outcomes is modest, cognitive consequences were much greater for (low / high)-SES children. Briefly explain why this is the case. (p. 296)

____

____

____

Heredity and Hormones

1. The ______________________ *gland,* located near the base of the brain, releases hormones affecting physical growth. (p. 297)

2. Describe the impact of *growth hormone (GH)* and *thyroid-stimulating hormone (TSH)* on body growth, and indicate the consequences of deficiencies of these hormones. (p. 297)

   GH: ____

   ____

   TSH: ____

   ____

Emotional Well-Being

1. Describe the cause and characteristics of *psychosocial dwarfism.* (p. 297)

   Cause: ____

   ____

   Characteristics: ____

   ____

   ____

2. True or False: Even when children with psychosocial dwarfism are removed from their emotionally inadequate environments at an early age, their growth is permanently stunted. (p. 297)

Sleep Habits and Problems

1. In the following list, circle the possible consequences of sleep deprivation in young children. (p. 298)

   impaired cognitive performance

   inhibited personality

   decreased attention

   lower intelligence test scores

   psychosocial dwarfism

   decreased speed of thinking

2. Total sleep time (increases / decreases) in early childhood. (p. 298)
3. Explain why bedtime is often a source of stress between parents and young children. (p. 298)

   ____

   ____

4. List three sleep problems of early childhood. (p. 299)

   A. ____

   B. ____

   C. ____

Nutrition

1. True or False: It is normal for children's appetite to decline in early childhood. Explain why or why not. (p. 299)

   ____

   ____

2. Provide an example of how the social and emotional climates influence young children's food preferences and eating habits. (p. 300)

   Social: ______________________________

   ____

   Emotional: ______________________________

   ____

3. List the most common dietary deficiencies during the preschool years. (p. 300)

   A. ______________________________
   B. ______________________________
   C. ______________________________
   D. ______________________________
   E. ______________________________
   F. ______________________________

4. Describe three ways to encourage good nutrition in early childhood. (p. 301)

   A. ______________________________

   ____

   B. ______________________________

   ____

   C. ______________________________

   ____

Infectious Disease

1. Describe the bidirectional relationship between infectious disease and malnutrition. (pp. 301–302)

   ____

   ____

   ____

2. Most developmental impairments and deaths due to diarrhea can be prevented with a nearly cost-free ______________________________, a glucose, salt, and water solution that quickly replaces fluids the body loses. (p. 302)

3. True or False: Nearly one-quarter of American preschoolers lack essential immunizations. (p. 302)

4. Provide two reasons why parents in the United States choose not to immunize their children. (p. 302)

   A. ______________________________
   B. ______________________________

Cultural Influences: Child Health Care in the United States and Other Western Nations

1. True or False: In the United States, nearly 10 percent of the child population is uninsured. Explain why. (p. 303)

   ____

   ____

2. Describe child health care initiatives in the Netherlands and Norway, two countries whose services stand in sharp contrast to those available in the United States. (p. 303)

   Netherlands: ______________________________

   ____

   ____

   Norway: ______________________________

   ____

   ____

3. Describe the Children's Health Insurance Program (CHIP), and note some of the barriers to health care that still exist for children who are enrolled in the program. (p. 303)

   Program: ______________________________

   ____

   Barriers: ______________________________

   ____

Social Issues: Health: Otitis Media and Development

1. Briefly explain how otitis media affects language development and academic progress. (p. 304)

   ____

   ____

   ____

2. List three factors linked to increased rates of otitis media. (p. 304)

   A. ______________________________

   B. ______________________________

   C. ______________________________

3. Cite four ways that parents can protect their children from otitis media. (p. 304)

   A. ______________________________

   B. ______________________________

   C. ______________________________

   D. ______________________________

Childhood Injuries

1. True or False: Unintentional injuries are the leading cause of childhood mortality in industrialized countries. (p. 305)

2. List three of the most common causes of injury during early childhood. (p. 305)

   A. ______________________________

   B. ______________________________

   C. ______________________________

3. Summarize individual, family, community, and societal factors linked to childhood injury. (pp. 305–306)
   Individual: ______________________________
   ____
   Family: ______________________________
   ____
   Community: ______________________________
   ____
   Societal: ______________________________
   ____

4. Provide one reason why child injury rates in the United States higher than in other developed nations. (p. 306)
   ____

5. List four ways to reduce unintentional injuries in early childhood. (pp. 306–307)
   A. ______________________________
   B. ______________________________
   C. ______________________________
   D. ______________________________

Motor Development

Gross-Motor Development

1. As children's bodies become more streamlined and their center of gravity shifts (upward / downward), ______________ improves greatly, paving the way for new motor skills involving large muscles of the body. (p. 308)

2. Match the following sets of gross-motor developments with the ages at which they are typically acquired. (p. 309)
   _____ Walks up stairs with alternating feet; flexes upper body when jumping and hopping; throws with slight involvement of upper body, still catches against chest; pedals and steers tricycle
   _____ Walks down stairs with alternating feet; gallops; throws ball with transfer of weight on feet; catches with hands; rides tricycle rapidly, steers smoothly
   _____ Hurried walk changes to run; jumps, hops, throws, and catches with rigid upper body; little steering
   _____ Engages in true skipping; displays mature throwing and catching pattern; rides bicycle with training wheels

   A. 2 to 3 years
   B. 3 to 4 years
   C. 4 to 5 years
   D. 5 to 6 years

Fine-Motor Development

1. To parents, fine-motor development is most evident in which two areas? (p. 309)
   A. ______________________ B. ______________________

2. Match the following sets of fine-motor developments with the ages at which they are typically acquired. (p. 309)
   _____ Draws first tadpole image of a person; copies vertical line and circle; uses scissors; fastens and unfastens large buttons
   _____ Draws a person with six parts; copies some numbers and words; ties shoes; uses knife
   _____ Copies triangle, cross, and some letters; cuts along line with scissors; uses fork effectively
   _____ Scribbles gradually become pictures; puts on and removes simple items of clothing; zips large zippers; uses spoon effectively

   A. 2 to 3 years
   B. 3 to 4 years
   C. 4 to 5 years
   D. 5 to 6 years

3. Describe the three-stage sequence in which drawing skills develop during early childhood, noting major milestones and competencies in each stage. (p. 310)

   A. ____

   ____

   B. ____

   ____

   C. ____

   ____

4. How do preschoolers come to learn that writing stands for language? (p. 312)

   ____

5. In addition to fine-motor control, what other skill contributes to printing ability? (p. 312)

   ____

Individual Differences in Motor Skills

1. In early childhood, (boys / girls) have an advantage in skills that emphasize force and power, while (boys / girls) excel in fine-motor skills and gross-motor skills that require good balance and foot movement. (p. 313)
2. Provide an example of how social pressures might exaggerate small genetically based sex differences in motor skills. (p. 313)

   ____

   ____

Enhancing Early Childhood Motor Development

1. True or False: Preschoolers exposed to formal lessons in motor skills are generally more advanced in their motor development than agemates who do not take such lessons. (p. 313)
2. List three ways to foster young children's motor development. (p. 313)

   A. ____

   B. ____

   C. ____

ASK YOURSELF . . .

For *Ask Yourself* questions for this chapter, along with feedback on the accuracy of your answers, please log on to MyDevelopmentLab (for registration and access, please visit mydevelopmentlab.com or follow the instructions on page ix).

(1) Select the Multimedia Library.

(2) Choose the explore option.

(3) Find your chapter from the drop down box.

(4) Click find now.

(5) Complete questions and choose "Submit answers for grading" or "Clear answers" to start over.

SUGGESTED READINGS

Cabeza, R., Nyberg, L., & Park, D. (2009). *Cognitive neuroscience of aging: Linking cognitive and cerebral aging.* New York: Oxford University Press. Examines a new scientific discipline, known as the cognitive neuroscience of aging. Topics include noninvasive measures of cerebral aging; the effects of cerebral aging on cognitive functions like perception, memory, and attention; and applications of brain research.

Coll, C. G., & Marks, K. (2009). *Immigrant stories: Ethnicity and academics in middle childhood.* New York: Oxford University Press. A longitudinal study of first- and second-generation immigrant youths, this book examines the unique challenges and strengths of these children and their families. Topics include cultural attitudes and identity development, academic achievement, the importance of community resources, and the importance of public policies for immigrant families.

Freeman, M., & Mathison, S. (2008). *Researching children's experiences.* New York: Guilford. Presents an extensive overview of research methods commonly used to study children and adolescents. The authors also present information on recruiting minors for research, the roles and responsibilities of researchers, the importance of understanding the child's developmental level, and ethical considerations and challenges.

CROSSWORD PUZZLE 8.1

Across

1. ____________ formation: brain structure that maintains alertness and consciousness
6. _____________ dwarfism is a growth disorder caused by extreme emotional deprivation.
8. The _____________ cerebral hemisphere of the brain is responsible for skilled motor action.
9. A pituitary hormone that stimulates the thyroid gland to release thyroxine, which is necessary for normal brain development and body growth (abbr.)

Down

2. A brain structure that aids in balance and control of body movements
3. Corpus ____________: large bundle of fibers that connects the two hemispheres of the brain
4. The ___________ gland, located near the base of the brain, releases hormones affecting physical growth.
5. A brain structure that helps to process emotional information
7. An inner-brain structure that plays a vital role in memory in spatial images we use to help us find our way

PRACTICE TEST #1

1. On average, preschoolers add _____ pounds to their weight each year. (p. 290)
   a. 2
   b. 5
   c. 7
   d. 10

2. In early childhood, girls __________ than boys. (p. 290)
   a. are more muscular
   b. retain more body fat
   c. are taller
   d. are heavier

3. Between ages 2 and 6, the brain increases from _____ percent of its adult weight to _____ percent. (p. 291)
   a. 50; 80
   b. 60; 80
   c. 70; 90
   d. 80; 90

4. As early as the tenth week of pregnancy, most fetuses __________ (p. 293)
   a. show a right-hand preference during thumb sucking.
   b. show a dominant right cerebral hemisphere.
   c. display smoother movement when reaching with their left arm.
   d. display signs of being ambidextrous.

5. Left-handed people __________ (p. 294)
   a. show a strong tendency to have left-handed children.
   b. usually house language in the left hemisphere only.
   c. are unlikely to develop outstanding verbal and mathematical talents.
   d. are slightly advantaged in speed and flexibility of thinking.

6. The __________ plays a vital role in memory and in images of space that help us find our way. (p. 294)
   a. cerebellum
   b. reticular formation
   c. hippocampus
   d. amygdala

7. The __________ supports smooth coordination of movements on both sides of the body and integration of many aspects of thinking, including perception, attention, memory, language, and problem solving. (p. 295)
   a. hippocampus
   b. amygdala
   c. reticular formation
   d. corpus callosum

8. Higher blood levels of __________ are associated with deficits in verbal and visual-motor skills and with distractibility, overactivity, poor organization, and behavior problems. (p. 296)
   a. zinc
   b. iron
   c. lead
   d. folic acid

9. Growth hormone is responsible for __________ (p. 297)
   a. the development of almost all body tissues.
   b. stimulating the release of thyroxine.
   c. normal growth of the hippocampus.
   d. body growth in infancy and toddlerhood only.

10. __________ is necessary for brain development and for the growth hormone to have its full impact. (p. 297)
    a. Cortisol
    b. Thyroxine
    c. Estrogen
    d. Insulin

11. When children with psychosocial dwarfism do not receive treatment or when treatment is delayed, __________ (p. 297)
    a. catch-up growth will not occur until adolescence.
    b. they may reach an average height of only 5 feet.
    c. they often develop muscle atrophy and brittle bones.
    d. dwarfism can be permanent.

12. Sleep difficulties __________ (p. 298)
    a. are more pronounced in middle-SES children.
    b. rarely have a lasting impact on body growth.
    c. are associated with impaired cognitive performance.
    d. occur in approximately 80 percent of U.S. children.

13. On average, 2- to 3-year-olds sleep __________ hours per day. (p. 298)
    a. 9 to 10
    b. 10 to 11
    c. 11 to 12
    d. 12 to 13

14. About one-third of preschoolers experience __________ (pp. 298–299)
    a. difficulty falling asleep.
    b. difficulty staying asleep.
    c. sleepwalking.
    d. sleep terrors.

15. Over the course of the day, preschoolers __________ (p. 299)
    a. compensate for eating little at one meal by eating more at a later one.
    b. naturally make well-balanced food choices.
    c. should limit snacks and avoid extra opportunities to eat.
    d. eat more than the average adult.

16. Repeated, unpressured exposure to a new food __________ (p. 300)
    a. decreases focus on the food.
    b. increases acceptance.
    c. increases the likelihood of overeating.
    d. increases the likelihood of undereating.

17. Ordinary childhood illnesses, like chicken pox and measles, __________ (p. 301)
    a. are no longer serious issues in developing countries.
    b. are no longer of concern in the U.S. because immunizations have stopped their spread.
    c. have no effect on physical growth in well-nourished children.
    d. do not contribute to malnutrition in undernourished children.

18. __________ children are more susceptible to childhood illnesses. (p. 301)
    a. Malnourished
    b. Western
    c. Middle-SES
    d. Immunized

19. Large-scale studies show __________ (p. 302)
    a. a strong link between mercury-based preservatives and autism.
    b. no association between mercury-based preservatives and autism.
    c. that routine immunizations are unnecessary for healthy children.
    d. that fewer than 10 percent of U.S. preschoolers lack essential immunizations.

20. For children, one of the greatest immediate benefits of the U.S. Health-Care Reform Act is __________ (p. 303)
    a. that employment-related health coverage is mandatory.
    b. that insurance companies can deny coverage for preexisting conditions.
    c. that everyone will be able to afford health insurance.
    d. the expansion of Medicaid.

21. Otitis media __________ (p. 304)
    a. can disrupt language and academic progress.
    b. is uncommon in the United States.
    c. occurs more often in children who stay at home than in those who attend child care.
    d. is more common in children of nonsmokers than in children whose parents smoke.

22. __________ is/are the leading cause of childhood mortality in industrialized nations. (p. 305)
    a. Cancer
    b. Intentional injuries
    c. Unintentional injuries
    d. Childhood illnesses

23. __________ is strongly associated with childhood injury. (p. 305)
    a. Ethnicity
    b. Poverty
    c. An inhibited temperament
    d. An avoidant attachment style

24. Which of the following is true about relying on children's knowledge of safety rules? (p. 306)
    a. Preschool children typically comply with safety rules explained to them by their parents.
    b. Even older preschoolers spontaneously recall only about 25 percent of the safety rules their parents teach them.
    c. Before age 6, few children have the cognitive skills necessary for understanding basic safety rules.
    d. Even with well-learned rules, children need supervision to ensure they comply.

25. During early childhood, __________, paving the way for new motor skills involving large muscles of the body. (p. 308)
    a. children gain 5 to 10 pounds of muscle
    b. involvement in organized sports increases
    c. the body becomes more top-heavy
    d. balance improves greatly

26. The average 2- to 3-year-old can __________ (p. 309)
    a. use scissors.
    b. gallop and skip with one foot.
    c. use a fork effectively.
    d. use a spoon effectively.

27. The average 3- to 4-year-old can __________ (p. 309)
    a. walk down stairs, alternating feet.
    b. walk down stairs, leading with one foot.
    c. engage in true skipping.
    d. draw a person with six parts.

28. The ability to draw the tadpole image of a person usually emerges at _____ years of age. (p. 310)
    a. 3–4
    b. 4–5
    c. 5–6
    d. 6–7

29. Western children begin to draw __________ (p. 310)
    a. around 9 months of age.
    b. between 10 and 12 months of age.
    c. during the second year.
    d. between 2 and 3 years of age.

30. Children represent salient object parts in their drawing __________ (p. 311)
    a. during early preschool.
    b. during late preschool and school years.
    c. before they use lines to represent boundaries.
    d. after they begin to use depth cues.

PRACTICE TEST #2

1. On average, children add _____ inches in height each year. (p. 290)
   a. 1 to 2
   b. 2 to 3
   c. 3 to 4
   d. 4 to 5

2. Doctors use X-rays of epiphyses to __________ (p. 290)
   a. estimate children's skeletal age.
   b. estimate children's future height.
   c. create growth norms.
   d. predict the emergence of permanent teeth.

3. Overabundance of synaptic connections supports __________ of the young brain. (p. 292)
   a. lateralization
   b. synaptic pruning
   c. plasticity
   d. myelination

4. Handedness __________ (p. 293)
   a. is not evident until children begin school.
   b. is weakest for complex skills requiring extensive training.
   c. occurs at the same rate across all cultures.
   d. is the greater capacity of a side of the brain to carry out skills.

5. The __________ contributes to improvements in sustained, controlled attention. (p. 294)
   a. cerebellum
   b. reticular formation
   c. hippocampus
   d. amygdala

6. The __________ aids in balance and control of body movement. (p. 294)
   a. cerebellum
   b. reticular formation
   c. hippocampus
   d. amygdala

7. The __________ plays a central role in the processing of emotional information. (p. 295)
   a. cerebellum
   b. reticular formation
   c. hippocampus
   d. amygdala

8. __________ is a highly toxic element that, at blood levels exceeding 60 micrograms per deciliter, causes brain swelling and hemorrhaging. (p. 296)
   a. Iron
   b. Zinc
   c. Lead
   d. Aluminum

9. The __________ plays a critical role in growth by releasing two hormones that induce growth. (p. 297)
   a. pituitary gland
   b. reticular formation
   c. hippocampus
   d. amygdala

10. In early childhood, emotional well-being __________ (p. 297)
    a. affects appetite and the ability to digest proteins.
    b. has little effect on physical growth and health.
    c. primarily affects height, not weight.
    d. can profoundly affect growth and health.

11. The impact of disrupted sleep on cognitive development is __________ (p. 298)
    a. almost always temporary, as the young brain is highly plastic.
    b. more pronounced for low-SES children.
    c. equally pronounced for low-, middle-, and high-SES children.
    d. difficult to identify in young children.

12. On average, 4- to 6-year-olds sleep __________ hours per day. (p. 298)
    a. 10 to 11
    b. 9 to 10
    c. 8 to 9
    d. 7 to 8

13. Bedtime routines are more common among __________ than __________ parents. (p. 298)
    a. Hispanic; Caucasian
    b. African-American; Caucasian
    c. Caucasian; Hispanic.
    d. non-Western; Western

14. __________ powerfully influences young children's food preferences. (p. 300)
    a. Body weight
    b. Temperament
    c. Parent–child attachment
    d. The social environment

15. By the school years, low-SES children in the United States are, on average, __________ than their economically advantaged counterparts. (p. 300)
    a. ½ to 1 inch taller
    b. ½ to 1 inch shorter
    c. 2 to 2½ inches taller
    d. 2 to 2½ inches shorter

16. Of the 10 million annual deaths of children under 5 worldwide, _____ percent are in developing countries. (p. 301)
    a. 60
    b. 70
    c. 85
    d. 98

17. Most developmental impairments due to chronic diarrhea __________ (p. 302)
    a. can be cured with zinc.
    b. can be prevented with oral rehydration therapy.
    c. are not preventable.
    d. can be prevented with growth hormone therapy.

18. Under the U.S. Health-Care Reform Act, health insurance in the United States will __________ (p. 303)
    a. be a mandatory cost for all employers.
    b. be more expensive for the average family.
    c. be affordable for most parents who work part-time.
    d. remain an optional employment-related fringe benefit.

19. Which of the following is true about immunizations? (p. 302)
    a. The United States lags behind many other industrialized nations in immunization.
    b. Over 90 percent of U.S. children are fully immunized.
    c. In the U.S., the immunization rates are higher for low-SES than middle-SES children.
    d. Nearly 50 percent of U.S. children lack access to routine immunizations.

20. The incidence of otitis media is greatest between __________ (p. 304)
    a. birth and 6 months.
    b. 6 months and 3 years.
    c. ages 4 to 5 years.
    d. ages 6 to 8 years.

21. Nearly 35 percent of U.S. childhood deaths are due to __________ (p. 305)
    a. cancer.
    b. childhood illnesses.
    c. intentional injuries.
    d. unintentional injuries.

22. __________ are the most frequent source of unintentional injury across all ages in the United States. (p. 305)
    a. Burns
    b. Auto collisions
    c. Falls
    d. Sports

23. Which of the following preschoolers is at greatest risk for injury? (p. 305)
    a. Tia, who lives in a large, extended-family household
    b. DeShawn, who is extremely inhibited and nonassertive
    c. Laci, who has three older brothers
    d. Paulie, who is inattentive and irritable

24. Twenty-seven percent of U.S. parents __________ (p. 306)
    a. fail to use child car safety seats.
    b. install infant safety seats improperly.
    c. install child booster seats improperly.
    d. consistently use child car safety seats.

25. Which of the following is true about realism in children's drawings? (p. 311)
    a. Realism in drawings appears spontaneously, at around 4 years of age.
    b. Preschoolers' free depiction of reality makes their artwork look fanciful and inventive.
    c. Use of depth cues increases during the early preschool years, regardless of drawing experience.
    d. Children's first attempt to represent a cube typically involves several squares, which stand for the cube's sides.

26. Children of the Jimi Valley of Paupa New Guinea did not draw the universal tadpole when asked to draw a person because __________ (p. 311)
    a. their culture has a rich artistic tradition.
    b. they instead learned to draw stick figures in school.
    c. they placed a greater emphasis on the head than most Western children do.
    d. their culture has no indigenous pictorial art.

27. When preschoolers first try to write, they __________ (p. 312)
    a. use separate forms arranged in a line on a page.
    b. use picturelike devices to represent words.
    c. scribble, making no distinction between writing and drawing.
    d. usually write their names.

28. Three-year-olds __________ (p. 312)
    a. display diverse pencil grip patterns and pencil angles.
    b. usually use an adult pencil grip pattern.
    c. usually use a fairly constant pencil angle.
    d. often grip a pencil with one finger on the top.

29. As children gain experience with written materials, they __________ (p. 312)
    a. scan a printed line from right to left.
    b. prefer cursive writing to basic print.
    c. tune in to mirror images.
    d. confuse letter pairs that are subtly different.

30. The U.S. National Association for Sport and Physical Education recommends that each day, preschoolers engage in unstructured physical activity for __________ (p. 313)
    a. 20 to 30 minutes.
    b. 30 to 45 minutes.
    c. no more than an hour.
    d. at least 60 minutes.

CHAPTER 9
COGNITIVE DEVELOPMENT IN EARLY CHILDHOOD

BRIEF CHAPTER SUMMARY

Early childhood brings dramatic advances in representational, or symbolic, activity. Piaget believed that children's cognitive change resulted primarily from sensorimotor activity. But other theorists disagree with Piaget, placing more emphasis on the link between language and thought. Make-believe play during the preschool years reflects the child's growing symbolic mastery and eventually includes sociodramatic play—make-believe with others.

Dual representation improves rapidly over the third year of life as children realize that models, drawings, and simple maps correspond to circumstances in the real world. Aside from gains in representation, Piaget described preschool children in terms of deficits rather than strengths. He identified egocentrism, animistic thinking, inability to conserve, and irreversibility as illogical features of preoperational thought. But newer research reveals that Piaget overestimated these deficiencies and that, when tasks are simplified and made relevant to their everyday experiences, preschoolers show the beginnings of logical, reflective thought. Evidence suggests that operational thought develops gradually, not abruptly, as Piaget had thought. But despite its limitations, Piaget's theory has had a powerful influence on education, promoting child-oriented approaches to teaching and learning.

Whereas Piaget believed that language is of little importance in cognitive development, Vygotsky, who emphasized the social context of cognitive development, regarded language as the foundation for all higher cognitive processes. Social interaction promotes cognitive development through intersubjectivity and scaffolding or, more broadly, guided participation. A Vygotskian classroom emphasizes not just independent discovery but also assisted discovery, including verbal support from teachers and peer collaboration.

A variety of information-processing skills improve during early childhood, including sustained attention, planning, and memory. Recognition memory becomes highly accurate, while recall develops more slowly because preschoolers are not yet effective users of memory strategies. Like adults, young children remember familiar, repeated events in terms of scripts. Between ages 3 and 6, they develop increasingly well-organized, detailed autobiographical memory, or memory for unique, meaningful events.

Preschoolers make great strides in problem-solving skills. Overlapping-waves theory describes how young children experiment with diverse problem-solving strategies, eventually selecting the best ones on the basis of two criteria: accuracy and speed. Around the same time, children begin to develop a theory of mind, or metacognition—a coherent set of ideas about mental activities. Preschoolers also develop a basic understanding of written symbols and mathematical concepts.

A stimulating home environment, warm parenting, and reasonable demands for mature behavior continue to predict gains in mental development in early childhood. Formal academic training in early childhood undermines motivation and other aspects of emotional well-being. Although test score gains resulting from early intervention programs like Head Start eventually decline, at-risk children show broader long-term benefits in school adjustment. High-quality child care can serve as effective intervention.

Educational media, including television, computers, and the Internet, are features of most children's lives in industrialized nations. Educational TV can promote literacy and number concepts, as well as general knowledge and social skills, but heavy viewing of entertainment TV detracts from children's school success and social experiences. Language development proceeds rapidly during early childhood. By the end of the preschool years, children have an extensive vocabulary, use most of the grammatical constructions of their language competently, and are effective conversationalists.

LEARNING OBJECTIVES

After reading this chapter, you should be able to:

9.1 Describe advances in mental representation during the preschool years, including changes in make-believe play. (pp. 318–320)

9.2 Describe what Piaget regarded as deficiencies of preoperational thought. (pp. 321–322)

9.3 Discuss recent research on preoperational thought, and note the implications of such findings for the accuracy of Piaget's preoperational stage. (pp. 323–328)

9.4 Describe educational principles derived from Piaget's theory. (pp. 328–329)

9.5 Describe Vygotsky's perspective on the social origins and significance of children's private speech, and contrast Piaget's view of children's private speech with that of Vygotsky. (pp. 329–330)

9.6 Discuss applications of Vygotsky's theory to education. (p. 332)

9.7 Summarize recent challenges to Vygotsky's theory, and evaluate his major ideas. (pp. 332–334)

9.8 Describe advances in attention, memory, and problem solving during early childhood. (pp. 334–338)

9.9 Discuss preschoolers' understanding of mental activities, noting factors that contribute to early metacognition, as well as limitations of the young child's theory of mind. (pp. 338–341)

9.10 Describe early literacy and mathematical development during the preschool years, and discuss appropriate ways to enhance children's development in these areas. (pp. 341, 343–346)

9.11 Summarize the content of early childhood intelligence tests, and explain the impact of home, preschool and kindergarten programs, child care, and educational media on mental development. (pp. 346–353)

9.12 Trace the development of vocabulary, grammar, and conversational skills in early childhood. (pp. 354–359)

9.13 Cite factors that support language learning in early childhood. (p. 359)

STUDY QUESTIONS

Piaget's Theory: The Preoperational Stage

1. As children move from the sensorimotor to the *preoperational stage,* the most obvious change is an extraordinary increase in ______________________________. (p. 318)

Advances in Mental Representation

1. True or False: Piaget believed that language is the most important factor in cognitive development. (p. 319)

Make-Believe Play

1. List three important changes in make-believe play during early childhood, and give an example of each. (p. 319)

   A. ______________________________

   Example: ______________________________

   B. ______________________________

   Example: ______________________________

   C. ______________________________

   Example: ______________________________

2. What is *sociodramatic play*? (p. 319)

   ____

   ____

3. Summarize contributions of make-believe play to children's cognitive and social development. (p. 319)

   Cognitive: ____

   ____

   Social: ____

   ____

4. True or False: Recent research indicates that the creation of imaginary companions is a sign of maladjustment. Explain your answer. (p. 319)

   ____

5. Describe three strategies for enhancing preschoolers' make-believe play. (p. 320)

   A. ____

   ____

   B. ____

   ____

   C. ____

   ____

Symbol–Real-World Relations

1. ____________________ refers to the ability to view a symbolic object as both an object in its own right and a symbol. Provide an example. (p. 320)

   ____

   ____

2. What factors contribute to children's understanding of *dual representation*? (pp. 320–321)

   ____

   ____

Limitations of Preoperational Thought

1. Piaget described preschoolers in terms of what they (can / cannot) understand. (p. 321)
2. According to Piaget, young children are not capable of ______________, or mental actions that obey logical rules. (p. 321)
3. Piaget believed that ________________, the inability to distinguish the symbolic viewpoints of others from one's own, is the most serious deficiency of preoperational thought. (p. 321)
4. The preoperational belief that inanimate objects have lifelike qualities, such as thoughts, wishes, and intentions, is called ____________________. (p. 321)
5. What is *conservation*? Provide an example. (pp. 321–322)

   Definition: ____

   ____

   Example: ____

   ____

6. The inability to conserve highlights three aspects of preoperational children's thinking. List and describe them. (p. 322)

   A. ____

   ____

   B. ____

   ____

   C. ____

   ____

7. The most important illogical feature of preoperational thought is ______________________, an inability to mentally go through a series of steps in a problem and then reverse direction, returning to the starting point. (p. 322)

8. Describe *hierarchical classification.* What Piagetian task demonstrates this limitation? (p. 322)

   A. ____

   ____

   B. ____

Follow-Up Research on Preoperational Thought

1. Current research (challenges / supports) Piaget's view of preschoolers as cognitively deficient. (p. 323)

2. Cite two examples of nonegocentric responses in preschoolers' everyday interactions. (p. 323)

   A. ____

   B. ____

3. Piaget (overestimated / underestimated) preschoolers' animistic beliefs. Provide evidence to support your answer. (p. 323)

   ____

   ____

4. Between 4 and 8 years of age, as familiarity with physical events and principles increases, children's magical beliefs (increase / decline). (p. 323)

5. Provide an example of how religion and culture contribute to how quickly children give up certain fantastic ideas. (p. 324)

   ____

   ____

6. Provide an example of how preschoolers are capable of logical thought when given tasks that are simplified and made relevant to their everyday lives. (p. 324)

   ____

   ____

   ____

7. Indicate the order in which categorization develops in most children. (p. 325)

   _____ General categories

   _____ Basic-level categories

   _____ Subcategories

8. List two factors that support preschoolers' impressive skill at categorizing. (p. 325)

   A. ____________________

   B. ____________________

9. How can adults strengthen children's categorical learning? (pp. 325, 326)

   ____

   ____

   ____

10. What factor largely accounts for young children's difficulty on appearance–reality problems? (p. 327)

    ____

Social Issues: Education: Children's Questions: Catalyst for Cognitive Development

1. At all ages between 1 and 5 years, the majority of children's questions are (information-seeking / non-information-seeking). (p. 326)

2. How does a child's questioning behavior change with age? (p. 326)

   ____

   ____

   ____

3. How do parents adjust the complexity of their answers to fit their children's maturity? (p. 326)

   ____

   ____

Evaluation of the Preoperational Stage

1. The finding that logical operations develop gradually across the preschool years (supports / challenges) Piaget's stage concept. (pp. 327–328)

2. Some neo-Piagetian theorists combine Piaget's stage concept with the information-processing emphasis on task-specific change. Briefly describe this viewpoint. (p. 328)

   ____

   ____

   ____

Piaget and Education

1. List and describe three educational principles derived from Piaget's theory. (pp. 328–329)

   A. ____________________

   ____

   B. ____________________

   ____

   C. ____________________

   ____

2. What is perhaps the greatest challenge to educational applications of Piaget's theory? (p. 329)

____

Vygotsky's Sociocultural Theory

Private Speech

1. Contrast Piaget's view of children's egocentric speech with Vygotsky's view of *private speech.* (p. 330)

   Piaget: ____

   ____

   Vygotsky: ____

   ____

2. Most research findings have supported (Piaget's / Vygotsky's) view of children's private speech. (p. 330)
3. Under what circumstances are children likely to use private speech? (p. 330)

   ____

   ____

Social Origins of Early Childhood Cognition

1. Vygotsky believed that children's learning takes place within a zone of proximal development. Explain what this means. (p. 330)

   ____

   ____

2. Explain how two features of social interaction, *intersubjectivity* and *scaffolding,* facilitate children's cognitive development. (p. 331)

   Intersubjectivity: ____

   ____

   Scaffolding: ____

   ____

3. Define the term *guided participation,* noting how it differs from scaffolding. (p. 331)

   ____

   ____

   ____

4. Describe features of effective adult scaffolding that foster children's cognitive development. (p. 332)

   ____

   ____

   ____

Vygotsky and Early Childhood Education

1. Vygotskian classrooms emphasize ____________________ discovery, in which teachers guide children's learning, and ______________________________, in which children of varying abilities and skill levels work together. (p. 332)

2. Vygotsky saw ______________________________ as the ideal social context for fostering cognitive development in early childhood. Explain why. (p. 332)

____

____

Evaluation of Vygotsky's Theory

1. List two contributions and two criticisms of Vygotsky's theory of cognitive development. (pp. 332, 333, 334)

   Contributions:

   A. ____

   B. ____

   Criticisms:

   A. ____

   B. ____

Cultural Influences: Children in Village and Tribal Cultures Observe and Participate in Adult Work

1. How do middle-SES parents' interactions with children compare to parents' interactions in village and tribal cultures? (p. 333)

____

____

____

____

2. Yucatec Mayan parents expect young children to be self-sufficient. Provide an example of this. (p. 333)

____

____

3. A(n) (American/Mayan) child is more likely to display attention-getting behaviors. (p. 333)

Information Processing

Attention

1. What factors are responsible for gains in sustained attention during early childhood? (p. 334)

____

____

2. How can a high-quality preschool curriculum assist in the development of sustained attention? (p. 335)

____

____

3. Describe preschoolers' ability to plan, including what they are likely to plan well, as well as limitations in their *planning*. (p. 335)

   Planning abilities: ______________________________

   ____

   ____

   Limitations: ______________________________

   ____

4. Explain how cultural tools support planning skills. (p. 335)

   ____

   ____

Memory

1. Preschoolers' recall memory is much (better / worse) than their recognition memory. (p. 336)
2. Explain why preschoolers are ineffective at using *memory strategies.* (p. 336)

   ____

   ____

3. Describe *episodic memory,* and provide an example. (p. 336)

   A. ______________________________

   B. ______________________________

4. Like adults, preschoolers remember familiar experiences in terms of ______________, general descriptions of what occurs and when it occurs in a particular situation. What are the benefits of using this strategy to aid memory and recall? (p. 336)

   ____

   ____

5. How does autobiographical memory change in early childhood? (p. 337)

   ____

   ____

6. Describe two styles adults use for promoting children's autobiographical narratives, and note which style leads to better memory of events over time. (p. 337)

   Elaborative: ______________________________

   ____

   Repetitive: ______________________________

   ____

7. How do cultural values influence children's narratives about past events? (p. 337)

   ____

   ____

Problem Solving

1. Describe Siegler's *overlapping-waves theory* of problem solving. (p. 338)

____

____

____

2. According to Siegler, what two criteria do children use to select problem-solving strategies? (p. 338)

A. ____

B. ____

3. List three factors that facilitate children's movement from less to more efficient problem-solving strategies. (p. 338)

A. ____

B. ____

C. ____

The Young Child's Theory of Mind

1. A theory of mind, also called ______________________________, is a coherent set of ideas about mental activities. (p. 339)

2. Number each milestone in children's theory of mind in the order that it is typically achieved. (p. 339)

_____ Realize that other people differ from each other and from themselves

_____ Realize that both beliefs and desires determine behavior; understand concept of false beliefs

_____ Able to view people as intentional beings who can share and influence one another's mental states

_____ Understand that thinking takes place inside their heads

3. List three benefits children derive from gaining an understanding of false belief. (p. 340)

A. ____

B. ____

C. ____

4. Name and briefly describe four factors that contribute to preschoolers' theory of mind. (p. 340)

A. ____

B. ____

C. ____

D. ____

5. Cite two ways in which preschoolers' awareness of inner cognitive activities is incomplete. (p. 341)

A. ____

B. ____

Biology and Environment: "Mindblindness" and Autism

1. Describe three core areas of functioning in which children with autism display deficits. (p. 342)

   A. ______________________________

   ____

   B. ______________________________

   ____

   C. ______________________________

   ____

2. True or False: Researchers agree that autism stems from abnormal brain functioning, usually due to genetic or prenatal environmental causes. (p. 342)

3. Growing evidence reveals that children with autism have a deficient theory of mind. Cite several consequences of this deficit. (p. 342)

   ____

   ____

   ____

4. How might impairments in executive processing affect the thinking and behavior of children with autism? (p. 342)

   ____

   ____

Early Literacy and Mathematical Development

1. True or False: Preschoolers cannot understand written language until they learn to read and write. (p. 341)

2. A young child's active effort to construct literacy knowledge through informal experiences is called ______________ *literacy.* (p. 343)

3. ______________________________ refers to the ability to reflect on and manipulate the sound structure of spoken language. (p. 343)

4. Why do preschoolers from low-SES families have fewer opportunities for literacy learning than their more affluent counterparts? (p. 343)

   ____

   ____

   ____

5. List four ways adults can help promote emergent literacy in early childhood. (p. 345)

   A. ______________________________

   B. ______________________________

   C. ______________________________

   D. ______________________________

6. Match each of the following milestones of mathematical reasoning with the age in which it typically develops. (p. 344)

_____	Children can count rows of about 5 objects.	A. 14 to 16 months
_____	Children display a beginning grasp of ordinality.	B. 2 to 3 years
_____	Children can use counting to solve simple arithmetic problems.	C. 3½ to 4 years
_____	Children display a beginning grasp of cardinality.	D. 4 to 5 years

7. When children understand basic arithmetic, they are able to ____________________, or generate approximate answers. (p. 345)

8. True or False: Basic arithmetic knowledge emerges in a universal sequence around the world. (p. 345)

Individual Differences in Mental Development

Early Childhood Intelligence Tests

1. What two types of tasks are commonly included on early childhood intelligence tests? (p. 346)

   A. ______________________________

   B. ______________________________

2. Why do minorities and children from low-SES homes sometimes do poorly on intelligence tests? What steps can be taken to help improve their performance? (pp. 346–347)

   A. ______________________________

   ____

   B. ______________________________

   ____

3. True or False: By age 6 or 7, scores on early childhood intelligence tests are good predictors of later IQ and academic achievement. (p. 347)

Home Environment and Mental Development

1. Describe the characteristics of homes that foster young children's intellectual growth. (p. 347)

   ____

   ____

   ____

2. Research suggests that the home environment (does / does not) play a major role in the generally poorer intellectual performance of low-SES children in comparison to their higher-SES peers. (p. 347)

Preschool, Kindergarten, and Child Care

1. The number of young children enrolled in preschool or child care has steadily (decreased / increased) over the past several decades, reaching nearly _____ percent in the United States. (p. 348)

2. A ____________________ is a program with planned educational experiences aimed at enhancing the development of 2- to 5-year-olds. In contrast, ____________________ includes a variety of arrangements for supervising children of employed parents. (p. 348)

3. In the following list, mark features of *child-centered preschools* with the letter C and features of *academic preschools* with the letter A. (p. 348)
   _____ Teachers allow children to select activities.
   _____ Literacy and mathematical skills are taught using drill and repetition.
   _____ Learning takes place through play.
   _____ Teachers structure children's learning.

4. True or False: Children in academic preschools demonstrate higher levels of achievement than those in child-centered preschools, including greater mastery of motor, academic, language, and social skills. (p. 348)

5. List four features of Montessori education, and discuss the benefits associated with this type of education. (p. 348)

   A. ______________________________

   B. ______________________________

   C. ______________________________

   D. ______________________________

   Benefits: ______________________________

   ____

6. Summarize the goal and program components of *Project Head Start.* (p. 349)

   Goal: ______________________________

   Components of the program: ______________________________

   ____

   ____

   ____

7. Cite two long-term benefits of preschool intervention. (p. 349)

   A. ______________________________

   B. ______________________________

8. Why do the benefits derived from Head Start typically disappear when children begin school? (p. 350)

   ____

   ____

   ____

9. Explain how parent involvement in early intervention contributes to improved school adjustment in children. (p. 350)

   ____

   ____

10. What is Jumpstart? What do evaluations indicate about preschoolers who experience Jumpstart? (p. 350)

    A. ______________________________

    B. ______________________________

    ____

11. True or False: Preschoolers exposed to poor-quality child care score lower on measures of cognitive and social skills and display more behavior problems. (p. 351)

12. List four characteristics of high-quality child care. (p. 352)

    A. ______________________________

    B. ______________________________

    C. ______________________________

    D. ______________________________

Educational Media

1. Describe the benefits of watching educational programs like *Sesame Street.* (pp. 351–352)

   ____

   ____

   ____

2. The average 2- to 6-year-old watches TV programs and videos from ____ to ____ hours a day. (p. 352)

3. What does research reveal about the effects of heavy TV viewing on children's cognitive development? (pp. 352–353)

   ____

   ____

4. Cite several benefits associated with children's use of educational computer programs. (p. 353)

   ____

   ____

Language Development

Vocabulary

1. At age 2, the average child has a spoken vocabulary of _______ words. By age 6, vocabulary grows to around ________ words. (p. 354)

2. What is *fast mapping,* and how does culture contribute to this process? (p. 354)

   A. ______________________________

   B. ______________________________

   ____

3. The principle of ______________________________ refers to an assumption made by children in the early stages of vocabulary growth that words refer to entirely separate (nonoverlapping) categories. (p. 355)

4. When children figure out the meaning of a word by observing how it is used in the structure of a sentence, they are using __________________ *bootstrapping.* (p. 355)

5. Discuss two ways adults support children's vocabulary growth during early childhood. (pp. 355–356)

   A. ______________________________

   ____

   B. ______________________________

   ____

6. Provide two explanations for vocabulary development during early childhood. (p. 356)

   A. ____

   ____

   B. ____

   ____

Grammar

1. True or False: English-speaking children show wide variability in the sequence in which they master grammatical markers. (p. 356)
2. When children overextend grammatical rules to words that are exceptions—for example, saying "I runned fast" instead of "I ran fast"—they are making an error called ____________________. (p. 357)
3. True or False: By the end of the preschool years, children use most of the grammatical constructions of their language competently, with the exception of passive expressions. (p. 357)
4. Briefly describe two differing perspectives in the debate over how children acquire grammar. (pp. 357–358)

   A. ____

   ____

   B. ____

   ____

Conversation

1. The practical, social side of language that is concerned with how to engage in effective and appropriate communication with others is known as ________________. (p. 358)
2. Preschoolers are skilled conversationalists. Provide an example to support this statement. (p. 358)

   ____

3. True or False: Having an older sibling facilitates the acquisition of pragmatic language. (p. 358)
4. Provide an example of a situation in which a preschooler is likely to experience a breakdown of conversational skills. (p. 358)

   ____

   ____

Supporting Language Learning in Early Childhood

1. Explain how adults can use *expansions* and *recasts* to promote preschoolers' language development. (p. 359)

   Expansions: ____

   ____

   Recasts: ____

   ____

ASK YOURSELF . . .

For *Ask Yourself* questions for this chapter, along with feedback on the accuracy of your answers, please log on to MyDevelopmentLab (for registration and access, please visit mydevelopmentlab.com or follow the instructions on page ix).

(1) Select the Multimedia Library.

(2) Choose the explore option.

(3) Find your chapter from the drop down box.

(4) Click find now.

(5) Complete questions and choose "Submit answers for grading" or "Clear answers" to start over.

SUGGESTED READINGS

Lawson, J. (2010). *The role of autism in shaping society*. Bristol, PA: Taylor & Francis. A compelling look at autism, this book examines various forms of autism, characteristics of the disorder, the impact of autism on children, families, and society, theories about its origin, and contemporary treatments and educational interventions.

Lillard, A. (2007). *Montessori: The science behind the genius.* New York: Oxford University Press. Presents an alternative to traditional educational practices by focusing on children's learning and cognition, their natural interest in learning, meaningful learning contexts, the importance of peers, and adult interaction styles and child outcomes.

Singer, D. Hirsh-Pasek, K., & Golinkoff, R. (Eds.). (2009). *Play = Learning: How play motivates and enhances children's cognitive and social-emotional growth.* New York: Oxford University Press. A collection of chapters highlighting the diverse benefits of play for children's learning. The authors argue that in trying to create a generation of "Einsteins," many parents and educators are overlooking the importance of play in early child development.

CROSSWORD PUZZLE 9.1

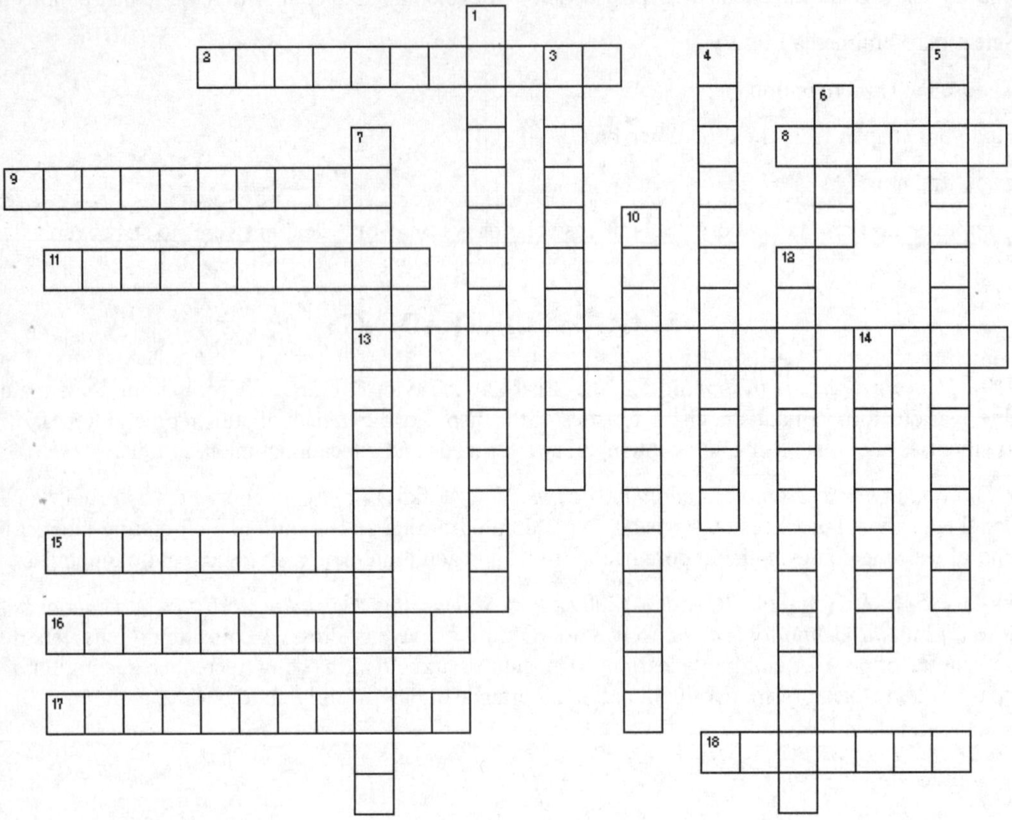

Across

2. The inability to distinguish the symbolic viewpoints of others from one's own
8. __________ participation refers to shared endeavors between more expert and less expert participants, without specifying the precise features of communication.
9. Tendency to focus on one aspect of a situation and neglect other important features
11. Memory __________: deliberate mental activities that improve our chances of remembering
13. Make-believe play with others (2 words)
15. __________ thinking: the belief that inanimate objects have lifelike qualities
16. __________ classification: organization of objects into classes and subclasses based on similarities and differences
17. Mutual __________ bias: assumption that words refer to entirely separate categories
18. General descriptions of what occurs and when it occurs in a particular situation

Down

1. The inability to mentally go through a series of steps and then reverse direction, returning to the starting point
3. Adjusting the quality of support over the course of a teaching session to fit the child's current level of performance
4. Understanding that certain physical features of an object remain the same, even when their outward appearance changes
5. Piaget's second stage; marked by rapid growth in representation
6. __________ representation: representations of a symbolic object as both an object in its own right and a symbol
7. Process by which two participants who begin a task with different understandings arrive at a shared understanding
10. Thinking about thought
12. Memory for everyday experiences (2 words)
14. Thinking out a sequence of acts ahead of time and allocating attention accordingly to reach a goal

CROSSWORD PUZZLE 9.2

Across

3. Adult responses that elaborate on a child's utterance, increasing its complexity
8. Preschools in which teachers provide a variety of activities from which children select; most of the day is devoted to free play (2 words, hyph.)
10. __________-waves theory: children generate a variety of strategies on challenging problems and gradually select those that result in rapid, accurate solutions.
12. Principle stating that the last number in a counting sequence indicates the quantity of items in the set
13. Fast ___________: connecting a new word with an underlying concept after only a brief encounter
15. Adult responses that restructure children's incorrect speech into a more appropriate form

Down

1. ___________ bootstrapping: figuring out grammatical rules by relying on word meanings
2. Project _____________ ____________ is a federal program that provides low-SES children with a year or two of preschool, along with nutritional and medical services. (2 words)
4. Application of regular grammatical rules to words that are exceptions
5. Preschools in which teachers structure the children's learning and teach through formal lessons
6. _________ speech: self-directed speech that children use to plan and guide their behavior
7. ___________ literacy refers to young children's active efforts to construct literacy knowledge through informal experiences.
9. Principle specifying order relationships between quantities
11. ___________ bootstrapping: figuring out word meanings by observing how words are used in the structure of sentences
13. The practical, social side of language that is concerned with how to engage in effective and appropriate communication with others

PRACTICE TEST #1

1. Toddlers' earliest pretend acts __________ (p. 319)
   a. are flexible.
   b. usually imitate adults' actions.
   c. use objects as symbols for other objects.
   d. are directed toward others.

2. Make-believe play becomes __________ as children realize that agents and recipients of pretend actions can be independent of themselves. (p. 319)
   a. less self-centered
   b. more self-focused
   c. less other-oriented
   d. less flexible

3. As Maggi hugs her stuffed pig, she says, "My pig is sad." Maggi is displaying __________ (p. 321)
   a. egocentrism.
   b. dual representation.
   c. self-centered play.
   d. animistic thinking.

4. The most illogical feature of preoperational thought is its __________ (p. 322)
   a. irreversibility.
   b. dynamic transformation.
   c. centration.
   d. animistic thinking.

5. Piaget __________ preschoolers' __________ thinking. (p. 323)
   a. underestimated; animistic
   b. overestimated; animistic
   c. underestimated; magical
   d. underestimated; egocentric

6. __________ play a role in how quickly children give up certain fantastic ideas. (p. 324)
   a. Heredity and environment
   b. Heredity and culture
   c. Religion and culture
   d. Religion and heredity

7. Which of the following is the most likely to be among a child's first categories? (p. 325)
   a. trucks
   b. dump trucks
   c. vehicles
   d. pickup trucks

8. In responding to children's questions, parents __________ (p. 326)
   a. give the same answers to children of different ages.
   b. often include additional irrelevant information.
   c. tend to give only prior cause explanations.
   d. usually respond informatively.

9. Which of the following is true about Piagetian classrooms? (pp. 328–329)
   a. Children are discouraged from spontaneously interacting with the environment.
   b. Teachers present ready-made knowledge through the use of worksheets.
   c. Teachers promote discovery learning through a rich variety of activities designed to promote exploration.
   d. Children are discouraged from engaging in sociodramatic play.

10. In Piagetian classrooms, teachers __________ (p. 329)
    a. introduce activities that build on children's current thinking.
    b. present ready-made knowledge verbally.
    c. rely exclusively on peer collaboration.
    d. evaluate children on the basis of normative standards.

11. Children's self-directed speech is now called __________ speech. (p. 330)
    a. egocentric
    b. private
    c. inner
    d. social

12. According to Vygotsky, to promote cognitive development, social interaction must have __________ and __________ (p. 331)
    a. intersubjectivity; dual representation.
    b. a zone of proximal development; dual representation.
    c. a zone of proximal development; egocentrism.
    d. intersubjectivity; scaffolding.

13. Children in Vygotskian classrooms __________ (p. 332)
    a. are evaluated on the basis of normative standards.
    b. work in groups, teaching and helping one another.
    c. work in whole class groups, rather than in small groups.
    d. sit in individual desks and work independently.

14. Vygotsky saw __________ as the ideal social context for fostering cognitive development in early childhood. (p. 332)
    a. early intervention programs
    b. independent discovery
    c. make-believe play
    d. the classroom setting

15. Yucatec Mayan children __________ (p. 333)
    a. are highly competent at self-care.
    b. engage in make-believe play for hours each day.
    c. converse and play with their parents more than Western children.
    d. have more behavioral problems than Western children.

16. Vygotsky's theory has been criticized for saying little about __________ (p. 334)
    a. the relationship between language and cognition.
    b. educational practices, such as peer collaboration.
    c. the role of parents in supporting cognitive development.
    d. the development of basic cognitive processes.

17. In *Tools of the Mind*—a preschool curriculum inspired by Vygotsky's theory—__________ is woven into virtually all classroom activities. (p. 335)
    a. math and science instruction
    b. scaffolding of attention skills
    c. independent discovery
    d. animistic thinking

18. Even preschoolers with good language skills __________ poorly because they are not skilled at using memory strategies. (p. 336)
    a. recognize
    b. use scripts
    c. recall
    d. remember one-time events

19. Preschoolers who experience the __________ style recall more information about past events and also produce more organized and detailed personal stories. (p. 337)
   a. overlapping-waves
   b. repetitive
   c. episodic
   d. elaborative

20. By age 3, children __________ (p. 339)
   a. realize that thinking takes place inside their heads.
   b. are not yet aware that a person can think something without seeing it.
   c. realize that both beliefs and desires determine behavior.
   d. do not yet understand that people have different likes and dislikes.

21. Make-believe play helps children develop a theory of mind because it __________ (p. 340)
   a. enables them to reason about the implications of situations that contradict reality.
   b. helps them solidify beliefs about animistic objects.
   c. allows them to share beliefs with playmates and acquire conversational skills.
   d. enables them to use mental-state words and apply memory strategies.

22. Children with autism __________ (p. 342)
   a. have smaller-than-average brains.
   b. often imitate an adult's novel behaviors.
   c. have delayed and stereotyped behavior.
   d. usually have a broad range of interests.

23. Three-year-old Grace writes a letter to her grandma. The writing consists of a string of pictures and letters. This demonstrates Grace's __________ (p. 343)
   a. emergent literacy.
   b. phonological awareness.
   c. theory of mind.
   d. grasp of ordinality.

24. When Donovan plays a game, he counts out four players and then gets out four game pieces. This demonstrates Donovan's grasp of __________ (p. 344)
   a. ordinality.
   b. cardinality.
   c. estimation.
   d. functionality.

25. Research shows that formal academic training __________ (p. 348)
   a. undermines preschoolers' motivation and emotional well-being.
   b. results in significantly higher IQ scores for most preschoolers.
   c. enhances preschoolers' motivation and emotional well-being.
   d. is especially beneficial to low-income preschoolers.

26. Poverty-stricken children who attended university preschool programs __________ than those who did not attend preschool. (p. 349)
   a. were more likely to be placed in special education
   b. were more likely to graduate high school
   c. scored 15 to 20 points higher on IQ tests
   d. experienced a faster "washout effect"

27. Using __________, children connect new words with their underlying concepts after only a brief encounter. (p. 354)
   a. dual representation
   b. the mutual exclusivity bias
   c. fast mapping
   d. overlapping-waves

28. Jane's father tells her that their new pet is a poodle. Jane does not know the word poodle, but she knows the word dog. To accept the concept that a poodle is a type of dog, Jane must overcome the __________ (p. 355)
    a. fast mapping bias.
    b. syntactic bootstrap.
    c. semantic bootstrap.
    d. mutual exclusivity bias.

29. Francis told her father, "We singed a song in church." This is an example of __________ (p. 357)
    a. fast mapping.
    b. overregularization.
    c. syntactic bootstrapping.
    d. semantic bootstrapping.

30. Some researchers question the importance of adults' recasts and expansions of children's speech because __________ (p. 359)
    a. restructuring and elaborating can discourage children from freely using language.
    b. those techniques are not used in all cultures and do not consistently affect children's usage.
    c. those techniques do not accurately model grammar or pragmatics.
    d. adults do not always apply grammatical rules consistently.

PRACTICE TEST #2

1. Preschoolers who spend more time in sociodramatic play are seen as _________ by their teachers. (p. 319)
   a. socially immature
   b. less intelligent
   c. more socially competent
   d. more intelligent

2. May attempts to put a doll's shoe on her own foot. May is having difficulty with _________ (p. 320)
   a. egocentrism.
   b. animistic thinking.
   c. conservation.
   d. dual representation.

3. Piaget's class inclusion problem demonstrates that preoperational children have difficulty with _________ (p. 322)
   a. irreversibility.
   b. dual representation.
   c. hierarchical classification.
   d. conservation.

4. Preoperational children often have difficulty with Piaget's conservation task because they _________ (p. 322)
   a. center on the height of the liquid, failing to realize that the width compensates for the changes in height.
   b. are rarely distracted by the perceptual appearance of objects.
   c. focus on the dynamic transformation of the liquid.
   d. mentally go through a series of steps in the problem and then reverse direction.

5. Follow-up research shows that _________ realize that what they see sometimes differs from what another person sees. (p. 327)
   a. even 2-year-olds
   b. not until age 4 do children
   c. preoperational children fail to
   d. not until they begin formal schooling do children

6. Evidence that preschool children can be trained to perform well on Piagetian problems challenges the idea of _________ (p. 327)
   a. egocentrism.
   b. dual representation.
   c. stages.
   d. animistic thinking.

7. From age 2 on, children _________ (p. 326)
   a. build on fact-oriented questions with follow-up questions that ask for causes and explanations.
   b. ask more non-information-seeking questions than fact-oriented questions.
   c. ask questions more often as a means of seeking attention than as a means of obtaining information.
   d. ask more theory of mind questions than fact-oriented questions.

8. Discovery learning in a Piagetian classroom _________ (pp. 328–329)
   a. involves the use of assisted discovery where teachers guide children's learning with explanations.
   b. is aided by peer collaboration, as children with varying abilities work in groups, teaching and helping one another.
   c. involves the use of teaching materials specially designed to promote academic achievement.
   d. encourages children to discover for themselves through spontaneous interaction with the environment.

9. In a Piagetian classroom, teachers _________ (p. 329)
   a. speed up development by imposing new skills according to normative standards.
   b. assume that all children go through the same sequence of development at the same rate.
   c. plan activities for individual children and small groups, as well as for the whole class.
   d. evaluate children's progress on the basis of average performance of same-age peers.

10. Research shows that children use more __________ when tasks are appropriately challenging—neither too easy nor too hard. (p. 330)
    a. dual representation
    b. make-believe play
    c. private speech
    d. animistic thinking

11. In shared endeavors between more expert and less expert participants, __________ allows for variations across situations and cultures. (p. 331)
    a. guided participation
    b. dual representation
    c. dynamic transformation
    d. symbolic communication

12. In Vygotskian classrooms, __________ (p. 332)
    a. teachers deemphasize the importance of individual differences.
    b. teachers promote assisted discovery.
    c. make-believe play is discouraged.
    d. teachers present ready-made knowledge verbally.

13. In Western cultures, parents assume much responsibility for children's __________ (p. 332)
    a. motivation.
    b. attention.
    c. memory.
    d. false beliefs.

14. Yucatec Mayan young children __________ (p. 333)
    a. display more attention-getting behaviors than Western children.
    b. spontaneously take responsibility for tasks beyond those assigned.
    c. are more dependent on their parents than Western children.
    d. are highly competent at make-believe play.

15. __________ predicts social maturity and reading and math achievement from kindergarten through high school. (p. 334)
    a. Resisting the "pull" of attention toward a dominant stimulus
    b. Access to educational media
    c. Being able to recognize and recall stimuli
    d. Intense academic instruction

16. Preschoolers can __________ (p. 335)
    a. hold on to pieces of information while simultaneously applying a strategy.
    b. remember five digits at a time in digit-span tasks.
    c. generate and follow a plan, as long as tasks are familiar and not too complex.
    d. search thoroughly when asked to compare detailed pictures.

17. Young children's __________ is poorer than their __________. (p. 336)
    a. recognition; recall
    b. recall; recognition
    c. recognition; episodic memory
    d. recognition; autobiographical memory

18. Preschoolers remember familiar, repeated events in terms of __________ (p. 336)
    a. scripts.
    b. overlapping-waves.
    c. dual representation.
    d. dynamic transformations.

19. As representation of the world, memory, and problem solving improve, children begin to construct __________ (p. 338)
    a. false beliefs about the world.
    b. a theory of mind.
    c. imaginary companions.
    d. phonological awareness.

20. Research on theory of mind shows that __________ predicts preschoolers' grasp of false belief. (p. 340)
    a. formal schooling
    b. access to early intervention
    c. language
    d. animistic thinking

21. Children with autism __________ (p. 342)
    a. have a well-developed theory of mind by age 5.
    b. have delayed verbal language but are exceptionally skilled at using nonverbal cues.
    c. engage in longer make-believe episodes than other children.
    d. engage in much less make-believe play than other children.

22. Four-year-old Sophia can "read" the signs at McDonald's and Wendy's. However, she spells her name S-F-A. This demonstrates Sophia's __________ (p. 343)
    a. emergent literacy.
    b. grasp of ordinality.
    c. phonological awareness.
    d. grasp of cardinality.

23. Four-year-old Honor likes to rhyme words and manipulate the sounds within words. This demonstrates Honor's __________ (p. 343)
    a. grasp of ordinality.
    b. grasp of cardinality.
    c. phonological awareness.
    d. ability to read.

24. In a(n) __________ program, teachers structure children's learning, teaching letters, numbers, colors, and shape through formal lessons. (p. 348)
    a. child-care
    b. academic
    c. child-centered
    d. Montessori

25. In a(n) __________ program, teachers allow long time periods for individual and small-group learning in child-chosen activities. (p. 348)
    a. child-care
    b. academic
    c. formal preschool
    d. Montessori

26. Head Start __________ (pp. 349–350)
    a. is less cost effective than other early intervention programs.
    b. children show greater academic gains than children who receive university-based services.
    c. children show more gains when parents are involved.
    d. participants show lasting gains in IQ and achievement test scores.

27. Evaluations indicate that preschoolers who experience __________ show greater end-of-year gains in language, literacy, task persistence, and social skills than comparison children. (p. 350)
    a. public child care
    b. private child care
    c. Head Start
    d. Jumpstart

28. Which of the following is true about child care? (p. 351)
    a. Psychological well-being declines when children experience the instability of several child-care settings.
    b. Most child care in the United States is average to above average in quality.
    c. Even preschoolers exposed to substandard child care show enhanced cognitive abilities.
    d. Good child care enhances social development in preschool, but gains quickly dissolve in elementary school.

29. About _____ percent of U.S. 2-year-olds regularly watch either TV or videos. (p. 352)
    a. 40
    b. 60
    c. 80
    d. 90

30. Children acquire the pragmatics of language as they __________ (p. 358)
    a. learn basic rules of grammar.
    b. engage in social interaction.
    c. master telegraphic speech.
    d. experiment with word strategies.

CHAPTER 10
EMOTIONAL AND SOCIAL DEVELOPMENT IN EARLY CHILDHOOD

BRIEF CHAPTER SUMMARY

Erikson's stage of initiative versus guilt offers an overview of the personality changes of early childhood. During the preschool years, children's self-concepts begin to take shape. Their self-esteem is high, supporting their enthusiasm for mastering new skills. As self-awareness strengthens, children begin to develop a self-concept, the set of attributes, abilities, attitudes, and values that an individual believes defines who he or she is. In early childhood, children gain in understanding of emotion, emotional self-regulation, capacity to experience self-conscious emotions, and capacity for empathy and sympathy. Cognition, language, and warm, sensitive parenting support these developments.

During the preschool years, peers provide an important context for the development of a wide range of social skills. Peer interaction increases, cooperative play becomes common, and children form first friendships. Preschoolers learn to use their new social problem-solving skills to resolve conflicts. Peer relations are influenced by parental guidance and the quality of sibling ties.

Three approaches to understanding early childhood morality—psychoanalytic, social learning, and cognitive-developmental—emphasize different aspects of moral understanding. Although most researchers reject Freud's view of conscience development, the power of inductive discipline is recognized. Social learning theorists believe that children learn to act morally through modeling, while the cognitive-developmental perspective regards children as active thinkers about social rules. A conflict-ridden family atmosphere, poor parenting practices, and heavy viewing of violent television and other media promote childhood aggression, which can develop into severe conduct problems.

Gender typing develops rapidly over the preschool years. Heredity contributes to gender-typed behavior, but environmental forces—including parents, teachers, and the broader social environment—also play powerful roles. Neither cognitive-developmental theory nor social learning theory provides a complete account of the development of gender identity. Gender schema theory is an information-processing approach that shows how environmental pressures and children's cognition combine to affect gender-role development.

Compared to children of authoritarian and permissive parents, children who experience authoritative child rearing are most likely to be well-adjusted and socially mature. Warmth, explanations, and reasonable demands for mature behavior account for the effectiveness of the authoritative style. Child-rearing beliefs and practices vary in different ethnic groups, so child-rearing styles should always be viewed in light of cultural values and the circumstances in which parents and children live.

Child maltreatment, including both abuse and neglect, is the combined result of factors within the family, the community, and the broader culture. Interventions at all of these levels are essential for preventing it.

LEARNING OBJECTIVES

After reading this chapter, you should be able to:

10.1 Describe personality changes that take place during Erikson's stage of initiative versus guilt. (p. 364)

10.2 Discuss preschoolers' self-concepts and the development of autobiographical memory and self-esteem. (pp. 364–367)

10.3 Identify changes in understanding and expressing emotion during early childhood, citing factors that influence those changes. (pp. 367–370)

10.4 Discuss the development of self-conscious emotions, empathy, and sympathy during early childhood, noting how parenting and temperament affect emotional development in these areas. (pp. 370–371)

10.5 Describe advances in peer sociability over the preschool years, with particular attention to Parten's play types, and discuss cultural variations in peer sociability. (pp. 372–374)

10.6 Describe the quality of preschoolers' first friendships, noting how parents and siblings influence early peer relations, and discuss the emergence of social problem solving during early childhood. (pp. 374–378)

10.7 Compare the central features of psychoanalytic, social learning, and cognitive-developmental approaches to moral development. (pp. 378–385)

10.8 Trace milestones in preschoolers' moral understanding, highlighting the importance of social experience. (pp. 384–385)

10.9 Describe the development of aggression in early childhood, including family and media influences, and cite ways to control aggressive behavior. (pp. 385–390)

10.10 Describe preschoolers' gender-stereotyped beliefs and behaviors, and discuss genetic and environmental influences on gender-role development. (pp. 390–395)

10.11 Describe and evaluate major theories that explain the emergence of gender identity, and cite ways to reduce gender stereotyping in young children. (pp. 395–398)

10.12 Describe three features that distinguish major styles of child rearing. Compare each style, indicating which is most effective, and discuss cultural variations in child-rearing beliefs and practices. (pp. 398–401)

10.13 Describe the multiple origins of child maltreatment, its consequences for development, and prevention strategies. (pp. 401–405)

STUDY QUESTIONS

Erikson's Theory: Initiative versus Guilt

1. Define *initiative versus guilt,* and describe how it is exhibited in preschoolers. (p. 364)

   A. ____

   ____

   B. ____

   ____

2. Describe two benefits of play for preschoolers. (p. 364)

   A. ____

   ____

   B. ____

   ____

3. According to Erikson, what leads to a negative outcome of the initiative-versus-guilt stage? (p. 364)

   ____

   ____

Self-Understanding

1. ____________________ refers to the set of attributes, abilities, attitudes, and values that an individual believes defines who he or she is. How does this mental representation of the self affect children's development? (pp. 364–365)

   ____

   ____

Foundations of Self-Concept

1. Which of the following self-descriptions are typical of preschool-age children? (p. 365)

_____ "I am 4-years-old."
_____ "I am trustworthy."
_____ "Sometimes I lose my temper."
_____ "I'm shy."
_____ "I am a girl."
_____ "I'm very good at swimming."
_____ "I have a new game."
_____ "I don't like scary cartoons."

2. Preschoolers with a secure attachment to their mothers are (more / less) likely to have a favorable self-concept. Briefly explain why. (p. 365)

____

____

____

3. True or False: Preschoolers are unable to view themselves as persisting over time and cannot imagine or plan for future events. (p. 365)

Cultural Influences: Cultural Variations in Personal Storytelling: Implications for Early Self-Concept

1. Discuss differences in storytelling practices between Chinese and Irish-American parents, and explain the influence on children's self-image. (p. 366)

Differences in storytelling: ____

____

Differences in self-image: ____

____

2. Although most Americans believe that favorable self-esteem is (crucial / unimportant) for healthy development, Chinese adults generally regard self-esteem as (crucial / unimportant). Explain the implications of this view for Chinese children's self-image. (p. 366)

____

____

Emergence of Self-Esteem

1. Define *self-esteem.* (p. 366)

____

____

2. Preschoolers generally rate their own ability as (higher / lower) than their actual competence and (overestimate / underestimate) the difficulty of tasks. Explain why. (pp. 366–367)

____

____

3. How does high self-esteem help preschoolers master new skills? (p. 367)

____

____

____

Emotional Development

1. Between the ages of 2 and 6, children make strides in the emotional abilities known, collectively, as ______________________. List the three ways in which this growth takes place. (p. 367)

   A. ______________________

   B. ______________________

   C. ______________________

Understanding Emotion

1. True or False: By age 4 to 5, children can correctly judge the causes of many basic emotions. (p. 368)
2. Do preschoolers recognize that thoughts and feelings are interconnected? Explain. (p. 368)

   ____

   ____

3. True or False: In situations with conflicting cues about how a person is feeling, preschoolers can easily reconcile this differing information. (p. 368)
4. Provide an example of how can parents can facilitate children's understanding of emotion. (p. 368)

   ____

   ____

   ____

5. Discuss how make-believe play, especially with siblings, contributes to emotional understanding. (pp. 368–369)

   ____

   ____

   ____

6. List four ways in which emotional knowledge helps children get along with their peers (p. 369)

   A. ______________________

   B. ______________________

   C. ______________________

   D. ______________________

Emotional Self-Regulation

1. Provide an example of how language contributes to preschoolers' improved emotional self-regulation. (p. 369)

   ____

   ____

2. Explain how effortful control helps young children manage emotion. (p. 369)

   ____

   ____

   ____

3. Cite two characteristics of emotionally reactive children. (p. 369)

   A. ______________________________

   B. ______________________________

4. How can parents foster preschoolers' emotional self-regulation? (pp. 369–370)

   ____

   ____

   ____

5. List two fears common in early childhood. (p. 370)

   A. ______________________________

   B. ______________________________

Self-Conscious Emotions

1. Preschoolers experience self-conscious emotions (more / less) often than do toddlers. (p. 370)
2. Beginning in early childhood, (guilt / shame) is associated with feelings of personal inadequacy and is linked with maladjustment. In contrast, (guilt / shame), as long as it occurs in appropriate circumstances, is related to positive adjustment, perhaps because it helps children resist harmful impulses. (p. 370)

Empathy and Sympathy

1. Empathy serves as an important motivator of __________________, or __________________ behavior—actions that benefit another person without any expected reward for the self. (p. 371)
2. Distinguish between empathy and *sympathy.* (p. 371)

   Empathy: ______________________________

   ____

   Sympathy: ______________________________

   ____

3. True or False: In some children, empathizing with an upset peer or adult escalates into personal distress. (p. 371)
4. Provide an example of how parenting contributes to the development of empathy and sympathy. (p. 371)

   ____

   ____

   ____

Peer Relations

Advances in Peer Sociability

1. Match each of the following types of social interaction with its correct description. (p. 372)

_____ Nonsocial activity	A.	An advanced type of social interaction in which children orient toward a common goal
_____ Parallel play	B.	Unoccupied, onlooker behavior and solitary play
_____ Associative play	C.	A limited form of social participation in which a child plays near other children with similar materials but does not try to influence their behavior
_____ Cooperative play	D.	A form of social interaction in which children engage in separate activities but exchange toys and comment on one another's behavior

2. True or False: Longitudinal research shows that play types emerge in the order Parten suggested, with later-appearing ones replacing earlier ones in a developmental sequence. (p. 373)

3. True or False: It is the *type,* rather than the *amount,* of solitary and parallel play that changes during early childhood. (p. 373)

4. What types of nonsocial activity in the preschool years are cause for concern? (p. 373)

5. Most preschoolers with low rates of peer interaction are not socially anxious. Cite research that supports this statement. (p. 373)

6. How does sociodramatic play support emotional and social development during early childhood? (p. 374)

7. True or False: Peer sociability takes essentially the same form in collectivist and individualistic cultures. Provide an example to support your answer. (p. 374)

First Friendships

1. Summarize children's understanding of friendship in early childhood. (p. 374)

2. Provide an example illustrating the unique quality of preschoolers' interactions with friends. (pp. 374–375)

Peer Relations and School Readiness

1. Kindergartners with friendly, __________ behavioral styles make new friends easily, whereas those with weak emotional self-regulation skills and argumentative, aggressive, or ______________ styles establish poor-quality relationships and make few friends. (p. 375)

2. Experts propose that readiness for kindergarten be assessed in terms of social skills as well as academic skills. What types of social skills are important to social maturity in early childhood? (p. 375)

____

____

____

Social Problem Solving

1. Explain how the resolution of peer conflicts promotes development during early childhood. (p. 375)

____

____

____

2. List the six steps in the *social problem-solving* model proposed by Crick and Dodge. (pp. 375–376)

   A. ____

   B. ____

   C. ____

   D. ____

   E. ____

   F. ____

3. Compare the behavior of children who are skilled at social problem solving with those who lack these skills. (p. 376)

   Skilled: ____

   ____

   Unskilled: ____

   ____

4. Provide an example of how social problem solving improves during the preschool and early school years. (p. 376)

____

____

____

5. Cite several ways that intervening with children who have weak social problem-solving skills can enhance development. (pp. 376–377)

____

____

____

Parental Influences on Early Peer Relations

1. List two ways that parents directly influence their children's social relationships. (p. 377)

   A. ____

   B. ____

2. Explain how parent–child attachment and parent–child play can promote children's peer interaction skills. (p. 377)

   Attachment: ____

   ____

   Play: ____

   ____

Foundations of Morality

1. List two points on which most theories of moral development are in agreement. (p. 378)

   A. ____

   B. ____

2. Match each of the following major theories of moral development with the aspect of moral functioning that it emphasizes. (p. 378)

   _____ Emotional side of conscience
   _____ Ability to reason about justice and fairness
   _____ Moral behavior

   A. Psychoanalytic theory
   B. Social learning theory
   C. Cognitive-developmental theory

The Psychoanalytic Perspective

1. True or False: Most researchers agree with Freud's assertion that fear of punishment and loss of parental love motivates children to behave morally. (p. 379)

2. A special type of discipline called ____________________ supports conscience development by pointing out the effects of the child's misbehavior on others. Cite four ways in which it does so. (p. 379)

   A. ____

   ____

   B. ____

   ____

   C. ____

   ____

   D. ____

   ____

3. What type of parenting interferes with the development of empathy and prosocial responding? (p. 379)

   ____

   ____

4. True or False: Twin studies suggest a modest genetic contribution to empathy and prosocial behavior. (p. 379)

5. True or False: Mild, patient tactics work equally well with anxious, fearful preschoolers and fearless, impulsive children. Explain your answer. (p. 380)

____

____

Social Learning Theory

1. Explain why operant conditioning is insufficient for children to acquire moral responses. (p. 380)

____

____

____

2. Social learning theorists believe that children learn to behave morally largely through ______________________— observing and imitating adults who demonstrate appropriate behavior. (p. 380)

3. List three characteristics of models that affect children's willingness to imitate them. (pp. 380–381)

   A. ____

   B. ____

   C. ____

4. True or False: Punishment promotes immediate compliance but does not produce long-lasting changes in children's behavior. (p. 381)

5. List five undesirable side effects of harsh punishment. (p. 381)

   A. ____

   B. ____

   C. ____

   D. ____

   E. ____

6. True or False: Studies have failed to find a link between corporal punishment and aggressive behavior. Explain your answer. (p. 382)

____

____

7. List two alternatives to harsh punishment. (p. 382)

   A. ____

   B. ____

8. Cite three ways that parents can increase the effectiveness of punishment when they do decide to use it. (p. 382)

   A. ____

   B. ____

   C. ____

9. Explain how effective discipline encourages good behavior. (p. 383)

____

____

____

10. Provide three examples of positive discipline. (p. 384)

A. ____

B. ____

C. ____

Cultural Influences: Ethnic Differences in the Consequences of Physical Punishment

1. Use of physical punishment is highest among (low-SES minority parents / middle-SES white parents). (p. 383)

2. Although corporal punishment is linked with a wide variety of negative child outcomes, exceptions do exist. Describe these exceptions. (p. 383)

____

____

____

3. Discuss differences in the ways that African-American and Caucasian-American families view physical punishment. (p. 383)

African-American: ____

____

____

Caucasian-American: ____

____

____

The Cognitive-Developmental Perspective

1. In what major way does the cognitive-developmental perspective of morality differ from the psychoanalytic and social learning approaches? (p. 384)

____

____

2. Preschoolers are able to distinguish ______________ *imperatives,* which protect people's rights and welfare, from two other forms of action: ______________ *conventions,* or customs determined solely by consensus, such as table manners and dress style, and *matters of* ___________________________, which do not violate rights or harm others, are not socially regulated, and therefore are up to the individual. (p. 384)

3. Provide an example of how young children learn to make distinctions between moral imperatives and social conventions. (p. 385)

____

____

____

4. List three features of parent communication that help children reason about morality. (p. 385)

   A. ____________________

   B. ____________________

   C. ____________________

The Other Side of Morality: Development of Aggression

1. By the end of the preschool years, two general types of aggression emerge. The most common is __________ *aggression,* aimed at obtaining an object, privilege, or space with no deliberate intent to harm. The other type is __________ *aggression,* which is intended to hurt another person. (p. 385)

2. Match the following types of hostile aggression with the appropriate descriptions. (pp. 385–386)

   _____ *Physical aggression*
   _____ *Verbal aggression*
   _____ *Relational aggression*

   A. Harms others through threats of physical aggression, name-calling, or hostile teasing
   B. Social exclusion, malicious gossip, or friendship manipulation
   C. Pushing, hitting, kicking, or punching others; destroying other's property

3. In early childhood, (physical / verbal) aggression gradually replaces (physical / verbal) aggression. What accounts for this change? (p. 386)

   ____

4. (Boys/Girls) display overall rates of aggression that are much higher than (boys'/girls'). (p. 386)

5. Cite three negative outcomes for highly aggressive children. (p. 386)

   A. ____________________

   B. ____________________

   C. ____________________

6. Provide an example of how a hostile family atmosphere creates a cycle of aggression. (p. 387)

   ____

   ____

   ____

7. True or False: Girls are more likely than boys to be targets of harsh physical discipline and parental inconsistency. (p. 387)

8. Compare deficits in social information-processing for children high in reactive aggression and those high in proactive aggression. (p. 387)

   Reactive: ____________________

   ____

   Proactive: ____________________

   ____

9. True or False: Violent content in children's programming occurs at above average rates, and cartoons are the most violent. (pp. 387–388)

10. Explain why young children are especially likely to be influenced by television. (p. 388)

   ____

   ____

   ____

11. True or False: Media violence hardens children to aggression, making them more willing to tolerate it in others. Briefly explain your response. (p. 388)

____

____

____

12. List three strategies parents can use to regulate children's TV viewing and computer use. (p. 389)

A. _______________

B. _______________

C. _______________

13. List several ways to help parents and children break the cycle of hostility between family members. (p. 389)

Parents:

A. _______________

B. _______________

Children:

A. _______________

B. _______________

Gender Typing

1. What is *gender typing?* (p. 390)

____

____

____

Gender-Stereotyped Beliefs and Behaviors

1. Preschoolers' gender stereotypes are (flexible / rigid). Explain your answer. (p. 391)

____

____

____

2. True or False: Most preschoolers believe that characteristics associated with each sex (for example, activities, clothes, hairstyles, and occupation) determine whether a person is male or female. (p. 391)

Biological Influences on Gender Typing

1. List four sex differences in play and personality traits that are widespread among mammalian species. (p. 391)

A. _______________ B. _______________

C. _______________ D. _______________

2. Eleanor Maccoby argues that _______________ affect human play styles, leading to rough, noisy movements among boys and calm, gentile actions among girls. (p. 391)

3. Girls exposed to high levels of androgens prenatally display (more / less) "masculine" behavior. (pp. 391–392)

Biology and Environment: David: A Boy Who Was Reared as a Girl

1. True or False: After sex reassignment surgery, Bruce—renamed Brenda—readily adopted feminine social and personality characteristics. (p. 392)
2. Explain how David Reimer's development confirms the impact of genetic sex and prenatal hormones on a person's sense of self as male or female. (p. 392)

   ____

   ____

3. What does David Reimer's childhood reveal about the importance of environmental influences on gender typing? (p. 392)

   ____

   ____

Environmental Influences on Gender Typing

1. Provide an example of how parents encourage gender-stereotyped beliefs and behavior in their children. (p. 393)

   ____

   ____

2. Of the two sexes, (girls / boys) are more clearly gender-stereotyped. Why might this be the case? (p. 393)

   ____

   ____

   ____

3. Provide an example of how preschool teachers contribute to children's gender-role learning. (p. 394)

   ____

   ____

4. Peer rejection is greater for (girls / boys) who frequently engage in "cross-gender" behavior. (p. 394)
5. Discuss the different styles of social influence promoted within gender-segregated peer groups. (p. 394)

   Boys: ____

   ____

   Girls: ____

   ____

6. Cite three factors that work together to sustain gender segregation and the gender typing that occurs within it. (p. 394)

   A. ____

   B. ____

   C. ____

7. How do TV and media influence children's endorsement of gender stereotypes? (p. 395)

   ____

   ____

   ____

Gender Identity

1. Define *gender identity,* and indicate how it is measured. (p. 395)

   A. ____

   ____

   B. ____

2. ____________________ refers to a type of gender identity in which the person scores highly on both masculine and feminine personality characteristics. (p. 395)

3. True or False: Children and adults with a feminine gender identity generally have higher self-esteem than individuals who identify as masculine or androgynous. Explain why or why not. (p. 395)

   ____

   ____

   ____

4. Contrast social learning and cognitive-developmental accounts of the emergence of gender identity. (p. 395)

   Social Learning: ____

   ____

   ____

   Cognitive-Developmental: ____

   ____

   ____

5. ____________________ refers to the understanding that sex is biologically based and remains the same even if clothing, hairstyles, and play activities change. (p. 395)

6. Match each stage in toddlers' mastering of *gender constancy* with its description. (pp. 395–396)

   _____ Gender labeling
   _____ Gender stability
   _____ Gender consistency

   A. Understanding that gender remains the same over time
   B. Realization that gender is not altered by superficial changes in clothing or activities
   C. Correct naming of one's own and others' sex

7. Is gender constancy responsible for children's gender-typed behavior? Why or why not? (p. 396)

   ____

   ____

   ____

8. Explain gender schema theory. (p. 396)

   ____

   ____

   ____

9. Define gender schemas, and explain how they influence gender-typed preferences and behavior. (p. 396)
   A. ____
   ____
   B. ____
   ____

10. How does gender-schematic thinking affect children's behavior? (p. 396)
   ____
   ____
   ____

Reducing Gender Stereotyping in Young Children

1. Cite three ways that parents and teachers can reduce gender stereotyping in young children. (p. 397)
   A. ____
   B. ____
   C. ____
   ____

Child Rearing and Emotional and Social Development

Styles of Child Rearing

1. Based on the research findings of Baumrind and others, cite three features that consistently differentiate between more and less effective child-rearing styles. (p. 398)
   A. ____
   B. ____
   C. ____

2. Match each child-rearing style with the appropriate description and associated child outcomes. (pp. 398–400)

Child-Rearing Style	Description	Associated Child Outcomes
_____ _____ *Uninvolved*	A. High acceptance and involvement, adaptive control techniques, and appropriate autonomy granting	1. Anxiety, low self-esteem and self-reliance, hostile reactions to frustration, high anger, dependence in girls, poor school performance
_____ _____ *Authoritative*	B. Warmth and acceptance combined with overindulgence or inattention	2. Poor emotional self-regulation, poor school achievement, antisocial behavior
_____ _____ *Permissive*	C. Low acceptance and involvement, little control, and general indifference to autonomy	3. Upbeat mood, self-control, persistence, cooperativeness, high self-esteem, academic success
_____ _____ *Authoritarian*	D. Low acceptance and involvement, high coercive control, and low autonomy granting	4. Impulsivity, disobedience, rebellion, dependent and nonachieving, antisocial behavior

3. (Authoritarian / Authoritative) parents engage in a subtle type of control called ______________ *control,* in which they intrude on and manipulate children's verbal expression, individuality, and attachments to parents. (p. 399)

4. Which child-rearing approach is the most successful, and why? (p. 400)

   A. ______________________________

   B. ______________________________

5. At its extreme, uninvolved parenting is a form of child maltreatment called ______________. (p. 400)

What Makes Authoritative Child Rearing Effective?

1. Cite four reasons that authoritative parenting is especially effective. (p. 400)

   A. ______________________________

   B. ______________________________

   C. ______________________________

   D. ______________________________

Cultural Variations

1. Describe how the parenting practices of the following cultural groups often differ from those of Caucasian Americans. (pp. 400–401)

   Chinese: ______________________________

   ____

   Hispanic, Asian Pacific Island, and Caribbean (of African and East Indian origin): ______________

   ____

   ____

   African-American: ______________________________

   ____

2. Cite several contextual factors that contribute to successful parenting. (p. 401)

   ____

   ____

Child Maltreatment

1. List and describe four forms of child maltreatment. (pp. 401–402)

   A. ______________________________

   B. ______________________________

   C. ______________________________

   D. ______________________________

2. (Parents / Strangers) commit more than 80 percent of abusive incidents. (p. 402)
3. True or False: Researchers have identified an "abusive" personality type. (p. 402)
4. List several parent, child, and family environment characteristics associated with an increased likelihood of abuse. (p. 402)

   Parent: ______________________________

   Child: ______________________________

   Family Environment: ______________________________

5. Cite two reasons that most abusive parents are isolated from supportive ties to their communities. (p. 403)

   A. ______________________________

   ____

   B. ______________________________

   ____

6. Societies that view violence as an appropriate way to solve problems set the stage for child abuse. These conditions (do / do not) exist in the United States and Canada. Explain your answer. (p. 403)

   ____

   ____

   ____

7. Summarize the consequences of child maltreatment for abused children. (pp. 403–404)

   ____

   ____

   ____

8. Discuss strategies for preventing child maltreatment in the family. (p. 404)

   ____

   ____

   ____

9. Explain how the Healthy Families America program works to reduce abuse and neglect. (pp. 404–405)

   ____

   ____

   ____

10. In child maltreatment cases, judges are often hesitant to remove the child from the family. List three reasons for their reluctance. (p. 405)

    A. ______________________________

    B. ______________________________

    C. ______________________________

ASK YOURSELF . . .

For *Ask Yourself* questions for this chapter, along with feedback on the accuracy of your answers, please log on to MyDevelopmentLab (for registration and access, please visit mydevelopmentlab.com or follow the instructions on page ix).

(1) Select the Multimedia Library.

(2) Choose the explore option.

(3) Find your chapter from the drop down box.

(4) Click find now.

(5) Complete questions and choose "Submit answers for grading" or "Clear answers" to start over.

SUGGESTED READINGS

Arsenio, W. F., & Lemerise, E. A. (2010). *Emotions, aggression, and morality in children: Bridging development and psychopathology.* Washington, DC: American Psychological Association. Presents a diverse range of topics on emotional development, including biological and environmental influences, the importance of empathy, early parent–child and peer relations, the development of morality and aggression, the long-term consequences of childhood aggression, and research-based interventions for aggressive children.

Hirsh-Pasek, K., Golinkoff, R. M., Berk, L. E., & Singer, D. G. (2009). *A mandate for playful learning in preschool: Presenting the evidence.* New York: Oxford University Press. Using the latest research on early child development, this book examines the importance of play for academic and social development. Although some parents and educators favor academic training over playtime, scientific evidence shows that unstructured free time and opportunities for play are ideal for fostering cognitive and social/emotional development in preschool-age children.

Perry, D. F., Knitzer, J., & Kaufmann, R. (Eds.). (2007). *Social and emotional health in early childhood: Building bridges between services and systems*. Baltimore, MD: Paul H. Brookes. A collection of chapters examining the link between social/emotional and cognitive development in young children. The book highlights the importance of social skills and emotional well-being for school readiness, peer relations, and favorable mental health across the school years.

CROSSWORD PUZZLE 10.1

Across

3. Actions that benefit another person without any expected reward for the self are known as ____________, or altruistic, behaviors.
5. Play that occurs near other children, with similar materials, but involves no interaction
7. Set of attributes, abilities, attitudes, and values that individuals believe define who they are (2 words, hyph.)
8. Aggression aimed at obtaining an object, privilege, or space with no intent to harm
9. Play that involves separate activities but exchange of toys and comments
10. A form of hostile aggression that does damage to another's peer relationships
12. Judgments we make about our own self-worth and the feelings associated with those judgments (2 words, hyph.)
13. Erikson regarded ____________ versus guilt as the critical psychological conflict of the preschool years.

Down

1. Feelings of concern or sorrow for another's plight
2. Activity involving unoccupied, onlooker behavior and solitary play
4. Aggression intended to harm another person
6. Play with others that is directed toward a common goal
9. Gender identity in which the person scores high on both masculine and feminine personality traits
11. ___________ problem solving: resolving conflicts in ways that are both acceptable to others and beneficial to the self

CROSSWORD PUZZLE 10.2

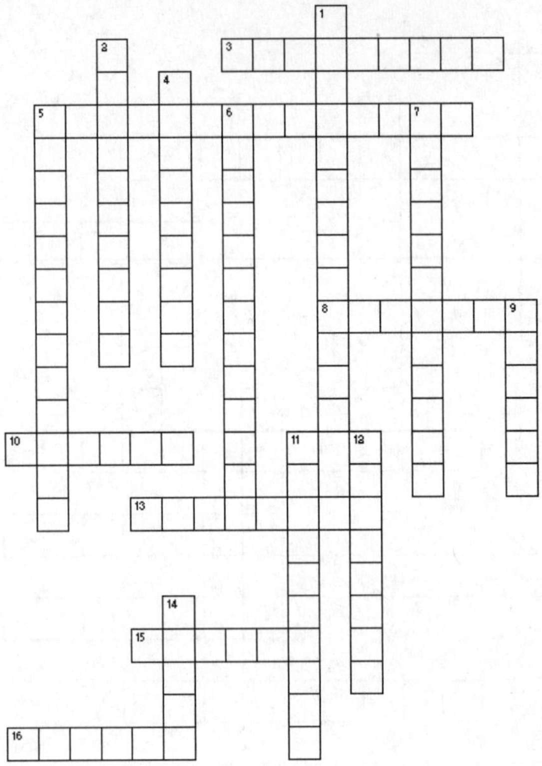

Across

3. Type of discipline that involves communicating the effects of the child's misbehavior on others
5. Matters of ___________ ___________: concerns that do not violate rights and are up to each individual, such as choice of friends or color of clothing (2 words)
8. Mild punishment involving removal of the child from the immediate setting until he/she is ready to behave appropriately (2 words)
10. Gender __________ theory: approach to gender typing that combines social learning and cognitive-developmental features
13. Gender _____________: image of oneself as relatively masculine or feminine in characteristics
15. ___________ conventions: customs determined solely by consensus, such as table manners
16. ___________ aggression: a form of hostile aggression that harms others through threats of physical aggression, name-calling, or hostile teasing

Down

1. Style of child rearing that involves high acceptance and involvement, adaptive control techniques, and appropriate autonomy granting
2. Style of child rearing that is high in acceptance but overindulging and inattentive, low in control, and lax rather than appropriate in autonomy granting
4. Gender ___________: understanding that sex remains the same even if outward appearance changes
5. __________ control: parental behaviors that intrude on and manipulate children's verbal expression, individuality, and attachment to parents
6. Style of child rearing that is low in acceptance and involvement, high in coercive control, and low in autonomy granting
7. ________-_________ styles: combinations of parenting behaviors that occur over a wide range of situations (2 words, hyph.)
9. Gender __________: the process of developing gender roles
11. Style of child rearing that combines low acceptance and involvement, little control, and indifference to autonomy granting
12. __________ aggression: a form of hostile aggression that harms others through physical injury to individuals or their property
14. ___________ imperatives: standards that protect people's rights and welfare

PRACTICE TEST #1

1. According to Erikson, the psychological conflict of the preschool years is __________ (p. 364)
   a. trust versus mistrust.
   b. initiative versus guilt.
   c. autonomy versus shame.
   d. industry versus inferiority.

2. Erikson regarded play as __________ (p. 364)
   a. a means through which young children learn about themselves and their social world.
   b. an idle use of time after age 4 or 5.
   c. a private inner life that is not accessible to others.
   d. a context in which young children practice representational schemes.

3. Preschoolers' self-concepts largely consist of characteristics, such as __________ (p. 365)
   a. shyness.
   b. physical appearance.
   c. helpfulness.
   d. family values.

4. Preschoolers usually rate their own ability to complete tasks as extremely high because they __________ (p. 366)
   a. have difficulty distinguishing between their desired and their actual competence.
   b. do not yet have a fully developed superego.
   c. have not yet experienced many setbacks or failures.
   d. are much better than they used to be at accomplishing tasks.

5. Chinese parents __________ (p. 366)
   a. believe that favorable self-esteem is crucial for healthy development.
   b. use storytelling to cultivate their child's individuality.
   c. use storytelling to guide their child toward socially responsible behavior.
   d. attribute a child's transgressions to spunk and assertiveness.

6. Preschoolers __________ (p. 368)
   a. cannot predict what a playmate expressing a certain emotion might do.
   b. can easily interpret situations that offer conflicting cues about how a person is feeling.
   c. cannot come up with effective ways to relieve others' negative feelings, such as hugging to reduce sadness.
   d. have an impressive ability to interpret, predict, and change others' feelings.

7. Lincoln covers his eyes when the villain appears during his favorite movie. Lincoln is using __________ (p. 369)
   a. empathy.
   b. emotional self-regulation.
   c. self-conscious awareness.
   d. altruism.

8. Eddie's parents repeatedly comment on his worth and his performance. Eddie is likely to experience __________ (p. 370)
   a. less pride after success.
   b. less shame after failure.
   c. more guilt after a transgression.
   d. less fear of the unknown.

9. Monica is sociable and assertive. Phoebe is shy and anxious. Monica is __________ (p. 371)
   a. less likely than Phoebe to help a friend in distress.
   b. less likely than Phoebe to display sympathetic concern.
   c. more likely than Phoebe to be overwhelmed by her feelings with faced with someone in need.
   d. more likely than Phoebe to share with a friend.

10. Charlie and Camdyn are playing with blocks. Charlie is building a spaceship. Camdyn is making a swimming pool. Although they are sitting near one another, they do not comment on each other's behavior or exchange blocks. Charlie and Camdyn are engaged in __________ play. (p. 372)
    a. nonsocial
    b. parallel
    c. associative
    d. cooperative

11. Macy is putting together a puzzle. She is engaged in __________ play. (p. 372)
    a. associative
    b. functional
    c. constructive
    d. make-believe

12. Winnie, a kindergartener, has a friendly, prosocial behavioral style. She will probably __________ (p. 375)
    a. make new friends easily.
    b. make few friends.
    c. spend a great deal of time in solitary play.
    d. prefer parallel to play to other forms of social interaction.

13. Children with peer difficulties __________ (p. 376)
    a. tend to be only children.
    b. request an explanation when they do not understand a peer's behavior.
    c. prefer solitary play over other forms of social interaction.
    d. attend selectively to social cues.

14. Accordingly to Freud, young children __________ (p. 378)
    a. adopt the moral standards of the other-sex parent.
    b. obey the superego to avoid identity confusion.
    c. identify with the same-sex parent.
    d. feel little guilt over minor transgressions.

15. With fearless, impulsive children, __________ (pp. 379–380)
    a. power assertion works best.
    b. mild, patient disciple tactics work best.
    c. requests, suggestions, and explanations are sufficient to prompt conscience development.
    d. gentle discipline has little impact.

16. Preschoolers are more likely to copy the prosocial actions of an adult who is __________ (p. 381)
    a. powerful.
    b. distant.
    c. inconsistent.
    d. male.

17. Which of the following children is the most likely to view spanking as a practice carried out with their best interests in mind? (p. 383)
    a. Kelly, a 3-year-old Caucasian-American girl
    b. Fenn, a 5-year-old Asian-American boy
    c. Molly, a 7-year-old Caucasian-American girl
    d. Jonathon, an 8-year-old African-American boy

18. Around age _____, children know that a person who expresses an insincere intention is lying. (p. 384)
    a. 2
    b. 4
    c. 6
    d. 8

19. Preschool children __________ (p. 385)
    a. cannot yet distinguish between moral imperatives and social conventions.
    b. consider violations of social conventions as more wrong than moral violations.
    c. tend to reason rigidly within the moral domain.
    d. tend to view not sharing as a more serious transgression than breaking a friend's toy.

20. Ron pushes Jane after Jane accidentally bumps into Ron. Ron is engaging in __________ aggression. (p. 385)
    a. proactive
    b. reactive
    c. relational
    d. indirect

21. Willow tells her friends that they should not speak to Maleena because she is poor. Willow is engaging in __________ aggression. (p. 386)
    a. reactive
    b. verbal
    c. relational
    d. physical

22. Preschool girls tend to play most often __________ (p. 391)
    a. with preschool boys.
    b. in large groups.
    c. in active, physical activities.
    d. in pairs.

23. The case of David Reimer confirms the __________ (p. 392)
    a. predominant influence of social experience on gender.
    b. close emotional connection of same-sex siblings.
    c. impact of genetic sex and prenatal hormones on a person's sense of sex and gender.
    d. fact that males are especially uncomfortable with gender stereotypes.

24. Parents tend to give their sons toys that stress __________ (p. 393)
    a. nurturance.
    b. competition.
    c. cooperation.
    d. dependence.

25. A child who identifies him or herself as affectionate, cheerful, competitive, and self-sufficient has a(n) __________ gender identity. (p. 395)
    a. androgynous
    b. masculine
    c. feminine
    d. permissive

26. When Gavin's brother wears a skirt to the Scottish festival, Gavin knows that his brother is still a boy. Gavin has developed a sense of gender __________ (p. 395)
    a. identity.
    b. constancy.
    c. orientation.
    d. stereotyping.

27. The most successful child rearing style is __________ (p. 398)
    a. uninvolved.
    b. permissive.
    c. authoritarian.
    d. authoritative.

28. Dennis is highly defiant and aggressive. When frustrated, he reacts with hostility. Dennis probably has parents who use a(n) __________ child-rearing style. (p. 399)
    a. uninvolved
    b. permissive
    c. authoritarian
    d. authoritative

29. A family characteristic strongly associated with child abuse is __________ (p. 403)
    a. partner abuse.
    b. exposure to violent TV.
    c. excessive reliance on nonfamily child care.
    d. a permissive child-rearing style.

30. The majority of abusive and neglectful parents __________ (p. 404)
    a. live in extended-family households.
    b. are isolated from social supports.
    c. have a permissive child-rearing style.
    d. have sick or premature children.

PRACTICE TEST #2

1. According to Erikson, the positive outcome of early childhood is __________ (p. 364)
   a. autonomy.
   b. industry.
   c. a sense of purposefulness.
   d. a strong gender identity.

2. For Erikson, the negative outcome of early childhood is __________ (p. 364)
   a. an overly strict superego.
   b. the development of mistrust.
   c. inferiority.
   d. isolation.

3. Four-year-old Aliyah is asked to describe herself. Which of the following is she most likely to say? (p. 365)
   a. "I am helpful."
   b. "I am shy."
   c. "I'm not mean."
   d. "I have two cats."

4. Which of the following children is most likely to describe himself as "helpful"? (p. 365)
   a. Matthew, an 8-year-old boy
   b. Bennie, a 3-year-old girl
   c. Fatima, a 4-year-old girl
   d. Joe, a 3-year-old boy

5. The more parents label emotions, the __________ (p. 365)
   a. fewer "emotion words" children use.
   b. fewer explanations for behavior they provide.
   c. better developed children's emotional understanding.
   d. more confused preschoolers are when asked to judge how others are feeling.

6. Compared to Irish-American parents, Chinese parents __________ (p. 366)
   a. downplay the seriousness of transgressions in stories.
   b. tell more stories about children's misdeeds.
   c. tell stories that cast the child's shortcomings in a positive light.
   d. tell more stories to promote self-esteem.

7. When parents intervene in sibling disputes by reasoning and negotiating, __________ (p. 369)
   a. they inadvertently contribute to sibling rivalry.
   b. the more often the siblings fight.
   c. they prevent the children from solving their own problems.
   d. the more often the children refer to their sibling's perspective.

8. Phobias __________ (p. 370)
   a. are sometimes linked to family problems and require counseling to reduce them.
   b. usually diminish without treatment as the child's capacity for emotional self-regulation improves.
   c. occur in approximately 60 percent of preschool-age children.
   d. probably stem from a fear of separation and can be reduced by warm encouragement.

9. When parents focus on how to improve performance, __________ (p. 370)
   a. children tend to give up easily on difficult tasks.
   b. children experience self-conscious emotions intensely.
   c. they induce moderate, adaptive levels of shame and pride.
   d. children develop feelings of personal inadequacy.

10. Jenny and Jack are playing in the sandbox. Jenny is using funnels to sift sand. Jack is "baking" a pie. They comment on one another's behavior and exchange toys. Jenny and Jack are engaged in __________ play. (p. 372)
    a. nonsocial
    b. parallel
    c. associative
    d. cooperative

11. Billy and Belinda are playing house. Billy is pretending to be the dad and Belinda is pretending to be the baby. Billy and Belinda are engaged in __________ play. (p. 372)
    a. nonsocial
    b. parallel
    c. associative
    d. cooperative

12. Social maturity in early childhood __________ (p. 375)
    a. tends to be higher in boys than girls.
    b. contributes to later academic performance.
    c. predicts favorable peer relationships but has no impact on academic performance.
    d. drops slightly as children transition from preschool to kindergarten.

13. Preschoolers whose parents frequently arrange informal peer play activities __________ (p. 377)
    a. tend to be more socially skilled.
    b. tend to have smaller peer networks.
    c. learn to value popularity above social competence.
    d. have difficulty making friends on their own.

14. Freud believed that moral development is largely complete by __________ (p. 378)
    a. birth.
    b. 1 to 2 years.
    c. 3 to 4 years.
    d. 5 to 6 years.

15. When Mason pushes his sister while she is walking, his mother says, "If you keep pushing her, she'll fall down and cry." Mason's mother is using __________ discipline. (p. 379)
    a. authoritarian
    b. inductive
    c. operant
    d. permissive

16. According to the cognitive-developmental view, preschoolers can distinguish moral imperatives from social conventions because they __________ (p. 384)
    a. actively think about social rules.
    b. have been reinforced for moral behavior.
    c. have likely been punished for committing moral transgressions.
    d. regularly observe adults modeling social rules.

17. Compared with Caucasian-American parents, African-American parents __________ (p. 383)
    a. are often rejecting of the child when delivering physical punishment.
    b. are often highly agitated when delivering physical punishment.
    c. approve of mild physical punishment aimed at helping children become responsible adults.
    d. reject spanking and other forms of harsh punishment.

18. Preschoolers consider violations of __________ as more wrong than violations of __________ (pp. 384–385)
    a. social conventions; moral imperatives.
    b. moral imperatives; matters of personal choice.
    c. matters of personal choice; individual rights.
    d. social conventions; matters of personal choice.

19. Renae, age 4, is most likely to select which of the following as the most wrong? (p. 385)
    a. eating on the floor
    b. lying about breaking a friend's bicycle
    c. eating ice cream with one's fingers
    d. going to school in one's pajamas

20. Jade calls Samantha a "big fat hog." Jade is engaging in __________ aggression. (p. 385)
    a. physical
    b. direct
    c. verbal
    d. relational

21. After arguing over a toy, Inez refuses to speak to Ruth. Inez is engaging in __________ aggression. (p. 386)
    a. physical
    b. indirect
    c. verbal
    d. direct

22. Most 3- to 6-year olds __________ (p. 391)
    a. are reluctant to be friends with a child who violates gender stereotypes.
    b. would say that it is okay for boys to play with Barbie dolls.
    c. have flexible gender-based beliefs and behaviors.
    d. would say that girls can be firefighters.

23. David Reimer's gender reassignment failed because __________ (p. 392)
    a. his male biology overwhelmingly demanded a consistent sexual identity.
    b. the surgery changed his gender identity from masculine to androgynous.
    c. he was not mentally stable and secure in his sexual identity.
    d. the androgen hormones did not sufficiently masculinize his body.

24. The more preschoolers play with same-sex peers, the __________ (p. 394)
    a. less gender-typed their toy choices.
    b. more accepting they become of gender-aschematic children.
    c. more gender-typed their behavior becomes.
    d. more responsive they become to other-sex adults.

25. Someone with a feminine identity scores high on which of the following personality traits in self-ratings? (p. 395)
    a. ambitious
    b. affectionate
    c. competitive
    d. self-sufficient

26. Bonnie is offered a toy truck to play with. She asks herself, "Do I like this toy?" She decides that she does, and she plays with the truck. Bonnie is a(n) __________ child. (p. 396)
    a. androgynous
    b. gender-schematic
    c. masculine
    d. gender-aschematic

27. Aaron's parents make few or no demands. They permit Aaron to make many decisions before he is ready. Aaron's parents use a(n) __________ style of child rearing. (p. 399)
    a. authoritative
    b. authoritarian
    c. permissive
    d. uninvolved

28. Joyce's parents are emotionally detached and withdrawn. They make few demands and are indifferent to Joyce's point of view. Joyce's parents use a(n) __________ style of child rearing. (p. 400)
    a. authoritative
    b. authoritarian
    c. permissive
    d. uninvolved

29. Hispanic and Asian Pacific Island families typically combine firm insistence on respect for parental authority with __________ (p. 401)
    a. permissiveness in all other areas.
    b. high parental warmth.
    c. psychological coercion.
    d. harsh punishment for moral transgressions.

30. The most common form of reported child maltreatment is __________ (p. 402)
    a. physical abuse.
    b. emotional abuse.
    c. sexual abuse.
    d. neglect.

CHAPTER 11
PHYSICAL DEVELOPMENT IN MIDDLE CHILDHOOD

BRIEF CHAPTER SUMMARY

Physical growth is slow and regular throughout middle childhood, although large individual and ethnic variations exist. Because of improved health and nutrition, children in industrialized nations are growing larger and reaching physical maturity earlier than their ancestors.

In middle childhood, bones continue to lengthen and broaden, and permanent teeth replace primary teeth. In the brain, white matter increases, especially in the prefrontal cortex. Gray matter declines as a result of synaptic pruning, and the accompanying reorganization and selection of brain circuits result in more efficient information processing.

Although children from economically advantaged homes are at their healthiest in middle childhood, health problems do occur. Vision and hearing difficulties, malnutrition, obesity, bedwetting, asthma, and unintentional injuries are the most frequent health concerns of the school years. Overweight and obesity have increased dramatically in both industrialized and developing nations, especially in the United States. Family-based interventions aimed at changing parents' and children's eating patterns and lifestyles are the most effective approaches to treating childhood obesity.

Growth in body size and muscle strength supports improved motor coordination in middle childhood. Gains in flexibility, balance, agility, force, and reaction time underlie improvements in children's gross-motor skills. Fine-motor coordination also increases. Children's writing becomes more legible, and their drawings show greater organization, more detail, and representation of depth. As in younger children, marked individual differences in motor capacities are evident in middle childhood.

The physical activities of school-age children reflect advances in the quality of their play. Child-organized games with rules become common and support emotional and social development. Increasingly, children participate in adult-organized youth sports. Some researchers are concerned that this trend may have an adverse effect on development. Rough-and-tumble play and the establishment of dominance hierarchies are aspects of children's interaction that reflect our evolutionary past. Wide individual differences in athletic performance exist, influenced by both genetic and environmental factors. Physical education classes help ensure that all children have access to the benefits of regular exercise and play. Many experts believe that schools should offer more frequent physical education classes and should shift their focus to enjoyable, informal games and individual exercise. In recent years, school recess has diminished to allow more time for academics, but research findings indicate that regular, unstructured recess fosters children's health and competence—physically, academically, and socially.

LEARNING OBJECTIVES

After reading this chapter, you should be able to:

11.1 Describe changes in body size, proportions, and skeletal maturity during middle childhood, noting secular trends in physical growth. (pp. 412–414)

11.2 Describe brain development in middle childhood, including the influence of neurotransmitters and hormones. (pp. 414–415)

11.3 Explain the causes and consequences of serious nutritional problems in middle childhood, giving special attention to obesity. (pp. 416–422)

11.4 Describe common vision and hearing problems in middle childhood. (p. 422)

11.5 Discuss factors that contribute to nocturnal enuresis and to asthma, noting how these health problems can be reduced. (pp. 422–424)

11.6 Describe changes in the occurrence of unintentional injuries during middle childhood, and cite effective interventions. (pp. 424–425)

11.7 Summarize ways parents and teachers can encourage good health practices in school-age children. (pp. 425, 427)

11.8 Cite major changes in gross- and fine-motor development during middle childhood. (pp. 427–429)

11.9 Describe individual differences in motor performance during middle childhood. (p. 430)

11.10 Discuss the quality of children's play during middle childhood, and identify features of children's physical activity that reflect our evolutionary past. (pp. 430–432)

11.11 Discuss research on physical education, and cite steps that schools can take to promote physical fitness in middle childhood. (pp. 432–434)

STUDY QUESTIONS

Body Growth

1. During middle childhood, children continue to add _____ inches in height and _____ pounds in weight each year. (p. 412)
2. Describe sex differences in body growth and proportions during middle childhood. (p. 412)

___

___

___

___

Worldwide Variations in Body Size

1. True or False: Growth norms in countries throughout the world reveal few cultural differences in body size. (p. 413)
2. List hereditary and environmental factors that account for differences in physical size among children around the world. (p. 413)

   Hereditary: ___

   ___

   Environmental: ___

   ___

Secular Trends in Physical Growth

1. What are secular trends in physical growth? (p. 413)

   ___

2. Summarize the factors responsible for current secular growth patterns. (p. 413)

   ___

   ___

   ___

Skeletal Growth

1. Describe advances in bone, muscle, and ligament growth during middle childhood. What unusual ability is evident during this time? (p. 414)

   Bone: ______________________________

   Muscle: ______________________________

   Ligament: ______________________________

   Ability: ______________________________

2. Between ages ___ and ___, all primary teeth are lost and replaced by permanent ones, with (boys / girls) losing their teeth slightly earlier than (boys / girls). (p. 414)

3. True or False: Over 50 percent of American children have some tooth decay. (p. 414)

4. One-third of school-age children suffer from ______________________, a condition in which the upper and lower teeth do not meet properly. List two causes of this condition. (p. 414)

   A. ______________________________

   B. ______________________________

Brain Development

1. True or False: The weight of the brain increases only 10 percent during middle childhood and adolescence. (p. 414)

2. Describe changes in white and gray matter during middle childhood. (p. 414)

   White matter: ______________________________

   ____

   Gray matter: ______________________________

   ____

3. Briefly summarize changes in neurotransmitters and hormones during middle childhood, noting their effects on brain functioning. (pp. 414–415)

   Neurotransmitters: ______________________________

   ____

   ____

   Hormones: ______________________________

   ____

   ____

Common Health Problems

1. __________________ is a powerful predictor of poor health during middle childhood, due to lack of health insurance and access to medical care. (p. 415)

Nutrition

1. The percentage of children who eat dinner with their families (drops / rises) sharply between ages 9 and 14. Cite the benefits of family dinnertimes. (p. 416)

   ____

   ____

2. What do school-age children say is a major barrier to healthy eating? (p. 416)

____

3. Summarize the effects of prolonged malnutrition that become apparent by middle childhood. (p. 416)

____

____

____

4. Malnutrition that persists from infancy or early childhood into the school years usually leads to (permanent / temporary) physical and mental deficits. (p. 416)

Overweight and Obesity

1. *Obesity* is a greater-than-______-percent increase over healthy weight, based on body mass index—a ratio of weight to height associated with body fat. (p. 416)
2. Obesity rates are increasing (slowly / rapidly) in developing countries. What factors are responsible for this trend? (p. 417)

____

____

3. True or False: With the transition to adolescence, most overweight children become normal-weight, and only about 40 percent of obese and overweight young people continue to be overweight in adulthood. (p. 417)
4. Circle the health problems in the following list that are associated with obesity. (p. 417)

high blood pressure

cerebral palsy

circulatory problems

deficient immunity

kwashiorkor

insulin resistance

respiratory difficulties

decreased cognitive skills

sleep disorders

type 2 diabetes

5. True or False: Heredity is the single most important contributing factor to childhood obesity. Explain your answer. (p. 417)

____

____

6. (Low-SES / Middle-SES) children are more likely to be overweight. Cite three factors that contribute to this trend. (p. 417)

A. ____

B. ____

C. ____

7. True or False: Children who were undernourished in their early years are at risk for later excessive weight gain. (p. 418)

8. Explain how parenting practices contribute to children's weight problems. (p. 418)

____

____

____

9. Describe two maladaptive eating habits that are often found in obese children. (p. 418)

A. ____

____

B. ____

____

10. Describe the relationship between TV viewing and obesity. (pp. 418–419)

____

____

____

11. Provide an example illustrating how the broader food environment affects the incidence of obesity. (p. 418)

____

____

12. Cite several emotional and social consequences of childhood obesity. (p. 419)

____

____

____

13. Describe the characteristics of effective interventions for childhood obesity. (pp. 420–421)

____

____

____

14. Provide an example of a strategy that schools can use to help reduce childhood obesity. (p. 422)

____

____

____

Social Issues: Health: The Obesity Epidemic: How Americans Became the Heaviest People in the World

1. ________ percent of American children and ________ percent of adults are overweight or obese. (p. 420)

2. Place an X next to each factor that has contributed to the widespread rapid weight gain in Western nations. (pp. 420–421)

_____ Fad diets
_____ Availability of cheap commercial fat and sugar
_____ Portion supersizing
_____ Declining rates of physical activity
_____ Increasingly busy lives
_____ Lack of access to high-quality diet products
_____ Social acceptance of overweight role models
_____ Snacking between meals

3. Cite six suggestions for combating obesity at the societal level. (p. 421)

   A. ______________________________

   B. ______________________________

   C. ______________________________

   D. ______________________________

   E. ______________________________

   F. ______________________________

Vision and Hearing

1. The most common vision problem of middle childhood is _______________, or nearsightedness. (p. 422)
2. Cite evidence indicating that both heredity and environment contribute to *myopia.* (p. 422)

   Heredity: ______________________________

   ____

   Environment: ______________________________

   ____

3. True or False: Repeated ear infections put children at risk for hearing loss. (p. 422)

Bedwetting

1. Ten percent of American school-age children suffer from ______________________________, or bedwetting during the night. (p. 422)
2. In the majority of cases, *nocturnal enuresis* is caused by (biological / environmental) factors. (p. 422)
3. Describe the most effective treatment for enuresis. (p. 423)

   ____

   ____

Illnesses

1. What accounts for the somewhat higher rate of illness during the first two years of elementary school? (p. 423)

   ____

2. The most common chronic illness, representing the most frequent cause of school absence and childhood hospitalization, is ______________________. (p. 423)
3. List characteristics of children who are at greatest risk for asthma. (p. 423)

   ____

   ____

   ____

4. Besides physical discomfort, what other negative consequences are associated with chronic childhood illness? (p. 423)

   ____

   ____

   ____

5. List five interventions for chronically ill children and their families that foster improvements in family interactions and child adjustment. (p. 424)

   A. ______________________________

   B. ______________________________

   C. ______________________________

   D. ______________________________

   E. ______________________________

Unintentional Injuries

1. List two environmental factors linked to high injury rates in childhood and adolescence. (p. 424)

   A. ______________________________

   B. ______________________________

2. What is the leading cause of injury during the school years? (p. 424)

   ____

3. Cite three characteristics of effective safety education programs. (p. 424)

   A. ______________________________

   B. ______________________________

   C. ______________________________

4. What simple safety precaution leads to a 25 percent reduction in risk of head injury? (p. 424)

   ____

5. Describe characteristics of children who are most at risk for injury in middle childhood. (p. 425)

   ____

   ____

   ____

Health Education

1. Why is the school-age period especially important for fostering healthy lifestyles? (p. 425)

   ____

   ____

   ____

2. List three reasons why efforts to impart health concepts to school-age children often have little impact on their behavior. (p. 425)

   A. ______________________________

   B. ______________________________

   C. ______________________________

3. Cite four strategies for fostering healthy lifestyles in school-age children. (p. 427)

   A. ______________________________

   B. ______________________________

   C. ______________________________

   D. ______________________________

Social Issues: Education: Children's Understanding of Health and Illness

1. Trace changes in children's understanding of health and illness from preschool into adolescence. (p. 426)

   Preschool and early school age (3- to 8-year-olds): ______________________________

   Older school age (9- to 10-year-olds): ______________________________

   Early adolescence (11- to 14-year-olds): ______________________________

2. Describe factors that affect children's understanding of health and illness. (p. 426)

3. Provide an example of how education can help children develop an accurate appreciation of disease transmission and prevention. (p. 426)

Motor Development and Play

Gross-Motor Development

1. List gains in four basic motor capacities that support improvements in gross-motor skills during middle childhood. (p. 428)

   A. ______________________________

   B. ______________________________

   C. ______________________________

   D. ______________________________

2. Explain how more efficient information processing contributes to the improved motor performance of school-age children. (p. 428)

Fine-Motor Development

1. Describe typical gains in writing and drawing during middle childhood. (p. 429)

   Writing: ____

   ____

   Drawing: ____

   ____

Individual Differences in Motor Skills

1. Discuss the influence of socioeconomic status on children's motor development. (p. 430)

   ____

   ____

   ____

2. In middle childhood, (boys / girls) are more skilled at handwriting, drawing, and gross-motor capacities that depend on balance and agility, while (girls / boys) excel at all other gross-motor skills, especially throwing and kicking. How do environmental factors contribute to these differences? (p. 430)

   ____

   ____

3. List two strategies that can help raise girls' participation, self-confidence, and sense of fair treatment in athletics. (p. 430)

   A. ____

   B. ____

Games with Rules

1. What cognitive capacity permits the transition to rule-oriented games during middle childhood? (p. 430)

   ____

2. Explain how child-invented games contribute to emotional and social development. (p. 430)

   ____

   ____

   ____

Adult-Organized Youth Sports

1. Compared with past generations, school-age children today spend less time gathering informally on sidewalks and in playgrounds. Explain why. (p. 431)

   ____

   ____

2. Participation on community athletic teams (is / is not) associated with increased self-esteem and social competence. (p. 431)

3. Cite four criticisms of adult-organized youth sports. (p. 431)

   A. ______________________________

   B. ______________________________

   C. ______________________________

   D. ______________________________

4. Explain four ways to ensure that organized sports provide positive, developmentally appropriate experiences for children. (p. 431)

   A. ______________________________

   ____

   B. ______________________________

   ____

   C. ______________________________

   ____

   D. ______________________________

   ____

Shadows of Our Evolutionary Past

1. ______________________________ is a form of peer interaction involving friendly chasing and play-fighting. (p. 431)

2. Describe sex differences in *rough-and-tumble play.* (pp. 431–432)

   ____

   ____

3. Explain how rough-and-tumble play assists children in establishing a *dominance hierarchy,* and note how this is adaptive for peer relations. (p. 432)

   A. ______________________________

   ____

   B. ______________________________

   ____

Physical Education

1. True or False: Nearly 90 percent of U.S. elementary schools have daily physical education. (pp. 432–433)

2. What kinds of activities should physical education classes emphasize to help the largest number of children develop active and healthy lifestyles? (p. 433)

   ____

   ____

3. List three benefits of being physically fit in childhood. (p. 434)

   A. ______________________________

   B. ______________________________

   C. ______________________________

Social Issues: Education: School Recess—A Time to Play, a Time to Learn

1. The amount of time that U.S. schoolchildren spend at recess has (increased / decreased) in recent years. (p. 433)
2. Discuss the physical, academic, and social benefits of recess periods for school-age children. (p. 433)

   Physical: ____

   ____

   Academic: ____

   ____

   Social: ____

   ____

ASK YOURSELF . . .

For *Ask Yourself* questions for this chapter, along with feedback on the accuracy of your answers, please log on to MyDevelopmentLab (for registration and access, please visit mydevelopmentlab.com or follow the instructions on page ix).

(1) Select the Multimedia Library.

(2) Choose the explore option.

(3) Find your chapter from the drop down box.

(4) Click find now.

(5) Complete questions and choose "Submit answers for grading" or "Clear answers" to start over.

SUGGESTED READINGS

Green, K. (2010). *Key themes in youth sports*. New York: Routledge. Using a multidisciplinary approach, this book examines the effects of sports, leisure, and exercise on child and adolescent development. The author also addresses public concerns over contemporary youth sports.

Heinberg, L. J., & Thompson, J. K. (2009). *Obesity in youth: Causes, consequences, and cures.* Washington, DC: American Psychological Association. Presents leading research on the obesity epidemic among American children, including genetic and environmental contributions; psychological and social consequences, such as poor body image and peer rejection; treatment options; and strategies for preventing overweight and obesity.

Hyder, A. A., Peden, M., Branche, C., Ozanne-Smith, J., & Rivara, F. (2009). *World report on child injury prevention.* Geneva: World Health Organization. Using data collected by the WHO and UNICEF, this book presents up-to-date research on child injury rates throughout the world, risk and protective factors, the importance of public policy, and the effectiveness of existing interventions. Recommendations for preventing common childhood injuries are also provided.

CROSSWORD PUZZLE 11.1

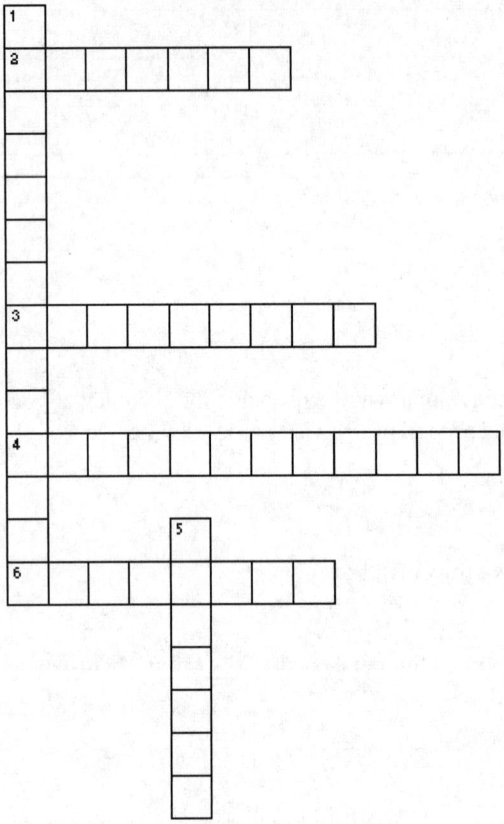

Across

2. A greater-than-20-percent increase over healthy weight, based on sex, age, and physical build
3. ____________ hierarchy: stable ordering of group members that predicts who will win when conflict arises
4. Condition in which the upper and lower teeth do not meet properly
6. Nocturnal ____________: repeated bedwetting during the night

Down

1. ________-_____-____________ play: a form of peer interaction involving friendly chasing and play-fighting (3 words, hyph.)
5. __________ trends in physical growth refer to changes in body size from one generation to the next.

PRACTICE TEST #1

1. At age 6, the average North American child is _____ feet tall. (p. 412)
   a. 3
   b. 3¼
   c. 3½
   d. 4

2. During middle childhood, the bones of the body __________ (p. 414)
   a. narrow.
   b. are firmly attached to the ligaments.
   c. lengthen and broaden.
   d. become flexible.

3. Malocclusion can be caused by __________ (p. 414)
   a. sitting too close to the television.
   b. finger sucking.
   c. wearing braces.
   d. tooth decay.

4. Children without health insurance are __________ as likely to have unmet dental needs as children with insurance. (p. 414)
   a. half
   b. just
   c. twice
   d. three times

5. The weight of the brain increases by _____ percent during middle childhood. (p. 414)
   a. 5
   b. 10
   c. 15
   d. 20

6. When neurotransmitters are not present in appropriate balances, children __________ (p. 415)
   a. may suffer serious developmental problems.
   b. are at-risk for early puberty.
   c. rapidly lose gray matter.
   d. compensate by producing more white matter.

7. Children say that a major barrier to healthy eating is the __________ (p. 416)
   a. lack of flavor in healthy foods.
   b. ready availability of unhealthy options.
   c. lack of availability of healthy foods in school lunches.
   d. lack of availability of healthy foods in their homes.

8. In research focusing on school-age children from middle- to high-SES families, insufficient dietary iron and folate predicted __________ (p. 416)
   a. hyperactivity in boys.
   b. slightly lower mental test performance.
   c. rapid weight gain.
   d. severe mood swings in girls.

9. In a longitudinal study of more than 1,000 U.S. children, overweight preschoolers were __________ times more likely than their normal weight peers to be overweight at age 12. (p. 417)
   a. two
   b. three
   c. four
   d. five

10. Portion supersizing __________ (p. 420)
    a. leads consumers to view huge portions as normal and appropriate.
    b. has been eliminated in many restaurants to help combat the obesity epidemic.
    c. prompts children to eat faster and chew their food less thoroughly.
    d. prompts children to eat smaller "child-sized" meals because the adult portions are so large.

11. Worldwide, myopia occurs far more frequently in __________ than in __________ populations. (p. 422)
    a. nonindustrialized; industrialized
    b. Caucasian; Asian
    c. Asian; Caucasian
    d. poor; wealthy

12. The most effective treatment for nocturnal enuresis is __________ (p. 422)
    a. consistent punishment for bedwetting.
    b. antidepressant drugs that reduce the amount of urine produced.
    c. gradual training of the muscles that govern urination.
    d. a urine alarm that wakes the child at the first sign of dampness.

13. Most school absences can be traced to __________ (p. 423)
    a. colds and flu viruses.
    b. a few students with chronic health problems.
    c. parental neglect.
    d. a lack of sleep.

14. Which of the following children is at greatest risk for asthma? (p. 423)
    a. Beth, who lives in an extended-family household
    b. Maecy, who lives in a rural community
    c. Lamar, who is African American
    d. Beni, who is Asian

15. In the United States, the leading cause of injury from middle childhood to adolescence is motor vehicle accidents, with __________ next in line. (p. 424)
    a. bicycle accidents
    b. aggressive contact sports
    c. pedestrian injuries
    d. physical abuse

16. Wearing protective helmets while bicycling, in-line skating, skateboarding or using scooters leads to a _____ percent reduction in head injuries. (p. 424)
    a. 15
    b. 25
    c. 35
    d. 45

17. Efforts to impart health concepts to school-age children __________ (p. 425)
    a. lead to improvements in overall health and nutrition.
    b. have been hampered by a lack of funding for schools.
    c. have little impact on behavior.
    d. often lead to anxiety over the possibility of becoming seriously ill.

18. School-age children may conclude that sneezing on someone can cause cancer because they __________ (p. 426)
    a. readily generalize from their knowledge of familiar diseases to less familiar ones.
    b. do not yet view illness from a biological perspective.
    c. tend to suggest moral causes for suffering.
    d. cannot yet name many internal organs or view them as an interconnected system.

19. Teaching school-age children about health concepts can be difficult because __________ (p. 425)
    a. they tend to be overly concerned about getting sick.
    b. they do not grasp biological explanations for health and illness.
    c. much health information is contradicted by other sources.
    d. most schools lack the resources for health education.

20. Along with body growth, __________ plays a vital role in improved motor performance during middle childhood. (p. 428)
    a. concern with fitness
    b. more efficient information processing
    c. social problem solving
    d. the dominance hierarchy

21. Six-year-old Joseph will probably have the most success at which of the following sports or games? (p. 428)
    a. baseball
    b. basketball
    c. kickball
    d. football

22. At first children's writing is large because they __________ (p. 429)
    a. make strokes with their wrists.
    b. make strokes with their fingers.
    c. have difficulty reading small print.
    d. make strokes with their arms.

23. Children whose parents enjoy physical exercise tend to __________ (p. 430)
    a. be more skilled.
    b. be excessively competitive.
    c. enjoy it less.
    d. play more child-invented games.

24. Boys outperform girls in __________ (p. 430)
    a. hopping.
    b. kicking.
    c. drawing.
    d. handwriting.

25. Child-invented games __________ (p. 430)
    a. permit children to try out different styles of cooperating and competing.
    b. typically involve contests of individual ability.
    c. are less important for emotional and social development than adult-organized youth sports.
    d. generally involve an element of personal risk.

26. Compared to past generations, children today __________ (p. 431)
    a. engage in more spontaneous play.
    b. engage in more child-invented games.
    c. play more adult-organized sports.
    d. play fewer adult-organized sports.

27. In middle childhood, rough-and-tumble play accounts for about _____ percent of free-play behavior. (p. 432)
    a. 3
    b. 5
    c. 10
    d. 25

28. A play behavior that limits aggression in childhood but becomes a context for hostility in adolescence is __________ play. (p. 432)
    a. solitary
    b. rough-and-tumble
    c. functional
    d. parallel

29. Recess is one of the few remaining contexts devoted to __________ (p. 433)
    a. child-organized games.
    b. minimizing sex differences in play.
    c. adult-organized sports.
    d. rough-and-tumble play.

30. Physical education that emphasizes training in competitive sports __________ (p. 433)
    a. is especially beneficial for overweight children.
    b. is more effective at promoting physical well-being than informal games.
    c. leads to significant gains in perspective-taking skills.
    d. is unlikely to reach the least physically fit children.

PRACTICE TEST #2

1. During the school years, children add about _____ pounds in weight each year. (p. 412)
   a. 2
   b. 3
   c. 5
   d. 7

2. After age 8, girls accumulate __________ at a faster rate than boys. (p. 413)
   a. muscle
   b. fat
   c. white matter
   d. gray matter

3. Secular gains in physical growth are smaller for low-income children because they __________ (p. 413)
   a. tend to have poorer diets and are more likely to suffer from growth-stunting illnesses.
   b. have lower rates of obesity than higher-income children.
   c. often come from shorter ethnic groups.
   d. are frequently born with thyroxine deficiencies.

4. Mason lost his first tooth. If Mason is a typical child, it was a(n) __________ (p. 414)
   a. molar.
   b. upper back tooth.
   c. cuspid.
   d. lower front tooth.

5. White matter consists mostly of __________ (p. 414)
   a. myelinated nerve fibers.
   b. neurons and supportive material.
   c. synapses.
   d. sex hormones.

6. As children acquire more complex abilities, __________ (p. 414)
   a. the number of myelinated neurons decreases.
   b. stimulated neurons increase in synaptic connections.
   c. the corpus callosum shrinks.
   d. neural fibers become less elaborate and myelinated.

7. The percentage of children who eat meals with their families __________ (p. 416)
   a. increases sharply in middle childhood.
   b. stabilizes in middle childhood.
   c. drops sharply between ages 9 and 14.
   d. is highest in affluent families.

8. A BMI above the _____ percentile for a child's age and sex is considered overweight. (p. 416)
   a. 55th
   b. 65th
   c. 75th
   d. 85th

9. Which of the following has led to increasing obesity rates in developing countries? (p. 417)
   a. environmental pollution
   b. lack of funding for health education
   c. diets high in milk and cheese products
   d. diets high in meat and refined foods

10. The 1970s saw two massive changes in the U.S. food economy that have encouraged widespread rapid weight gain, the mass production of __________ and the importation of __________. (p. 420)
    a. high-fructose corn syrup; palm oil
    b. sugar; corn oil
    c. artificial sweeteners; corn oil
    d. soft drinks; sugar

11. School-age children with low birth weights show an especially high rate of __________ (p. 422)
    a. malnutrition.
    b. otitis media.
    c. myopia.
    d. nocturnal enuresis.

12. In the school-age population, otitis media is __________ (p. 422)
    a. more frequent than in infancy.
    b. less frequent than in early childhood.
    c. extremely rare.
    d. a frequent cause of hospitalization.

13. Ten percent of U.S. school children suffer from __________ (p. 422)
    a. being overweight.
    b. obesity.
    c. myopia.
    d. nocturnal enuresis.

14. Of the following chronic childhood illnesses, which is the most frequent cause of school absence and childhood hospitalization? (p. 423)
    a. diabetes
    b. influenza
    c. asthma
    d. type 2 diabetes

15. By middle childhood, the greatest risk-takers tend to be those __________ (p. 424)
    a. whose parents do not act as safety-conscious models.
    b. who suffer from low self-esteem and depression.
    c. who are athletically skilled.
    d. whose parents place a high value competition.

16. Compared with girls, boys __________ (p. 425)
    a. engage in less risk-taking behavior.
    b. pay less attention to injury risk cues.
    c. judge risky play activities as more likely to result in injury.
    d. engage in about the same amount of risk-taking behavior.

17. In middle childhood, health __________ (p. 425)
    a. becomes an important goal for children.
    b. is seldom an important goal for children.
    c. education should emphasize simple biological concepts.
    d. is more important to boys than girls.

18. Bindi, an Indian child, is asked why a man probably got sick. Bindi is most likely to say which of the following? (p. 426)
    a. "He went outside without his coat on when it was cold outside."
    b. "He breathed in a virus."
    c. "His sinuses filled with mucus. So did his lungs."
    d. "He is being punished by God for his bad behavior."

19. Compared with preschoolers, school-age children are physically __________ (p. 428)
    a. more elastic.
    b. less pliable.
    c. less agile.
    d. clumsy.

20. The height children can jump increases by _____ inches from ages 6 to 12. (p. 428)
    a. 3
    b. 6
    c. 8
    d. 12

21. By age 6, most children can __________ (p. 429)
    a. write the letters of the alphabet using upper and lowercase letters.
    b. print their first and last names.
    c. master cursive writing.
    d. accurately copy a three-dimensional form.

22. Girls outperform boys in __________ (p. 430)
    a. running.
    b. jumping.
    c. catching.
    d. skipping.

23. Boys are __________ (p. 430)
    a. less positive than girls about the value of sports.
    b. more likely than girls to regard boys' advantage in sports as unjust.
    c. more positive than girls about their own sports ability.
    d. less concerned about athletic ability than girls.

24. When parents and coaches emphasize __________, young athletes enjoy sports more and exert greater effort to improve their skills. (p. 431)
    a. competition
    b. winning
    c. physical fitness
    d. effort

25. Child-invented games usually __________ (p. 430)
    a. involve complex rules and physical skills.
    b. involve gender-segregated activities.
    c. rely on a sizable element of luck.
    d. are contests of individual ability.

26. Friendly chasing and play-fighting on the playground usually involves __________ play. (p. 431)
    a. rough-and-tumble
    b. aggressive
    c. adult-structured
    d. parallel

27. A stable ordering of group members that predicts who will win when conflict arises is a __________ (p. 432)
    a. clique.
    b. peer group.
    c. dominance hierarchy.
    d. popularity contest.

28. U.S. elementary schools __________ (p. 432)
    a. devote at least two hours a week to recess.
    b. have cut back on recess.
    c. offer physical education five days a week.
    d. provide enough physical activity for good health.

29. Research on recess indicates that __________ (p. 433)
    a. school-age children are more attentive in the classroom after recess than before it.
    b. boys are less disruptive in the classroom after recess than before it.
    c. recess time reinforces the lessons learned in gym classes.
    d. that most U.S. public schools provide at least 30 minutes of daily recess.

30. Many experts believe that schools should not only offer more frequent physical education classes but also change the content of these programs to include greater emphasis on __________ (p. 433)
    a. competitive sports.
    b. weight training.
    c. activities demanding a high level of skill.
    d. enjoyable, informal games.

CHAPTER 12
COGNITIVE DEVELOPMENT IN MIDDLE CHILDHOOD

BRIEF CHAPTER SUMMARY

During Piaget's concrete operational stage, from about age 7 to 11, thought becomes more logical, flexible, and organized than in early childhood. This is evident in children's grasp of concepts like conservation, classification, and seriation, as well as in improvements in spatial reasoning. However, concrete operational children think logically only when dealing with concrete, tangible information, and mastery of concrete operational tasks occurs gradually. Specific cultural practices, especially those associated with schooling, promote mastery of Piagetian tasks.

Some information-processing theorists argue that the development of operational thinking can best be understood in terms of gains in information-processing speed rather than a sudden shift to a new stage. Brain development contributes to gains in processing speed and capacity, as well as in inhibition, which facilitate diverse aspects of thinking. During middle childhood, attention becomes more sustained, selective, and adaptable, and the use of memory strategies becomes more effective. Children learn much about planning by collaborating with more expert planners. Memory strategies are promoted by learning activities in school and are not used by children in non-Western cultures who have no formal schooling.

Children's theory of mind, or metacognition, becomes much more elaborate and refined in middle childhood, increasing children's ability to reflect on their own mental life. School-age children, unlike preschoolers, regard the mind as an active, constructive agent and are conscious of mental inferences and mental strategies. Cognitive self-regulation—the ability to monitor progress toward a goal and redirect unsuccessful efforts—develops gradually. In both reading and mathematics, academic instruction that combines an emphasis on meaning and understanding with training in basic skills may be most effective.

Intelligence tests for children measure overall IQ, as well as separate intellectual factors. Sternberg's triarchic theory of intelligence defines three broad, interacting intelligences (analytical, creative, and practical); intelligent behavior involves balancing all three. Gardner's theory of multiple intelligences identifies at least eight mental abilities. It has been helpful in understanding and nurturing children's talents and in stimulating efforts to define, measure, and foster emotional intelligence, a set of capacities for dealing with people and understanding oneself.

Heritability estimates and adoption research show that both genetic and environmental factors contribute to individual differences in intelligence. Because of different communication styles and lack of familiarity with test content, IQ scores of low-SES ethnic minority children often do not reflect their true abilities. Stereotype threat also has a negative effect. Supplementing IQ tests with measures of adaptive behavior and adjusting testing procedures to account for cultural differences—for example, through dynamic assessment—can reduce test bias.

Language development continues during the school years. At this age, children develop metalinguistic awareness—the ability to think about language as a system. Vocabulary increases rapidly, and pragmatic skills are refined. Bilingual children are advanced in cognitive development and metalinguistic awareness.

Schools are powerful forces in children's development. Class size, the school's educational philosophy, teacher–pupil interaction, grouping practices, and the way computers are used in classrooms all affect motivation and achievement in middle childhood. Teachers face special challenges in meeting the needs of children who have learning difficulties as well as those with special intellectual strengths. In international studies, U.S. students typically display average or below-average performance. Efforts are currently underway to upgrade the quality of American education.

LEARNING OBJECTIVES

After reading this chapter, you should be able to:

12.1 Describe the major characteristics of concrete operational thought, including cognitive limitations during this stage. (pp. 437–440)

12.2 Discuss follow-up research on concrete operational thought, noting the implications of recent findings for the accuracy of Piaget's concrete operational stage. (pp. 440–442)

12.3 Cite basic changes in information processing during middle childhood. (pp. 442–443)

12.4 Describe changes in attention and memory during middle childhood. (pp. 443, 434, 446–447)

12.5 Describe the school-age child's theory of mind and capacity to engage in cognitive self-regulation. (pp. 447–449)

12.6 Discuss applications of information processing to academic learning, noting current perspectives on teaching reading and mathematics to elementary school children. (pp. 450–453)

12.7 Describe the Stanford-Binet Intelligence Scale and the Wechsler Intelligence Scale for Children-IV. (pp. 453–454)

12.8 Discuss recent efforts to define intelligence, including componential analysis, Sternberg's triarchic theory of successful intelligence, and Gardner's theory of multiple intelligences. (pp. 454–458)

12.9 Cite evidence indicating that both heredity and environment contribute to intelligence. (pp. 458–459)

12.10 Describe cultural influences on intelligence test performance, and discuss efforts to overcome cultural bias in intelligence testing. (pp. 459–462)

12.11 Summarize changes in metalinguistic awareness, vocabulary, grammar, and pragmatics during middle childhood. (pp. 462–464)

12.12 Discuss the major issues surrounding bilingual development and bilingual education, noting the advantages of bilingualism in childhood. (pp. 464–466)

12.13 Discuss the impact of class size, educational philosophies, teacher–student interaction, and grouping practices on student motivation and academic achievement. (pp. 466–471)

12.14 Describe educational benefits of computer use as well as concerns about computers. (pp. 472–473)

12.15 Summarize the conditions under which placement of mildly mentally retarded and learning disabled children in regular classrooms is successful. (pp. 473–474)

12.16 Describe the characteristics of gifted children, and discuss current efforts to meet their educational needs. (pp. 474–476)

12.17 Compare the U.S. cultural climate for academic achievement with that of other industrialized nations. (pp. 476–477)

STUDY QUESTIONS

Piaget's Theory: The Concrete Operational Stage

Achievements of the Concrete Operational Stage

1. How does thought change as children enter the *concrete operational stage*? (p. 438)

____

2. Match the following terms with the appropriate descriptions and examples. (p. 438)

_____ The ability to order items along a quantitative dimension, such as length or weight
_____ The ability to focus on relations between a general category and two specific categories
_____ The ability to seriate mentally
_____ The ability to focus on several aspects of a problem and relate them rather than centering on just one aspect

A. Decentration
B. *Reversibility*
C. Classification
D. *Seriation*
E. *Transitive inference*

3. Advances in spatial reasoning are evidenced by the creation of _______________, or mental representations of familiar large scale spaces. Summarize the features of children's maps at each age listed below. (pp. 438–439)

   Preschool: ______________________________

   ____

   Ages 8–10: ______________________________

   ____

   Ages 10–12: ______________________________

   ____

4. Explain how cultural frameworks influence children's map making. (p. 439)

   ____

   ____

Limitations of Concrete Operational Thought

1. Describe the major limitation of concrete operational thought. (p. 440)

   ____

   ____

2. Children master concrete operational tasks (step-by-step / all at once). Explain your answer. (p. 440)

   ____

   ____

Follow-Up Research on Concrete Operational Thought

1. Cite two examples that illustrate how culture and schooling contribute to children's mastery of conservation and other Piagetian tasks. (p. 440)

   A. ______________________________

   ____

   B. ______________________________

   ____

2. Briefly summarize Case's information-processing view of cognitive development. (p. 441)

   ____

   ____

   ____

   ____

3. What are central conceptual structures? (p. 441)

   ____

   ____

4. Based on Case's theory, cite two reasons why children's understandings appear in specific situations at different times rather than being mastered all at once. (p. 441)

   A. ______________________________

   ____

   B. ______________________________

   ____

Evaluation of the Concrete Operational Stage

1. Many researchers believe that two types of change may be involved in the school-age child's approach to Piagetian problems. List these two changes. (p. 442)

   A. ______________________________

   B. ______________________________

Information Processing

1. What two factors underlie every act of cognition? (p. 442)

   A. ______________ B. ______________

2. List two ways in which brain development contributes to changes in information processing. (pp. 442–443)

   A. ______________________________

   B. ______________________________

Attention

1. Cite three ways in which attention changes during middle childhood. (p. 443)

   A. ______________________________

   B. ______________________________

   C. ______________________________

2. Indicate the order in which children acquire selective, adaptable attentional strategies. (p. 443)

   _____ Utilization deficiency

   _____ Production deficiency

   _____ Effective strategy use

   _____ Control deficiency

3. Provide an example illustrating how school-age children's attentional strategies become more planful. (p. 444)

   ____

   ____

4. Explain how children typically learn planning skills, and discuss what adults can do to foster the development of planning in school-age children. (pp. 444–445)

   A. ______________________________

   ____

   B. ______________________________

   ____

Biology and Environment: Children with Attention-Deficit Hyperactivity Disorder

1. Describe typical characteristics of children with *attention-deficit hyperactivity disorder (ADHD).* (p. 444)

   A. ____

   ____

   B. ____

   ____

2. True or False: Children with ADHD perform as well as other children on tests of intelligence. (p. 444)

3. Researchers agree that deficient executive processing underlies ADHD symptoms. Briefly describe the two views that contribute to this theory. (p. 444)

   A. ____

   ____

   B. ____

   ____

4. Cite evidence that ADHD is influenced by both heredity and environment. (pp. 444–445)

   Heredity: ____

   ____

   Environment: ____

   ____

5. List three treatments for ADHD, noting which method is the most <u>common</u> and which method is the most <u>effective</u>. (p. 445)

   A. ____

   B. ____

   C. ____

6. True or False: ADHD is a lifelong disorder, with problems usually persisting into adulthood. (p. 445)

Memory Strategies

1. List two memory strategies that emerge during middle childhood. (p. 446)

   A. ____

   B. ____

2. Cite two factors required for perfecting memory strategies. (p. 446)

   A. ______________________ B. ______________________

3. How is young children's use of memory strategies adaptive? (p. 446)

   ____

   ____

4. What is *elaboration*, and how does it help children expand working memory and retrieval? (p. 446)

   A. ______________________________

   B. ______________________________

   ____

The Knowledge Base and Memory Performance

1. Provide an example of how extensive knowledge and use of memory strategies are closely related to and support one another. (p. 446)

   ____

   ____

2. True or False: Knowledge is not the most important factor in children's memory processing. Explain your answer. (p. 447)

   ____

   ____

Culture, Schooling, and Memory Strategies

1. True or False: Children in non-Western cultures who have no formal schooling benefit more from instruction in memory strategies than Western children do. (p. 447)
2. Discuss how culture and schooling are related to the development of memory strategies. (p. 447)

   ____

   ____

   ____

The School-Age Child's Theory of Mind

1. Provide an example of how a school-age child's theory of mind differs from that of a preschooler. (pp. 447–448)

   ____

   ____

   ____

2. How does the ability to make mental inferences assist children in understanding others' perspectives? (p. 448)

   ____

   ____

   ____

3. What are second-order false beliefs, and how do they contribute to perspective taking? (p. 448)

   A. ______________________________

   ____

   B. ______________________________

   ____

4. How does schooling contribute to theory of mind? (p. 448)

____

____

Cognitive Self-Regulation

1. What is *cognitive self-regulation,* and how do researchers study it? (p. 449)

   A. ____

   ____

   B. ____

   ____

2. School-age children (are / are not) good at cognitive self-regulation. Explain your answer. (p. 449)

____

____

3. Why does cognitive self-regulation develop gradually during middle childhood? (p.449)

____

____

____

4. Provide an example of how parents and teachers can foster self-regulation. (p. 449)

____

____

5. Children who acquire effective self-regulatory skills develop a sense of ____________________, confidence in their own ability, which supports future self-regulation. (p. 449)

Applications of Information Processing to Academic Learning

1. List the diverse information-processing skills that contribute to the process of reading. (p. 450)

____

____

2. How does the *whole language* approach to reading instruction differ from the *phonics approach*? (p. 450)

____

____

____

3. Explain why combining phonics with whole language is often the best strategy for teaching children to read. (pp. 450–451)

____

____

____

4. Match each of the following age ranges with the reading skills that emerge during that time period. (p. 451)

_____	Masters basic decoding skills, reads about 3,000 words	A. 2 to 6 years
_____	Reads with self-defined purpose	B. 6 to 7 years
_____	Pretends to read and write	C. 7 to 8 years
_____	Reads widely, taps material with diverse viewpoints	D. 9 to 14 years
_____	Masters letter-sound correspondences, reads simple stories	E. 15 to 17 years
_____	Reads to learn new knowledge, usually without questions	F. 18 years and older

5. Arguments about how to teach mathematics closely resemble those in reading. Briefly summarize these arguments. (p. 451)

   A. ____

   ____

   B. ____

   ____

6. Research has shown that when teachers emphasize (conceptual knowledge / rote memorization of mathematical rules) children are more successful in learning to solve arithmetic problems. (p. 452)

7. Briefly explain why students in Asian countries often excel at both math reasoning and computation. (p. 452)

   ____

   ____

   ____

Individual Differences in Mental Development

Defining and Measuring Intelligence

1. List the types of items commonly included on intelligence tests for children. (p. 453)

   ____

   ____

2. Distinguish between group- and individually administered intelligence tests, and cite the advantages of each. (p. 453)

   Group administered: ____

   ____

   ____

   Individually administered: ____

   ____

   ____

3. Match each of the following intelligence tests with the appropriate descriptions. (Each answer will be used more than once.) (p. 454)

_____ Appropriate for individuals age 6–16
_____ Appropriate for individuals between 2 years of age and adulthood
_____ Assesses four broad intellectual factors: verbal reasoning, perceptual reasoning, working memory, and processing speed
_____ Assesses five broad intellectual factors: general knowledge, quantitative reasoning, visual-spatial processing, working memory, and basic information processing
_____ First test to be standardized on samples representing the total population of the United States, including ethnic minorities
_____ Appropriate for children 2 years 6 months through 7 years 3 months

A. Stanford-Binet Intelligence Scales
B. Wechsler Intelligence Scale for Children-IV
C. Wechsler Preschool and Primary Scale of Intelligence—Revised

Recent Efforts to Define Intelligence

1. What is a *componential analysis,* and why is it used? (p. 454)

A. ______________________________

____

B. ______________________________

____

2. Besides efficient thinking, what other factors are important in predicting IQ? (p. 455)

____

3. What is the major shortcoming of the componential approach? (p. 455)

____

____

4. List and briefly describe the three broad intelligences outlined in Sternberg's *triarchic theory of successful intelligence.* (pp. 455–456)

A. ______________________________

____

B. ______________________________

____

C. ______________________________

____

5. Provide an example of how Sternberg's theory responds to the limitations of current intelligence tests. (p. 456)

____

____

6. Define Gardner's *theory of multiple intelligences,* and list his eight independent intelligences. (p. 456)

____

____

A. ____________________ B. ____________________

C. ____________________ D. ____________________

E. ____________________ F. ____________________

G. ____________________ H. ____________________

7. True or False: In Gardner's theory, intelligence has a purely biological basis and is not affected by cultural values or learning opportunities. (p. 456)

8. Gardner's theory (is / is not) firmly grounded in research. (p. 457)

Social Issues: Education: Emotional Intelligence

1. Define *emotional intelligence,* and explain how researchers measure it. (p. 457)

   A. ____

   ____

   B. ____

   ____

2. True or False: Emotional intelligence is modestly related to IQ, and it is positively associated with self-esteem, empathy, prosocial behavior, and life satisfaction. (p. 457)

3. How can teachers help foster social and emotional intelligence in school-age children? (p. 457)

____

____

Explaining Individual and Group Differences in IQ

1. Briefly summarize evidence related to ethnic and SES differences in IQ. (p. 458)

   Ethnic differences: ____

   ____

   ____

   SES differences: ____

   ____

   ____

2. What do kinship studies reveal about the role of heredity in IQ? (p. 458)

____

____

____

3. What do adoption studies suggest about the contribution of environmental factors in IQ? (pp. 458–459)

____

____

____

4. Research shows a dramatic secular trend in mental test performance. Explain what this means. (p. 459)

____

____

5. What is test bias? Briefly discuss the controversy surrounding test bias and ethnic differences in IQ. (p. 459)

   A. ____

   ____

   B. ____

   ____

6. Provide an example of how ethnic minority families often use communication styles that differ from those used in most classrooms and testing situations. (p. 459)

____

____

7. Ethnic minority parents without extensive schooling prefer a (collaborative / hierarchical) style of communication. With increasing education, parents establish a collaborative / hierarchical) style. (p. 460)

8. True or False: Using nonverbal intelligence tests that tap spatial reasoning and performance skills considerably raises the scores of ethnic minority children. Explain your answer. (p. 460)

____

____

9. Define *stereotype threat,* and explain how it is likely to influence low-SES minority children's performance on intelligence tests. (pp. 460–461)

   Definition: ____

   ____

   Influence: ____

   ____

10. Cite two components of self-discipline that predict school performance at least as well as, and sometimes better than, IQ does. (p. 461)

   A. ______________________ B. ______________________

Reducing Cultural Bias in Testing

1. Children's ability to cope with the demands of their everyday environments is called ______________________. Why is assessment of this trait especially important for minority children? (p. 461)

____

____

2. Describe *dynamic assessment,* and discuss its effectiveness for reducing cultural bias in testing. (p. 461)

   A. ____

   ____

   B. ____

   ____

3. True or False: Dynamic assessment is more effective than traditional tests in predicting academic achievement. Explain your answer. (pp. 461–462)

   ____

   ____

Language Development

1. School-age children develop ____________________ *awareness,* the ability to think about language as a system. (p. 462)

Vocabulary

1. True or False: The rate of vocabulary growth during the school years exceeds that of early childhood. (p. 462)
2. Cite four strategies that assist school-age children in building their vocabularies. (p. 463)

   A. ____

   B. ____

   C. ____

   D. ____

3. Provide an example illustrating the school-age child's more reflective and analytic approach to language. (p. 463)

   ____

   ____

Grammar

1. Cite two grammatical achievements of middle childhood. (p. 463)

   A. ____

   B. ____

Pragmatics

1. Describe three advances in pragmatic speech that take place during middle childhood. (p. 464)

   A. ____

   ____

   B. ____

   ____

   C. ____

   ____

2. Summarize cultural differences in children's narrative styles of communication. (p. 464)

____

____

____

Learning Two Languages

1. Cite two ways in which children can become bilingual. (p. 464)

   A. ____

   B. ____

2. True or False: When bilingual children engage in code switching, they do not violate the grammar of either language. Briefly explain your response. (p. 465)

____

____

3. True or False: There is a sensitive period for second-language development. (p.465)

4. List the cognitive benefits of bilingualism. (p. 465)

____

____

____

5. Briefly describe the structure and benefits of Canada's language immersion programs. (p. 465)

____

____

6. Summarize the current debate regarding how American ethnic minority children with limited English proficiency should be educated. (p. 465)

____

____

____

____

7. List several benefits of combining children's native language with English in the classroom. (pp. 465–466)

____

____

____

Children's Learning in School

1. List four characteristics of high-quality education in elementary school. (p. 466)

   A. ______

   B. ______

   C. ______

   D. ______

Class Size

1. According to research on 6,000 Tennessee kindergartners, what is an ideal class size for facilitating children's learning? (p. 466)

   ______

2. List two reasons why small class size is beneficial. (p. 467)

   A. ______

   B. ______

Educational Philosophies

1. Describe *traditional classrooms* and *constructivist classrooms,* noting how students' progress is evaluated in each. (pp. 467–468)

   Traditional: ______

   ______

   ______

   Constructivist: ______

   ______

   ______

2. True or False: Constructivist classroom settings are associated with gains in critical thinking, social and moral maturity, and positive attitudes. (p. 468)

3. Describe the nature of *social-constructivist* classrooms. (p. 468)

   ______

   ______

4. List three Vygotskian-inspired teaching methods. (p. 468)

   A. ______

   B. ______

   C. ______

5. ______________________ refers to a method of learning in which a teacher and 2 to 4 students form a cooperative group and take turns leading dialogues on the content of a text passage. Describe four cognitive strategies that group members apply during these dialogues. (pp. 468–469)

   A. ______________________

   B. ______________________

   C. ______________________

   D. ______________________

6. What are *communities of learners,* and what is the philosophy behind this educational approach? (p. 469)

   Description: ______________________

   ____

   Philosophy: ______________________

   ____

Teacher–Student Interaction

1. Describe how teachers interact differently with high-achieving, well-behaved students versus low-achieving, disruptive students. (p. 470)

   High-achieving, well-behaved students: ______________________

   ____

   Low-achieving, disruptive students: ______________________

   ____

2. What are *educational self-fulfilling prophecies,* and how do they affect students' motivation and performance? (p. 470)

   Definition: ______________________

   ____

   Effects: ______________________

   ____

   ____

3. Why do teacher expectations have a greater impact on low-achieving than high-achieving students? (p. 470)

   ____

   ____

Grouping Practices

1. What are homogeneous groups, and how can they be a potential source of self-fulfilling prophecies? (p. 470)

   A. ______________________

   B. ______________________

   ____

2. Discuss the benefits of multigrade classrooms, noting how student training in *cooperative learning* contributes to the success of such classrooms. (pp. 470, 471)

   Benefits: ______________________________

   Training in cooperative learning: ______________________________

Social Issues: Education: Magnet Schools: Equal Access to High-Quality Education

1. True or False: Since U.S. public schools were desegregated in the 1950s, most African-American and Hispanic children attend schools that are ethnically diverse. (p. 471)
2. Explain why inner-city schools are likely to be disadvantaged in funding. (p. 471)

   ____

3. What is a magnet school? (p. 471)

   ____

4. Why are magnet schools more diverse than mainstream public schools? (p. 471)

   ____

Computers and Academic Learning

1. Explain how the use of word-processing programs can be beneficial to children as they learn to read and write. (p. 472)

   ____

2. On average, children and adolescents use the computer a _____ hour a day for schoolwork and _____ hour a day for pleasure. (p. 472)
3. Provide an example of a sex difference in computer use and choice of activities. (p. 472)

   ____

4. True or False: Children who are skilled in the use of computers usually acquire an adult-level understanding of the technical complexity of the Internet by age 7. (p. 472)

Teaching Children with Special Needs

1. What is an *inclusive classroom*? (p. 473)

____

____

____

2. List characteristics of children with mild mental retardation and *learning disabilities.* (p. 473)

   A. ____

   ____

   B. ____

   ____

3. True or False: Nearly all students benefit academically from full inclusion. Explain your answer. (pp. 473–474)

____

____

4. True or False: Special-needs children placed in regular classrooms often do best when they receive instruction in a resource room for part of the day and in the regular classroom for the remainder of the day. (p. 474)

5. Cite two ways in which teachers can promote peer acceptance in inclusive classrooms. (p. 474)

   A. ____

   B. ____

6. Describe the characteristics of *gifted* children. (p. 474)

____

____

7. ____________________ refers to the ability to produce work that is original yet appropriate. (p. 474)

8. Distinguish between *convergent* and *divergent thinking.* (p. 474)

   Convergent: ____

   ____

   Divergent: ____

   ____

9. ____________________ refers to outstanding performance in a particular field. (p. 474)

10. Describe family characteristics that foster *talent.* (p. 475)

____

____

____

11. Summarize risk factors associated with extreme giftedness, noting sex differences. (p. 475)

____

____

____

12. List three models for educating gifted children. (pp. 475–476)

    A. ____________________

    B. ____________________

    C. ____________________

How Well-Educated Are U.S. Children?

1. Cite three reasons why U.S. children lag behind students in other countries. (p. 476)

    A. ____________________

    B. ____________________

    C. ____________________

2. List several factors that have led to academic success for Finnish students. (p. 477)

    ____

    ____

3. In contrast to their Asian counterparts, American parents and teachers tend to believe that children's (native ability / hard work) is central to academic success. (p. 477)

4. Cite five strategies for improving the U.S. education system. (p. 477)

    A. ____________________

    B. ____________________

    C. ____________________

    D. ____________________

    E. ____________________

ASK YOURSELF . . .

For *Ask Yourself* questions for this chapter, along with feedback on the accuracy of your answers, please log on to MyDevelopmentLab (for registration and access, please visit mydevelopmentlab.com or follow the instructions on page ix).

(1) Select the Multimedia Library.

(2) Choose the explore option.

(3) Find your chapter from the drop down box.

(4) Click find now.

(5) Complete questions and choose "Submit answers for grading" or "Clear answers" to start over.

SUGGESTED READINGS

Cartledge, G. Y., Gardner, R., & Ford, D. Y. (2008). *Teaching diverse learners*. Newark, NJ: Prentice Hall. A collection of chapters focusing on the educational needs of culturally and racially diverse learners, including children with special needs. Other topics include research on gifted and talented students, assessment and testing, and strategies for enhancing social and academic skills.

Johnson, A. W. (2009). *Objectifying measures: The dominance of high-stakes testing and the politics of schooling.* Philadelphia, PA: Temple University Press. A compelling look at the high-stakes testing movement, this book examines the effects of standardized testing on educational quality in the United States. The author also presents research how on high-stakes testing affects minority students from low-SES backgrounds.

Stewart-Brown, S., & Edmunds, L. (2007). *Educating people to be emotionally intelligent.* Westport, CT: Praeger. Highlights the importance of emotional intelligence for favorable adjustment throughout the lifespan. The authors also present strategies for enhancing emotional development in both children and adults.

CROSSWORD PUZZLE 12.1

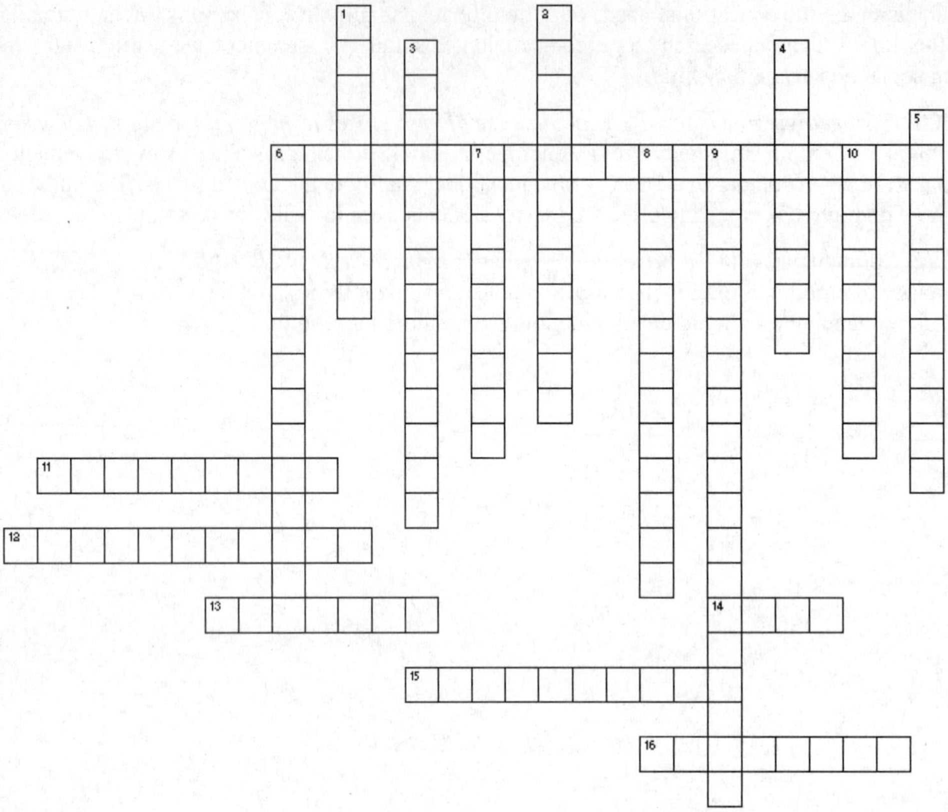

Across

6. Classroom in which children participate in a wide range of challenging activities with teachers and peers to jointly construct understandings (2 words, hyph.)
11. Memory strategy of repeating information
12. Memory strategy of creating a relation between two or more items that are not members of the same category
13. ____________ deficiency: inability to consistently execute a mental strategy
14. Disorder involving inattentiveness, impulsivity, and excessive motor activity that results in academic and social problems (abbr.)
15. ____________ deficiency: failure to use a mental strategy when it could be helpful
16. Piaget's ______________ operational stage is marked by logical, flexible, and organized thought.

Down

1. ____________ strategy use: consistent use of a mental strategy that leads to improved performance
2. Memory strategy of grouping together related items
3. The ability to think about language as a system is known as ______________ awareness.
4. The ability to order items along a quantitative dimension
5. ____________ deficiency: inability to improve performance even with consistent use of a mental strategy
6. Cognitive __________-_____________: process of continually monitoring progress toward a goal, checking outcomes, and redirecting unsuccessful efforts (2 words, hyph.)
7. ___________ maps: children's mental representation of familiar, large-scale spaces, such as their school or neighborhood
8. Ability to mentally go through a series of steps in a problem and then reverse direction, returning to the starting point
9. Resolving differences of opinion, sharing responsibilities, considering one another's ideas, and providing one another with sufficient explanations to correct misunderstandings while working in a group (2 words)
10. Transitive ____________: ability to mentally order items along a quantitative dimension

CROSSWORD PUZZLE 12.2

Across

1. Vygotsky-inspired method of teaching in which a teacher and 2 to 4 students form a cooperative learning group
3. In _____________ classrooms, children are passive learners who acquire information presented by teachers.
5. _________ of learners: teachers guide the overall learning process, but otherwise, no distinction is made between adult and child contributors
6. Classrooms in which students with learning disabilities learn alongside typical students
8. Learning ______________: specific disorders leading to poor academic achievement
9. ____________ thinking: generation of a single correct answer to a problem
10. The ability to produce work that is original yet appropriate
12. Educational ______-_____________ prophecy: children adopt teachers' positive or negative attitudes toward them and start to live up to these expectations
13. _________ thinking: generation of multiple and unusual possibilities when faced with a problem
14. In _____________ classrooms, children construct their own knowledge and are viewed as active agents who reflect on and coordinate their own thoughts rather than absorbing those of others.
17. Approach to beginning reading that parallels children's natural language learning (2 words, hyph.)
18. Stereotype ____________: fear of being judged on the basis of a negative stereotype
19. Gardner's theory of _____________ intelligences proposes at least eight independent intelligences.

Down

2. A set of abilities that enable individuals to process and adapt to emotional information (2 words)
4. Outstanding performance in a particular field
7. Displaying exceptional intellectual strengths, including high IQ, creativity, and talent
11. ___________ assessment: individualized teaching is introduced into the testing situation to see what the child can attain with social support.
15. Sternberg's ____________ theory of intelligence states that information-processing skills, ability to learn efficiently in novel situations, and contextual factors interact to determine intelligent behavior.
16. An approach to beginning reading instruction that emphasizes coaching children on the basic rules for translating written symbols into sounds is called the __________ approach.

PRACTICE TEST #1

1. Piaget's __________ stage extends from about 7 to 11 years. (p. 438)
   a. sensorimotor
   b. preoperational
   c. concrete operational
   d. formal operational

2. India can think through a series of steps and then mentally reverse directions, returning to the starting point. This means that India is capable of __________ (p. 438)
   a. decentration.
   b. reversibility.
   c. conservation.
   d. class inclusion.

3. The experience of __________ seems to promote mastery of Piagetian tasks. (p. 440)
   a. growing older
   b. living in an agricultural region
   c. spending time in independent play
   d. going to school

4. Some neo-Piagetians argue that the development of operational thinking can best be understood in terms of gains in __________ (p. 441)
   a. information-processing speed.
   b. convergent thinking.
   c. sensorimotor abilities.
   d. white matter.

5. Strides in __________ occur in middle childhood as the prefrontal cortex develops further. (p. 443)
   a. social referencing
   b. metacognition
   c. inhibition
   d. pragmatics

6. Hattie, a preschooler, rarely engages in attentional strategies. Hattie has a(n) __________ deficiency. (p. 443)
   a. production
   b. control
   c. utilization
   d. organizational

7. Gregory executes attentional strategies consistently, but his performance does not improve. Gregory has a(n) __________ deficiency. (p. 443)
   a. production
   b. control
   c. utilization
   d. organizational

8. ADHD __________ (p. 444)
   a. runs in families and is highly heritable.
   b. usually subsides by adolescence or early adulthood.
   c. is often caused by prenatal alcohol exposure.
   d. affects academic learning but has little impact on social and emotional development.

9. Lance knows that doing well on a task depends on focusing his concentration and exerting effort. Lance's __________ has become more refined. (p. 447)
   a. attribution style
   b. theory of mind
   c. ability to elaborate
   d. ability to conserve

10. Mr. Van Dalen believes that children should first be coached on the basic rules for translating written symbols into sounds before they are exposed to complex reading materials. Mr. Van Dalen probably uses a __________ approach to teaching reading. (p. 450)
    a. phonics
    b. whole-language
    c. reading to learn
    d. constructivist

11. Arguments on how to teach mathematics pit __________ against __________ (p. 451)
    a. whole-number learning; computational drill.
    b. number sense; whole-number learning.
    c. computational drill; rote memorization.
    d. computational drill; number sense.

12. Around age 6, IQ correlates with academic achievement around _____ to _____ (p. 453)
    a. .10; .20.
    b. .30; .40.
    c. .50; .60.
    d. .70; .80.

13. Group-administered intelligence tests __________ (p. 453)
    a. are useful in instructional planning.
    b. demand considerable training to administer correctly.
    c. are primarily used to identify children who may be gifted.
    d. cannot be given by classroom teachers.

14. According to Sternberg, __________ intelligence consists of the information-processing components that underlie all intelligent acts. (p. 455)
    a. practical
    b. analytical
    c. creative
    d. logico-mathematical

15. Horace scored high in Gardner's spatial intelligence. A good career for Horace might be a __________ (p. 456)
    a. journalist.
    b. mathematician.
    c. navigator.
    d. salesperson.

16. When her friend is excluded from attending a birthday party, Greta comforts her and says, "If you aren't invited, I'm not going either." Greta probably excels at __________ intelligence. (p. 457)
    a. relational
    b. social
    c. analytical
    d. emotional

17. On the basis of kinship evidence, researchers estimate that about __________ the differences in IQ among children can be traced to their genetic makeup. (p. 458)
    a. 10 percent of
    b. a quarter of
    c. half
    d. three-quarters of

18. Many ethnic minority parents without extensive schooling prefer a(n) __________ style of communication. (p. 459)
    a. collaborative
    b. elaborative
    c. hierarchical
    d. analytical

19. Mayar's fear of being judged on the basis of her religion triggers performance anxiety on a test. Mayar is experiencing a __________ (p. 460)
    a. secular trend.
    b. stereotype threat.
    c. dynamic trend.
    d. metacognitive threat.

20. During the elementary school years, vocabulary __________ (p. 462)
    a. doubles.
    b. triples.
    c. increases fourfold.
    d. increases tenfold.

21. Children of bilingual parents who teach them both languages in infancy and early childhood __________ (p. 465)
    a. attain early language milestones according to a typical timetable.
    b. generally take 3 or 4 years to attain speaking skills on par with those of native-speaking agemates.
    c. generally take 5 to 7 years to attain speaking skills on par with those of native-speaking agemates.
    d. do not learn either language proficiently when compared with monolingual agemates.

22. Providing instruction in English and a child's native tongue __________ (p. 465)
    a. leads to inadequate proficiency in both languages.
    b. lets the child know that her heritage is respected.
    c. results in the gradual loss of the child's native language.
    d. is the bilingual education approach used in most U.S. schools.

23. In a study of Tennessee students, placing kindergarteners through third graders in classes of _____ to _____ students predicted substantially higher achievement fourth through ninth grade. (p. 466)
    a. 13; 17
    b. 18; 22
    c. 23; 25
    d. 26; 30

24. In a traditional classroom, __________ (p. 467)
    a. students are agents of their own knowledge.
    b. the teacher guides and supports in response to children's needs.
    c. the teacher is the sole authority for knowledge and decision making.
    d. students are evaluated by considering their progress in relation to their own prior development.

25. Magnet schools offer a solution to the problem of racial segregation in public schools by __________ (p. 471)
    a. reducing cultural test bias and emphasizing rote instruction.
    b. attracting students from outside the neighborhood to schools in low-income areas.
    c. increasing inclusion and offering special programs for students with learning problems.
    d. teaching to the standardized tests and increasing school funding.

26. School assignments written using computer word processing programs tend to __________ than assignments written by hand. (p. 472)
    a. be of poorer quality and contain more spelling errors
    b. take longer for students to complete
    c. be less successful in promoting language skills
    d. be longer and of higher quality

27. Shelby has an average IQ, but has low reading achievement scores. Shelby probably has __________ (p. 473)
    a. mild mental retardation.
    b. moderate mental retardation.
    c. a learning disability.
    d. a behavioral disability.

28. __________ children show outstanding performance in a specific field. (pp. 474–475)
    a. Gifted
    b. Creative
    c. Talented
    d. Few

29. Gifted children thrive in learning environments that __________ (p. 475)
    a. permit them to take intellectual risks.
    b. allow them to work independently.
    c. only include other gifted students.
    d. permit them to be passive learners.

30. In contrast to American parents, Asian parents __________ (p. 477)
    a. regard native ability as the key to academic success.
    b. spend fewer hours helping their children with homework.
    c. value individual accomplishment over effort.
    d. believe that all children can succeed academically as long as they try hard.

PRACTICE TEST #2

1. Matthew can focus on several aspects of a problem and relate them, rather than focusing on just one. This means that Matthew is capable of __________ (p. 438)
   a. decentration.
   b. reversibility.
   c. class inclusion.
   d. seriation.

2. Micah can seriate mentally. This means that Micah has mastered __________ (p. 438)
   a. conservation.
   b. classification.
   c. transitive inference.
   d. spatial reasoning.

3. Ten- to twelve-year-olds are able to grasp the concept of __________ due to experience with reading maps. (p. 439)
   a. route of travel
   b. directionality
   c. navigation
   d. scale

4. A child who often listens to and tells stories but rarely draws pictures displays __________ advanced conceptual structures in __________. (p. 441)
   a. more; drawing
   b. more; storytelling
   c. few; storytelling
   d. no; thinking

5. One reason Kaylee is able to memorize her family's important phone numbers at 12 but had trouble doing so at 7 is that she has made gains in __________ (pp. 442–443)
   a. digit span.
   b. seriation.
   c. inhibition.
   d. class inclusion.

6. Brenda sometimes produces attentional strategies, but not consistently. She has a(n) __________ deficiency. (p. 443)
   a. production
   b. control
   c. utilization
   d. organizational

7. By the mid-elementary school years, Vanessa uses attentional strategies consistently and performance improves. Vanessa __________ (p. 443)
   a. may still have a production deficiency.
   b. will continue to demonstrate a control deficiency.
   c. is probably very creative.
   d. is engaging in effective strategy use.

8. Boys are diagnosed with ADHD about __________ times as often as girls. (p. 444)
   a. two
   b. three
   c. four
   d. five

9. Mia memorizes a list of state capitals by repeating them to herself. This is called __________ (p. 446)
   a. elaboration.
   b. organization.
   c. rote memorization.
   d. rehearsal.

10. School-age children have difficulty translating metacognition into action because __________ (p. 449)
    a. they lack the expertise to utilize memory strategies.
    b. they are not yet good at cognitive self-regulation.
    c. the prefrontal cortex is still developing.
    d. public-school curriculum does not emphasize these skills.

11. Studies indicate that children learn to read faster when __________ (p. 450)
    a. given lessons in both phonics and the whole-language approach.
    b. taught using the phonics approach only, with emphasis on pronunciation.
    c. placed in multigrade classrooms with multiple instructors.
    d. given storybooks with fewer pictures and larger type.

12. Intelligence test designers use __________ to identify the various abilities that intelligence tests measure. (p. 453)
    a. intelligence clusters
    b. meaningful chunking
    c. factor analysis
    d. a standard bell curve

13. According to the test designers, the __________ is the most "culture-fair" intelligence test available. (p. 454)
    a. Stanford-Binet Intelligence Scales, Fifth Edition
    b. Wechsler Preschool and Primary Scale of Intelligence-Revised
    c. Kaufman Assessment Battery for Children-II
    d. Wechsler Intelligence Scale for Children-IV

14. According to Sternberg, __________ intelligence is goal-oriented activity aimed at adapting to, shaping, or selecting environments. (p. 455)
    a. practical
    b. analytical
    c. creative
    d. logico-mathematical

15. Marci scored high in Gardner's naturalist intelligence. This means Marci probably is __________ (p. 456)
    a. sensitive to the sounds, rhythms, and meaning of words.
    b. able to recognize and classify all varieties of animals and plants.
    c. able to discriminate complex inner feelings and knows her own desires.
    d. able to detect and respond appropriately to the moods of others.

16. Emotional intelligence is __________ (p. 457)
    a. strongly related to IQ.
    b. positively associated with leadership skills.
    c. negatively associated with self-esteem.
    d. positively associated with aggressive behavior.

17. Arthur Jensen claims that __________ is largely responsible for variations in intelligence. (p. 458)
    a. heredity
    b. SES
    c. gender
    d. the environment

18. With increasing education, parents establish a(n) __________ style of communication, like that of classrooms and tests. (p. 460)
    a. collaborative
    b. elaborative
    c. hierarchical
    d. analytical

19. Dynamic assessment is consistent with which theory of development? (p. 461)
    a. information-processing theory
    b. the behaviorist perspective
    c. psychoanalytic theory
    d. Vygotsky's sociocultural theory

20. The school years bring dramatic gains in pragmatics, which refers to __________ (p. 463)
    a. the mastery of complex grammatical constructions.
    b. the communicative side of language.
    c. language decoding skills.
    d. word-learning strategies.

21. Bilingual adults frequently code switch to __________ (p. 465)
    a. express cultural identity.
    b. attain better writing skills.
    c. violate the rules of grammar.
    d. gain appreciation for a second language.

22. Mastery of a second language must begin __________ for full development to occur. (p. 465)
    a. at birth
    b. by age 2
    c. by kindergarten
    d. sometime in childhood

23. In a constructivist classroom, __________ (p. 467)
    a. students complete teacher-assigned tasks.
    b. students are active agents of their own knowledge.
    c. the teacher is the sole authority for rules and knowledge.
    d. the teacher does most of the talking.

24. In __________, a teacher and two to four students form a cooperative group and lead dialogues on the content of a text passage. (p. 468)
    a. reciprocal teaching
    b. a social-constructivist classroom
    c. a community of learners
    d. a traditional classroom

25. Research shows that __________ (p. 471)
    a. schools in low-income neighborhoods usually emphasize a back-to-basics approach to teaching.
    b. magnet schools usually serve only the neighborhood student population.
    c. a less segregated education enhances minority student achievement.
    d. magnet schools benefit middle- and higher-SES students, but low-SES students show fewer gains.

26. The more low-SES middle-school students use home computers to access the Internet for information gathering, the __________ (p. 472)
    a. lower their school grades.
    b. higher their reading achievement scores.
    c. lower their math achievement scores.
    d. more likely they are to cheat on assignments.

27. Derek, who has Down syndrome, spends all of his school day working alongside typical students in a regular educational setting. Derek's classroom is __________ (p. 473)
    a. probably unable to meet his unique needs.
    b. fully integrated.
    c. fully inclusive.
    d. consistent with a constructivist approach.

28. The standard definition of giftedness includes children whose IQ scores exceed _____ (p. 474)
    a. 100.
    b. 120.
    c. 130.
    d. 150.

29. When faced with a task or problem, Kristin generates multiple and unusual possible solutions. Kristin __________ (p. 474)
    a. thinks divergently.
    b. is probably between the ages of 7 and 9.
    c. thinks convergently.
    d. is formal operational.

30. International studies reveal that, compared with students in top-achieving nations, U.S. students __________ (p. 476)
    a. are about equal with Canadian students.
    b. focus more on absorbing facts.
    c. perform significantly better in science and language arts.
    d. focus more on effort than grades.

CHAPTER 13
EMOTIONAL AND SOCIAL DEVELOPMENT IN MIDDLE CHILDHOOD

BRIEF CHAPTER SUMMARY

According to Erikson, children who successfully resolve the psychological conflict of industry versus inferiority develop a sense of competence at useful skills and tasks, learn the value of division of labor, and develop a sense of moral commitment and responsibility. During middle childhood, psychological traits and social comparisons appear in children's self-concepts, and a hierarchically organized self-esteem emerges. Attribution research has identified adult communication styles that affect children's explanations for success and failure and, in turn, their academic self-esteem, motivation, and task performance. Gains occur in self-conscious emotions, understanding of emotional states, and emotional self-regulation. Perspective taking improves greatly, supported by cognitive maturity and experiences in which adults and peers explain their viewpoints. An expanding social world, the capacity to consider more information when reasoning, and perspective taking lead moral understanding to advance during middle childhood.

In middle childhood, the society of peers becomes an increasingly important context for development. Friendships become more complex and psychologically based, with a growing emphasis on mutual trust and assistance. Peer acceptance is a powerful predictor of current and future psychological adjustment. Rejected children tend to engage in antisocial behavior that leads agemates to dislike them. During the school years, boys' masculine gender identities strengthen, whereas girls' identities become more flexible. Cultural values and parental attitudes influence these trends.

During middle childhood, the amount of time children spend with parents declines dramatically. Child rearing shifts toward coregulation as parents grant children more decision-making power while still retaining general oversight. Sibling rivalry tends to increase in middle childhood, and siblings often attempt to reduce it by striving to be different from one another. Only children are no less well-adjusted than children with siblings and are advantaged in self-esteem and achievement motivation. Children of gay and lesbian parents are well-adjusted, and the large majority are heterosexual. The situations of children in never-married, single-parent families can be improved by strengthening social support, education, and employment opportunities for parents.

When children experience divorce—often followed by entry into blended families as a result of remarriage—child, parent, and family characteristics all influence how well they fare. Growing up in a dual-earner family can have many benefits for school-age children, particularly when mothers enjoy their work, when work settings and communities support parents in their child-rearing responsibilities, and when high-quality child care is available, including appropriate after-school programs as an alternative to self-care.

As children experience new demands in school and begin to understand the realities of the wider world, their fears and anxieties are directed toward new concerns, including physical harm, media events, academic failure, parents' health, and peer rejection. Child sexual abuse has devastating consequences for children and is especially difficult to treat. The personal characteristics of children, a warm family life that includes authoritative parenting, and school and community resources predict resilience—the capacity to overcome adversity.

LEARNING OBJECTIVES

After reading this chapter, you should be able to:

13.1 Explain Erikson's stage of industry versus inferiority, noting major personality changes. (p. 482)

13.2 Describe school-age children's self-concept and self-esteem, and discuss factors that affect their achievement-related attributions. (pp. 482–488)

13.3 Cite changes in the expression and understanding of emotion in middle childhood. (pp. 489–491)

13.4 Trace the development of perspective taking in middle childhood, and discuss the relationship between perspective taking and social skills. (pp. 491–492)

13.5 Describe changes in moral understanding during middle childhood, including children's understanding of diversity and inequality. (pp. 492–497)

13.6 Discuss changes in peer sociability during middle childhood, including characteristics of peer groups and friendships and the contributions of each to social development. (pp. 497–500)

13.7 Describe the four categories of peer acceptance, noting how each is related to social behavior, and discuss ways to help rejected children. (pp. 500–503)

13.8 Summarize changes in gender-stereotyped beliefs and gender identity during middle childhood, noting sex differences and cultural influences. (pp. 503–506)

13.9 Discuss changes in the parent–child relationship during middle childhood. (pp. 506–507)

13.10 Describe changes in sibling relationships during middle childhood, and compare the experiences and developmental outcomes of only children with those of children with siblings. (pp. 507–508)

13.11 Describe gay and lesbian families, and discuss the developmental outcomes of children raised in such families. (pp. 508–509)

13.12 Describe the characteristics of never-married, single-parent families, and explain how living in a single-parent household affects children. (pp. 509–510)

13.13 Explain children's adjustment to divorce and blended families, noting the influence of parent and child characteristics and social supports within the family and surrounding community. (pp. 510–515)

13.14 Discuss the impact of maternal employment and dual-earner families on school-age children's development, noting the influence of environmental supports, and summarize research on child care for school-age children. (pp. 515–517)

13.15 Discuss common fears and anxieties in middle childhood. (pp. 517–518)

13.16 Discuss factors related to child sexual abuse, its consequences for children's development, and its prevention and treatment. (pp. 519–520)

13.17 Cite factors that foster resilience in middle childhood. (pp. 520, 522–523)

STUDY QUESTIONS

Erikson's Theory: Industry versus Inferiority

1. According to Erikson, the combination of what two factors sets the stage for the psychological conflict of middle childhood, *industry versus inferiority*? (p. 482)

   A. ______________________________

   B. ______________________________

2. Describe the positive resolution of the industry versus inferiority stage. (p. 482)

   ____

   ____

3. Explain how the beginning of formal schooling puts some children at risk for developing a sense of inferiority during middle childhood. (p. 482)

   ____

   ____

   ____

Self-Understanding

Self-Concept

1. List three ways in which self-concept changes during middle childhood. (p. 482)

   A. ______

   B. ______

   C. ______

2. Provide an example of a *social comparison.* (p. 483)

   ______

   ______

Cognitive, Social, and Cultural Influences on Self-Concept

1. Describe changes in the structure of the self during middle childhood. (p. 483)

   ______

   ______

2. Provide an example of how perspective-taking skills affect the development of self-concept. (p. 483)

   ______

   ______

3. Explain the importance of parental support for self-development in middle childhood. (p. 483)

   ______

   ______

4. True or False: Children in collectivist societies often define themselves according to group membership, while Western children usually focus on personal attributes. (p. 483)

Self-Esteem

1. List four self-evaluations that children form by the age of 6 or 7. (p. 484)

   A. ______

   B. ______

   C. ______

   D. ______

2. True or False: Once children's self-esteem takes on a hierarchical structure, separate self-evaluations contribute equally to general self-esteem. (p. 484)

3. During childhood and adolescence, perceived (academic competence / physical appearance) correlates more strongly with overall self-worth than does any other self-esteem factor. (p. 484)

4. Self-esteem (rises / drops) during the early elementary school years. Explain why. (p. 485)

   ______

   ______

   ______

Influences on Self-Esteem

1. Provide an example of an ethnic difference and a sex difference in children's self-esteem. (p. 485)

   Ethnic: ______________________________

   ____

   Sex: ______________________________

   ____

2. Differentiate child-rearing practices associated with high versus low self-esteem in middle childhood. (p. 486)

   High: ______________________________

   ____

   Low: ______________________________

   ____

3. What is the best way to foster a positive, secure self-image in school-age children? (p. 486)

   ____

4. ______________ are our common, everyday explanations for the causes of behavior. (p. 486)

5. Children who are high in academic self-esteem make ______________ attributions, in which successes are credited to ability. In contrast, children who hold a fixed view of ability develop ______________ and attribute their failures to lack of ability. (pp. 486–487)

6. Briefly explain how children's attributions affect their goals. (p. 487)

   ____

   ____

   ____

7. Summarize how communication from parents and teachers influences children's attributional style. (p. 487)

   Parents: ______________________________

   ____

   Teachers: ______________________________

   ____

8. True or False: Girls and low-income ethnic minority children are especially vulnerable to *learned helplessness.* (p. 487)

9. Provide an example of how cultural values affect the likelihood that children will develop learned helplessness. (p. 488)

   ____

   ____

10. ______________________ is an intervention that encourages learned-helpless children to believe that they can overcome failure by exerting more effort. Briefly describe this technique. (p. 488)

    ____

    ____

    ____

11. List four ways to foster a *mastery-oriented* approach to learning in middle childhood. (p. 489)

    A. ____________________

    B. ____________________

    C. ____________________

    D. ____________________

Emotional Development

Self-Conscious Emotions

1. Discuss changes in how children experience pride and guilt during middle childhood. (pp. 489–490)

2. Under what circumstances are pride and guilt beneficial? (p. 490)

3. Intense feelings of ____________________ can lead to a sharp drop in self-esteem, withdrawal, depression, and anger. (p. 490)

Emotional Understanding

1. List three advances in school-age children's understanding of emotions. (p. 490)

    A. ____________________

    B. ____________________

    C. ____________________

2. How do cognitive development and social experiences contribute to gains in emotional understanding? (p. 490)

Emotional Self-Regulation

1. Differentiate between *problem-centered* and *emotion-centered* coping strategies, noting the circumstances in which children are likely to use one strategy versus the other. (p. 490)

    Problem-centered: ____________________

    Emotion-centered: ____________________

2. When the development of emotional self-regulation has gone well, young people acquire a sense of emotional ______________________________—a feeling of being in control of their emotional experience. (p. 491)

3. Distinguish characteristics of emotionally well-regulated children versus children with poor emotional regulation. (p. 491)

   Well-regulated: ______________________________

   ____

   Poorly regulated: ______________________________

   ____

4. Briefly explain the role of culture in the development of self-regulation. (p. 491)

   ____

   ____

Understanding Others: Perspective Taking

1. Define *perspective taking.* (p. 491)

   ____

   ____

2. Match each of Selman's stages of perspective taking with the appropriate descriptions. (p. 492)

   _____ Recognize that self and others can have different perspectives, but confuse the two
   _____ Understand that different perspectives may be due to access to different information
   _____ Can imagine how the self and others are viewed from the perspective of an impartial third person
   _____ Can view own thoughts, feelings, and behavior from others' perspectives
   _____ Understand that third-party perspective taking can be influenced by larger societal values

   A. Undifferentiated
   B. Social-informational
   C. Self-reflective
   D. Third-party
   E. Societal

3. Cite factors that contribute to individual differences in perspective-taking skill. (p. 492)

   ____

   ____

   ____

Moral Development

Moral and Social-Conventional Understanding

1. Provide an example illustrating cultural differences in children's appreciation of moral rules. (p. 492)

   ____

   ____

2. School-age children develop a (flexible / rigid) approach to moral rules. (p. 492)

3. How do children interpret the relationship between moral imperatives and social conventions? (p. 493)

   ____

   ____

   ____

Understanding Individual Rights

1. How do notions of personal choice enhance children's moral understandings? (p. 493)

2. Provide an example showing how older school-age children place limits on individual choice. (pp. 493–494)

Culture and Moral Understanding

1. True or False: Children in Western and non-Western cultures use similar criteria to distinguish moral and social-conventional concerns. Explain your answer. (p. 494)

Cultural Influences: Children's Understanding of God

1. Trace children's understanding of God from preschool through adolescence. (p. 495)

   Preschool and school-age children:

   Adolescents:

2. Explain how the research strategies used to study children's understanding of God influence their responses. (p. 495)

3. Children's understanding of God (is / is not) limited to an anthropomorphic, "big person" image. (p. 495)

Understanding Diversity and Inequality

1. True or False: Young schoolchildren often derive their racial attitudes from the media and from implicit messages in their environments rather than from parents and friends. (p. 494)
2. True or False: Many ethnic-minority children show a pattern of reverse favoritism, in which they assign positive characteristics to the privileged white majority and negative characteristics to their own group. (p. 496)
3. List three personal and situational factors that influence the extent to which children hold racial and ethnic biases. (p. 496)

   A.

   B.

   C.

4. Describe two ways to reduce prejudice in school-age children. (p. 497)

   A. ____

   ____

   B. ____

   ____

Peer Relations

Peer Groups

1. Describe the characteristics of *peer groups.* (p. 498)

   ____

   ____

   ____

2. How does the creation of a "peer culture" lead to a sense of group identity? (p. 498)

   ____

   ____

   ____

   ____

3. Explain how school-age children view peer exclusion, noting gender differences. (p. 498)

   ____

   ____

   ____

4. Describe the social and emotional consequences of being excluded from a peer group. (p. 498)

   Social: ____

   ____

   Emotional: ____

   ____

Friendships

1. Describe the nature of friendship during the school years. (p. 499)

   ____

   ____

2. Cite the defining feature of friendship in middle childhood. (p. 499)

   ____

3. True or False: New ideas about the meaning of friendship lead school-age children to be less selective in their choice of friends than they were at younger ages. (p. 499)

4. High-quality friendships (do / do not) tend to remain stable over middle childhood. (p. 499)

5. List characteristics of aggressive children's friendships. (pp. 499–500)

   Aggressive girls: ______________________________

   ____

   Aggressive boys: ______________________________

   ____

Peer Acceptance

1. Define *peer acceptance*, noting how it is different from friendship. (p. 500)

   ____

   ____

   ____

2. Explain how researchers commonly assess peer acceptance. (p. 500)

   ____

   ____

3. Name and briefly describe four categories of peer acceptance. (p. 500)

   A. ______________________________

   B. ______________________________

   C. ______________________________

   D. ______________________________

4. True or False: All school-age children fit into one of the four categories of peer acceptance described in Question 3. (p. 500)

5. Identify and describe two subtypes of *popular children.* (pp. 500–501)

   A. ______________________________

   ____

   B. ______________________________

   ____

6. Describe the social behavior of *rejected-aggressive* and *rejected-withdrawn* children. (p. 501)

   Aggressive: ______________________________

   ____

   Withdrawn: ______________________________

   ____

7. Cite four consequences of peer rejection. (p. 501)

   A. ______________________________

   B. ______________________________

   C. ______________________________

   D. ______________________________

8. True or False: *Controversial children* are hostile and disruptive but also engage in high rates of positive, prosocial acts. (p. 501)

9. True or False: *Neglected children* are often poorly adjusted and display less socially competent behavior than their peers. Explain your answer. (p. 501)

____

____

10. List three interventions designed to help rejected children. (pp. 502–503)

A. ____

B. ____

C. ____

Biology and Environment: Bullies and Their Victims

1. What is *peer victimization*? (p. 502)

____

____

2. True or False: Twenty to 40 percent of middle-school students report they have experienced "cyberbullying"—bullying through e-mail or other electronic media. (p. 502)

3. Describe typical characteristics of bullies. (p. 502)

____

____

____

4. Describe characteristics of victimized children. (p. 502)

____

____

____

5. True or False: Victims of peer victimization are rarely, if ever, aggressive. Explain your answer. (p. 502)

____

____

____

6. Discuss individual and environment-based interventions for peer victimization. (p. 502)

Individual: ____

____

Environment-based: ____

____

Gender Typing

Gender-Stereotyped Beliefs

1. Gender-stereotyping of personality traits (decreases / increases) steadily during middle childhood. (p. 503)
2. Provide an example illustrating how parents contribute to children's stereotyping of personality traits. (p. 503)

   ____

   ____

3. Differentiate academic subjects and skills that children regard as either masculine or feminine. (p. 503)

   Masculine: ____

   Feminine: ____

4. True or False: As school-age children extend their knowledge of gender stereotypes, they become more closed-minded about what males and females can do. (p. 504)
5. True or False: School-age children regard certain violations of gender roles—such as boys dressing in girls' clothing—as nearly as bad as moral transgressions. (p. 504)

Gender Identity and Behavior

1. Contrast the gender identity development of girls and boys during middle childhood, and note implications for behavior. (p. 505)

   Girls: ____

   ____

   Boys: ____

   ____

2. List three self-evaluations that influence gender identity and adjustment in middle childhood. (p. 505)

   A. ____

   B. ____

   C. ____

3. Discuss two competing approaches to helping children who are gender-atypical. (p. 506)

   A. ____

   ____

   B. ____

   ____

Family Influences

Parent–Child Relationships

1. In middle childhood, the amount of time that children spend with their parents (declines / increases) dramatically. (p. 506)
2. During the school years, child rearing becomes easier for those parents who established a(n) ______________________ style during the early years. (p. 507)

3. What is *coregulation,* and how does it foster a cooperative relationship between parent and child? (p. 507)

   A. ______________________________

   ____

   B. ______________________________

   ____

4. How do mothers and fathers differ in interactions with their children? (p. 507)

   Mothers: ______________________________

   ____

   Fathers: ______________________________

   ____

Siblings

1. During middle childhood, sibling rivalry tends to (increase / decrease). Explain your answer. (p. 507)

   ____

   ____

2. School-age siblings (do / do not) usually rely on each other for companionship and assistance. Explain your answer. (p. 508)

   ____

   ____

Only Children

1. True or False: Research indicates that sibling relationships are essential for normal development. (p. 508)
2. Discuss the adjustment of children in one-child families. (p. 508)

   ____

   ____

   ____

Gay and Lesbian Families

1. True or False: Research shows that gay and lesbian parents are as committed to and effective at child-rearing as are heterosexual parents. Provide evidence to support your response. (p. 509)

   ____

   ____

   ____

2. True or False: Children from gay and lesbian families are more likely than their peers to be homosexual as adults. (p. 509)
3. Are most children of gay and lesbian parents stigmatized by their parents' sexual orientation? Explain. (p. 509)

   ____

   ____

Never-Married Single-Parent Families

1. What group constitutes the largest proportion of never-married parents, and what factors may contribute to this trend? (p. 509)

   A. ______________________________

   B. ______________________________

2. Cite outcomes associated with children raised in never-married single-parent families. (p. 510)

   ____

   ____

   ____

Divorce

1. True or False: The United States has the highest divorce rate in the world. (p. 510)
2. Of the 45 percent of American marriages that end in divorce, ______ percent involve children. (p. 510)
3. Your text points out that divorce is not "a single event in the lives of parents and children." Explain what this means. (p. 510)

   ____

   ____

   ____

4. Provide an example of an immediate consequence of divorce on the home environment. (p. 511)

   ____

   ____

5. Discuss how children's ages affect their reactions to divorce. (p. 511)

   Older children: ______________________________

   ____

   Younger children: ______________________________

   ____

6. Summarize sex differences in children's reactions to divorce. (pp. 511–512)

   Boys: ______________________________

   ____

   ____

   Girls: ______________________________

   ____

   ____

7. (Boys / Girls) of divorcing parents receive less emotional support from mothers, teachers, and peers. (p. 512)
8. Most children show improved adjustment by ________ years after their parents' divorce. (p. 512)

9. Summarize the potential long-term negative consequences of parental divorce, noting who is most at risk for such adjustment difficulties. (p. 512)

____

____

____

____

10. What is the overriding factor in positive adjustment following divorce? (p. 512)

____

11. Explain why a good father–child relationship is important for both boys and girls following divorce. (p. 512)

Girls: ____

____

Boys: ____

____

12. True or False: Making the transition to a low-conflict, single-parent household is better for children than staying in a high-conflict intact family. (p. 512)

13. Describe *divorce mediation,* and explain why it is likely to have benefits for children. (p. 513)

____

____

____

____

14. In ______________________________, the court grants the mother and father equal say in important decisions regarding the child's upbringing. Describe common living arrangements associated with this option, noting their impact on children's adjustment. (p. 513)

Living arrangements: ____

____

Impact: ____

____

15. List four ways to help children adjust to divorce. (p. 514)

A. ____

B. ____

C. ____

D. ____

Blended Families

1. What is a *blended,* or *reconstituted, family*? (p. 513)

____

____

2. List two reasons why blended families present adjustment difficulties for many children. (p. 513)

   A. ______________________________

   ____

   B. ______________________________

   ____

3. The most frequent form of blended family is a(n) ______________ arrangement. Contrast boys' and girls' adjustment in this family arrangement. (p. 514)

   Boys: ______________________________

   ____

   Girls: ______________________________

   ____

4. Explain why older children and adolescents of both sexes living in mother–stepfather families display more irresponsible, acting out, and antisocial behavior than do their agemates in nonstepfamilies. (p. 514)

   ____

   ____

   ____

5. Remarriage of noncustodial fathers often leads to (reduced / increased) contact with children. (p. 515)

6. Cite two reasons why children tend to react negatively to the remarriage of custodial fathers. (p. 515)

   A. ______________________________

   B. ______________________________

7. (Girls / Boys) have an especially hard time getting along with stepmothers. Briefly explain your response. (p. 515)

   ____

   ____

   ____

8. Explain how family life education and counseling can help parents and children in blended families adapt to the complexities of their new circumstances. (p. 515)

   ____

   ____

   ____

   ____

9. The divorce rate for second marriages is (higher / lower) than for first marriages. (p. 515)

Maternal Employment and Dual-Earner Families

1. In the United States, more than _______ percent of mothers with school-age children are employed. (p. 515)

2. Describe potential benefits of maternal employment for school-age children, and note the circumstances under which such outcomes are achieved. (p. 515)

____

____

____

3. True or False: Maternal employment results in more time with fathers, who take greater responsibility for child care. (p. 515)

4. List four supports that help parents juggle the demands of work and child rearing. (p. 516)

   A. ____

   B. ____

   C. ____

   D. ____

5. Cite characteristics of *self-care children* who fare well and those who fare poorly. (p. 516)

   Children who fare well: ____

   ____

   Children who fare poorly: ____

   ____

6. Before age ______ or ______, children should not be left unsupervised because most are not yet competent to handle emergencies. (p. 516)

7. True or False: After-school enrichment programs are especially common in inner-city neighborhoods. (p. 517)

Some Common Problems of Development

Fears and Anxieties

1. Summarize new fears and anxieties that emerge in middle childhood. (p. 517)

____

____

____

2. What do children in Western nations mention as the most common source of their fears? (p. 517)

____

3. An intense, unmanageable fear that leads to persistent avoidance of the feared situation is called a(n) ______________. (p. 517)

4. Describe the symptoms associated with school phobia. (p. 517)

____

____

5. Distinguish common causes of school phobia in early childhood from those in later childhood and adolescence, noting implications for treatment. (p. 518)

   Early childhood: ______

   Later childhood and adolescence: ______

Cultural Influences: The Impact of Ethnic and Political Violence on Children

1. Discuss the immediate and long-term consequences faced by children of war. (p. 518)

2. What is the best safeguard against lasting problems for children exposed to ethnic and political violence? (p. 518)

3. Provide an example of an intervention used to help children from Public School 31 in Brooklyn, New York, in the wake of the September 11 attack on the World Trade Center. (p. 518)

Child Sexual Abuse

1. Sexual abuse is committed against children of both sexes, but more often against (girls / boys). (p. 519)
2. List typical characteristics of sexual abusers. (p. 519)

3. Describe the characteristics of children who are especially vulnerable to abuse. (p. 519)

4. Discuss the adjustment problems of sexually abused children, noting differences between younger children and adolescents. (p. 519)

   Younger children: ______

   Adolescents: ______

5. Describe common behavioral characteristics of sexually abused children as they move into young adulthood. (pp. 519–520)

6. Why is it difficult to treat victims of child sexual abuse? (p. 520)

7. Discuss the role of educational programs in preventing child sexual abuse. (p. 520)

Social Issues: Health: Children's Eyewitness Testimony

1. True or False: Children as young as age 3 are frequently asked to provide testimony in court cases involving child abuse and neglect. (p. 521)
2. Briefly summarize age differences in children's ability to provide accurate testimony. (p. 521)

3. Identify several reasons why young children are more prone to memory problems than older children. (p. 521)

4. True or False: When adults lead children by suggesting incorrect information, they increase the likelihood of incorrect reporting among preschool and school-age children alike. (p. 521)
5. True or False: Special interviewing methods involving the use of anatomically correct dolls have been successful in prompting more accurate recall of sexual abuse experiences, particularly among preschoolers. (p. 521)
6. Provide an example of an intervention that can be used to assist child witnesses. (p. 521)

Fostering Resilience in Middle Childhood

1. Cite personal, family, school, and community resources that foster resilience in middle childhood. (p. 521)

   Personal: ______________________________

   ____

   Family: ______________________________

   ____

   School: ______________________________

   ____

   Community: ______________________________

   ____

2. Summarize components of the *Resolving Conflicts Creatively Program,* and note program outcomes for child behavior. (p. 521)

   Components: ______________________________

   ____

   ____

   Outcomes: ______________________________

   ____

   ____

ASK YOURSELF . . .

For *Ask Yourself* questions for this chapter, along with feedback on the accuracy of your answers, please log on to MyDevelopmentLab (for registration and access, please visit mydevelopmentlab.com or follow the instructions on page ix).

(1) Select the Multimedia Library.

(2) Choose the explore option.

(3) Find your chapter from the drop down box.

(4) Click find now.

(5) Complete questions and choose "Submit answers for grading" or "Clear answers" to start over.

SUGGESTED READINGS

Feerick, M. M., & Silverman, G. B. (Eds.). (2007). *Children exposed to violence.* Baltimore, MD: Paul H. Brookes. With an emphasis on domestic violence, community violence, and war and terrorism, this book explores the effects of violence on all aspects of child development, including physical health, psychological well-being, academic achievement, and social competence.

Nucci, L. (2008). *Nice is not enough: Facilitating moral development.* Upper Saddle River, NY: Prentice Hall. Written by a leading expert in moral development, this book provides an extensive overview of developmental changes in moral understanding and explains how moral education can be incorporated into day-to-day classroom activities. Includes research-based strategies and sample lesson plans.

Pedro-Carroll, J. (2010). *Putting children first: Proven parenting strategies for helping children thrive through divorce.* New York: Avery/Penguin. Using up-to-date research findings, this book examines the short- and long-term consequences of parental divorce on children's development. Topics include preparing children for the separation, dealing with parent–child conflict, supporting children's resilience, and navigating new relationships and remarriage.

CROSSWORD PUZZLE 13.1

Across

3. __________-centered coping: appraising a situation as changeable, identifying the difficulty, and deciding what to do about it
5. Social _____________: judgments of appearance, abilities, behavior, and other characteristics in relation to those of others
6. ___________ taking: the capacity to imagine what others may be thinking and feeling
7. ___________ versus inferiority: Erikson's psychological conflict of middle childhood
8. Learned ______________: attributions that credit success to luck and failure to low ability
9. __________-centered coping: internal, private, and aimed at controlling distress when little can be done about an outcome

Down

1. Attribution __________ is an intervention aimed at modifying the attributions of learned-helpless children.
2. An intense, unmanageable fear that leads to persistent avoidance of a feared situation
4. __________-__________ attributions: credit success to high ability and failure to insufficient effort (2 words, hyph.)

CROSSWORD PUZZLE 13.2

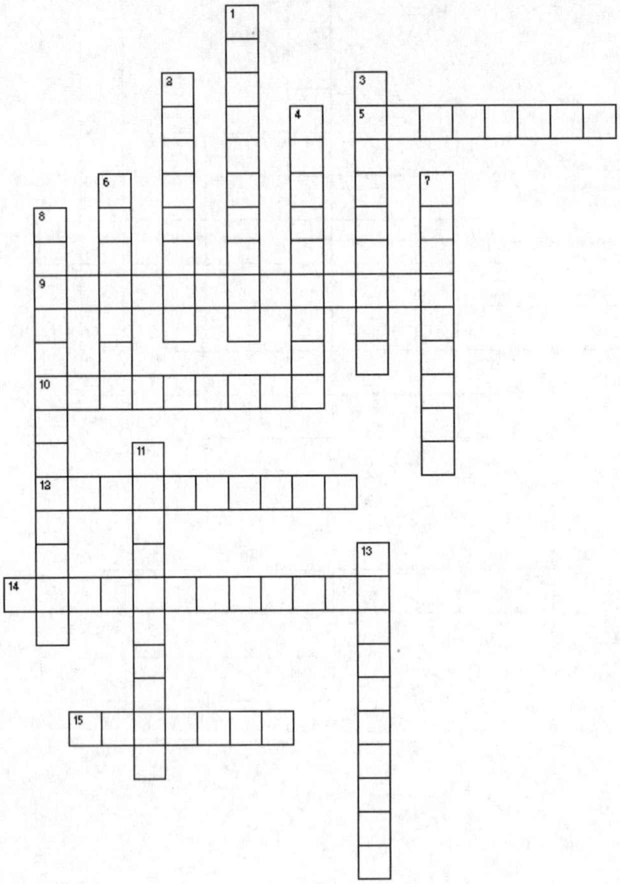

Across

5. Children who are actively disliked and get many negative votes on sociometric measures of peer acceptance
9. Children who get a large number of positive and negative votes on sociometric measures of peer acceptance
10. Divorce ___________ attempts to settle disputes of divorcing adults while avoiding legal battles that intensify family conflict.
12. Peer ____________: the extent to which a child is viewed by a group of agemates as a worthy social partner
14. Supervision in which parents exercise general oversight but permit children to manage moment-to-moment decisions
15. Children who get many positive votes on sociometric measures of peer acceptance

Down

1. Rejected-_____________ children are a subgroup of rejected children who engage in high rates of conflict, hostility, hyperactivity, inattention, and impulsivity.
2. ______-________ children look after themselves while their parents are at work. (2 words, hyph.)
3. Popular-____________ children: good students who communicate with peers in sensitive, friendly, and cooperative ways
4. Rejected-____________ children are a subgroup of rejected children who are passive and socially awkward.
6. Family structure resulting from cohabitation or remarriage that includes parent, child, and steprelatives; also called "reconstituted family"
7. Children who are seldom chosen, either positively or negatively, on sociometric measures of peer acceptance
8. Peer __________: certain children become frequent targets of verbal and physical attacks or other forms of abuse.
11. Social units of peers who generate unique values and standards for behavior and a social structure of leaders and followers (2 words)
13. Popular-____________ children: highly aggressive, yet viewed by peers as "cool"

PRACTICE TEST #1

1. According to Erikson, __________ is the positive resolution of the psychological conflict of middle childhood. (p. 482)
   a. autonomy
   b. trust
   c. industry
   d. identity

2. Chyna observed that she was "better at spelling" than her peers but "not as good at science." Chyna is __________ (p. 483)
   a. making social comparisons.
   b. engaging in perspective-taking.
   c. exhibiting learned helplessness.
   d. exhibiting poor self-esteem.

3. When school-age children become better at reading others' messages and internalizing their expectations, they form a(n) __________ that they use to evaluate their real self. (p. 483)
   a. social comparison
   b. inflated self-esteem
   c. mastery-oriented self
   d. ideal self

4. Self-esteem __________ few years of elementary school. (p. 484)
   a. is extremely high during the first
   b. declines during the first
   c. declines steadily during the last
   d. increases greatly during the first

5. Children whose parents use a(n) __________ child-rearing style feel especially good about themselves. (p. 486)
   a. authoritative
   b. authoritarian
   c. permissive
   d. uninvolved

6. During the school years, children typically report feeling guilt __________ (p. 489)
   a. only when adults are present.
   b. for any mishap in which they were involved.
   c. only for intentional wrongdoing.
   d. only to peers but not to adults.

7. Feelings of __________ motivate children to take on further challenges. (p. 490)
   a. guilt
   b. fear
   c. pride
   d. shame

8. Hermione understands that different perspectives may result because people have access to different information. Hermione is in Selman's stage of __________ perspective taking. (p. 492)
   a. undifferentiated
   b. social-informational
   c. self-reflective
   d. third-party

9. By age 7 or 8, most children say that __________ (pp. 492–493)
   a. truth telling is always good.
   b. it is OK to bluntly tell a classmate you do not like her drawing.
   c. lying is always bad, regardless of your reasons.
   d. intentions are important in deciding whether to tell the truth or lie.

10. By the early school years, children __________ (p. 494)
    a. associate power and privilege with all people, regardless of race.
    b. associate inferior status with people of color.
    c. evaluate their own racial group as less favorable than other groups.
    d. express out-group favoritism.

11. Children view God as __________ (p. 495)
    a. a parentlike figure in the sky.
    b. having only anthropomorphic characteristics.
    c. having a mix of tangible and intangible features.
    d. a being governed by human rules.

12. Peer groups organize on the basis of __________ (p. 498)
    a. proximity.
    b. temperament.
    c. family structure.
    d. moral values.

13. School-age children state that a good friendship is based on __________ (p. 499)
    a. proximity.
    b. acts of kindness.
    c. peer popularity.
    d. similar likes and dislikes.

14. On children's self-reports of peer acceptance, __________ children are seldom mentioned, either positively or negatively. (p. 500)
    a. rejected
    b. controversial
    c. neglected
    d. average

15. Popular-prosocial children __________ (pp. 500–501)
    a. include athletically skilled but poor students who cause trouble and defy adult authority.
    b. show high rates of physical and relational aggression.
    c. are passive and socially awkward.
    d. combine academic and social competence.

16. Controversial children __________ (p. 501)
    a. combine academic and social competence.
    b. include relationally aggressive children who enhance their own status by excluding others.
    c. display a blend of positive and negative social behaviors.
    d. are passive and socially awkward.

17. Research indicates that most bullies are __________ (p. 502)
    a. low-SES children eager to increase their status among peers.
    b. boys who use both physical and verbal attacks.
    c. children who were initially admired for some special ability but later rejected.
    d. girls who bombard a vulnerable classmate with verbal and relational hostility.

18. Max feels a high degree of similarity to other boys. Max is __________ (p. 505)
    a. gender stereotyped.
    b. gender typical.
    c. gender content.
    d. gender atypical.

19. __________ support(s) and protect(s) children while preparing them for adolescence, when they will make many important decisions themselves. (p. 507)
    a. Indulgent parenting
    b. Authoritarian child rearing
    c. Peer groups
    d. Coregulation

20. Parental comparisons of siblings are more frequent for __________ (p. 507)
    a. other-sex siblings who are close in age.
    b. same-sex siblings who are close in age.
    c. other-sex siblings who are far apart in age.
    d. same-sex siblings who are far apart in age.

21. Compared to children with siblings, only children in China __________ (p. 508)
    a. are more advanced in cognitive development.
    b. do poorer in school.
    c. feel less emotionally secure.
    d. are less accepted by their peers.

22. Children of never-married mothers who lack a father's involvement __________ than children in low-SES first-marriage families. (p. 510)
    a. achieve better in school
    b. do not suffer more adjustment problems
    c. engage in more antisocial behavior
    d. have more close friends

23. Children of divorce spend an average of _____ years in a single-parent home. (p. 510)
    a. 2
    b. 3
    c. 4
    d. 5

24. Which of the following children is the most likely to fear that both parents may abandon them following a divorce? (p. 511)
    a. Asher, age 4
    b. Beatrice, age 8
    c. Christa, age 12
    d. Dimitri, age 16

25. Self-care __________ (p. 516)
    a. decreases with age.
    b. is uncommon in the United States.
    c. increases with SES.
    d. children have few fears.

26. Nighttime fears __________ (p. 517)
    a. are most common in the preschool years.
    b. increase between ages 7 and 9.
    c. increase between ages 10 and 12.
    d. are most common in adolescence.

27. Outcomes for children exposed to ethnic and political violence, such as anxiety, depression, aggression, and antisocial behavior, appear to be __________ (p. 518)
    a. similar in all cultures worldwide.
    b. more pronounced in impoverished countries.
    c. less severe for girls than for boys.
    d. worse in collectivist societies.

28. The typical child sexual offender is a __________ (p. 519)
    a. female parent or stepparent who the victim trusts.
    b. female the victim does not know well.
    c. male the victim does not know well.
    d. male parent, or someone the parent knows well.

29. Children testifying in court cases are more likely to remember an event if __________ (p. 521)
    a. it is distinctive and personally relevant.
    b. it occurred during the past six months.
    c. they are prompted by leading questions.
    d. they are over the age of 10.

30. Which of the following is a typical personal characteristic of a stress-resilient child? (p. 520)
    a. being an only child
    b. having older siblings
    c. above-average intelligence
    d. emotion-centered coping style

PRACTICE TEST #2

1. According to Erikson, if the psychological conflict of middle childhood is resolved negatively, children develop a sense of __________ (p. 482)
   a. mistrust.
   b. shame.
   c. guilt.
   d. inferiority.

2. By age 6 to 7, children in diverse Western cultures have formed at least four broad self-evaluations, including __________ (p. 484)
   a. academic competence, social competence, physical/athletic competence, and physical appearance.
   b. emotional competence, social competence, cognitive competence, and spiritual competence.
   c. language competence, mathematical competence, physical appearance, and athletic ability.
   d. prosocial competence, athletic ability, spiritual competence, academic ability.

3. Self-esteem typically declines during the first few years of elementary school because __________ (p. 485)
   a. peer relationships become more complicated, often involving exclusion and rejection.
   b. children's performance is more frequently judged in relation to that of others.
   c. parents' expectations increase and become more rigid.
   d. children have less opportunity for physical activity and make-believe play.

4. Children who develop __________ attribute their failures, not their successes, to ability. (p. 487)
   a. learned helplessness
   b. mastery-oriented attributions
   c. an incremental view of ability
   d. overly high self-esteem

5. __________ encourages learned-helpless children to believe they can overcome failure by exerting more effort. (p. 488)
   a. Coregulation
   b. Mastery-orientation
   c. Attribution retraining
   d. Having an inflated self-esteem

6. School-age children tend to feel __________ when their violation of a standard is not under their control. (p. 489)
   a. guilt
   b. shame
   c. pride
   d. anger

7. Janice's emotional self-regulation has developed well. She feels in control of her emotional experiences. Janice __________ (p. 491)
   a. is engaging in problem-centered coping.
   b. is engaging in emotion-centered coping.
   c. is using coregulation.
   d. has acquired a sense of emotional self-efficacy.

8. Greta recognizes that she can have different thoughts and feelings than others, but she frequently confuses the two. According to Selman's stages of perspective taking, Greta is displaying __________ perspective taking. (p. 492)
   a. undifferentiated
   b. social-informational
   c. self-reflective
   d. third-party

9. With age, children realize that people's __________ and __________ affect the moral implications of violating a social convention. (p. 493)
   a. direct actions; knowledge of the rules
   b. direct actions; the presence of authority
   c. intentions; the context of their actions
   d. knowledge of the rules; the presence of authority

10. In middle childhood, children realize that responsibility for moral transgressions may differ according to a person's __________ (p. 493)
    a. sense of purposeful social convention.
    b. gender.
    c. sense of equity and benevolence.
    d. knowledge.

11. Ideas about God differ radically from ideas about ordinary experiences because they __________ (p. 495)
    a. are culturally transmitted.
    b. violate real-world assumptions.
    c. are highly detailed.
    d. involve moral concepts.

12. When peer groups are tracked for 3 to 6 weeks, __________ (p. 498)
    a. substantial change can occur.
    b. about half of the group members remain the same.
    c. membership changes very little.
    d. competition becomes increasingly common.

13. School-age children's friendships are __________ (p. 499)
    a. selective.
    b. diverse.
    c. based on proximity.
    d. unstable.

14. About __________ of students in a typical elementary school classroom are average in peer acceptance. (p. 500)
    a. one-quarter
    b. one-third
    c. half
    d. two-thirds

15. Rejected-aggressive children __________ (p. 501)
    a. are often admired for their athletic skills.
    b. are socially adept yet belligerent.
    c. are usually deficient in perspective taking.
    d. are passive and socially awkward.

16. Surprisingly, __________ children are usually well-adjusted. (p. 501)
    a. popular-antisocial
    b. rejected-withdrawn
    c. controversial
    d. neglected

17. Chronic victims of bullying have histories of __________ (p. 502)
    a. avoidant attachment.
    b. overly controlling child rearing.
    c. authoritative child rearing.
    d. nonfamily child care.

18. Riley is happy with her gender assignment and feels comfortable being a girl. Riley is gender __________ (p. 505)
    a. typical.
    b. atypical.
    c. content.
    d. stereotyped.

19. In middle childhood, child rearing becomes easier for parents who established a(n) __________ style during the early years. (p. 507)
    a. authoritative
    b. authoritarian
    c. permissive
    d. uninvolved

20. Only children are __________ than children with siblings. (p. 508)
    a. more often spoiled
    b. higher in self-esteem
    c. lower in achievement motivation
    d. less likely to go to college

21. According to research, children of homosexual parents __________ children of heterosexual parents. (p. 509)
    a. are as well adjusted as
    b. experience more mental health problems than
    c. are more likely to experience harsh discipline than
    d. are more confused about their gender identity than

22. Which of the following is true about never-married single-parent families? (p. 509)
    a. About 30 percent of U.S. children live with a single parent who has never married and does not have a partner.
    b. About 85 percent of never-married single parents are mothers and 15 percent are fathers.
    c. In the United States, Caucasian young women make up the largest group of never-married parents.
    d. Asian-American women postpone marriage more and childbirth less than women in other U.S. ethnic groups.

23. Which of the following is true about divorce rates in the United States? (p. 510)
    a. Between 2000 and 2010, the divorce rate rose dramatically.
    b. The United States has the lowest divorce rate of Western nations.
    c. About 45 percent of American marriages end in divorce, and half involve children.
    d. Nearly 60 percent of American marriages now end in divorce, with the majority involving children.

24. Divorced parents who __________ greatly improve their children's chances of growing up competent, stable, and happy. (p. 513)
    a. remarry
    b. engage in coparenting
    c. avoid divorce mediation
    d. agree to sole maternal custody

25. Which of the following is true about blended families? (p. 515)
    a. Girls, especially, have a hard time getting along with their stepmothers.
    b. Boys, especially, have a hard time getting along with their stepfathers.
    c. Parents do not usually treat their biological children differently from stepchildren.
    d. The longer children live in father–stepmother households, the greater the conflict.

26. As children become old enough to look after themselves, those who __________ appear responsible and well-adjusted. (p. 516)
    a. are left to their own devices
    b. have a history of maternal overprotection
    c. have a history of indulgent child rearing
    d. have regular after-school chores

27. Most cases of school phobia appear around age _____ to _____ (p. 517)
    a. 5; 7.
    b. 8; 10.
    c. 11; 13.
    d. 14; 17.

28. When war and social crises are temporary, most children _________ (p. 518)
    a. do not show long-term emotional difficulties.
    b. are emotionally unaffected by the trauma.
    c. become desensitized to violence.
    d. continue to show long-term mental health problems.

29. In about 25 percent of cases of sexual abuse, the offender is a _________ (p. 519)
    a. stepfather and the victim is a girl in middle childhood.
    b. mother, more often with a son.
    c. male relative and the victim is a child of the same sex.
    d. male acquaintance who the parents do not know well.

30. Which of the following is true about children's eyewitness testimony in court cases involving child abuse and neglect, child custody, and other matters? (p. 521)
    a. Until recently, children under 18 were not assumed fully competent to testify.
    b. Even in the face of biased interviewing, children and adolescents are resistant to suggestibility.
    c. When properly questioned, even 3-year-olds can recall recent events accurately.
    d. When adults use a confrontational questioning style, they increase the likelihood of correct reporting.

CHAPTER 14
PHYSICAL DEVELOPMENT IN ADOLESCENCE

BRIEF CHAPTER SUMMARY

Adolescence is a time of dramatic physical change leading to an adult-sized body and sexual maturity. Although early biologically based theories viewed puberty as a period of emotional turmoil, recent research shows that serious psychological disturbance is not common during the teenage years. A balanced point of view regards adolescent development as a joint product of biological, psychological, and social forces.

The dramatic physical changes of puberty are regulated by hormonal processes. On average, girls reach puberty two years earlier than boys, but wide individual differences exist. The first outward sign of puberty is the growth spurt, accompanied by changes in physical features related to sexual functioning. Heredity, nutrition, exercise, and overall health contribute to the timing of puberty. A secular trend toward earlier maturation has occurred in industrialized nations as physical well-being has increased.

Growth and myelination of stimulated neural fibers in the brain accelerate, and linkages between brain regions expand and attain rapid communication. However, changes in the brain's emotional/social network outpace development of the cognitive-control network, resulting in self-regulation difficulties.

The arrival of puberty brings new health concerns. For some teenagers, the cultural ideal of thinness combines with family and psychological problems to produce two serious eating disorders: anorexia nervosa and bulimia nervosa. The rate of unintentional injuries rises in adolescence as a result of risk taking, with automobile accidents as the leading killer of American teenagers. In the United States, firearms cause the majority of other fatal injuries. Sports-related injuries are also common.

U.S. attitudes toward adolescent sex are relatively restrictive, and the social environment—parents, schools, and mass media—delivers contradictory messages. Early, frequent teenage sexual activity is linked to personal, family, peer, and educational characteristics. Adolescent contraceptive use has risen in recent years, but many teenagers fail to take precautions, putting them at risk for unintended pregnancy. Sexual orientation is affected strongly by heredity and prenatal hormone levels. Adolescents have the highest rate of sexually transmitted diseases of all age groups. Although AIDS education has provided teenagers with basic information about AIDS, most have limited understanding of other STDs and are poorly informed about how to protect themselves. Adolescent pregnancy and parenthood rates are higher in the United States than in any other industrialized nation. Life conditions linked to economic disadvantage, along with personal attributes, contribute to adolescent childbearing. Although the majority of teenagers engage in some experimentation with alcohol and drugs, a minority make the transition from use to abuse.

LEARNING OBJECTIVES

After reading this chapter, you should be able to:

14.1 Discuss changing conceptions of adolescence over the past century, and identify the three phases of adolescence recognized in modern industrialized nations. (pp. 530–531)

14.2 Describe physical changes associated with puberty, including hormonal changes, body growth, and sexual maturation. (pp. 531–536)

14.3 Cite factors that influence the timing of puberty. (pp. 536–537)

14.4 Describe brain development and changes in the organization of sleep and wakefulness during adolescence. (pp. 537–539)

14.5 Cite factors that influence adolescents' reactions to the physical changes of puberty. (pp. 539–542)

14.6 Discuss the impact of maturational timing on adolescent adjustment, noting sex differences, as well as immediate and long-term consequences. (pp. 542–543)

14.7 Summarize the nutritional needs of adolescents. (pp. 544–545)

14.8 Describe the symptoms of anorexia nervosa and bulimia nervosa, and cite personal and environmental factors that contribute to these disorders. (pp. 545–546)

14.9 Cite common unintentional injuries in adolescence. (p. 547)

14.10 Discuss social and cultural influences on adolescent sexual attitudes and behavior. (pp. 548–552)

14.11 Discuss biological and environmental contributions to sexual orientation. (pp. 552, 554)

14.12 Discuss factors related to sexually transmitted diseases in adolescence, particularly AIDS, and cite strategies for STD prevention. (pp. 554–555)

14.13 Summarize factors related to adolescent pregnancy, consequences of early childbearing for adolescent parents and their children, and strategies for preventing adolescent pregnancy. (pp. 555–559)

14.14 Distinguish between substance use and abuse, including personal and social factors related to each, discuss the consequences of substance abuse, and cite strategies for prevention and treatment. (pp. 560–562)

STUDY QUESTIONS

1. Define *adolescence* and *puberty.* (pp. 529–530)

   Adolescence: ______________________________

   Puberty: ______________________________

Conceptions of Adolescence

The Biological Perspective

1. Describe G. Stanley Hall and Anna Freud's biological perspective of adolescence. (p. 530)

   Hall: ______________________________

   ____

   Freud: ______________________________

   ____

The Social Perspective

1. True or False: Rates of psychological disturbance increase dramatically during adolescence, supporting the conclusion that it is a period of storm and stress. (p. 530)
2. What conclusion did Margaret Mead make about Samoan adolescents? Have follow-up studies confirmed Mead's conclusion? Explain. (p. 530)

   A. ______________________________

   B. ______________________________

   ____

A Balanced Point of View

1. True or False: The length of adolescence is the same in all cultures. Briefly explain your response. (p. 531)

   ____

   ____

2. List and describe the three phases of adolescence. (p. 531)

   A. ______________________________

   B. ______________________________

   C. ______________________________

Puberty: The Physical Transition to Adulthood

Hormonal Changes

1. During sexual maturation, the boy's testes release large quantities of the androgen ____________________, which leads to muscle growth, body and facial hair, and other male sex characteristics, as well as contributing to gains in body size. (p. 531)

2. The release of ____________________ from the girl's ovaries causes the breasts, uterus, and vagina to mature, the body to take on feminine proportions, and fat to accumulate. (p. 531)

Body Growth

1. The first outward sign of puberty is the rapid gain in height and weight known as the ____________________. (p. 532)

2. On average, the adolescent *growth spurt* is underway for girls in the United States shortly after age ________ and for boys around age ________. (p. 532)

3. True or False: During puberty, the cephalocaudal trend reverses, with hands, legs, and feet growing first, followed by growth of the torso. (p. 533)

4. Describe sex differences in body proportions and muscle–fat makeup during adolescence. (pp. 533–534)

   Boys: ______________________________

   ____

   Girls: ______________________________

   ____

Motor Development and Physical Activity

1. Briefly summarize sex differences in gross-motor development during adolescence. (p. 534)

   Boys: ______________________________

   ____

   Girls: ______________________________

   ____

2. True or False: Use of creatine and anabolic steroids improves teenagers' athletic performance while having no adverse side effects. (p. 534)

3. Among American youths, rates of physical activity (rise / decline) during adolescence. (p. 534)

4. Cite several benefits of sports participation and exercise during adolescence. (pp. 534–535)

   ____

   ____

5. What is one of the best predictors of adult physical exercise, and why? (p. 535)

   A. ______________________________

   B. ______________________________

Sexual Maturation

1. Distinguish between *primary* and *secondary sexual characteristics.* (p. 535)

   Primary: ______________________________

   ____

   Secondary: ______________________________

   ____

2. ______________ is the scientific name for first menstruation. It typically happens around ________ years of age for American girls. (p. 536)

3. List early signs of puberty in boys. (p. 536)

   ____

   ____

4. The growth spurt occurs much (earlier / later) in the sequence of pubertal events for boys than for girls. (p. 536)

5. Around age 13½, __________________, or first ejaculation, occurs in boys. (p. 536)

Individual Differences in Pubertal Growth

1. Provide an example of how heredity, nutrition, and exercise contribute to the timing of puberty. (p. 536)

   Heredity: ______________________________

   Nutrition: ______________________________

   Exercise: ______________________________

2. Describe how SES and ethnicity influence pubertal growth. (pp. 536–537)

   ____

   ____

   ____

3. List an example of how early family experiences might contribute to the timing of puberty. (p. 537)

   ____

   ____

The Secular Trend

1. Describe the secular trend in pubertal timing in industrialized nations, and list factors believed to be responsible for it. (p. 537)

   Secular trend: ______________________________

   ____

   Factors responsible: ______________________________

Brain Development

1. During adolescence, growth and myelination of stimulated neural fibers accelerates, strengthening connections between regions of the brain. What effect does this have on teenagers' cognitive abilities? (p. 538)

____

____

2. Adolescents perform less well than adults on tasks requiring (A) ____________, (B) ____________, and (C) ____________ due to immaturity of the prefrontal cognitive-control network. (p. 538)

3. True or False: Heightened sensitivity to oxytocin leads adolescents to become self-conscious, and also encourages receptiveness to peer influences. (p. 538)

Changing States of Arousal

1. Describe the sleep "phase delay," noting factors that contribute to it. (p. 539)

   A. ____

   ____

   B. ____

   ____

2. List the negative consequences of sleep deprivation in adolescence. (p. 539)

____

____

The Psychological Impact of Pubertal Events

Reactions to Pubertal Changes

1. Discuss two factors that affect girls' reactions to *menarche.* (p. 539)

   A. ____

   B. ____

2. Overall, boys seem to get (more / less) social support for the physical changes of puberty than girls. (p. 540)

3. Many tribal and village societies celebrate puberty with a(n) ____________________, a community-wide event that marks an important change in privilege and responsibility. Briefly contrast this experience with that of adolescents in Western societies. (p. 540)

____

____

Pubertal Change, Emotion, and Social Behavior

1. Research shows that adolescents report (more / less) favorable moods than school-age children and adults. (p. 540)

2. Cite factors associated with high and low points in mood during adolescence. (p. 541)

   High points: ____

   ____

   Low points: ____

   ____

3. When do teenagers' frequent reports of negative mood level off, and what accounts for this change? (p. 541)

   A. ____

   B. ____

4. How might parent–child conflict during adolescence serve an adaptive function? (p. 541)

   ____

   ____

5. True or False: During adolescence, parent–daughter conflict tends to be more intense than parent–son conflict. (p. 541)

Pubertal Timing

1. For each description, indicate if it pertains to early-maturing girls (EG), early-maturing boys (EB), late-maturing girls (LG), or late-maturing boys (LB). (p. 542)

   _____ Relaxed, independent, self-confident, and popular but report more problem behaviors than on-time counterparts
   _____ Regarded as physically attractive, lively, and sociable
   _____ Unpopular, withdrawn, lacking in self-confidence, and hold few leadership roles
   _____ Perceived as immature and express more anxiety and depression than on-time counterparts

2. List two factors that largely account for trends in the effects of maturational timing. (p. 542)

   A. ____

   B. ____

3. Discuss the impact of maturational timing on adolescent *body image,* noting ethnic differences. (p. 542)

   ____

   ____

   ____

   ____

4. Early-maturing adolescents of both sexes tend to seek (younger / older) companions. Describe the consequences of this trend in peer relations. (p. 543)

   ____

   ____

5. The young person's environmental context greatly (decreases / increases) the likelihood that early pubertal timing will lead to (negative / positive) outcomes. Provide an example to support your response. (p. 543)

   ____

   ____

   ____

6. Provide two examples of the long-term effects of maturational timing on psychological well-being. (p. 543)

   A. ______________________________

   ____

   B. ______________________________

   ____

Health Issues

Nutritional Needs

1. Of all age groups, the eating habits of adolescents are the (best / poorest). What factors contribute to this trend? (p. 544)

   ____

   ____

2. What is the most common nutritional problem of adolescence? (p. 544)

   ____

3. Frequency of ______________________________ is strongly associated with healthy eating in teenagers. (p. 545)

Eating Disorders

1. What is the strongest predictor of the onset of an eating disorder in adolescence? (p. 545)

   ____

2. Describe the physical and behavioral symptoms of *anorexia nervosa.* (p. 545)

   ____

   ____

   ____

3. Provide an example of how forces within the person, family, and larger culture contribute to anorexia nervosa. (pp. 545–546)

   Person: ______________________________

   Family: ______________________________

   Culture: ______________________________

4. What is the most successful treatment method for anorexia? (p. 546)

   ____

5. Describe characteristics of *bulimia nervosa.* (p. 546)

   ____

   ____

   ____

6. Bulimia is (more / less) common than anorexia. (p. 546)

7. Identify similarities and differences between persons with anorexia and bulimia. (p. 546)

   Similarities: ______________________________

   ____

   Differences: ______________________________

   ____

Injuries

1. The total rate of unintentional injuries (increases / decreases) during adolescence. Why? (p. 547)

   ____

   ____

   ____

2. Most adolescent deaths are due to ______________________, with the majority of the remainder caused by ______________________. (p. 547)

3. How do coaches often contribute to sports injuries in adolescents? (p. 547)

   ____

   ____

Sexual Activity

1. Contrast the messages that adolescents receive from parents and the media regarding sexual activity, and note the impact of such contradictory messages on adolescents' understanding of sex. (pp. 548–549)

   Parents: ______________________________

   ____

   Media: ______________________________

   ____

   Impact: ______________________________

   ____

2. The sexual attitudes and behavior of American adolescents have become (more / less) liberal over the past 40 years. (p. 549)

3. Cite personal, familial, peer, and educational variables linked to early and frequent teenage sexual activity. (p. 549)

   Personal: ______________________________

   Family: ______________________________

   Peer: ______________________________

   Educational: ______________________________

4. Early sexual activity is (more / less) common among low-SES adolescents. Explain why. (p. 549)

   ____

   ____

5. Early and prolonged father absence predicts (higher / lower) rates of intercourse and pregnancy among adolescent girls. Explain why. (p. 550)

6. Discuss cognitive and social factors that may contribute to adolescents' reluctance to use contraception. (pp. 551–552)

   Cognitive: ______

   Social: ______

7. Cite characteristics of adolescents who are more likely to use contraception. (p. 552)

8. About ______ percent of young people identify as lesbian, gay, or bisexual. (p. 552)

9. Describe evidence suggesting that both heredity and prenatal biological influences contribute to homosexuality. (p. 552)

   Heredity: ______

   Prenatal biological influences: ______

10. List several stereotypes and misconceptions about homosexuality. (p. 552)

Social Issues: Education: Parents and Teenagers (Don't) Talk About Sex

1. True or False: On average, only half of adolescents say that their parents talk to them about sex. (p. 550)
2. Explain why many parents avoid discussing sexual issues with their teenage children. (p. 550)

3. Why are adolescents reluctant to discuss sex with their parents? (p. 550)

4. Describe qualities of successful parent–child communication about sex. (p. 551)

____

____

____

Biology and Environment: Gay, Lesbian, and Bisexual Youths: Coming Out to Oneself and Others

1. Identify the three-phase sequence that homosexual adolescents and adults move through in coming out to themselves and others. (p. 553)

   A. ____

   B. ____

   C. ____

2. For homosexual individuals, a first sense of their sexual orientation typically appears between the ages of ______ and ______. In what context does this typically occur? (p. 553)

   ____

3. True or False: Most adolescents resolve their feelings of confusion and discomfort at being attracted to same-sex individuals by crystallizing a gay, lesbian, or bisexual identity quickly—with a flash of insight into their sense of being different. (p. 553)

4. True or False: Most parents respond to their adolescent child's disclosure of homosexuality with severe rejection. (p. 553)

5. Explain how coming out has the potential to foster psychological growth in homosexual adolescents. (p. 553)

   ____

   ____

   ____

Sexually Transmitted Diseases

1. True or False: Adolescents have the highest incidence of sexually transmitted disease (STD) of any age group. (p. 554)

2. Which teenagers are at greatest risk of contracting STDs? (p. 555)

   ____

3. True or False: Nearly all cases of AIDS that appear in young adulthood originate in adolescence. (p. 555)

4. Cite four strategies for preventing STDs. (p. 555)

   A. ____

   B. ____

   C. ____

   D. ____

Adolescent Pregnancy and Parenthood

1. An estimated ______ percent of sexually active teenage girls in the United States become pregnant annually, a rate higher than any other industrialized country. (p. 556)

2. List three factors that heighten the incidence of adolescent pregnancy. (p. 556)

   A. ______

   B. ______

   C. ______

3. Summarize personal characteristics and life conditions that contribute to adolescent childbearing. (p. 556)

   Personal characteristics: ______

   Life conditions: ______

4. Briefly describe the educational attainment, marital patterns, and economic circumstances of adolescent parents. (pp. 556–557)

   Educational attainment: ______

   Marital patterns: ______

   Economic circumstances: ______

5. Why are teenage girls especially likely to experience prenatal and birth complications? (p. 557)

   ______

6. True or False: Adolescent mothers are just as effective at interacting with their children as adult mothers. (p. 557)

7. Cite four factors that protect teenage mothers and their children from long-term difficulties. (p. 557)

   A. ______

   B. ______

   C. ______

   D. ______

8. List four components of effective sex education programs. (p. 557)

   A. ______

   B. ______

   C. ______

   D. ______

9. What is the most controversial aspect of adolescent pregnancy prevention programs, and why? (pp. 557, 558)

   A. ______

   B. ______

10. True or False: In European countries where contraception is readily available to teenagers, sexual activity is not more common than in the United States but pregnancy, childbirth, and abortion rates are much lower. (p. 558)
11. In addition to sex education and access to contraceptives, what other strategies are essential for preventing adolescent pregnancy and parenthood? (p. 559)

____

____

12. List characteristics of school programs that increase adolescent mothers' educational success and prevent additional childbearing. (p. 559)

____

____

13. Older adolescent mothers display (more / less) effective parenting when they establish their own residence with the assistance of relatives. (p. 559)
14. True or False: Fewer than one-fourth of adolescent fathers maintain regular contact into the child's school-age years. (p. 559)
15. Under what circumstances are fatherhood interventions especially effective? (p. 559)

____

____

Social Issues: Health: Like Parent, Like Child: Intergenerational Continuity in Adolescent Parenthood

1. Research indicates that first-generation mothers' age at first childbirth (does / does not) predict the age at which second-generation young people became parents. (p. 558)
2. Describe three family conditions and personal characteristics that are associated with second-generation adolescent parenthood. (p. 558)

   A. ____

   ____

   B. ____

   ____

   C. ____

   ____

Substance Use and Abuse

1. Explain why adolescent drug use in the United States has declined since the mid-1990s. (p. 560)

____

____

2. Why do so many young people subject themselves to the health risks of alcohol and drugs? (p. 560)

____

____

3. Describe characteristics of minimal experimenters. (p. 560)

____

____

4. Explain how cultural factors affect adolescent substance use. (p. 560)

____

____

____

5. Provide an example of an environmental factor that contributes to adolescent substance abuse. (p. 560)

____

6. Cite three life-long consequences of adolescent substance abuse. (p. 561)

   A. ______________________________

   B. ______________________________

   C. ______________________________

7. List three features of school and community programs that reduce drug experimentation. (p. 561)

   A. ______________________________

   B. ______________________________

   C. ______________________________

8. Provide an example of a prevention strategy and a treatment strategy for adolescent drug abuse. (pp. 561–562)

   Prevention: ______________________________

   ____

   Treatment: ______________________________

   ____

ASK YOURSELF . . .

For *Ask Yourself* questions for this chapter, along with feedback on the accuracy of your answers, please log on to MyDevelopmentLab (for registration and access, please visit mydevelopmentlab.com or follow the instructions on page ix).

(1) Select the Multimedia Library.

(2) Choose the explore option.

(3) Find your chapter from the drop down box.

(4) Click find now.

(5) Complete questions and choose “Submit answers for grading” or “Clear answers” to start over.

SUGGESTED READINGS

Blyth, D., & Simmons, R. G. (2008). *Moving into adolescence: The impact of pubertal change and school context.* Piscataway, NJ: Rutgers. Examines the pubertal experience for young people in Western societies. The authors discuss the developmental milestones associated with the transition to adulthood, including how parents and schools can support adolescents during this exciting and challenging time of life.

Borkowski, J. G., Whitman, T. L., Weed, K., Keogh, D. A., & Farris, J. R. (Eds.). (2007). *Risk and resilience: Adolescent mothers and their children grow up.* Mahwah, NJ: Erlbaum. In 1984, the University of Notre Dame began a longitudinal study to examine the social and psychological consequences of adolescent parenthood. This edited volume presents findings from that study, highlighting the long-term consequences of adolescent parenthood for both parents and children.

Kirke, D. M. (2008). *Teenagers and substance use: Social networks and peer influence.* New York: Palgrave Macmillan. An insightful look at teenagers who abuse alcohol and drugs, this book explores how adolescents' peer groups and social networks contribute to or buffer against substance abuse.

CROSSWORD PUZZLE 14.1

Across

1. ____________ nervosa: eating disorder in which individuals starve themselves due to a compulsive fear of becoming fat and a distorted body image
2. ___________ sexual characteristics are features visible on the outside of the body that do not involve the reproductive organs.
3. First menstruation
4. First ejaculation of seminal fluid
6. Biological changes at adolescence leading to an adult-size body and sexual maturity
7. ____________ sexual characteristics directly involve the reproductive organs
8. Body ____________: conception of and attitude toward one's physical appearance

Down

1. Transition between childhood and adulthood
2. Growth _________: rapid gains in height and weight during adolescence
5. ___________ nervosa: eating disorder in which individuals engage in strict dieting and excessive exercise accompanied by binge eating, often followed by deliberate vomiting or purging with laxatives

PRACTICE TEST #1

1. The beginning of adolescence is marked by __________ (p. 530)
   a. severe moodiness.
   b. puberty.
   c. an identify crisis.
   d. menarche and spermarche.

2. Middle adolescence is a period __________ (p. 531)
   a. of rapid pubertal change.
   b. when a young person achieves full adult appearance.
   c. when pubertal change is nearly complete.
   d. when a young person assumes an adult role.

3. Growth in body size is complete for most girls by age _____ (p. 532)
   a. 14.
   b. 15.
   c. 16.
   d. 18.

4. During adolescence, __________ decreases in adolescent boys. (p. 533)
   a. arm and leg fat
   b. muscle strength
   c. speed
   d. endurance

5. Which of the following is a secondary sexual characteristic? (p. 535)
   a. appearance of underarm hair
   b. enlargement of the penis
   c. development of the uterus
   d. development of the testes

6. The first sign of puberty in boys is __________ (p. 536)
   a. a height spurt.
   b. the appearance of pubic hair.
   c. spermarche.
   d. enlargement of the testes.

7. Menarche is greatly delayed in __________ (p. 536)
   a. obese girls.
   b. poverty-stricken regions.
   c. industrialized nations.
   d. higher-income families.

8. Children with warm, stable family ties tend to reach puberty __________ (p. 537)
   a. very early.
   b. slightly early.
   c. on time.
   d. relatively late.

9. In humans and other mammals, __________ during puberty. (p. 538)
   a. neurons become more responsive to excitatory neurotransmitters
   b. gray matter increases and white matter decreases
   c. growth and myelination of stimulated neural fibers decrease
   d. brain plasticity rises sharply

10. For girls who have no advance information, menarche __________ (p. 539)
    a. is mildly surprising.
    b. can be disturbing.
    c. is usually a joyful time.
    d. is met with mixed feelings.

11. Boys who had advance information say that their first ejaculation __________ (p. 540)
    a. was shocking.
    b. was traumatic.
    c. occurred earlier than they expected.
    d. was something they told friends about.

12. Later-maturing boys tend to be __________ than their early-maturing counterparts. (p. 542)
    a. less popular
    b. less moody
    c. more self-confident
    d. more relaxed

13. Later-maturing girls tend to be __________ than their early-maturing counterparts. (p. 542)
    a. less popular
    b. more withdrawn
    c. less confident
    d. more sociable

14. Skipping breakfast is linked to __________ (p. 544)
    a. healthy weight.
    b. obesity.
    c. vegetarianism.
    d. a decrease in daily caloric intake.

15. __________ is associated with reduced fast-food consumption. (p. 545)
    a. Skipping lunch
    b. Eating meals with peers
    c. Frequency of family meals
    d. Increased availability of diet products

16. About _____ percent of North American and Western European teenage girls are affected with anorexia nervosa. (p. 545)
    a. 1
    b. 3
    c. 5
    d. 7

17. Individuals with __________ lose between 25 and 50 percent of their body weight. (p. 545)
    a. bulimia nervosa
    b. diabetes
    c. anorexia nervosa
    d. iron deficiency

18. After automobile injuries, __________ cause the majority of other fatal injuries in U.S. teens. (p. 547)
    a. sports
    b. firearms
    c. suicides
    d. STDs

19. Typically, parents in the United States __________ (p. 548)
    a. provide a lot of information about sex.
    b. are permissive about sex.
    c. have highly restrictive sexual attitudes.
    d. rarely talk about sex in children's presence.

20. Rates of extramarital sex among U.S. young people are __________ they were a decade ago. (p. 549)
    a. much higher than
    b. slightly higher than
    c. about the same as
    d. lower than

21. __________ more often dominate conversations about sexual matters than about everyday matters, especially when talking to __________ (p. 550)
    a. Mothers; sons.
    b. Fathers; sons.
    c. Fathers; daughters.
    d. Mothers; daughters.

22. __________ are more likely than __________ to share a homosexual orientation. (p. 552)
    a. Fraternal twins; identical twins
    b. Biological relatives; adoptive relatives
    c. Adoptive brothers; biological sisters
    d. Biological non-twin sisters; identical twin brothers

23. In research on ethnically diverse gay, lesbian, and bisexual youths, awareness of a same-sex physical attraction occurred, on average between ages _____and _____ for girls. (p. 553)
    a. 10; 11
    b. 12; 13
    c. 14; 15
    d. 16; 17

24. For which of the following sexually transmitted diseases (STDs) is there no cure? (p. 554)
    a. herpes simplex 2
    b. chlamydia
    c. gonorrhea
    d. syphilis

25. In contrast to other Western nations, __________ (p. 555)
    a. the incidence of AIDS among Americans under age 30 is much lower.
    b. the incidence of AIDS among Americans under age 30 is much higher.
    c. few U.S. high school students are aware of the basic facts about AIDS.
    d. 90 percent of U.S. middle school students are aware of the basic facts about AIDS.

26. An estimated _____ percent of teenage girls who have sexual intercourse become pregnant. (p. 556)
    a. 5
    b. 10
    c. 15
    d. 20

27. Parenthood before age 18 __________ the likelihood of __________ (p. 556)
    a. increases; contraceptive use after the birth.
    b. reduces; divorce.
    c. reduces; maternal unemployment.
    d. increases; marital instability.

28. Intergenerational continuity in adolescent parenthood is far greater when teenage mothers __________ (p. 558)
    a. remain unmarried.
    b. finish high school.
    c. marry teenage fathers.
    d. cohabit with their baby's father.

29. Of all teenage drug habits, __________ has received the least attention. (p. 560)
    a. inhalant use
    b. alcohol abuse
    c. cigarette smoking
    d. OxyContin abuse

30. To effectively reduce drug experimentation, school and community prevention programs should __________ (p. 561)
    a. implement abstinence programs, much like in sex education.
    b. teach skills for resisting peer pressure.
    c. emphasize facts and statistics.
    d. focus exclusively on teens, not parents.

PRACTICE TEST #2

1. __________ viewed the teenage years as a biologically based, universal "developmental disturbance." (p. 530)
   a. Erik Erikson
   b. Margaret Mead
   c. Lawrence Kohlberg
   d. Sigmund Freud

2. During __________, a young person achieves full adult appearance and anticipates assumption of adult roles. (p. 531)
   a. middle childhood
   b. early adolescence
   c. middle adolescence
   d. late adolescence

3. The __________ gland releases growth hormones and stimulates other glands to produce hormones that act on body issues, causing them to mature. (p. 531)
   a. adrenal
   b. pituitary
   c. thyroid
   d. pineal

4. On average, the growth spurt is underway for North American and Western European girls shortly after age _____ (p. 532)
   a. 8.
   b. 10.
   c. 12.
   d. 14.

5. During puberty, boys' __________ broaden relative to the __________ (p. 533)
   a. shoulders; hips.
   b. hips; shoulders.
   c. hips; waist.
   d. waist; hips.

6. For girls, gains in motor development level off by age _____ (p. 534)
   a. 10.
   b. 12.
   c. 14.
   d. 16.

7. In females, a sharp rise in __________ may trigger sexual maturation. (p. 536)
   a. body fat
   b. muscle strength
   c. height
   d. physical endurance

8. Children with a history of family conflict, harsh parenting, or parental separation tend to __________ (p. 537)
   a. reach puberty late.
   b. reproduce late.
   c. reach puberty early.
   d. experience interruptions in pubertal growth.

9. fRMI evidence reveals that adolescents tend to __________ than adults do. (p. 538)
   a. perform better on tasks requiring inhibition, planning, and future orientation
   b. recruit the prefrontal cortex's network of connections with other brain areas less effectively
   c. handle challenging self-regulation situations more effectively
   d. react less strongly to stressful events and experience pleasure less intensely

10. In the United States today, most girls __________ puberty. (pp. 539–540)
    a. have a traumatic reaction to
    b. do not tell friends about the onset of
    c. do not talk to their mothers about
    d. are informed about

11. Adolescent mood swings are __________ (p. 541)
    a. strongly related to situational changes.
    b. a myth and unsupported by research.
    c. less intense than mood swings in middle childhood.
    d. frequent and completely unpredictable.

12. Which of the following teens is the most likely to have a negative body image? (p. 543)
    a. Sabrina, an early-maturing Hispanic girl
    b. Adele, a late-maturing African-American girl
    c. Deana, an early-maturing Caucasian girl
    d. Wayne, an early-maturing Caucasian boy

13. Jenna, a(n) __________-maturing girl will probably feel most comfortable with girls who are __________ in maturation. (p. 543)
    a. later; early
    b. early; later
    c. early; early
    d. early; on-time

14. During the growth spurt, boys require __________ (p. 544)
    a. less protein than they did earlier.
    b. more protein than girls.
    c. fewer calories than girls.
    d. about 2,200 calories per day.

15. Of all age groups, __________ are the most likely to eat on the run. (p. 544)
    a. young children
    b. school-age children
    c. adolescents
    d. young adults

16. Which of the following individuals is at the greatest risk for developing an eating disorder? (p. 544)
    a. Sammie, an early-maturing girl
    b. Dennis, an early-maturing boy
    c. Fiona, a later-maturing girl
    d. Jason, a later-maturing boy

17. Less than _____ percent of people with anorexia recover fully. (p. 546)
    a. 50
    b. 60
    c. 70
    d. 80

18. __________ are especially vulnerable to sport-related injuries. (p. 547)
    a. Young adolescents
    b. Middle adolescents
    c. Older adolescents
    d. Teens who underestimate their abilities

19. Hormonal changes—in particular the production of __________ in young people of both sexes—lead to an increase in sex drive. (p. 548)
    a. estrogens
    b. androgens
    c. thyroxine
    d. oxytocin

20. The majority of young people learn about sex from __________ (p. 548)
    a. their mothers.
    b. their fathers.
    c. both parents.
    d. their friends or the media.

21. The high rate of sexual activity among African-American teenagers is largely accounted for by __________ in the black population. (pp. 549–550)
    a. intergenerational continuity
    b. widespread poverty
    c. limited access to birth control
    d. ineffective sex education programs

22. Parent-based sex education __________ (p. 551)
    a. is less effective than school-based sex education.
    b. is less effective for girls than for boys.
    c. has many advantages for both sexes.
    d. is less effective for boys than for girls.

23. __________ homosexuality tends to be more common on the __________ side of families. (p. 552)
    a. Male; paternal
    b. Female; paternal
    c. Male; maternal
    d. Female; maternal

24. Realizing that homosexuality has personal relevance generally sparks __________ in adolescents. (p. 553)
    a. confusion
    b. gender-role reversal
    c. atypical gender-typing
    d. self-acceptance

25. Which of the following sexually transmitted diseases can be cured using antibiotic drugs? (p. 554)
    a. chlamydia
    b. cytomegalovirus
    c. herpes simplex 2
    d. human papillomavirus

26. Most U.S. adolescents __________ (p. 555)
    a. are unaware of the basic facts about AIDS and other STDs.
    b. underestimate their own susceptibility to AIDS.
    c. are well-informed about how to protect themselves from AIDS.
    d. have extensive knowledge about STDS.

27. The U.S. adolescent pregnancy rate __________ (p. 556)
    a. has risen sharply in the past decade.
    b. is lower than that of any other industrialized country.
    c. is highest among middle-SES teens.
    d. has steadily declined since 1991.

28. First-generation mothers' age at first childbirth __________ the age at which second-generations young people become parents. (p. 558)
    a. weakly correlates to
    b. has no correlation to
    c. strongly predicts
    d. weakly predicts

29. Research reveals that U.S. teenagers are __________ likely to use __________ than European teenagers. (p. 560)
    a. more; alcohol
    b. more; illegal drugs
    c. more; cigarettes
    d. less; marijuana

30. Longitudinal evidence reveals drug abusers' impulsive, disruptive, hostile style is __________ (p. 561)
    a. rarely present before early adolescence.
    b. almost always linked to environmental factors.
    c. often present in drug experimenters as well.
    d. often evident in the early childhood.

CHAPTER 15
COGNITIVE DEVELOPMENT IN ADOLESCENCE

BRIEF CHAPTER SUMMARY

During Piaget's formal operational stage, young people develop the capacity for abstract, systematic, scientific thinking. They become capable of hypothetico-deductive reasoning, in which they begin with a hypothesis, or prediction, from which they deduce logical inferences. Piaget used the term propositional thought to describe adolescents' ability to evaluate the logic of verbal statements without referring to real-world circumstances. However, follow-up research reveals that school-age children already have some capacity for hypothetico-deductive reasoning, although they are less competent at it than adolescents. Cross cultural research challenges Piaget's view of formal operations as a universal change in cognition. Rather, it may be a culturally transmitted way of reasoning specific to literate societies and fostered by school experiences.

According to the information-processing perspective, cognitive change in adolescence is based on specific mechanisms supported by brain development and experience, including selective attention, improved inhibition, more effective strategies, increased knowledge, expanded metacognition, improved cognitive self-regulation, and increased thinking and processing speed. Metacognition, in particular, is central to adolescent cognitive development.

Adolescent cognitive changes lead to dramatic revisions in the ways adolescents see themselves, others, and the larger world. They develop distorted images of the relationship between self and other and are able to construct visions of ideal worlds. The dramatic cognitive changes of adolescence are reflected in many aspects of everyday behavior, including self-consciousness and self-focusing, idealism and criticism, and difficulties with planning and decision making.

Although boys and girls do not differ in general intelligence, they do vary in specific mental abilities. Throughout adolescence, girls continue to score higher than boys on tests of verbal ability, while boys continue to have an advantage in mathematical performance. These differences are related to heredity but also reflect cultural factors, including social pressures.

Language development continues during adolescence, in subtle but important ways that are influenced by improvements in metalinguistic awareness—the ability to think about language as a system. Vocabulary expands as adolescents add many abstract words. They also master irony and sarcasm, figurative language, and more complex grammatical constructions. As a result, communication skills improve.

School transitions create adjustment problems for adolescents, especially girls. Teenagers who must cope with added stresses are at greatest risk for adjustment problems following school change. Enhanced support from adults and peers eases the strain of school transition. Academic achievement reflects both personal traits and environmental factors, including child-rearing styles, parent–school partnerships, peer influences, and the responsiveness of school environments. A significant number of young people, more often boys than girls, drop out of school, often with dire consequences. School dropout is related to a variety of student, family, school, and community characteristics that undermine chances for success.

During late adolescence, young people face a major life decision: the choice of a suitable work role. Young people move through several periods of vocational development. Factors influencing adolescents' vocational choices include personality, family, teachers, and gender stereotypes in the larger social environment, as well as access to vocational information. High quality vocational preparation for non-college-bound adolescents is scarce in America compared with some European nations. A national apprenticeship system would improve the transition to work for those who terminate their education with a high school diploma.

LEARNING OBJECTIVES

After reading this chapter, you should be able to:

15.1 Describe the major characteristics of formal operational thought. (pp. 566–567)

15.2 Discuss recent research on formal operational thought and its implications for the accuracy of Piaget's formal operational stage. (pp. 567–569)

15.3 Explain how information-processing researchers account for the cognitive changes in adolescence. (pp. 569–570)

15.4 Summarize the development of scientific reasoning during adolescence. (pp. 570–571)

15.5 Describe typical reactions of adolescents that result from their advancing cognition. (pp. 571–574)

15.6 Describe sex differences in mental abilities at adolescence, along with factors that influence them. (pp. 575–578)

15.7 Describe changes in vocabulary, grammar, and pragmatics during adolescence. (pp. 578–580)

15.8 Discuss the impact of school transitions on adolescent adjustment, and cite strategies for easing the strain of these transitions. (pp. 580–582)

15.9 Discuss family, peer, and school influences on academic achievement during adolescence. (pp. 582–587).

15.10 Describe personal, family, and school factors related to dropping out, and cite ways to prevent early school leaving. (pp. 587–590)

15.11 Trace the development of vocational choice, and describe the factors that influence adolescents' vocational decisions. (pp. 590–593)

15.12 Discuss the problems faced by U.S. non-college bound youths in making the transition from school to work, along with ways to help them adjust. (pp. 593–595)

STUDY QUESTIONS

Piaget's Theory: The Formal Operational Stage

1. What is the basic difference between concrete and *formal operational* reasoning? (p. 566)

___

___

___

Hypothetico-Deductive Reasoning

1. Piaget believed that at adolescence, young people first become capable of ________________ reasoning. Provide an example of this type of reasoning. (p. 566)

___

___

2. Adolescents' performance on Piaget's famous ________________ illustrates their new approach to problem solving. (p. 566)

3. How do concrete operational children attempt to solve the pendulum problem? (p. 567)

___

___

Propositional Thought

1. Describe *propositional thought.* (p. 567)

___

___

___

2. True or False: Even though Piaget did not view language as playing a central role in young children's cognitive development, he acknowledged its importance in adolescence. (p. 567)

Follow-Up Research on Formal Operational Thought

1. Cite examples illustrating that school-age children show signs of hypothetico-deductive reasoning and propositional thought but are not yet as competent at it as adolescents. (pp. 567–568)

   Hypothetico-deductive reasoning: ______________________________

   ____

   Propositional thought: ______________________________

   ____

2. Children fail to grasp the ____________________ of propositional reasoning—that the accuracy of conclusions drawn from premises rests on the rules of logic, not real-world confirmation. (p. 568)

3. List three advances in reasoning during adolescence that illustrate their ability to apply logic. (p. 568)

   A. ______________________________

   B. ______________________________

   C. ______________________________

4. Explain why so many adults are not fully formal operational. (p. 568)

   ____

   ____

   ____

5. True or False: Despite few opportunities to solve hypothetical problems, most people in tribal and village societies still master formal operational tasks. (p. 569)

An Information-Processing View of Adolescent Cognitive Development

1. Information-processing theorists refer to seven specific mechanisms that underlie cognitive change in adolescence. List them. (p. 569)

   A. ____________________ B. ____________________

   C. ____________________ D. ____________________

   E. ____________________ F. ____________________

   G. ____________________

2. Which of the above mechanisms do researchers regard as central to adolescent cognitive development? (p. 570)

   ____

Scientific Reasoning: Coordinating Theory with Evidence

1. True or False: Kuhn's research into the development of scientific reasoning indicates that children as young as third grade are able to alter their theories to reflect conflicting evidence. (p. 570)

2. Cite major changes in scientific reasoning from childhood into adolescence and adulthood. (p. 570)

____

____

____

How Scientific Reasoning Develops

1. Identify two factors that support adolescents' skill at coordinating theory with evidence. (p. 570)

   A. ____

   B. ____

2. The number of years that a child spends in school has a (weak / strong) influence on the development of scientific reasoning. (p. 570)

3. Briefly explain how advances in metacognitive understanding promote adolescents' cognitive development. (p. 571)

____

____

____

4. True or False: Like Piaget, information-processing theorists maintain that scientific reasoning develops from an abrupt, stagewise change. (p. 571)

Consequences of Adolescent Cognitive Changes

1. List four ways to handle the consequences of teenagers' new cognitive capacities. (p. 572)

   A. ____

   B. ____

   C. ____

   D. ____

Self-Consciousness and Self-Focusing

1. Piaget's followers suggest that two distorted images of the relationship between self and other appear in adolescence. The __________ refers to adolescents' belief that they are the focus of everyone else's attention and concern. The __________ refers to teenagers' belief that they are special and unique. (p. 572)

2. The imaginary audience and personal fable (do / do not) result from egocentrism, as Piaget suggested. Explain your response. (p. 572)

____

____

3. List several positive aspects of the imaginary audience and personal fable. (pp. 572–573)

   Imaginary audience: ____

   ____

   Personal fable: ____

   ____

4. True or False: Adolescents who score highly on evaluations of the personal fable and levels of sensation-seeking tend to engage in more risky behavior than that of their agemates. (p. 573)

Idealism and Criticism

1. Provide an example of how the development of idealism leads adolescents to become overly critical. (p. 573)

2. How are idealism and criticism advantageous to teenagers? (p. 573)

Decision Making

1. True or False: Teenagers struggle with planning and decision making because they find it difficult to think rationally and inhibit their emotions. (p. 573)
2. Good decision making involves four steps. List them. (p. 573)
   A.
   B.
   C.
   D.
3. When making decisions, adolescents often emphasize (short-term / long-term) goals. (p. 574)
4. Why is adult supervision important as adolescents refine their decision-making skills? (p. 574)

Sex Differences in Mental Abilities

Verbal Abilities

1. (Boys / Girls) score higher than (boys / girls) on tests of verbal ability throughout childhood and adolescence. (p. 575)
2. True or False: The gap in reading and writing achievement between young men and women is believed to be a major factor in the changing gender demographic of college campuses in the United States. (p. 575)
3. Explain why the gender gap in verbal abilities exists, citing both biological and environmental reasons. (p. 575)
   Biological:
   Environmental:

Mathematical Abilities

1. Provide an example of a sex difference in mathematic ability. (p. 576)

2. Summarize how heredity and social pressures contribute to the gender gap in mathematics. (pp. 576–577)

   Heredity: ______________________________

   ____

   Social pressures: ______________________________

   ____

3. Cite three strategies used to promote girls' interest in and confidence at math and science. (p. 578)

   A. ______________________________

   B. ______________________________

   C. ______________________________

Biology and Environment: Sex Differences in Spatial Abilities

1. Describe two spatial tasks on which individuals evidence a notable sex difference in performance. (p. 576)

   A. ______________________________

   ____

   B. ______________________________

   ____

2. True or False: Sex differences in spatial abilities persist throughout the lifespan. (p. 576)

3. List biological and environmental factors that may contribute to sex differences in spatial abilities. (p. 577)

   Biological: ______________________________

   ____

   Environmental: ______________________________

   ____

4. True or False: Training and early intervention have little effect on girls' performance on spatial tasks, leading researchers to conclude that sex differences in these areas are biologically determined. (p. 577)

Language Development

Vocabulary and Grammar

1. Identify three changes in adolescents' vocabularies. (p. 579)

   A. ______________________________

   B. ______________________________

   C. ______________________________

2. Provide an example illustrating gains in grammatical development during the teenage years. (p. 579)

   ____

   ____

3. Explain why overt grammar instruction in U.S. schools is making a comeback. (p. 579)

____

____

Pragmatics

1. Summarize gains in adolescents' communication skills. (p. 579)

____

____

____

2. Explain the social function of teenage slang. (pp. 579–580)

____

____

Learning in School

School Transitions

1. List several reasons why adolescents' grades decline with the transition to secondary school. (p. 580)

   A. ____

   B. ____

   C. ____

2. (Boys / Girls) tend to have more difficulty with school transitions and experience a greater drop in self-esteem. Why is this the case? (p. 580)

____

____

3. What are some characteristics of an adolescent whose school performance remains low or drops sharply after school transition? (p. 581)

____

____

4. List three ways that parents, teachers, and peers can ease the strain of school transitions. (p. 581)

   A. ____

   B. ____

   C. ____

5. Identify several small changes that promote favorable adjustment after a school transition. (p. 581)

____

____

Academic Achievement

1. List four environmental factors that support high academic achievement in adolescence. (p. 582)

   A. ____________________

   B. ____________________

   C. ____________________

   D. ____________________

2. How do each of the four child-rearing styles contribute to adolescents' academic achievement? Which is the most effective, and why? (p. 582)

   Authoritative: ____________________

   Authoritarian: ____________________

   Permissive: ____________________

   Uninvolved: ____________________

   Most effective: ____________________

3. How does combining parental warmth with moderate to high control promote school success? (p. 582)

   ____

   ____

4. How do parent–school partnerships foster academic achievement? (pp. 582–583)

   ____

   ____

5. List four ways schools can strengthen parent–school partnerships. (p. 583)

   A. ____________________

   B. ____________________

   C. ____________________

   D. ____________________

6. Provide an example of how peers contribute to adolescent achievement. (p. 583)

   ____

   ____

7. Of the diverse characteristics on which friends resemble each other, ____________________ has the strongest association with future adjustment. (p. 583)

8. Provide an example of how peer support for high achievement depends on the overall climate of the peer culture. (p. 583)

   ____

   ____

9. How can schools promote academic achievement among ethnic minority students? (p. 584)

   ____

   ____

   ____

10. Compare the classroom experiences of adolescents who make gains in academic motivation and cognitive self-regulation versus students who show a decline in these areas. (p. 584)

    Increase in motivation and cognitive self-regulation: ____________________

    ____

    Decrease in motivation and cognitive self-regulation: ____________________

    ____

11. A (large / small) number of low-SES minority students are assigned to noncollege tracks in high school. What effect does this have on student achievement? (pp. 585–586)

    ____

    ____

    ____

12. Explain how tracking in the United States differs from that in Japan, China, and many Western European nations, and note the impact of these differences on student outcomes. (p. 587)

    Differences: ____________________

    ____

    Impact: ____________________

    ____

Social Issues: Education: Media Multitasking Disrupts Attention and Learning

1. Define "media multitasking." (p. 585)

   ____

   ____

2. Provide an example of how media multitasking reduces the efficiency of learning. (p. 585)

   ____

   ____

   ____

3. True or False: Adolescents who frequently engage in media multitasking are usually able to focus on a single task, such as studying for a test, if they work in an environment without any distractions. (p. 585)

Social Issues: Education: High-Stakes Testing

1. Explain how the U.S. No Child Left Behind Act broadens high-stakes testing. (p. 586)

   ____

   ____

   ____

2. Summarize potential benefits of high-stakes testing. (p. 586)

   ____

   ____

   ____

3. Evidence indicates that high-stakes testing (undermines / upgrades) the quality of education. (p. 586)

4. Identify a concern about high-stakes testing. (p. 586)

   ____

5. True or False: High-stakes testing has increased the emphasis on teaching for deeper understanding. (p. 586)

Dropping Out

1. The U.S. dropout rate is higher among (boys / girls) and is particularly high among (low-SES ethnic minority / learning-disabled) students. (p. 587)

2. Cite two consequences of dropping out of high school. (pp. 587–588)

   A. ____

   B. ____

3. Identify several student, family, and school and community characteristics related to dropping out. (p. 588)

   Student: ____

   ____

   Family: ____

   ____

   School and community: ____

   ____

4. Describe the school experiences of academically marginal students who drop out. (p. 588)

   ____

   ____

5. List four strategies to prevent school dropout. (p. 589)

   A. ____

   B. ____

   C. ____

   D. ____

6. Over the second half of the twentieth century, the percentage of American adolescents completing high school has (increased / decreased) steadily. (p. 590)

7. True or False: About one-third of high school dropouts eventually return to finish their secondary education. (p. 590)

Vocational Development

Selecting a Vocation

1. Describe the three phases of vocational development, noting the developmental period at which each occurs. (pp. 590–591)

   Fantasy period: ______________________________

   ____

   Tentative period: ______________________________

   ____

   Realistic period: ______________________________

   ____

Factors Influencing Vocational Choice

1. Match each of the following personality types that affect vocational development with the appropriate description. (p. 591)

   _____ Likes well-structured tasks and values social status; tends to choose business occupations
   _____ Prefers real-world problems and work with objects; tends toward mechanical occupations
   _____ Adventurous, persuasive, and a strong leader; drawn toward sales and supervisory positions
   _____ Enjoys working with ideas; likely to select scientific occupations
   _____ Has high need for emotional and individual expression; drawn toward fields like writing, music, and the visual arts

   A. Investigative
   B. Social
   C. Realistic
   D. Artistic
   E. Conventional
   F. Enterprising

2. The relationship between personality and vocational choice is (weak / moderate / strong). (p. 591)

3. Identify three reasons why young people's vocational aspirations correlate strongly with their parents' jobs. (pp. 591–592)

   A. ______________________________

   B. ______________________________

   C. ______________________________

4. Explain how teachers influence adolescents' career decisions. (p. 592)

   ____

   ____

5. Women's progress in entering and excelling at male-dominated professions has been (slow / rapid). (p. 592)

6. True or False: Sex differences in vocational achievement can be directly attributed to differences in ability. Explain your answer. (p. 593)

   ____

   ____

7. Cite two ways in which girls can be encouraged to maintain high career aspirations. (p. 593)

   A. ______________________________

   ____

   B. ______________________________

   ____

Vocational Preparation of Non-College-Bound Adolescents

1. Non-college-bound high school graduates have (more / fewer) work opportunities than they did several decades ago. (p. 593)

2. Describe the nature of most jobs held by adolescents, and discuss the impact of heavy job commitment on adolescents' attitudes and behaviors. (p. 594)

   A. ______________________________

   ____

   B. ______________________________

   ____

3. Briefly summarize the features of Germany's work–study apprenticeship system, noting how it creates a smooth transition from school to work. (p. 594)

   ____

   ____

   ____

   ____

   ____

4. Identify three major challenges to the implementation of a national apprenticeship program in the United States. (p. 594)

   A. ______________________________

   B. ______________________________

   C. ______________________________

ASK YOURSELF . . .

For *Ask Yourself* questions for this chapter, along with feedback on the accuracy of your answers, please log on to MyDevelopmentLab (for registration and access, please visit mydevelopmentlab.com or follow the instructions on page ix).

(1) Select the Multimedia Library.

(2) Choose the explore option.

(3) Find your chapter from the drop down box.

(4) Click find now.

(5) Complete questions and choose "Submit answers for grading" or "Clear answers" to start over.

SUGGESTED READINGS

Blyth, D., & Simmons, R. G. (2008). *Moving into adolescence: The impact of pubertal change and school context.* Piscataway, NJ: Rutgers. Examines the pubertal experience for young people in Western societies. The authors discuss the developmental milestones associated with the transition to adulthood, including how parents and schools can support adolescents during this exciting and challenging time of life.

Ceci, S. J., & Williams, W. M. (2010). *The mathematics of sex: How biology and society conspire to limit talented women and girls.* New York: Oxford University Press. Presents leading research on the ongoing controversy over sex differences in math achievement and math-oriented careers. The authors examine biological and social factors contributing these differences, as well as strategies for increasing girls' interest and involvement in mathematics.

Wing, Y., & Noguera, P. A. (Eds.). (2008). *Closing the racial achievement gap in our schools.* Hoboken, NJ: Wiley. A compelling look at racial inequalities in public education, this book examines racial and academic segregation in U.S. high schools. Topics include: factors contributing to academic inequality, the importance of parent involvement, student reflections on the high school experience, and strategies for increasing academic engagement in minority students.

CROSSWORD PUZZLE 15.1

Across

4. An adolescent's belief that he or she is the focus of everyone's attention and concern is referred to as the ___________ audience.
5. The period of vocational development in which children explore career options through make-believe play
7. ___________-deductive reasoning begins with a hypothesis, from which logical inferences can be deducted and then tested in a systematic fashion.
8. The period of vocational development in which adolescents weigh vocational options against their interests, abilities, and values
9. The period of vocational development in which adolescents focus on a general career category and eventually settle on a single occupation

Down

1. ___________ operational stage: Piaget's final stage, in which adolescents develop the capacity for abstract, scientific thinking.
2. ___________ necessity: specifies that the accuracy of conclusions drawn from premises rests on the rules of logic, not on real-world confirmation.
3. ___________ thought: evaluating the logic of verbal statements without referring to real-world circumstances.
6. The personal ______________ refers to adolescents' belief that they are special and unique.

PRACTICE TEST #1

1. According to Piaget, when adolescents engage in hypothetico-deductive reasoning, they __________ (p. 566)
   a. form a prediction about variables that might affect an outcome.
   b. focus on the most difficult aspects of a problem.
   c. solve problems through trial-and-error.
   d. focus on concrete aspects of a task.

2. Research indicates that when given a situation involving no more than two causal variables, 6-year-olds __________ (p. 567)
   a. are unable to deduce logical, testable inferences.
   b. understand that hypotheses must be confirmed by appropriate evidence.
   c. engage in high rates of abstract reasoning.
   d. ignore concrete aspects of the task.

3. The fact that college coursework leads to improvements in formal reasoning related to course content suggests that, contrary to Piaget's conclusions, __________ (p. 568)
   a. the majority of young people are fully formal operational.
   b. the basic rules of formal logic are innate concepts that emerge in late adolescence.
   c. operational thought involves verbal reasoning about abstract concepts.
   d. formal operational reasoning does not emerge all at once, but is specific to situation and task.

4. Follow-up research on formal operational thought shows that __________ (p. 569)
   a. school-age children are as competent as adolescents in hypothetico-deductive reasoning.
   b. the capacity for formal operational thought appears at puberty.
   c. schooling and practice lead to gains in formal operational thinking.
   d. nearly all adults are fully formal operational.

5. Researchers regard __________ as central to adolescent cognitive development. (p. 570)
   a. attention
   b. inhibition
   c. metacognition
   d. knowledge

6. According to Deanna Kuhn's findings, the capacity to reason like a scientist __________ (p. 570)
   a. levels off in the late teens.
   b. improves faster for boys than girls.
   c. improves with age.
   d. peaks in middle childhood.

7. Which of the following statements reflects the imaginary audience? (p. 572)
   a. "I don't care if my new haircut is bad. I'm going to the party anyway."
   b. "I can't go to the party with a huge pimple on my cheek! Everyone will make fun of me!"
   c. "My parents don't understand how hard school is for me!"
   d. "No one will care if I can't afford a new dress for the prom. I'll just wear the same one I wore last year."

8. Research on the imaginary audience and personal fable indicates that they __________ (p. 573)
   a. result from egocentrism, as Piaget suggested.
   b. may serve positive, protective functions.
   c. do not affect contemporary teens.
   d. are an indication of psychological disturbance.

9. Fifteen-year-old Kate seems to find fault with everything; she is critical of the way her parents dress, the food they buy, the cars they drive, and the manner in which they spend their free time. Kate's fault-finding results from adolescent __________ (p. 573)
   a. idealism.
   b. realism.
   c. egocentrism.
   d. perspective-taking.

10. Which of the following statements about adolescent decision making is true? (p. 573)
   a. Adolescents are just as skilled as adults in day-to-day decision making.
   b. Adolescents are more likely than adults to seek advice in solving real-world problems.
   c. Adolescents are more likely than adults to fall back on well-learned intuitive judgments.
   d. Adolescents rarely consider their options or think about the consequences of their decisions.

11. Which of the following statements about gender differences in reading and writing achievement is true? (p. 575)
   a. Girls attain higher scores in reading and writing until adolescence, when boys start to outperform girls.
   b. The area of the brain where language is localized develops earlier in girls than in boys.
   c. Despite receiving more verbal stimulation from their mothers, boys lag behind girls in reading and writing achievement.
   d. The area of the brain where language is localized develops earlier in boys than in girls.

12. Girls tend to be advantaged in __________ (p. 576)
   a. tests of complex reasoning.
   b. geometry.
   c. mental rotation tasks.
   d. arithmetic computation.

13. Sex differences in spatial abilities __________ (p. 576)
   a. emerge in early childhood.
   b. emerge in adolescence.
   c. are evident only in Western cultures.
   d. are primarily determined by biological factors.

14. Kristiana, an eighth grader, believes that her peers will judge her negatively if she does well in math. This is an example of __________ (p. 577)
   a. a self-fulfilling prophecy.
   b. propositional thought.
   c. metacognitive understanding.
   d. stereotype threat.

15. As with other aspects of semantic development, __________ fosters adolescents' understanding of proverbs. (p. 579)
   a. whole language instruction
   b. reading proficiency
   c. phonics instruction
   d. false-belief understanding

16. Teenagers use slang __________ (p. 580)
   a. as a sign of group belonging.
   b. because they lack grammatical understanding.
   c. when confronted with uncomfortable social situations.
   d. equally with parents and peers.

17. Research shows that students rate their __________ (p. 580)
   a. high school teachers as more sensitive and caring than their elementary school teachers.
   b. high school friends as more supportive and caring than their parents.
   c. middle- and high-school learning experiences more favorably than their elementary school experiences.
   d. middle- and high-school learning experiences less favorably than their elementary school experiences.

18. One strategy for helping adolescents adjust to school transitions is to __________ (p. 581)
    a. require at least one semester of extracurricular involvement each year of high school.
    b. form large units within smaller schools to promote student interaction.
    c. set up homerooms in which teachers offer academic and personal counseling.
    d. break up cliques that reject younger students or students who are new to the school.

19. Research on adolescents shows that both authoritarian and permissive parenting styles are linked to __________ (p. 582)
    a. high academic achievement but low self-esteem.
    b. lower grades.
    c. higher grades and high self-esteem.
    d. the poorest grades and worsening school performance over time.

20. In a nationally representative sample of U.S. adolescents, students' grade point average in tenth grade was strongly predicted by __________ (p. 583)
    a. SES and previous academic achievement.
    b. an authoritarian child-rearing style.
    c. their parents' school involvement in eighth grade.
    d. their parents' willingness to grant autonomy.

21. According to one study, integration into the school peer network predicted higher grades among __________ (p. 583)
    a. Asians and African Americans.
    b. Caucasians and Hispanics.
    c. Native Americans and African Americans.
    d. children of Asian and European immigrants.

22. Teenagers' __________ is an aspect of contemporary peer-group life that poses risks to achievement. (p. 584)
    a. involvement in school-based cliques and crowds
    b. use of text messaging and e-mail to remain continuously in touch with peers
    c. emphasis on enhancing their own popularity
    d. use of homeroom periods for gossiping and interacting with friends

23. In a survey of a nationally representative sample of U.S. 8- to 18-year-olds, __________ reported engaging in two or more media activities at once, some or most of the time. (p. 585)
    a. ten percent
    b. thirty percent
    c. more than half
    d. nearly two-thirds

24. Proponents of high-stakes testing believe that it __________ (p. 586)
    a. enhances teacher-training and qualifications.
    b. introduces greater rigor into the classroom teaching.
    c. improves the performance of marginal but not high-achieving students.
    d. emphasizes teaching for deeper understanding, similar to Asian schools.

25. Longitudinal research following thousands of U.S. students from eighth to twelfth grade revealed that assignment to a vocational or general education track __________ (p. 586)
    a. speeds up academic progress.
    b. facilitates motivation in low-achieving students.
    c. is primarily used with students with special learning needs.
    d. decelerates academic progress.

26. Research suggests that risk factors that predict later dropout can appear as early as __________ (p. 588)
    a. preschool.
    b. first grade.
    c. middle school.
    d. the first year of high school.

27. The most powerful way to prevent school dropout is to __________ (p. 589)
    a. address the academic and social problems of at-risk students in elementary school, and to involve their parents.
    b. place at-risk students in a college preparatory track, regardless of their prior achievement.
    c. eliminate high-stakes testing from public schools and improve the quality of special education services.
    d. limit at-risk students' participation in extracurricular activities so that they have more time to focus on academic work.

28. During the fantasy period of vocational development, children __________ (p. 590)
    a. gather information about possibilities that blend with their personal characteristics.
    b. tend to have career preferences that are very different from those of their parents.
    c. have career preferences based largely on familiarity, glamour, and excitement.
    d. begin to show an interest in the personal and educational requirements for different vocations.

29. Students with academic and behavior problems generally have __________ (p. 592)
    a. neither family nor teacher supports.
    b. closer relationships with family members than with teachers.
    c. relationships with peers that are strong, though not necessarily positive.
    d. limited access to special education or vocational services.

30. One of the major challenges to implementing an apprenticeship system in the United States is __________ (p. 594)
    a. overcoming employers' reluctance to assume part of the responsibility for vocational training.
    b. preventing qualifying examinations from becoming just another form of high-stakes testing.
    c. overcoming the widespread perception of such systems as low-status.
    d. gaining parental support for students' enrollment in apprenticeship programs.

PRACTICE TEST #2

1. When given a task that assesses hypothetico-deducting reasoning, school-age children, in contrast to adolescents, __________ (p. 567)
   a. typically fail to notice variables that are not immediately suggested by the concrete materials of the task.
   b. will often avoid the task altogether or will give up after several attempts to solve the problem.
   c. will test each variable separately and, if necessary, also in combination.
   d. engage in a form of problem solving which begins with a possibility and proceeds to reality.

2. A researcher hides a poker chip in her hand and asks participants to indicate whether the following statement is true, false, or uncertain: "Either the chip in my hand is green or it is not green." The researcher is assessing __________ (p. 567)
   a. hypothetico-deductive reasoning.
   b. propositional reasoning.
   c. concrete operational thought.
   d. metacognition.

3. Although Piaget did not view __________ as playing a central role in cognitive development, he acknowledged its importance in adolescence. (p. 567)
   a. metacognition
   b. social interaction
   c. language
   d. abstract reasoning

4. Ten-year-old Elliot does not yet understand that the accuracy of conclusions drawn from premises rests on the rules of logic, not real-world confirmation. Elliot fails to grasp the __________ (p. 568)
   a. logical necessity of propositional reasoning.
   b. the concrete nature of advanced problem-solving.
   c. illogical nature of hypothetico-deductive reasoning.
   d. scientific relevance of abstract problem-solving.

5. Information-processing findings confirm that scientific reasoning __________ (p. 571)
   a. results from abrupt, stagewise change.
   b. develops gradually out of different experiences.
   c. is possible even without sophisticated metacognitive understanding.
   d. is a biological capacity that first appears at adolescence, regardless of experiences.

6. Sixteen-year-old Michael feels that his experiences are extraordinary and that he is special and unique. He tells his parents, "You'll never understand what it's like to be me!" This is an example of __________ (p. 572)
   a. the personal fable.
   b. the imaginary audience.
   c. hypothetico-deductive reasoning.
   d. idealism.

7. Fourteen-year-old Octavia is sometimes highly critical of her family, which creates tension with her parents. The best way to respond to Octavia's critical comments is to __________ (p. 572)
   a. criticize her back so she understands what it feels like.
   b. ground her or remove privileges until her behavior improves.
   c. be patient and point out positive features of targets.
   d. ignore her until her attitude improves.

8. In the heat of the moment, when making good decisions requires them to inhibit "feel-good" behavior, adolescents are far more likely than adults to __________ (p. 574)
   a. rate the risks of that behavior higher than peers who have not tried it.
   b. assess the likelihood of various possible outcomes.
   c. ask for advice about what they should do.
   d. emphasize short-term over long-term goals.

9. Sex differences in __________ are believed to be major contributors to a widening gender gap in college enrollments. (p. 575)
   a. literacy skills
   b. spatial skills
   c. IQ
   d. scientific reasoning

10. Some research suggests that high-achieving African-American boys are particularly likely to have __________ (p. 575)
   a. mothers who provide verbal stimulation starting in the preschool years.
   b. access to computers equipped with educational software.
   c. fathers who are warm, verbally communicative, and demanding of achievement.
   d. parents who routinely discipline them for poor school performance.

11. Which of the following statements about sex differences in math abilities is true? (p. 576)
   a. Beginning in elementary school, boys consistently outperform girls in math achievement.
   b. The gender gap between boys and girls in math scores has grown in the past quarter-century.
   c. In most non-Western nations, adolescent girls outperform their male counterparts in math achievement.
   d. Boys start to outperform girls in math during early adolescence, when math concepts become more abstract and spatial.

12. Sex differences in spatial abilities __________ (p. 576)
   a. emerge in early childhood, persist through the lifespan, and are evident in many cultures.
   b. first appear in early adolescence and strengthen across the lifespan.
   c. are caused by biological differences between boys and girls and cannot be modified with experience or training.
   d. are primarily due to boys' interest in playing video games that require rapid mental rotation of visual images.

13. Mastery of __________ gives adolescents new ways to express themselves through language. (p. 579)
   a. grammar
   b. sarcasm and irony
   c. conversational turn-taking
   d. prose

14. In U.S. schools, __________, out of favor since the 1970s, is making a comeback. (p. 579)
   a. higher-level phonics instruction
   b. the whole language approach
   c. overt grammar instruction
   d. an emphasis on figurative language

15. Studies show that as a result of the transition from elementary school to middle or junior high school, __________ (p. 580)
   a. girls' self-esteem rises slightly, whereas boys' drops to an all-time low.
   b. most young people feel more academically competent, and their liking for school and motivation increases.
   c. many young people feel less academically competent, and their liking for school and motivation declines.
   d. boys, but not girls, tend to report that teachers care less about them and stress competition more.

16. To help ease the strain of school transition, parents __________ (p. 581)
   a. should enroll their adolescent in a private high school.
   b. can encourage their adolescent to seek a vocational track.
   c. should emphasize grades over mastery of subject matter.
   d. can gradually grant their adolescents more autonomy.

17. Research on the relationship between employment and academic achievement in adolescence indicates that __________ (p. 582)
   a. job commitment should be limited to less than 15 hours per week.
   b. full-time jobs help teenagers to become more independent and responsible.
   c. job commitment should not exceed 30 hours per week.
   d. full-time jobs help teenagers develop a strong work ethic, which carries over to schoolwork.

18. Mr. and Mrs. Hun want to know how they can best support their son's high achievement in adolescence. Research indicates that Mr. and Mrs. Hun should __________ (p. 583)
    a. select their son's high school classes for him.
    b. limit their contact with teachers unless there is a problem.
    c. have frequent contact with the school.
    d. limit their son's extracurricular involvement.

19. In classrooms emphasizing competition and public comparison of students, __________ (p. 584)
    a. low-achieving students develop higher levels of academic motivation.
    b. declines in motivation and self-regulation tend to occur.
    c. students become well-prepared for the transition to college.
    d. high-achieving students tend to experience a sharp decline in grades.

20. Research shows that frequent media multitaskers __________ (p. 585)
    a. often demonstrate an especially rapid rate of information processing, which leads to higher IQ scores.
    b. are especially skilled at filtering out irrelevant stimuli when solving complex problems.
    c. have a harder time filtering out irrelevant stimuli when they are not multitasking.
    d. have higher academic achievement and are more socially skilled than their peers.

21. Students most likely to score poorly on high-stakes tests are __________ (p. 586)
    a. adolescent boys.
    b. adolescent girls.
    c. high-achieving students with test anxiety.
    d. minority youths living in poverty.

22. Breaking out of a low academic track is __________ (p. 587)
    a. easier for female students, as they tend to receive more individualized instruction.
    b. difficult, as teachers and counselors often lack the time to reconsider individual cases.
    c. easier for minority youths, as they tend to be more motivated to succeed than their peers.
    d. more difficult in European countries than in the United States.

23. Among U.S. young people, about _____ percent leave high school without a diploma. (p. 587)
    a. 4
    b. 6
    c. 8
    d. 17

24. Students in __________ are three times as likely to drop out as those in __________. (p. 588)
    a. general education and vocational tracks; a college preparatory track
    b. rural schools; inner-city schools
    c. large, departmentalized schools; medium-sized schools
    d. public schools; private schools

25. In their late teens and early twenties, young people typically crystallize their vocations when they __________ (p. 591)
    a. focus on a general vocational category, within which they experiment for a time before settling on a specific occupation.
    b. first begin to gather information about career possibilities that blend with their personal characteristics.
    c. gain insight into a variety of career options by fantasizing about them.
    d. begin to think about possible careers in terms of their abilities and values.

26. According to John Holland, the realistic person __________ (p. 591)
    a. enjoys working with facts and ideas and is likely to select a career in science or math.
    b. likes interacting with people and gravitates toward a career in human services.
    c. prefers working with objects rather than people and tends to choose a mechanical occupation.
    d. is adventurous and persuasive and is drawn to supervisory positions.

27. Young people preparing for or engaged in careers requiring extensive education often report that __________ influenced their choice. (p. 592)
   a. peers
   b. siblings
   c. monetary needs
   d. teachers

28. Statistics shows that women __________ (p. 593)
   a. write more books, make more discoveries, and produce more works of art than men.
   b. have higher career aspirations during their college years than their male classmates.
   c. have made rapid progress in entering and excelling at male-dominated professions.
   d. remain concentrated in less-well-paid, traditionally feminine occupations.

29. Compared to several decades ago, non-college-bound high school graduates __________ (p. 593)
   a. are more likely to participate in apprenticeship programs.
   b. have more work opportunities.
   c. have fewer work opportunities.
   d. are viewed as more skilled by employers.

30. Teenagers who are heavily committed to low-level jobs __________ than their peers. (p. 594)
   a. have better school attendance
   b. report more drug and alcohol use
   c. are less likely to drop out of high school
   d. have closer relationships with their parents

CHAPTER 16
EMOTIONAL AND SOCIAL DEVELOPMENT IN ADOLESCENCE

BRIEF CHAPTER SUMMARY

Erikson defined the psychological conflict of adolescence as identity versus role confusion. Unlike Erikson, contemporary theorists do not view the typical process of developing a mature identity as a "crisis," but rather as a process of exploration followed by commitment. Self-concept changes as adolescents unify separate traits into more abstract generalizations about themselves, with more emphasis on social virtues and inclusion of enduring beliefs and plans. Self-esteem further differentiates in adolescence and tends to rise, while individual differences in self-esteem become increasingly stable. These advances in self-concept and self-esteem provide the cognitive foundation for forming an identity.

Researchers identify four identity statuses typical of adolescents: identity achievement, moratorium, foreclosure, and diffusion. Identity achievement and moratorium are both adaptive statuses, while teenagers who remain in a state of identity foreclosure or diffusion are likely to have adjustment difficulties. Positive identity development is promoted by the adolescent's own personality characteristics and influenced by parents, peers, school and community opportunities, and cultural values.

Lawrence Kohlberg, inspired by the research of Piaget, identified three levels of moral development, each with two stages. According to Kohlberg, moral development is a gradual process that occurs as the individual actively grapples with moral issues and achieves gains in perspective taking. Although Kohlberg's theory emphasizes a "masculine" morality based on rights and justice rather than a "feminine" morality based on care, it does not underestimate the moral maturity of females. Child-rearing practices, schooling, peer interaction, and culture all contribute to moral development. Maturity of moral reasoning is only modestly related to moral behavior. Moral action is also influenced by the individual's empathy and guilt, temperament, and history of morally relevant experiences.

Biological, social, and cognitive forces combine to make early adolescence a period of gender intensification. Over the adolescent years, relationships with parents and siblings change as teenagers strive to establish a healthy balance between family connection and separation. As adolescents spend more time with peers, intimacy and loyalty become central features of friendship. The Internet has expanded teenagers' opportunities for friendships beyond their schools and communities, but also poses dangers. Adolescent peer groups are typically organized into cliques, tightly knit groups of close friends, who may come together with other cliques sharing similar values and interests to form a crowd, which gives the adolescent an identity within the larger social structure of the school. Early adolescent dating relationships tend to be shallow and stereotyped, but dating that does not begin too soon provides valuable lessons in cooperation, etiquette, and other aspects of relationships. Peer pressure rises in early adolescence, but most teenagers do not blindly conform to the dictates of agemates.

The most common psychological problem of adolescence is depression, which results from a combination of diverse biological and environmental factors. Severe depression can lead to suicidal thoughts, and the suicide rate increases dramatically at adolescence. Although many teenagers become involved in some delinquent activity, only a few become serious, repeat offenders. Personal, family, school, peer, and neighborhood factors are related to delinquency.

LEARNING OBJECTIVES

After reading this chapter, you should be able to:

16.1 Discuss Erikson's theory of identity development, noting the major personality achievement of adolescence. (p. 600)

16.2 Describe changes in self-concept and self-esteem during adolescence. (pp. 601–603)

16.3 Describe the four identity statuses, noting how each is related to psychological adjustment, and summarize factors that promote identity development. (pp. 603–606)

16.4 Describe Kohlberg's theory of moral development, and evaluate its accuracy. (pp. 608–611)

16.5 Evaluate claims that Kohlberg's theory does not adequately represent the morality of females, with particular attention to Gilligan's argument. (pp. 611–612)

16.6 Describe influences on moral reasoning and its rleationship to moral behavior. (pp. 613–615, 617)

16.7 Summarize challenges to Kohlberg's theory. (pp. 617–618)

16.8 Explain why early adolescence is a period of gender intensification. (pp. 618–619)

16.9 Discuss familial influences on adolescent development, including changes in the parent–child and sibling relationships. (pp. 619–622)

16.10 Describe adolescent friendships, peer groups, and dating relationships and their consequences for development. (pp. 622–628)

16.11 Discuss conformity to peer pressure in adolescence, noting how parental behavior is related to adolescent conformity. (pp. 628–629)

16.12 Cite factors related to adolescent depression and suicide, along with prevention strategies and treatments. (pp. 629–633)

16.13 Discuss factors related to delinquency, and cite strategies for prevention and treatment. (pp. 633–635)

16.14 Review factors that foster resilience in adolescence. (pp. 636–637)

STUDY QUESTIONS

Erikson's Theory: Identity versus Role Confusion

1. Explain how young people construct an *identity.* (p. 600)

____

____

2. Discuss Erikson's notion of an identity crisis. (p. 600)

____

____

3. Describe the negative outcome of Erikson's psychological conflict of adolescence—*role confusion*. (p. 600)

____

____

____

4. Current theorists (do / do not) agree with Erikson that the process of identity development constitutes a "crisis." (p. 600)

Self-Understanding

Changes in Self-Concept

1. Provide an example illustrating how early adolescents unify separate traits into more abstract descriptors. (p. 601)

____

2. Compared to school-age children, teenagers place (more / less) emphasis on social virtues, such as being friendly, considerate, kind, and cooperative. Explain why. (p. 601)

____

____

Changes in Self-Esteem

1. Cite three new dimensions of self-esteem that emerge during adolescence. (p. 602)

   A. ______________________________

   B. ______________________________

   C. ______________________________

2. True or False: Except for temporary declines associated with school transitions, self-esteem rises in most adolescents. (p. 602)

3. Certain self-esteem factors are more strongly related to adjustment. Provide an example to support this statement. (p. 602)

   ____

   ____

Influences on Self-Esteem

1. Of those young people whose self-esteem declines in adolescence, most are girls. Explain why. (p. 602)

   ____

   ____

2. Explain how both parents and the larger social environment influence adolescents' self-esteem. (pp. 602–603)

   Parents: ______________________________

   ____

   Social environment: ______________________________

   ____

Paths to Identity

1. Which two key criteria from Erikson's theory do researchers use to evaluate progress in identity development? (p. 603)

   A. ______________________________

   B. ______________________________

2. Match each of the following identity statuses with the appropriate description. (p. 603)

_____ Commitment in the absence of exploration	A. *Identity achievement*
_____ Exploration without having reached commitment	B. *Identity moratorium*
_____ Commitment to values, beliefs, and goals following a period of exploration	C. *Identity foreclosure*
_____ An apathetic state characterized by lack of both exploration and commitment	D. *Identity diffusion*

3. Most adolescents start out at "lower" statuses, such as ____________ and ____________, but by late adolescence, they have moved toward "higher" statuses, including ____________ and ____________. (p. 604)

4. True or False: Most adolescent girls follow a different path to identity formation than do boys. They postpone the task of establishing an identity, focusing instead on intimacy development. (p. 604)

Identity Status and Psychological Well-Being

1. True or False: Research supports the conclusion that identity achievement and moratorium are psychologically healthy routes to a mature self-definition, whereas long-term identity foreclosure and identity diffusion are maladaptive. (p. 604)

2. List personality characteristics associated with each identity status. (pp. 604–605)

Identity achievement and moratorium: ______________________________

____

Identity foreclosure: ______________________________

____

Identity diffusion: ______________________________

____

Factors Affecting Identity Development

1. Match the following identity statuses with the appropriate description of associated personality and family factors. Descriptions may apply to more than one identity status. (p. 605)

_____ Assume that absolute truth is always attainable
_____ Lack confidence in the prospect of ever knowing anything with certainty
_____ Appreciate that they can use rational criteria to choose among alternatives
_____ Feel attached to parents but are also free to voice their own opinions
_____ Have close bonds with parents but lack healthy separation
_____ Report the lowest levels of warm, open communication at home

A. Identity achievement
B. Identity moratorium
C. Identity foreclosure
D. Identity diffusion

2. Provide an example of how peers contribute to adolescent identity development. (p. 605)

____

____

3. Describe ways schools can foster identity development during adolescence. (p. 605)

____

____

____

4. Which aspect of mature identity is not captured by the identity-status approach? (p. 605)

____

5. List five ways that adults can support healthy identity development in adolescents. (p. 605)

A. ______________________________

B. ______________________________

C. ______________________________

D. ______________________________

E. ______________________________

Cultural Influences: Identity Development Among Ethnic Minority Adolescents

1. What is an *ethnic identity*? (p. 607)

____

____

2. Psychological distress resulting from conflict between the minority and the host culture is called ______________________________. (p. 607)

3. Explain why ethnic minority adolescents often experience unique problems in developing a sense of identity. (p. 607)

______

______

______

4. List three ways that society can help minority adolescents resolve identity conflicts constructively. (p. 607)

   A. ______

   B. ______

   C. ______

5. Cite several benefits of a strong, secure ethnic identity. (p. 607)

______

______

6. What is a *bicultural identity,* and how does it benefit minority adolescents? (p. 607)

   A. ______

   B. ______

______

Moral Development

Kohlberg's Theory of Moral Development

1. To study moral development, Lawrence Kohlberg used a clinical interviewing procedure in which he presented 10- to 16-year-old boys with ______. (p. 608)

2. True or False: Kohlberg emphasized that it is the way an individual reasons about a dilemma, not the content of the response, that determines moral maturity. (p. 608)

3. List two factors that Kohlberg believed to promote moral understanding. (p. 608)

   A. ______

   B. ______

4. Explain the basic characteristics of moral reasoning at each of Kohlberg's three levels: (pp. 609–610)

   Preconventional: ______

   ______

   Conventional: ______

   ______

   Postconventional: ______

   ______

5. Match each of the following moral orientations with the appropriate description. (pp. 609–610)

_____ Laws must be obeyed under all circumstances; rules must be enforced in the same even-handed manner for everyone, and each member of society has a personal duty to uphold them
_____ Right action is defined by self-chosen ethical principles of conscience that are valid for all humanity, regardless of law and social agreement
_____ Ignore people's intentions and focus on fear of authority and avoidance of punishment as reasons for behaving morally
_____ Desire to obey rules because they promote social harmony
_____ Regard laws and rules as flexible and emphasize fair procedures for interpreting and changing the law in order to protect individual rights and the interests of the majority
_____ View right action as flowing from self-interest; reciprocity is understood as equal exchange of favors

A. Punishment and obedience orientation
B. Instrumental purpose orientation
C. "Good boy–good girl" orientation
D. Social-order-maintaining orientation
E. Social contract orientation
F. Universal ethical principle orientation

6. True or False: Longitudinal research suggests that individuals do not move through the stages of moral development in the order in which Kohlberg suggested. (p. 611)

7. True or False: The development of moral understanding is very slow and gradual. (p. 611)

8. (Few / Many) people reach Kohlberg's postconventional stage. What are the implications of this for Kohlberg's theory? (p. 611)

____

____

9. How are Kohlberg's moral stages similar to Piaget's stages? (p. 611)

____

____

Are There Sex Differences in Moral Reasoning?

1. Carol Gilligan believes that feminine morality emphasizes an "ethic of care" that is devalued in Kohlberg's model. Explain what she meant by this. (p. 612)

____

____

____

2. True or False: Research supports Gilligan's claim that Kohlberg's approach underestimates females' moral maturity. (p. 612)

3. According to a recent Australian study, under what condition did gender differences in moral reasoning emerge? (p. 612)

____

____

Coordinating Moral, Social-Conventional, and Personal Concerns

1. Provide an example of a matter of personal choice. Does concern with matters of personal choice differ across cultures? Explain. (p. 613)

A. ____

B. ____

____

2. Provide an example of how moral reasoning changes in adolescence. (p. 613)

3. Adolescents think (less / more) intently about conflicts between personal choice and community obligations. Briefly explain your response. (p. 613)

Influences on Moral Reasoning

1. Provide an example of how having a flexible, open-minded approach to new information and experiences fosters gains in moral reasoning. (p. 613)

2. Describe child-rearing practices that promote gains in moral development. (pp. 613–614)

3. True or False: Years of schooling is one of the most powerful predictors of moral maturity. (p. 614)
4. Cite characteristics of peer interaction that promote moral understanding and movement to higher moral stages. (p. 614)

5. True or False: Cross-cultural research shows that individuals in industrialized nations move through Kohlberg's stages more quickly and advance to higher levels of moral reasoning than individuals in village societies. Based on your response, provide a possible explanation. (pp. 614–615)

Moral Reasoning and Behavior

1. There is a (weak / moderate / strong) relationship between moral thought and action. (p. 615)
2. Define *moral self-relevance,* and cite factors that may contribute to a sense of moral self-relevance. (p. 615)

   A.

   B.

3. What is a just educational environment? (p. 615)

Social Issues: Education: Development of Civic Responsibility

1. What is civic responsibility? List its three components. (p. 616)

   Definition: ______

   A. ______

   B. ______

   C. ______

2. List examples of family, school, and community influences on adolescents' civic responsibility. (p. 616)

   Family: ______

   School: ______

   Community: ______

3. Cite two aspects of involvement in extracurricular activities and youth organizations that account for their lasting impact. (p. 616)

   A. ______

   B. ______

4. What are service-learning programs, and what are the consequences of participation? (p. 616)

   A. ______

   B. ______

Religious Involvement and Moral Development

1. During adolescence, formal religious involvement (increases / declines). (p. 617)
2. Summarize the benefits associated with involvement in a religious community. (p. 617)

   ______

3. What factors make religious involvement beneficial for adolescents? (p. 617)

   ______

Further Challenges to Kohlberg's Theory

1. Summarize the pragmatic approach to morality that has been suggested by Kohlberg's detractors. (p. 617)

   ______

2. Identify an argument that refutes the pragmatic approach to morality. (pp. 617–618)

Gender Typing

1. What is *gender intensification,* and when is it strongest? (p. 618)

   A.

   B.

2. Although it occurs in both sexes, gender intensification is stronger for (boys / girls). (p. 618)
3. Identify a biological, social, and cognitive factor associated with gender intensification. (p. 618)

   Biological:

   Social:

   Cognitive:

4. (Androgynous / Gender-typed) adolescents tend to be psychologically healthier. (pp. 618–619)

The Family

1. During adolescence, ______________________—establishing oneself as a separate, self-governing individual—becomes a salient task. (p. 619)

Parent–Child Relationships

1. Provide an example of a change in the parent–child relationship during adolescence. (p. 619)

2. Describe parenting practices that foster adolescent competence. (p. 620)

3. Explain how parents' own development can lead to friction with teenagers. (p. 620)

4. True or False: The quality of the parent–child relationship is the most consistent predictor of mental health throughout adolescence. (p. 621)
5. Explain how mild parent–child conflict is beneficial during adolescence. (p. 621)

6. True or False: The drop in time spent with the family during adolescence occurs in all cultures worldwide. Briefly explain your response. (p. 621)

___

___

Family Circumstances

1. Parents who are financially secure and content in their jobs and marriages find it (easier / more difficult) to grant teenagers *autonomy* and experience (more / less) conflict. (p. 621)
2. Explain how personal and environmental factors can help teenagers thrive despite stressful family situations. (pp. 621–622)

___

___

Siblings

1. During adolescence, teenagers invest (more / less) time and energy in siblings. Explain your answer. (p. 622)

___

___

2. Sibling relationships become (more / less) intense during adolescence, in both positive and negative feelings. (p. 622)
3. True or False: Mild sibling differences in perceived parental affection do not trigger jealousy but, rather, predict an increase in sibling warmth. Provide a possible explanation. (p. 622)

___

___

Peer Relations

Friendships

1. Cite the three characteristics of friendship emphasized by teenagers. (pp. 622–623)

   A. ___

   B. ___

   C. ___

2. Self-disclosure between friends tends to (increase / decrease) over the teenage years. (p. 623)
3. List three changes that result from adolescents' increased concern for their friends and effort in maintaining the relationship between them. (p. 623)

   A. ___

   B. ___

   C. ___

4. Briefly discuss how friendships change during the transition to middle or junior high school. (p. 624)

___

___

___

5. Provide an example of a sex difference in the nature of adolescents' close friendships. (p. 624)

6. True or False: Androgynous boys are just as likely as girls to form intimate same-sex ties, whereas boys who identify strongly with the traditional masculine role are less likely to do so. (p. 624)

7. Describe the potential benefits and costs of closeness in adolescent friendship. (p. 624)

   Benefits:

   Costs:

8. Discuss both the benefits and dangers of adolescent friendships on the Internet. (p. 625)

   Benefits:

   Dangers:

9. Cite four reasons why gratifying childhood and adolescent friendships are related to psychological health and competence in emerging adulthood. (pp. 625–626)

   A.

   B.

   C.

   D.

Cliques and Crowds

1. Differentiate between *cliques* and *crowds,* noting the characteristics of each. (p. 626)

   Cliques:

   Crowds:

2. Provide some examples of typical high school crowds. (p. 626)

3. True or False: Peer group values are often an extension of values learned in the home. (p. 627)

4. Describe the function of mixed-sex cliques in early adolescence. (p. 627)

5. True or False: Crowds increase in importance from early to late adolescence. (p. 627)

Dating

1. Describe younger and older adolescents' different reasons for dating. (p. 627)

   Younger: ____

   ____

   Older: ____

   ____

2. True or False: Early dating is positively associated with social maturity. Explain your answer. (p. 628)

   ____

   ____

3. Cite factors associated with dating violence. (p. 628)

   ____

   ____

4. Cite several unique challenges faced by homosexual adolescents in initiating and maintaining romances. (p. 628)

   ____

   ____

5. Summarize the benefits of adolescent dating. (p. 628)

   ____

   ____

Peer Conformity

1. True or False: Peer pressure to engage in antisocial and destructive behavior is much stronger than pressure to engage in proadult behavior, such as getting good grades in school. (p. 628)
2. Cite personal characteristics of adolescents who are less susceptible to peer pressure. (p. 629)

   ____

   ____

   ____

3. Summarize the link between parenting behavior and adolescents' conformity to peer pressure. (p. 629)

   ____

   ____

   ____

Problems of Development

Depression

1. About _____ to ______ percent of U.S. teenagers experience mild to moderate feelings of depression, while ______ to ______ percent have experienced one or more depressive episodes and ______ to ______ percent are chronically depressed. (p. 629)

2. Explain why adolescents' depressive symptoms tend to be overlooked by parents and teachers. (p. 629)

3. Cite biological and environmental factors related to adolescent depression. (p. 630)

   Biological:

   Environmental:

4. Adolescent (boys / girls) are twice as likely as adolescent (boys /girls) to experience persistent depressed mood, a trend that continues from adolescence throughout the lifespan. Why is this the case? (pp. 630–631)

Suicide

1. True or False: Suicide is currently the leading cause of death among young people in the United States. (p. 631)
2. True or False: Adolescent suicide rates are roughly equivalent in all industrialized countries. (p. 631)
3. Discuss sex differences in suicidal behavior, noting whether boys or girls are more likely to kill themselves. (p. 631)

4. What accounts for ethnic differences in adolescent suicide rates? (pp. 631–632)

5. True or False: Gay, lesbian, and bisexual youth are three times more likely to attempt suicide than heterosexual youth. (p. 632)
6. Identify two types of young people who tend to commit suicide. (p. 632)

   A.

   B.
7. Explain how biology and environment jointly contribute to adolescent suicidal behavior. (p. 632)

8. Cite cognitive changes that contribute to the rise in suicide among adolescents. (p. 632)

9. List five warning signs of suicide. (p. 632)
   A. ______________________________
   B. ______________________________
   C. ______________________________
   D. ______________________________
   E. ______________________________

10. Identify four ways of responding to an adolescent who might be suicidal. (p. 633)
    A. ______________________________
    B. ______________________________
    C. ______________________________
    D. ______________________________

11. Following a suicide, why must adults keep an especially watchful eye on vulnerable adolescents? (p. 633)

Delinquency

1. Explain why delinquency rises during early adolescence and then declines into young adulthood. (p. 634)

2. Provide an example of a sex difference in adolescent delinquency. (p. 634)

3. Do low-SES ethnic minority youths engage in more antisocial acts than their higher-SES white and Asian counterparts? Explain. (p. 634)

4. List personal factors associated with chronic delinquency. (p. 634)

5. Explain how ineffective parenting contributes to adolescent aggression and delinquency. (p. 634)

6. Aggressive young people often report (very high / very low) self-esteem. (p. 634)

7. What are zero tolerance policies? Are they effective? Explain. (p. 635)
   A. ______________________________
   B. ______________________________

8. List characteristics of the most effective treatment programs for adolescent delinquency. (p. 635)

9. Briefly describe multisystemic therapy, and discuss its effectiveness. (p. 635)
   A.
   B.

Biology and Environment: Two Routes to Adolescent Delinquency

1. Identify two paths to adolescent delinquency. (p. 636)
   A.
   B.
2. Differentiate between early-onset delinquent children who go on to follow the life-course path of delinquency versus those who show a decline in aggression and violence. (p. 636)

3. List characteristics that distinguish early-onset from late-onset delinquent youth. (pp. 636–637)
   Early-onset:
   Late-onset:

At The Threshold

1. List five factors that foster resilience in adolescence. (p. 637)
   A.
   B.
   C.
   D.
   E.

ASK YOURSELF . . .

For *Ask Yourself* questions for this chapter, along with feedback on the accuracy of your answers, please log on to MyDevelopmentLab (for registration and access, please visit mydevelopmentlab.com or follow the instructions on page ix).

(1) Select the Multimedia Library.

(2) Choose the explore option.

(3) Find your chapter from the drop down box.

(4) Click find now.

(5) Complete questions and choose "Submit answers for grading" or "Clear answers" to start over.

SUGGESTED READINGS

Brandt, D., & Kazdin, A. E. (2007). *Delinquency, development, and social policy*. New Haven: Yale University Press. An ecological approach to understanding antisocial behavior in adolescence, this book examines the origins and pathways of delinquency. The authors argue that early intervention that addresses the developmental needs of children and adolescents is more effective in preventing antisocial behavior than referral to juvenile courts or incarceration.

Deutsch, N. (2008). *Pride in the projects: Teens building identities in urban contexts*. New York: New York University Press. Based on four years of field research, this book examines identity development in inner-city youth. Although many of these young people encounter significant obstacles in their daily life, such as exposure to gangs and violence, discrimination, and poverty, having access to community resources and high-quality after-school programs can help foster resilience and favorable identity development.

Jamieson, P. E. (2008). *The changing portrayal of adolescents in the media since 1950*. New York: Oxford University Press. Presents a compelling look at how adolescents have been portrayed in the media for the past 60 years, including how these portrayals contribute to adolescent behavior. The author contends that a drastic increase in media consumption—from television to music to the Internet—has contributed to current trends in gender and ethnic representation, sexuality, substance use, violence, and even suicidal behavior among teens.

CROSSWORD PUZZLE 16.1

Across

2. Identity constructed by adolescents who explore and adopt values from both their subculture and the dominant culture
6. __________ identity: aspect of the self that includes sense of ethnic group membership and attitudes associated with that membership
7. Acculturative _________: psychological distress resulting from conflict between the minority culture and the host culture
9. A well-organized conception of the self made up of values, beliefs, and goals to which the individual is solidly committed
10. Kohlberg's highest level of moral development in which morality is defined in terms of abstract principles and values that apply to all situations and societies
13. Identity status of individuals who are exploring alternatives in an effort to find values and goals to guide their life
14. Identity ___________: identity status of individuals who have no commitments to values and goals and are not actively trying to reach them
15. Sense of self as a separate, self-governing individual
16. Identity versus role ____________: Erikson's psychological conflict of adolescence
17. Small group of 5 to 8 members who are good friends

Down

1. Kohlberg's first level of moral development in which moral understanding is based on rewards, punishments, and the power of authority figures
3. Gender _________: increased gender stereotyping of attitudes and behavior
4. Identity ____________: identity status of individuals who have explored and committed themselves to self-chosen values and goals
5. Kohlberg's second level of moral development in which moral understanding is based on conforming to social rules to ensure positive relationships and social order
8. Identity _____________: identity status of individuals who have accepted ready-made values and goals that authority figures have chosen for them
11. Moral _______-___________: the degree to which morality is central to an individual's self-concept (2 words, hyph.)
12. A large, loosely organized group consisting of several cliques whose membership is based on reputation and stereotype

PRACTICE TEST #1

1. Erikson was the first to recognize __________ as the major personality achievement of adolescence. (p. 600)
   a. intimacy
   b. rationality
   c. self-esteem
   d. identity

2. Current theorists agree with Erikson that __________ (p. 600)
   a. the questioning of values, plans, and priorities is necessary for a mature identity.
   b. most people develop a mature identity by middle adolescence.
   c. identity development is traumatic and disturbing.
   d. the process of identity development is similar across cultures.

3. Of those young people whose self-esteem declines in adolescence, most are __________ (p. 602)
   a. boys.
   b. girls.
   c. African Americans.
   d. immigrants.

4. T. J. is an identity-diffused teenager. When asked about his career goals, T. J. is likely to say, __________ (p. 603)
   a. "I have always wanted to be a doctor, just like my father and grandfather."
   b. "I don't know. I haven't really thought about it too much."
   c. "I'm trying to decide. I used to want to be a musician, and now I just don't know if that's practical."
   d. "I've really thought hard about that, and I've decided I want to work in schools and make them better places for children."

5. Research on identity construction indicates that __________ (p. 604)
   a. most adolescents experience a serious identity crisis, which is vital for psychological well-being.
   b. adolescents typically retain the same identity status across adolescence and early adulthood.
   c. adolescents who go to work after high school settle on an identity status later than college-bound youths.
   d. adolescents who go to work after high school settle on an identity status earlier than college-bound youths.

6. Adolescents in moratorium resemble identity-achieved individuals in __________ (p. 604)
   a. using an active, information-gathering cognitive style.
   b. using a diffuse, avoidant cognitive style.
   c. relying on emotion-centered coping.
   d. relying on adults to make decisions for them.

7. Identity-foreclosed teenagers usually __________ (p. 605)
   a. feel attached to their parents but also free to voice their own opinions.
   b. report low levels of parental support.
   c. have close bonds with their parents.
   d. have ample opportunities for healthy separation from their parents.

8. Thanh's family immigrated to the United States from Vietnam when she was 5. Now, at age 15, Thanh identifies with American culture and resists her parents' efforts to keep her from full assimilation. The conflict between Thanh and her parents is an example of __________ (p. 607)
   a. acculturative stress.
   b. bicultural identity.
   c. ethnic-identity diffusion.
   d. in-group prejudice.

9. When confronted with the Heinz dilemma, 14-year-old Andrew reasons, "Heinz should obey the law and not steal the medicine because if everybody just stole whenever they wanted, our whole society would break down." According to Kohlberg's theory of moral development, Andrew's answer reflects __________ (pp. 609–610)
   a. a postconventional level of moral reasoning.
   b. a conventional level of moral reasoning.
   c. the instrumental purpose orientation.
   d. the universal ethical principle orientation.

10. Research on Kohlberg's theory indicates that __________ (p. 611)
    a. moral development takes place in a neat, stepwise fashion.
    b. moral development is abrupt and uneven.
    c. few people move beyond Stage 4.
    d. most young people reach Stage 6 by the end of adolescence.

11. When faced with moral dilemmas, adolescent girls and women __________ (p. 612)
    a. tend to emphasize justice, whereas males tend to emphasize care.
    b. emphasize care over justice in hypothetical situations, but not in real-life.
    c. display reasoning at a lower stage than male agemates, regardless of culture.
    d. display reasoning at the same stage and often at a higher stage than male agemates.

12. Research on influences on moral reasoning indicates that __________ is a powerful predictor of movement to Kohlberg's Stage 6 or higher. (p. 614)
    a. schooling
    b. gender
    c. identity status
    d. close friendship

13. When asked about the causes of social problems such as unemployment or poverty, adolescents with a strong sense of civic responsibility __________ (p. 616)
    a. usually stress individual factors.
    b. usually stress situational and societal factors.
    c. have difficulty acknowledging the complexity of the issues.
    d. are more knowledgeable in their responses than non-civic-minded peers.

14. Teenagers affiliated with a religious community __________ than nonaffiliated teenagers. (p. 617)
    a. are no more moral in their values or behavior
    b. are more advantaged in moral values and behavior
    c. have fewer trusting relationships with adults
    d. develop moral self-relevance at a slower pace

15. Critics of the pragmatic approach to morality point out that __________ (p. 617)
    a. sometimes people use moral judgments for immoral purposes.
    b. people tend to act first, and then make a retrospective moral judgment.
    c. automatic moral judgments are extremely rare.
    d. people frequently rise above self-interest to defend others' rights.

16. During early adolescence, gender intensification is __________ (p. 618)
    a. stronger for boys.
    b. stronger for girls.
    c. equally strong for both boys and girls.
    d. not yet an important issue.

17. An improved ability to reason about social relationships leads teenagers to __________ (p. 619)
    a. bend to parental authority.
    b. resist opportunities for autonomy.
    c. deidealize their parents.
    d. deemphasize the importance of their friendships.

18. Throughout adolescence, the most consistent predictor of mental health is __________ (p. 621)
    a. the quality of the parent–child relationship.
    b. development of positive peer relationships.
    c. popularity and social status.
    d. success in academic efforts.

19. In adolescence, sibling relationships often become __________ (p. 622)
    a. more conflicted and competitive.
    b. less intense, in both positive and negative feelings.
    c. more intense, in both positive and negative feelings.
    d. closer, particularly among other-sex siblings.

20. When asked about the meaning of friendship, teenagers stress three characteristics: __________ (pp. 622–623)
    a. generosity, sincerity, and trust.
    b. helpfulness, proximity, and shared goals.
    c. fun, compatibility, and opportunity for growth or change.
    d. intimacy, mutual understanding, and loyalty.

21. Corumination __________ (p. 624)
    a. decreases intimacy among friends.
    b. triggers anxiety and depression.
    c. is a common feature of boys' friendships.
    d. is a major benefit of intimacy.

22. Clique membership __________ (p. 626)
    a. predicts academic and social competence among girls.
    b. predicts academic and social problems for both sexes.
    c. is equally important to boys and girls in early adolescence.
    d. becomes increasingly important throughout adolescence.

23. Between tenth and twelfth grade, __________ (p. 627)
    a. mixed-sex cliques begin to form.
    b. crowds increase in importance.
    c. deviant high school crowds lose members.
    d. cliques begin to form into crowds.

24. In early adolescence, dating __________ (p. 627)
    a. is done for recreational purposes, as well as to achieve status among agemates.
    b. is focused on psychological intimacy and shared interests.
    c. fosters social maturity, particularly for highly conflicted youths.
    d. protects teens against drug use, delinquency, and poor school performance.

25. Which of the following statements about peer conformity is true? (p. 629)
    a. In adolescence, peer pressure to engage in prosocial, proadult behavior is strong.
    b. Parents can control teenagers' day-to-day choices, but peers have more impact on their life values.
    c. Parental pressures and peer pressures are usually extremely divergent.
    d. Teenagers whose parents exert excessive control over them tend to resist negative peer pressure.

26. Teenage girls are __________ boys to report persistent depressed mood. (p. 630)
    a. much less likely than
    b. as likely as
    c. twice as likely as
    d. four times as likely as

27. Suicide rates __________ (p. 631)
    a. peak at adolescence, then stabilize.
    b. peak at adolescence, then decline.
    c. increase slightly in adolescence and then decline over the lifespan.
    d. increase over the lifespan, jumping sharply at adolescence.

28. Teenagers who have committed a law-breaking offense __________ (p. 634)
    a. account for a small minority of the adolescent population.
    b. score low on ratings of moral understanding.
    c. often become recurrent offenders.
    d. overwhelmingly become law-abiding citizens.

29. Children with early-onset behavior problems __________ (p. 636)
    a. usually decline in aggression over time.
    b. usually increase in aggression over time.
    c. are more likely than late-onset children to become well-adjusted adults.
    d. rarely respond to positive parenting practices.

30. Compared to several decades ago, today's young people in industrialized nations __________ (p. 637)
    a. have fewer options for success.
    b. lack a sense of moral self-relevance.
    c. face more complex choices.
    d. engage in significantly higher rates of delinquent behavior.

PRACTICE TEST #2

1. According to Erikson, the development of identity in adolescence is __________ (p. 600)
   a. similar in all the world's cultures.
   b. unrelated to the resolution of earlier conflicts.
   c. experienced as a "crisis" in complex societies.
   d. more likely to be positively resolved in societies that limit personal choices.

2. Compared with younger children, adolescents __________ when describing themselves. (p. 601)
   a. are more negative
   b. more often mention contradictory traits
   c. are less likely to use qualifiers, such as "fairly" or "kind of."
   d. place less emphasis on social virtues

3. When asked whether he ever had doubts about his religious beliefs, Cody said, "No. I have gone to the same church my whole life, and I know what the truth is and what my values are." Cody is __________ (p. 603)
   a. identity achieved.
   b. in moratorium.
   c. identity foreclosed.
   d. identity diffused.

4. Young people who are identity-achieved or in moratorium tend to __________ (p. 605)
   a. be advanced in moral reasoning.
   b. display a dogmatic cognitive style.
   c. go along with the crowd.
   d. be immature in identity development.

5. Identity development __________ (p. 606)
   a. occurs independently from personality characteristics.
   b. is mainly influenced by schools and communities.
   c. results directly from parental responsiveness and attachment.
   d. is influenced by a wide variety of factors.

6. Which group of adolescents is most likely to achieve a strong, secure ethnic identity? (p. 607)
   a. biracial adolescents who interact with peers of different ethnicities
   b. nonminority adolescents who interact frequently with same-ethnicity peers
   c. monoracial minority adolescents who interact frequently with same-ethnicity peers
   d. monoracial minority adolescents who interact mainly with nonminority peers

7. To assess moral reasoning, Kohlberg __________ (p. 608)
   a. presented 10- to 16-year-old boys with hypothetical moral dilemmas.
   b. observed school-age children and adolescents during peer disputes.
   c. presented 5- to 18-year-old boys and girls with real-life moral dilemmas.
   d. observed his own children as they grappled with hypothetical and real-life conflicts.

8. When an individual's moral reasoning stems from self-interest, which stage of Kohlberg's theory would best characterize her level of moral understanding? (p. 609)
   a. Stage 2: The instrumental purpose orientation
   b. Stage 3: The "good boy-good girl" orientation
   c. Stage 4: The social-order-maintaining orientation
   d. Stage 6: The universal ethical principle orientation

9. Follow-up research on Kohlberg's stages of moral understanding reveals that __________ (p. 611)
   a. individuals move through the first four of Kohlberg's stages in different orders.
   b. contrary to Kohlberg's belief, most adults reach Stage 6 of moral reasoning.
   c. Kohlberg's moral stages are loosely organized and overlapping.
   d. Kohlberg's moral stages are mostly immune to situational factors.

10. Teenagers who __________ show little or no change in moral reasoning over time. (p. 614)
    a. have warm, demanding, communicative parents
    b. have parents who lecture or threaten
    c. report many close friendships with other teenagers
    d. interact with peers who have differing viewpoints

11. The connection between moral reasoning and moral action is __________ (p. 615)
    a. weak.
    b. modest.
    c. strong.
    d. nil.

12. Which of the following statements about youth involvement in community service is true? (p. 616)
    a. Compared with the youth in other developed nations, U.S. youth are less likely to engage in community service.
    b. When adolescents are required to serve their communities, they are unlikely to want to remain engaged beyond the mandated time.
    c. Low-SES, inner-city youths are far less likely than higher-SES youth to express interest in community service participation.
    d. Low-SES, inner-city youths express interest in community service but score substantially lower than higher-SES youths in civic knowledge and participation.

13. During adolescence, formal religious involvement __________ (p. 617)
    a. declines.
    b. changes very little.
    c. increases.
    d. is rare.

14. Androgynous adolescents, particularly girls, tend to be __________ (pp. 618–619)
    a. identity foreclosed.
    b. psychologically healthy.
    c. unpopular.
    d. rejected by their peers.

15. Research suggests that in adolescence, urban low- and middle-SES African-American youths __________ (p. 621)
    a. show no decline in hours spent with family.
    b. show an especially sharp decline in hours spent with family.
    c. adjust more favorably when parents maintain loose control over them.
    d. have less trusting relationships with their parents than white youths do.

16. Self-disclosure __________ (p. 623)
    a. between friends declines steadily over the adolescent years.
    b. between friends rises steadily over the adolescent years.
    c. to parents rises in early adolescence, then declines.
    d. to parents remains stable throughout adolescence.

17. Which of the following is true of gender differences in adolescent friendships? (p. 624)
    a. Boys' closest same-sex friendships tend to be of shorter duration than girls'.
    b. Emotional closeness is equally common for girls and boys.
    c. Boys' friendships tend to focus on achievement and status, and girls' friendships tend to focus on communal concerns.
    d. Highly masculine boys are more likely than highly feminine girls to form intimate same-sex ties.

18. Which of the following teenagers' Internet use poses the most danger? (p. 625)
    a. Morgan constantly instant messages her friends, sometimes ignoring her family.
    b. Kaley, who suffers from bulimia, frequents a message board about eating disorders.
    c. Scott has conflict with his family and spends a lot of time on the Internet.
    d. Omar has encountered racial slurs in an unmonitored chat room he occasionally visits.

19. In early adolescence, cliques __________ (p. 626)
    a. are fairly unimportant to their members.
    b. serve as a context for relational aggression.
    c. are used by girls to express emotional closeness.
    d. often lead to delinquency.

20. "Jocks," "brains," and "partyers" are examples of __________ (p. 626)
    a. typical high school crowds.
    b. traditional cliques.
    c. mixed-sex cliques.
    d. negative peer networks.

21. __________ determine when and how adolescent dating begins. (p. 627)
    a. School policies
    b. Hormonal changes
    c. Peer group values
    d. Cultural expectations

22. The first dating relationships of homosexual youths tend to be short-lived and involve little emotional commitment. This is largely because they __________ (p. 628)
    a. are often less mature than their heterosexual peers.
    b. fear peer harassment and rejection.
    c. are still questioning their sexual identity.
    d. are looking for relationships that are fun and recreational.

23. Research on peer conformity indicates that __________ (p. 628)
    a. individuals are less likely to conform to peer pressure during adolescence than during childhood and early adulthood.
    b. peers exert more influence on teenagers' basic life values and educational plans than parents do.
    c. adolescents feel the greatest pressure to conform to obvious aspects of the peer culture, such as style of dress.
    d. adolescents who experience authoritative parenting are more likely to rely on advice from friends in making decisions.

24. Teenagers who follow parental rules and resist peer pressure tend to have parents who __________ (p. 629)
    a. use frequent punishment.
    b. exert oversight within a supportive environment.
    c. permit independent decision making in most areas of adolescent life.
    d. closely monitor adolescents' activities and encourage obedience.

25. What is the most common psychological problem of adolescence? (p. 629)
    a. gender confusion
    b. delinquency
    c. anxiety
    d. depression

26. Teenage girls who __________ are especially prone to depression. (p. 630)
    a. live in developing nations
    b. are androgynous
    c. identify with "feminine" traits
    d. are late-maturing

27. Which of the following is true of suicide among teenagers? (p. 631)
    a. Boys are three to four times more likely to kill themselves than girls.
    b. African Americans have higher suicide rates than Caucasian Americans.
    c. Rates of teenage suicide are the same among all industrialized nations.
    d. Boys make more unsuccessful suicide attempts than girls.

28. Which of the following is a major reason for the decline in delinquency after middle adolescence? (p. 634)
    a. The desire for peer approval becomes stronger in late adolescence.
    b. Moral reasoning improves in late adolescence.
    c. Teenage lawbreakers are usually incarcerated by late adolescence.
    d. Older adolescents are more adept at escaping detection of their crimes.

29. Which of the following is a consistent finding in research on juvenile delinquency? (p. 634)
    a. Low-SES and minority youths are much more likely to commit violent crimes than higher-SES white and Asian youths.
    b. Violent crime is equally common among adolescent boys and girls, though boys' violent crimes are of a more serious nature.
    c. Families of delinquent youths tend to be have harsh, inconsistent discipline tactics and low monitoring.
    d. Delinquent youths are usually identity-foreclosed and have controlling, authoritarian parents.

30. __________ is the main factor in transforming biologically based self-control difficulties into long-lasting hostility and defiance. (p. 636)
    a. Juvenile incarceration
    b. Peer pressure
    c. Inept parenting
    d. Academic failure

CHAPTER 17
EMERGING ADULTHOOD

BRIEF CHAPTER SUMMARY

Emerging adulthood is a recently identified period of development that is marked by great challenge and uncertainty. Young people between the ages of 18 and 25 in industrialized nations prolong identity development as they explore alternatives in education, work, personal values, and love.

Cultural changes have contributed to the appearance of emerging adulthood. Increased education required for entry-level positions in many fields, gains in economic prosperity and life expectancy, reduced need for young people's labor, and globalization have prompted the appearance and spread of emerging adulthood. These benefits, however, are not always available to many low-SES and ethnic minority youths.

To make a successful transition to adulthood, emerging adults must acquire new knowledge and skills. Research on postformal thought has shown that college students make substantial strides in cognition. The cognitive gains of the late teens and early twenties are supported by further brain development, especially of the prefrontal cortex. Older students make more effective use of relativistic thinking than younger students, as they are more aware of the existence of multiple truths. Exposure to a variety of viewpoints encourages young people to look at themselves. As self-understanding increases, emerging adults experience advances in identity in the areas of love, work, and worldview. Despite self-focused themes in their worldviews, many emerging adults also want to improve their communities, nation, and world and participate in community service.

Taking a more active role in their own development and participating in vigorous explorations, emerging adults face increased risks. Also, loneliness peaks in emerging adulthood. Certain personal attributes and social supports increase resilience and foster successful passage through this period.

LEARNING OBJECTIVES

After reading this chapter, you should be able to:

17.1 Describe emerging adulthood, noting characteristics of this new transitional period of development. (pp. 644–645)

17.2 Explain how cultural changes have contributed to the appearance of emerging adulthood and why this period is only applicable to certain groups of young people. (pp. 645–646)

17.3 Discuss cognitive, emotional, and social changes that take place during emerging adulthood. (pp. 647–656)

17.4 Discuss the risks faced by emerging adults, and summarize factors that foster resilience and a successful transition to adulthood. (pp. 656–658)

STUDY QUESTIONS

1. Describe the new phase of development known as *emerging adulthood.* (p. 644)

____

____

____

A Period of Unprecedented Exploration

1. True or False: About 85 percent of American young people who enroll in higher education earn their bachelor's degree by age 25. (p. 644)
2. The average age of first marriage is (increasing / declining) in industrialized nations. (p. 644)
3. Explain how extended education and delayed career entry and marriage create residential instability for emerging adults. (p. 645)

____

____

____

4. True or False: Most emerging adults remain financially dependent on their parents. (p. 645)

Cultural Change, Cultural Variation, and Emerging Adulthood

1. Cite two cultural factors that have contributed to emerging adulthood. (pp. 645–646)

A. ____

B. ____

2. True or False: Emerging adulthood is largely limited to industrialized nations. Briefly explain your response. (p. 646)

____

____

3. Emerging adulthood (is / is not) common in low-SES and ethnic minority youths. Explain why or why not. (p. 646)

____

____

____

4. Explain how globalization is expected to impact emerging adulthood. (p. 646)

____

____

Cultural Influences: Is Emerging Adulthood Really a Distinct Period of Development?

1. Briefly summarize three arguments that refute the concept of emerging adulthood, providing evidence for each. (p. 647)

   A. ______________________________

   ____

   B. ______________________________

   ____

   C. ______________________________

   ____

2. Why do some researchers argue that emerging adulthood is a crucial and distinct period of development? (p. 647)

   ____

   ____

   ____

Development in Emerging Adulthood

Cognitive Changes

1. What is *postformal thought,* and how does college contribute to it? (p. 648)

   A. ______________________________

   B. ______________________________

2. Briefly describe *epistemic cognition.* (p. 648)

   ____

   ____

   ____

3. Trace changes in thought that occur across the college years. Be sure to include *dualistic thinking* and *relativistic thinking* in your response. (p. 648)

   Younger students: ______________________________

   ____

   Older students: ______________________________

   ____

4. What is *commitment within realitivistic thinking,* and what factors support its development? (pp. 648–649)

   A. ______________________________

   ____

   B. ______________________________

   ____

5. How do gains in metacognition support epistemic cognition? (p. 649)

   ____

   ____

6. Explain why peer interaction and reflection are especially important for cognitive development in emerging adulthood. (p. 649)

____

____

Emotional and Social Changes

1. Provide an example of how emerging adults explore both in breadth and in depth as they construct an identity. (pp. 649–650)

____

____

2. What is personal agency, and how does it contribute to emerging adults' emotional and social development? (p. 650)

   A. ____

   B. ____

   ____

3. According to Erikson, ____________________ is a major task of the early adulthood years. (p. 650)

4. Explain how dating relationships change from adolescence into emerging adulthood. (p. 650)

____

____

5. Provide an example of how partner similarity and communication affect the likelihood of forming an intimate romantic bond during emerging adulthood. (p. 651)

   Partner similarity: ____

   ____

   Communication: ____

   ____

6. Although half of American young couples cohabit, their relationships are more likely to break up within two years than those of Western European cohabitors. Explain why. (p. 652)

____

____

____

7. Provide an example of how work-related goals and pursuits differ for young men and women. (p. 652)

____

____

____

8. Identify four experiences common to women who continue to achieve at a high level during the college years. (p. 653)

   A. ____

   B. ____

   C. ____

   D. ____

9. Provide an example of how the experience of emerging adulthood differs between ethnic minority young people and their Caucasian peers. (p. 653)

10. List a strategy for improving college success for low-income, ethnic minority students. (p. 653)

11. True or False: Racial bias and discrimination in career opportunities has lessened, especially for college graduates. (p. 653)

12. Why do ethnic minority women have an especially difficult time realizing their career potential? (p. 654)

13. True or False: Emerging adults report that constructing a worldview, or set of beliefs and values to live by, is more important than finishing their education and settling into a career or marriage. (p. 654)

14. The Millennial generation is (more / less) narcissistic than previous generations. Explain why or why not. (p. 654)

15. Compared to previous generations, far fewer American young people vote and engage in political party activities. Explain why. (p. 655)

16. True or False: Religious involvement is at its lowest level during the late teens and early twenties. (p. 655)

17. How do parental relationships affect religious development in young adulthood? (p. 656)

Risk and Resilience in Emerging Adulthood

1. Cite several risks associated with emerging adults' vigorous explorations. (p. 656)

2. True or False: Feelings of loneliness peak during the late teens and early twenties. Explain your answer. (pp. 656–657)

3. Provide several examples of personal attributes and social supports that foster development during emerging adulthood. (p. 657)

   Cognitive attributes: ____

   ____

   Emotional and social attributes: ____

   ____

   Social supports: ____

   ____

4. Explain circumstances in which the parental bond can both support and undermine development during emerging adulthood. (pp. 657–658)

   Support: ____

   ____

   Undermine: ____

   ____

ASK YOURSELF . . .

For *Ask Yourself* questions for this chapter, along with feedback on the accuracy of your answers, please log on to MyDevelopmentLab (for registration and access, please visit mydevelopmentlab.com or follow the instructions on page ix).

(1) Select the Multimedia Library.

(2) Choose the explore option.

(3) Find your chapter from the drop down box.

(4) Click find now.

(5) Complete questions and choose "Submit answers for grading" or "Clear answers" to start over.

SUGGESTED READINGS

Settersten, R., Furstenberg, F. F., & Rumbart, R. G. (Eds.). (2008). *On the frontier of adulthood.* Chicago, IL: University of Chicago Press. Presents leading research on early adult development, including factors related to substance use, the college experience, selecting a vocation, and public policies aimed at helping young people with the transition to adulthood.

Watt, H. M., & Eccles, J. S. (Eds.). (2008). *Gender and occupational outcomes*. Washington, DC: American Psychological Association. Examines longitudinal trends in gender inequality in the workplace. Although women have made great strides in entering traditionally male-dominated professions, there continues to be gender-related disparities in math, science, and technology careers, with women rarely sharing the salary and status of men in similar positions. An excellent resource for students, educators, policymakers, and anyone interested in vocational development.

CROSSWORD PUZZLE 17.1

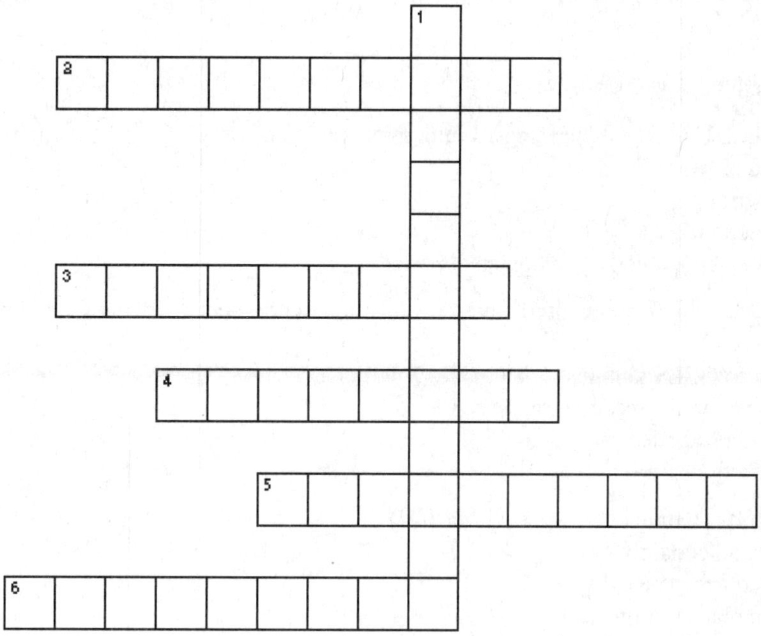

Across

2. ________________ within relativistic thinking: the mature individual's formulation of a perspective that synthesizes contradictions between opposing views, rather than choosing between them
3. The view that knowledge is made up of separate beliefs and propositions, whose truth can be determined by comparing them with objective standards is called ______________ thinking
4. A new period of development, extending from the late teens to the twenties, during which young people have left adolescence but have not yet assumed full adult responsibilities is called _____________ adulthood.
5. Development beyond Piaget's formal operational stage is called _____________ thought.
6. _____________ cognition: reflections on how one arrived at facts, beliefs, and ideas

Down

1. _______________ thinking: the view that knowledge is embedded in a framework of thought and that multiple truths can exist, each relative to its context

PRACTICE TEST #1

1. Hans, a German 20-year-old college student, is asked whether he considers himself to have reached adulthood. Hans is most likely to answer, __________ (p. 643)
   a. "Yes, I reached it at age 18."
   b. "No."
   c. "Yes and no."
   d. "Yes, I reached it at age 20."

2. American psychologist, Jeffrey Arnett, regards emerging adulthood as a __________ (p. 644)
   a. distinct period of life.
   b. floundering period.
   c. global construction.
   d. modern trend, but not a new developmental period.

3. Young people __________ explore alternatives in education, work, personal values, and love more intensely than they did as teenagers. (p. 644)
   a. who come for low-SES families
   b. who have the economic resources to do so
   c. from collectivist societies
   d. with a foreclosed identity

4. Emerging adulthood is a time of __________ (p. 644)
   a. intense focus and certainty.
   b. immaturity and irresponsibility.
   c. career development and financial growth.
   d. great challenge and uncertainty.

5. For more than half of 18- to 25-year-olds in the United States, the preferred way of entering into a committed intimate partnership is __________ (p. 645)
   a. cohabitation.
   b. marriage.
   c. sexual experimentation.
   d. extended friendship before romance.

6. Among African-American, Hispanic, and Native-American groups, rates of leaving home are lower because __________ (p. 645)
   a. young people in these groups nearly always attend colleges close to home.
   b. of high rates of early marriage and divorce.
   c. young people in these groups experience an extended adolescence.
   d. of poverty and a cultural tradition of extended family.

7. In the United States today, about __________ of young people enroll in colleges and universities in the first year after high school graduation. (p. 646)
   a. one-quarter
   b. one-third
   c. two-thirds
   d. three-quarters

8. The massive expansion of higher education has __________ (p. 646)
   a. shortened the time period for emerging adulthood.
   b. delayed financial independence and career commitment.
   c. shortened the time period for exploring work options.
   d. resulted in greater financial stability for young adults.

9. Dramatic gains in __________ in prosperous nations have contributed to emerging adulthood. (p. 646)
   a. drug use
   b. gross national product
   c. population
   d. life expectancy

10. Disagreement exists over whether __________ (p. 646)
    a. cultural change has prolonged the transition to adult roles for many young people.
    b. attending college facilitates postformal thought.
    c. emerging adulthood is really a distinct period of development.
    d. most of the world's youths are limited in education.

11. One criticism of the concept of emerging adulthood is that __________ (p. 647)
    a. it fails to describe the experiences of most of the world's young people.
    b. it primarily occurs in low-SES young people.
    c. most individuals consider themselves fully adult by age 18.
    d. most research has been conducted on college-age males from the United States.

12. Researchers who study __________ thought have found that college students make impressive strides in cognition. (p. 648)
    a. preoperational
    b. formal operational
    c. postoperational
    d. postformal

13. To facilitate exploration, college exposes students to __________ (p. 648)
    a. idealistic worldviews.
    b. a form of culture shock.
    c. mandatory civic engagement.
    d. dualistic thinking.

14. __________ thinking divides information, values, and authority into right and wrong, good and bad, we and they. (p. 648)
    a. Dualistic
    b. Relativistic
    c. Postformal
    d. Epistemic

15. Brenda gave up the possibility of absolute truth in favor of multiple truths. She views all knowledge as embedded in a framework of thought. Brenda uses __________ thinking. (p. 648)
    a. dualistic
    b. relativistic
    c. postformal
    d. epistemic

16. When considering which of two television shows deserves an Emmy, Omar moves beyond the stance that everything is a matter of opinion and generates rational criteria against which options can be evaluated. Omar is using __________ (p. 648)
    a. dualistic thinking.
    b. relativistic thinking.
    c. commitment within relativistic thinking.
    d. epistemic cognition.

17. Advances in epistemic cognition depend on gains in metacognition, which are more likely to occur in situations that __________ (p. 649)
    a. encourage young people to affirm their personal beliefs and values.
    b. induce young people to consider the rationality of their thought processes.
    c. allow young people to express their opinions with greater intensity.
    d. allow young people to receive guidance from a likeminded mentor.

18. _________ remain(s) a highly effective basis for education in emerging adulthood. (p. 649)
    a. Peer collaboration
    b. Full inclusion
    c. A lecture format
    d. Standardized testing

19. During college, students' attitudes and values _________ (p. 649)
    a. narrow.
    b. become egocentric.
    c. become polarized.
    d. broaden.

20. Compared to their peers, college students who spend a lot of time exploring in breadth without making commitments tend to be _________ (pp. 649–650)
    a. happier.
    b. poorly adjusted.
    c. less anxious.
    d. higher in self-esteem.

21. According to Erikson, _________ is the major task of the emerging adulthood years. (p. 650)
    a. initiative
    b. trust
    c. intimacy
    d. industry

22. About _____ percent of emerging adults have had only one sexual partner in the previous year. (p. 651)
    a. 30
    b. 40
    c. 50
    d. 60

23. An important feature of a couple's commitment is _________ (p. 651)
    a. constructive conflict resolution.
    b. the ability to tolerate criticism from one other.
    c. avoidance of negative emotion.
    d. dependence on each other.

24. To help realize their career dreams, young people generally _________ (p. 652)
    a. turn to their parents for help.
    b. form a relationship with a mentor.
    c. seek career support from a romantic partner.
    d. rely only on themselves.

25. Women in male-dominated careers _________ (p. 652)
    a. earn less than women in traditionally "feminine" careers.
    b. are usually reliant on others.
    c. typically have "masculine" traits.
    d. are usually unsure about whether their efforts will result in success.

26. Many college dropouts _________ (p. 653)
    a. leave school to begin a career.
    b. live in campus housing.
    c. return to college after getting married.
    d. leave within the first six weeks.

27. Most emerging adults say that __________ is the most important thing in attaining adult status. (p. 654)
    a. constructing a worldview
    b. finishing their education
    c. settling into a career
    d. getting married and having children

28. Compared to students not engaged in community service, those who volunteer have a __________ (p. 655)
    a. stronger individualistic orientation.
    b. stronger pluralistic orientation.
    c. greater aversion to having their views challenged.
    d. narrow-minded approach to societal problems.

29. Which of the following is true about religion and spirituality in emerging adulthood? (p. 655)
    a. Young people attend more religious services in college than they do in later adulthood.
    b. Only about 10 percent of U.S. emerging adults sustain regular, formal religious activities.
    c. Emerging adults who feel securely attached to their parents are more likely to question their religious beliefs.
    d. Many young people begin to construct their own individualized faith.

30. Loneliness __________ (p. 656)
    a. is uncommon among emerging adults.
    b. is associated with greater sensitivity to others.
    c. can motivate young people to reach out to others.
    d. in emerging adulthood rarely affects self-esteem.

PRACTICE TEST #2

1. During emerging adulthood, adult milestones __________ (p. 644)
   a. occur earlier in women than men.
   b. are highly diverse in timing and order across individuals.
   c. are universal across diverse SES and ethnic groups.
   d. occur earlier in high-SES than low-SES young people.

2. __________ of young people who enroll in higher education have earned their bachelor's degree by age 25. (p. 644)
   a. About 20 percent
   b. Thirty percent
   c. Only about half
   d. Two-thirds

3. Today, the majority of Americans view marriage and parenthood as __________ (p. 645)
   a. crucial markers of adult status.
   b. a means of attaining financial security.
   c. obstacles to career and self-exploration.
   d. personal choices among a range of possible lifestyles.

4. Together, extended education, delayed career entry, and later marriage lead to __________ (p. 645)
   a. great residential instability.
   b. future marriage instability.
   c. high rates of depression and anxiety.
   d. a sharp rise in self-involvement and narcissism.

5. Usually, __________ cause(s) 18- to 25-year-olds to return to their parents' home for brief periods after first leaving. (p. 645)
   a. a brush with the law
   b. parental pressure
   c. role transitions
   d. loneliness

6. Emerging adulthood is limited to cultures that __________ (p. 646)
   a. are not prosperous.
   b. postpone entry into adult roles until the twenties.
   c. have shorter-living populations.
   d. have a brief period of adolescence.

7. __________ college students believe that becoming less self-oriented and conducting oneself responsibly are as important as self-sufficiency. (p. 646)
   a. Asian
   b. Hispanic
   c. Protestant
   d. Mormon

8. In Western nations, for young people who __________, emerging adulthood is limited or nonexistent. (p. 646)
   a. pursue vocational training
   b. are burdened by early parenthood
   c. attend graduate school
   d. attend community college

9. Some researchers predict that emerging adulthood will become increasingly common as __________ accelerates. (p. 646)
   a. globalization
   b. the economic recession
   c. political unrest
   d. drug and alcohol abuse

10. Skeptics note that emerging adulthood is unlikely to become a prominent period of life in __________ (p. 647)
    a. Western nations.
    b. poverty-stricken areas.
    c. developing nations that play a role in the global economy.
    d. industrialized regions.

11. Researchers who study postformal thought maintain that college serves as a(n) __________ (p. 648)
    a. "developmental testing ground."
    b. "rollercoaster ride of emotions."
    c. "period of moral uncertainty."
    d. "experiment with alternative lifestyles."

12. William Perry provided a starting point for an expanding research literature on the development of __________ (p. 648)
    a. postformal thought.
    b. formal operational thought.
    c. epistemic cognition.
    d. dualistic thinking.

13. Younger students tend to engage in __________ (p. 648)
    a. dualistic thinking.
    b. relativistic thinking.
    c. commitment within relativistic thinking.
    d. postformal thought.

14. As a result of relativistic thinking, older college students become __________ (p. 648)
    a. disillusioned with society.
    b. more flexible and tolerant.
    c. more critical and idealistic.
    d. strong leaders.

15. Eventually, most mature individuals progress to __________ (p. 648)
    a. dualistic thinking.
    b. relativistic thinking.
    c. commitment within relativistic thinking.
    d. preoperational thought.

16. Few college students reach __________ (p. 649)
    a. dualistic thinking.
    b. relativistic thinking.
    c. commitment within relativistic thinking.
    d. preoperational thought.

17. Attainment of commitment within relativism occurs more often in young people who __________ (p. 649)
    a. have no formal school.
    b. pursue advanced graduate education.
    c. take some college classes, but do not obtain a degree.
    d. live in collectivist societies.

18. When college students were asked to devise the most effective solution to a difficult logical problem, those who arrived at the best answer worked __________ (p. 649)
    a. alone.
    b. with one partner.
    c. in a large group.
    d. in a small group.

19. Exposure to multiple viewpoints in college __________ (p. 649)
    a. encourages young people to look more closely at themselves.
    b. erodes students' values by encourage them to question and experiment.
    c. confuses young people, delaying their commitment to educational and career goals.
    d. polarizes young people by pushing them to extreme viewpoints.

20. Emerging adults who move toward exploration in depth and certainty of commitment are __________ (pp. 649–650)
    a. lower in self-esteem.
    b. higher in academic adjustment.
    c. lower in social adjustment.
    d. higher in anxiety.

21. With age, emerging adults' romantic ties involve __________ (p. 650)
    a. less trust.
    b. greater support.
    c. less commitment.
    d. less emotional closeness.

22. Success rates for relationships involving couples who meet over the Internet are __________ than with conventional strategies. (p. 651)
    a. much lower
    b. slightly lower
    c. slightly higher
    d. much higher

23. Which of the following cohabiting couples is the most likely to break up within two years? (p. 652)
    a. Alt and Amalia, from the Netherlands
    b. Kai and Gerta, from Norway
    c. Jane and John, from the United States
    d. Anders and Elin, from Sweden

24. Mathematically talented college women __________ (p. 652)
    a. frequently choose nonscience majors.
    b. generally choose math or science majors.
    c. rarely have concerns about combining work with family.
    d. have no doubt they can succeed in male-dominated fields.

25. __________ with __________ mentors tend to be more successful. (p. 653)
    a. Women; male
    b. Men; female
    c. Men; no
    d. Women; female

26. Racial bias in career opportunities __________ (p. 653)
    a. now involves a bias against Caucasians.
    b. has been eradicated by equal opportunity employment laws.
    c. remains strong.
    d. still exists, but is weak.

27. Analyses of large, nationally representative samples of U.S. young people, suggest that compared to past generations, the Millennial generation reports __________ (p. 654)
    a. less narcissism.
    b. greater valuing of money.
    c. greater empathy for the less fortunate.
    d. less interest in leisure pursuits.

28. Compared to previous generations, fewer young people today __________ (p. 655)
    a. vote.
    b. discuss controversial issues.
    c. have a desire to volunteer.
    d. lack faith in the political process.

29. Emerging adults who view their parents as having a(n) __________ style of parenting are more likely to hold religious or spiritual beliefs similar to those of their parents. (p. 656)
    a. authoritarian
    b. uninvolved
    c. authoritative
    d. permissive

30. __________ has an especially wide-ranging influence on resilience in emerging adulthood. (p. 657)
    a. Good academic performance
    b. A secure, affectionate parent–emerging adult bond
    c. Development of strong dualistic thinking skills
    d. A variety of romantic ties

CROSSWORD PUZZLE SOLUTIONS

PUZZLE 1.1

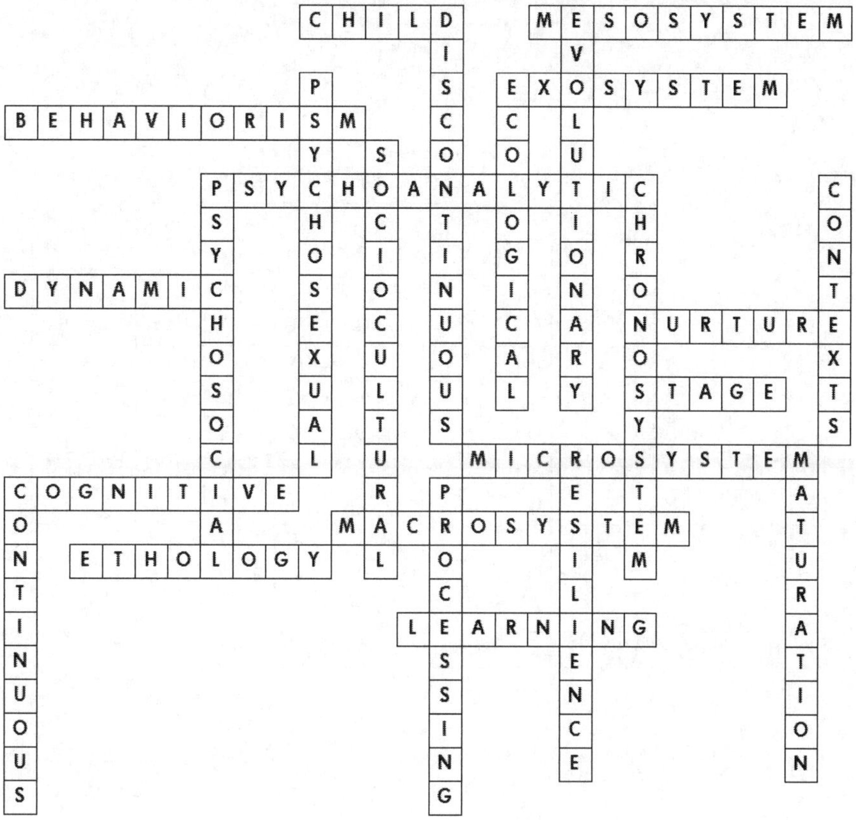

PUZZLE 1.2

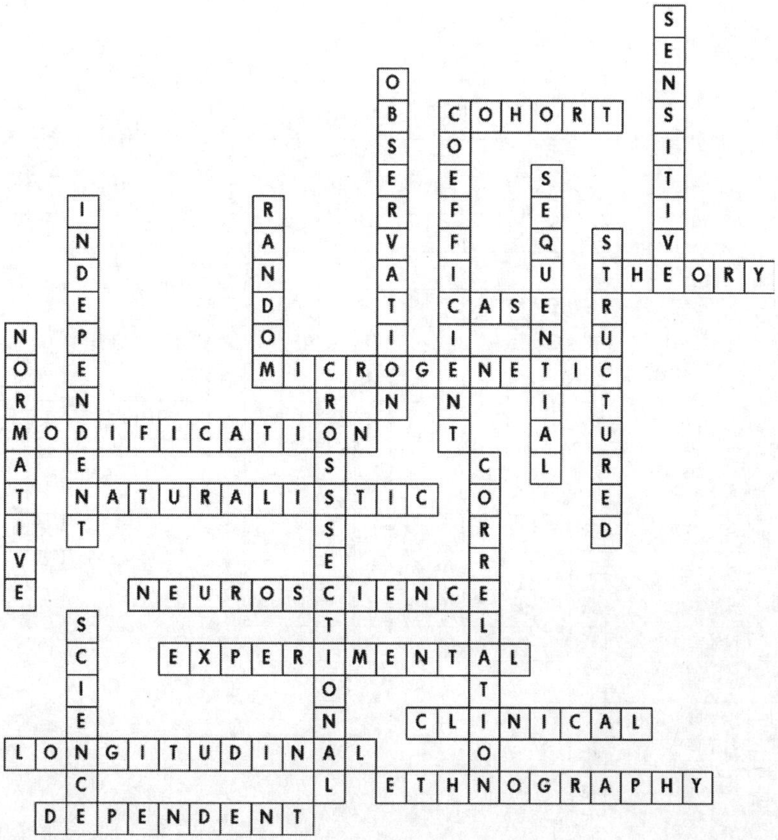

PUZZLE 2.1

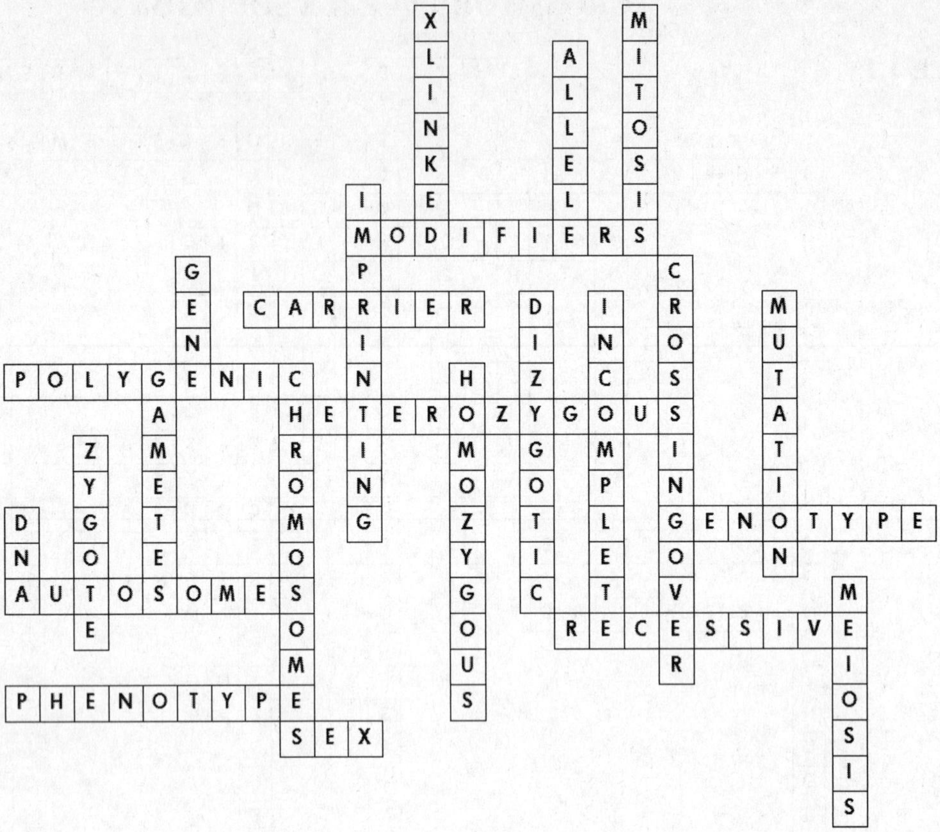

PUZZLE 2.2

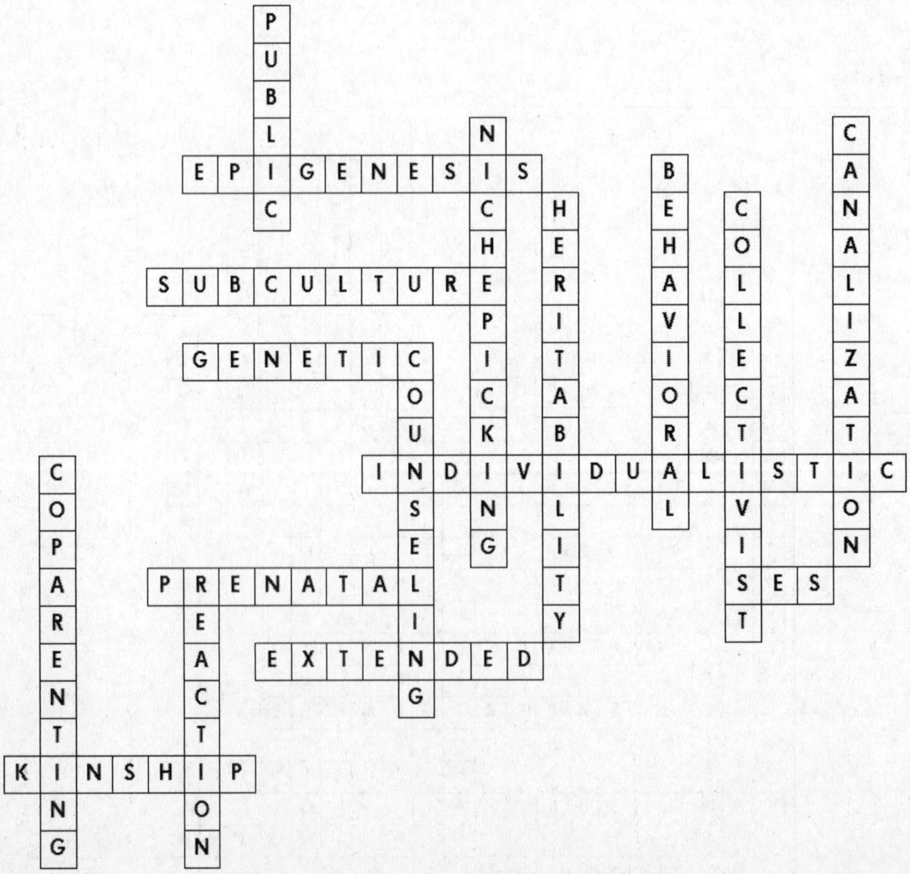

PUZZLE 3.1

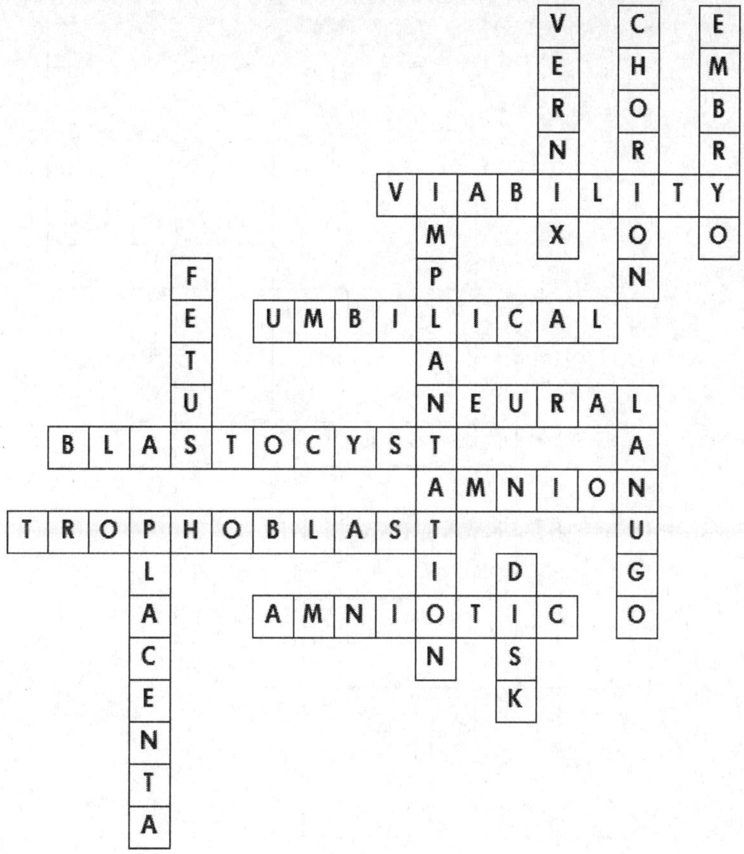

PUZZLE 3.2

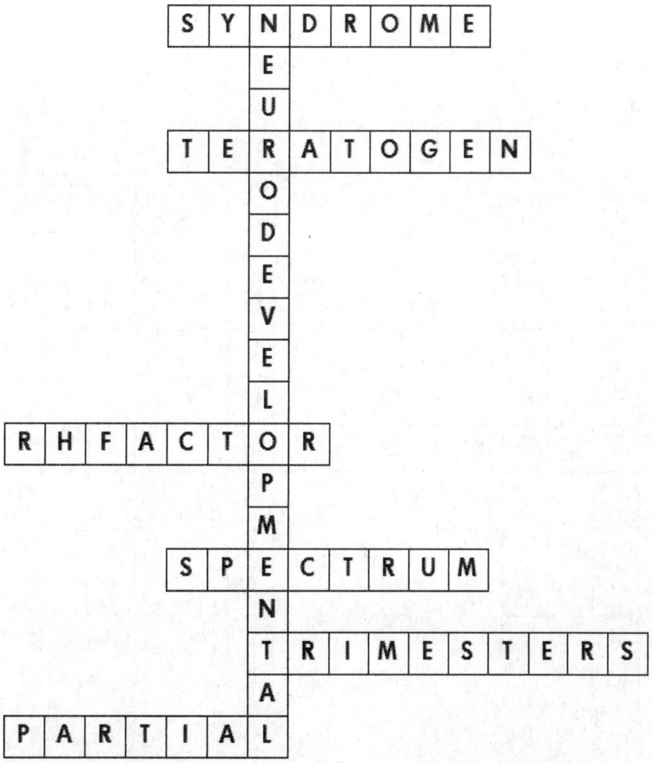

PUZZLE 4.1

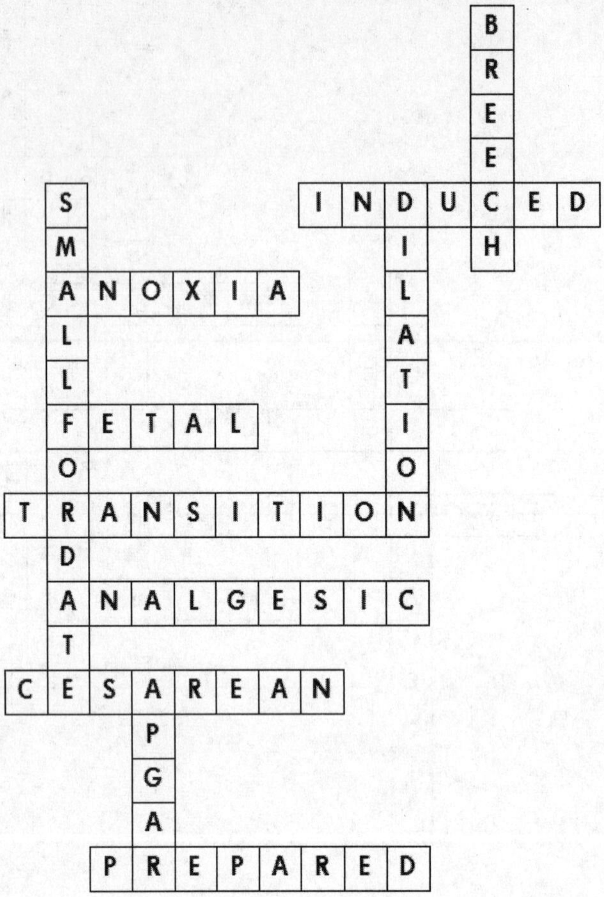

PUZZLE 4.2

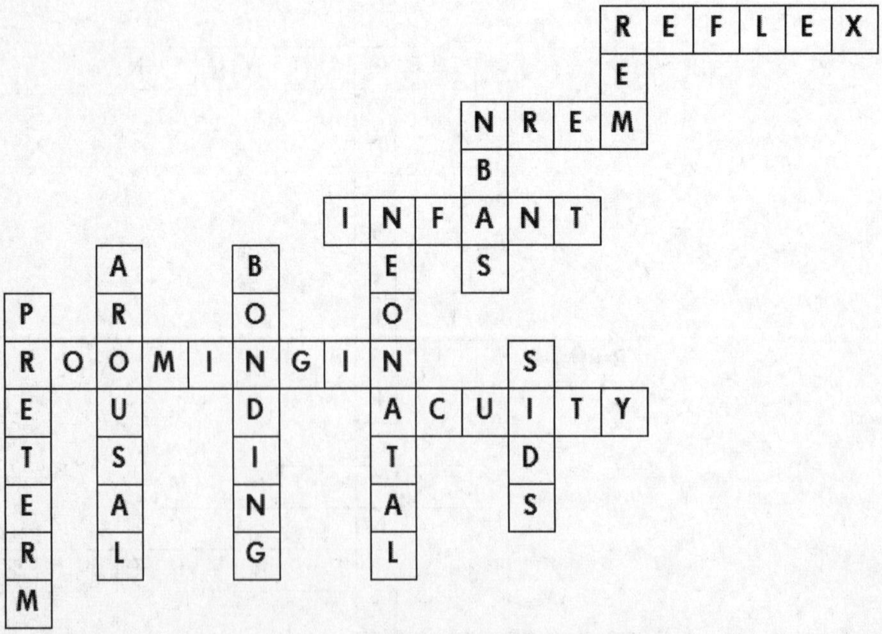

PUZZLE 5.1

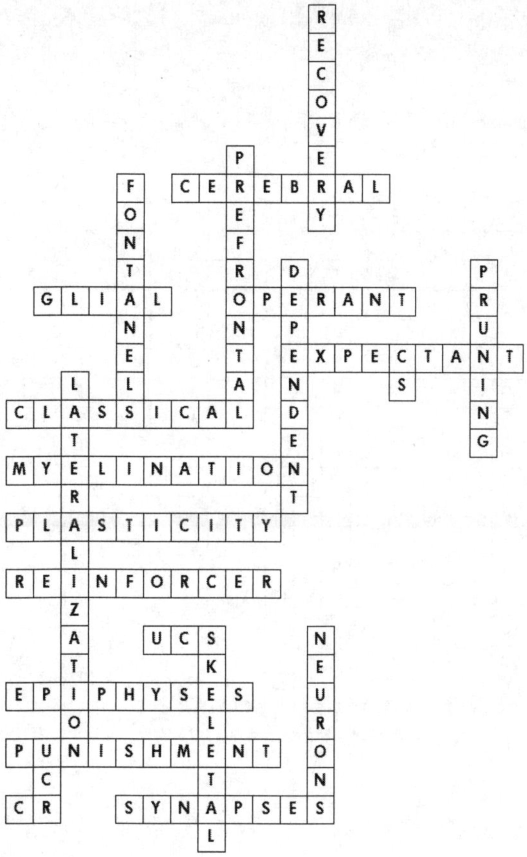

PUZZLE 5.2

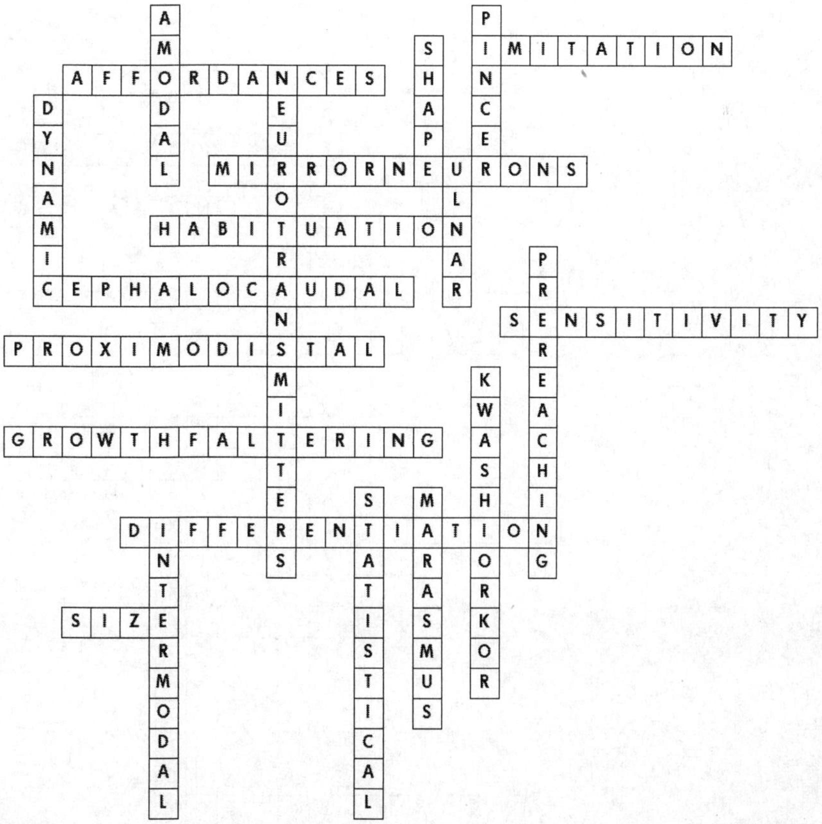

PUZZLE 6.1

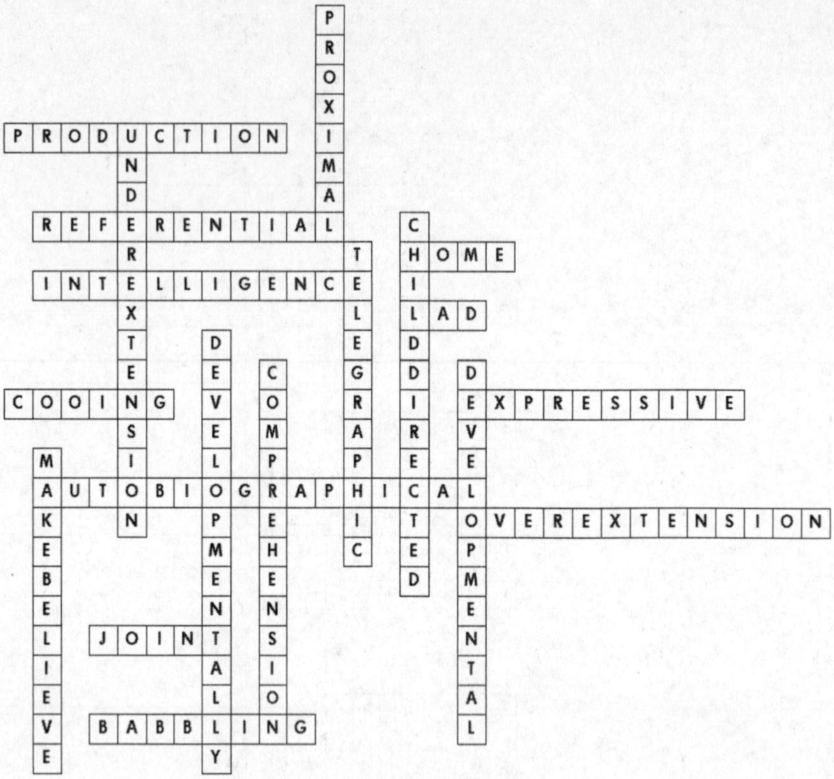

PUZZLE 6.2

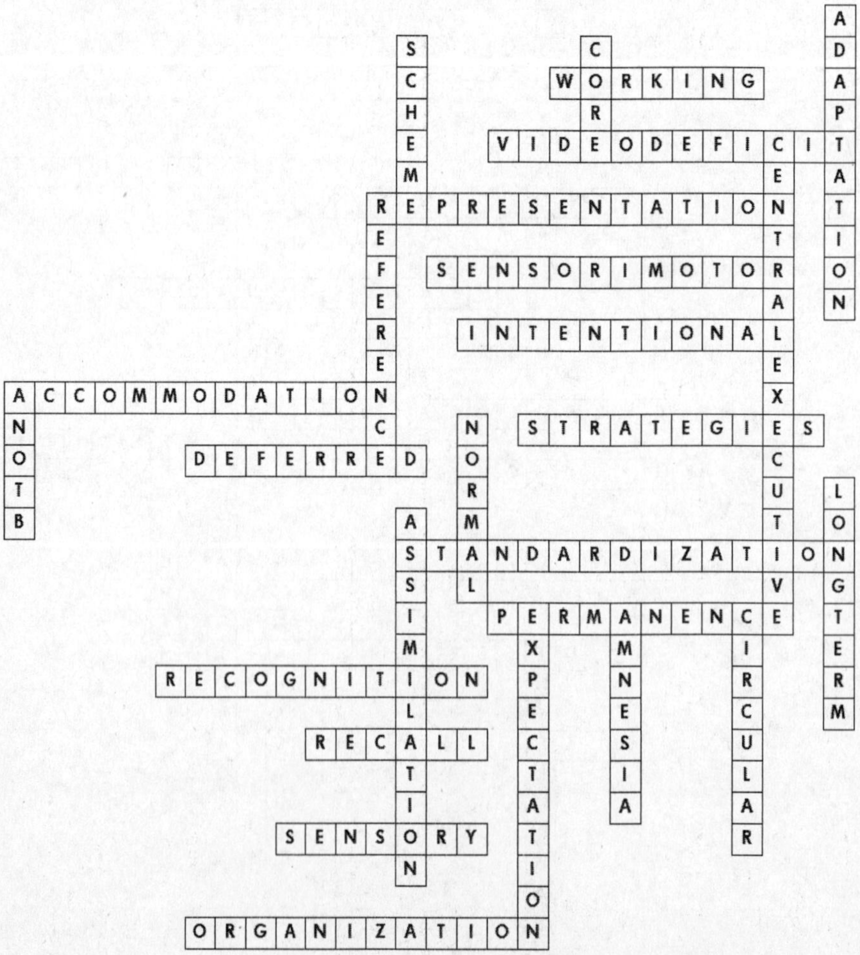

PUZZLE 7.1

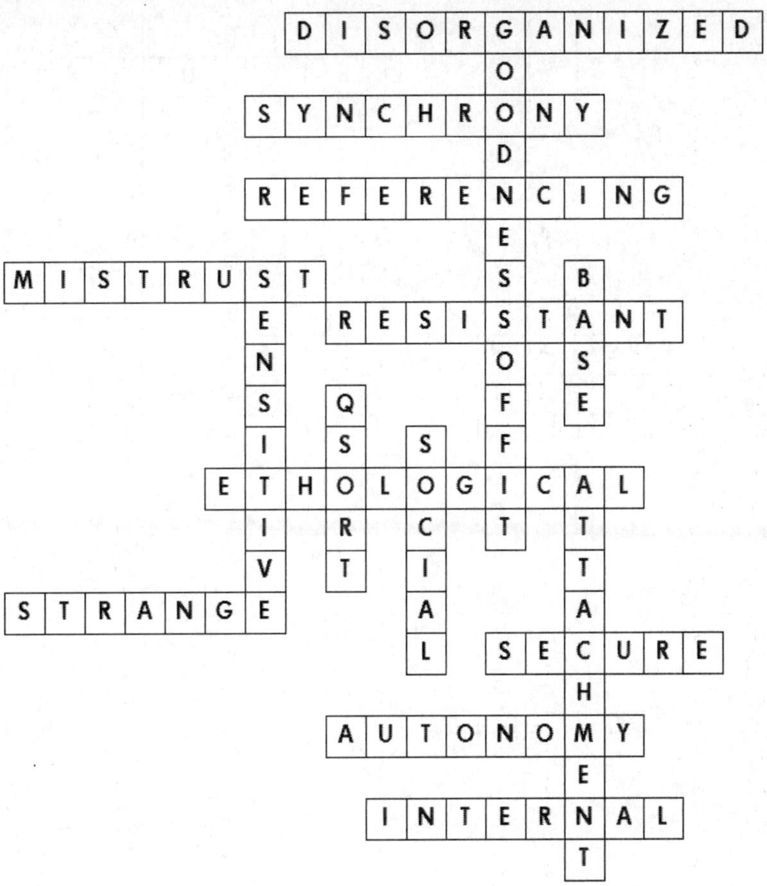

PUZZLE 7.2

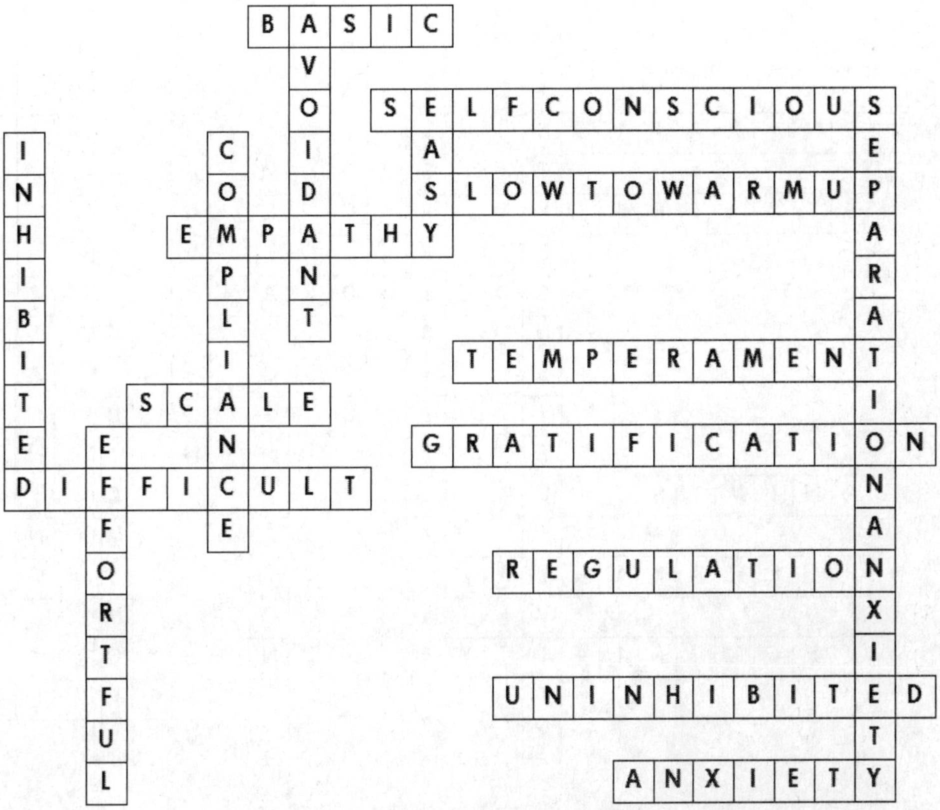

PUZZLE 8.1

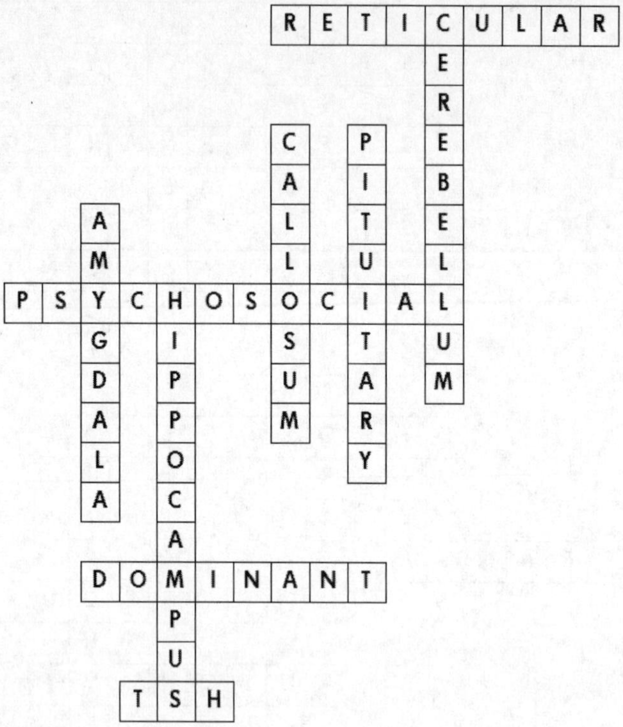

PUZZLE 9.1

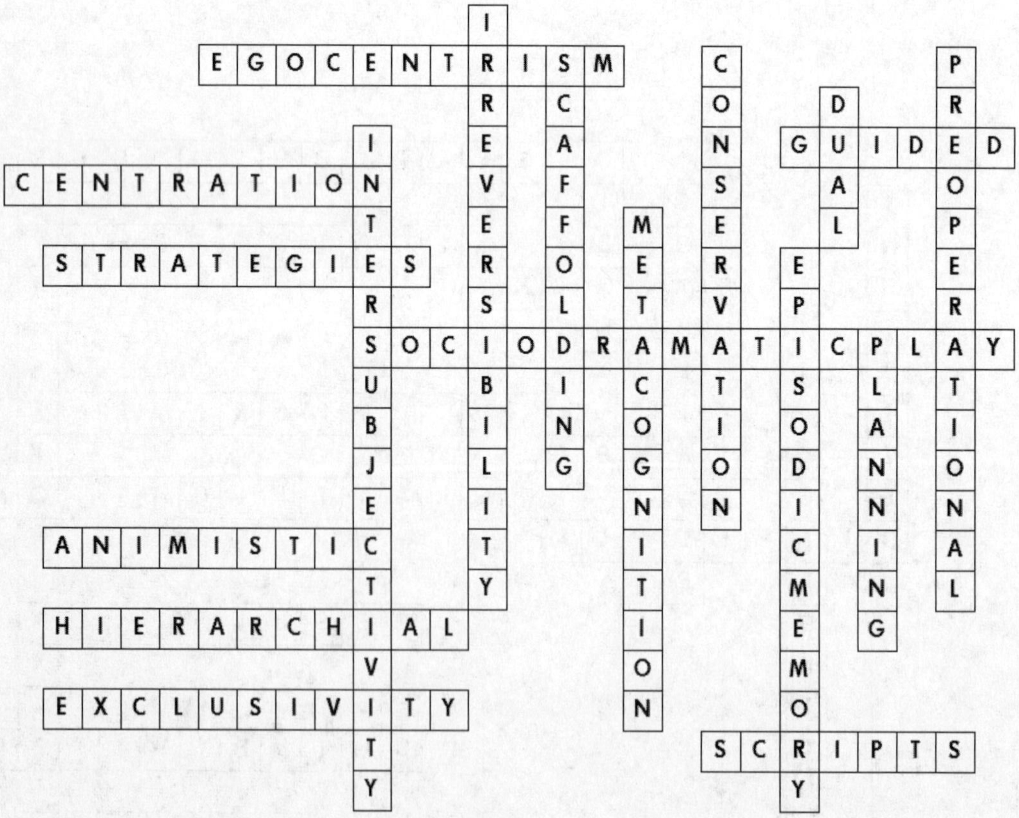

PUZZLE 9.2

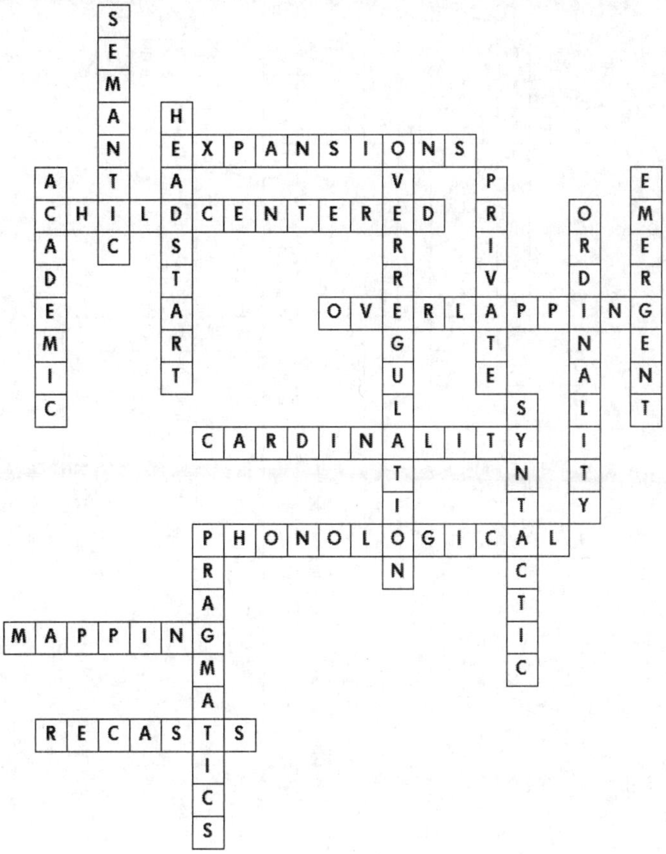

PUZZLE 10.1

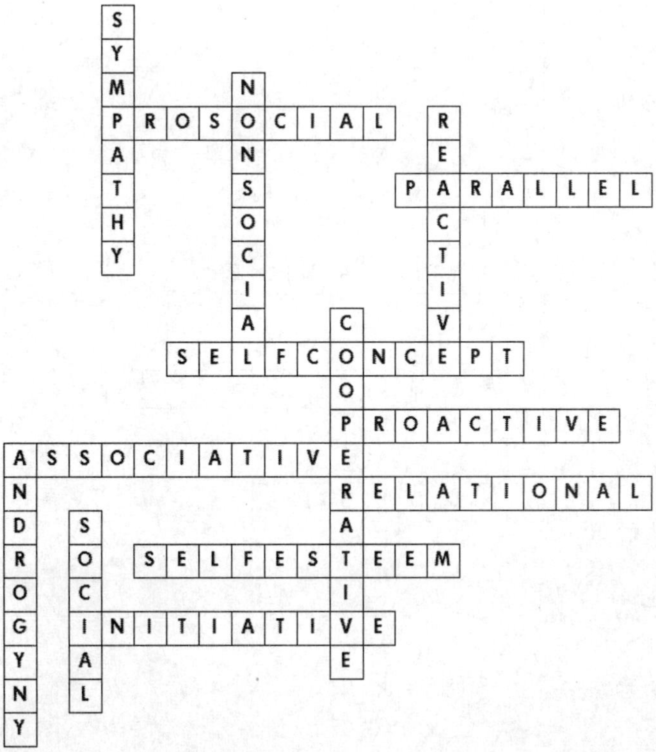

PUZZLE 10.2

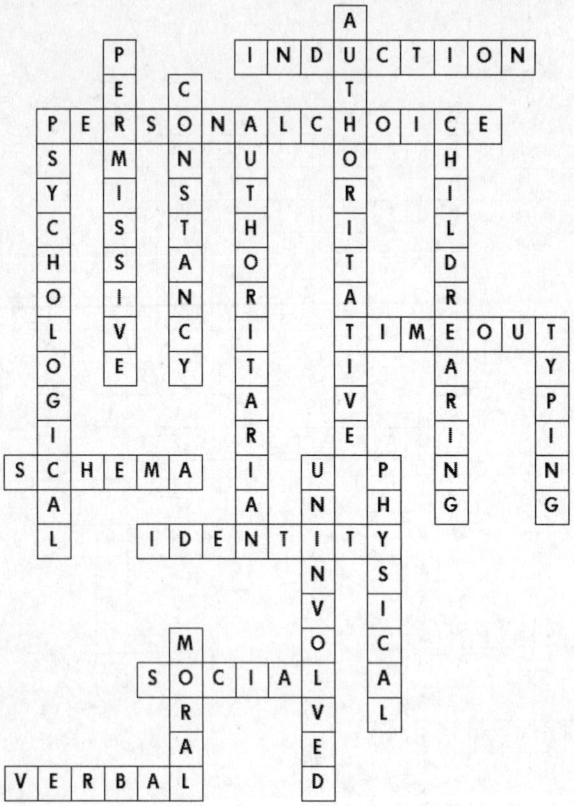

PUZZLE 11.1

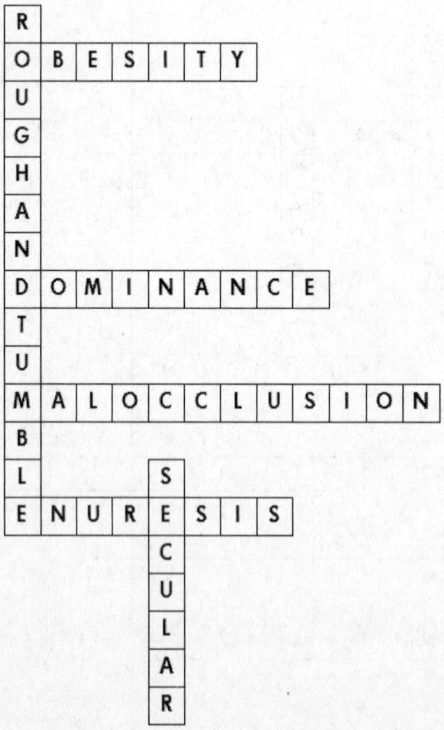

PUZZLE 12.1

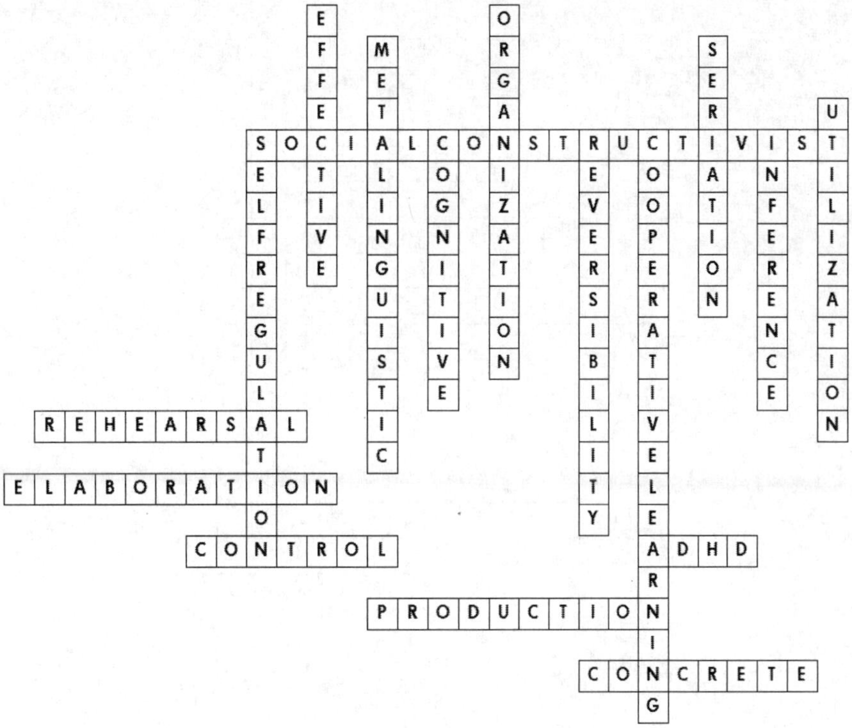

PUZZLE 12.2

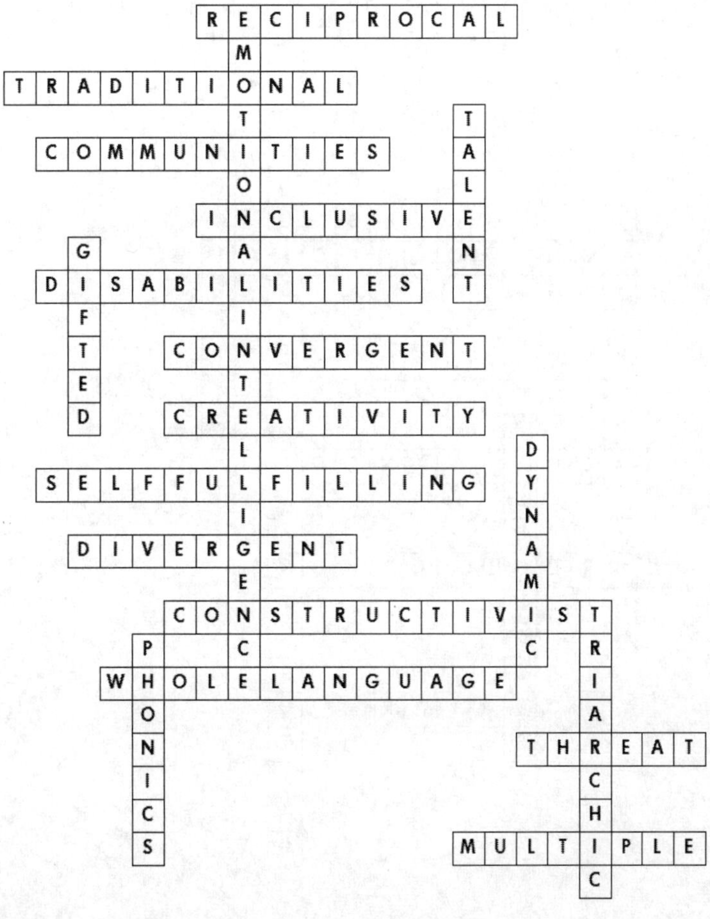

PUZZLE 13.1

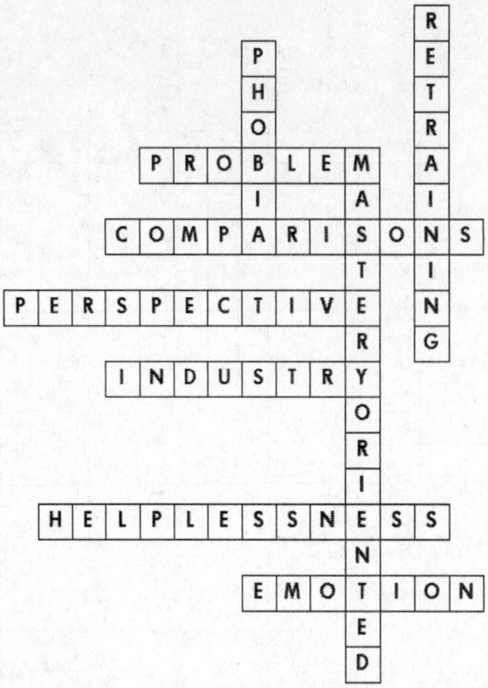

PUZZLE 13.2

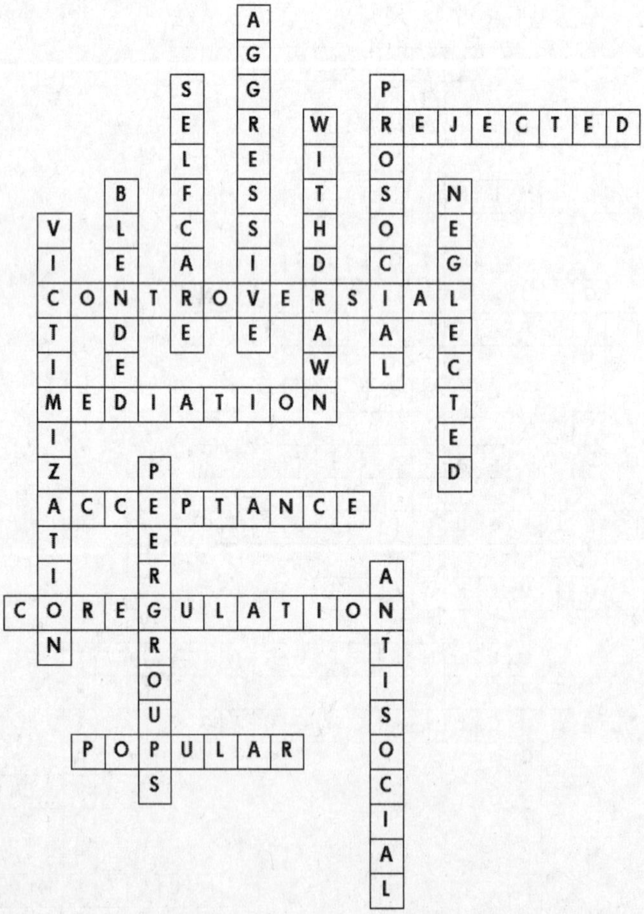

PUZZLE 14.1

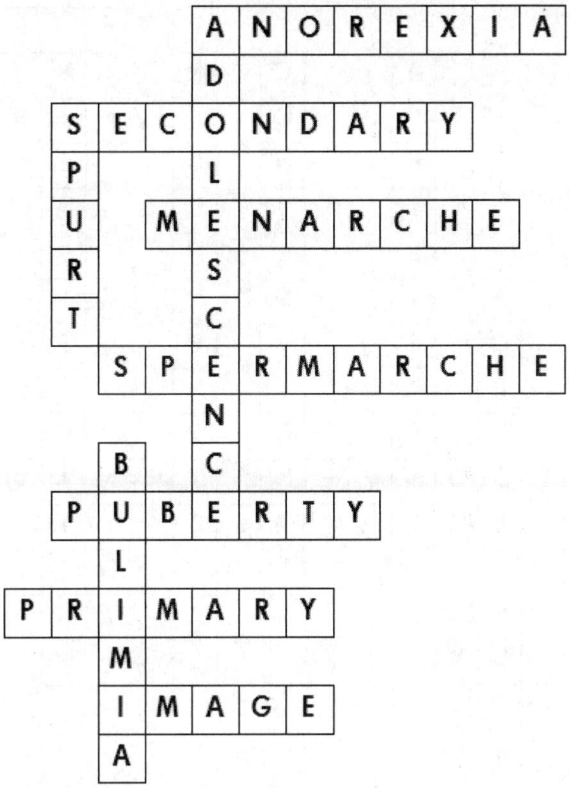

PUZZLE 15.1

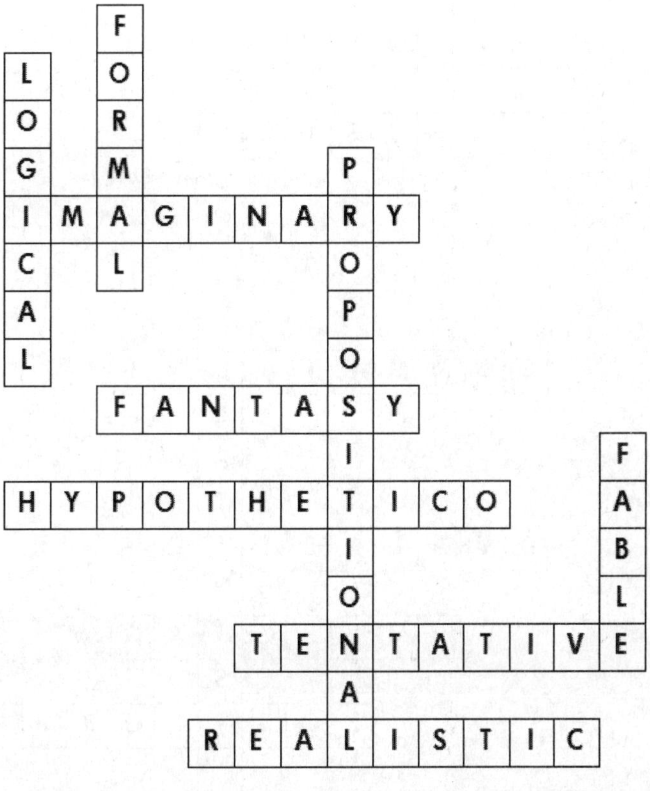

PUZZLE 16.1

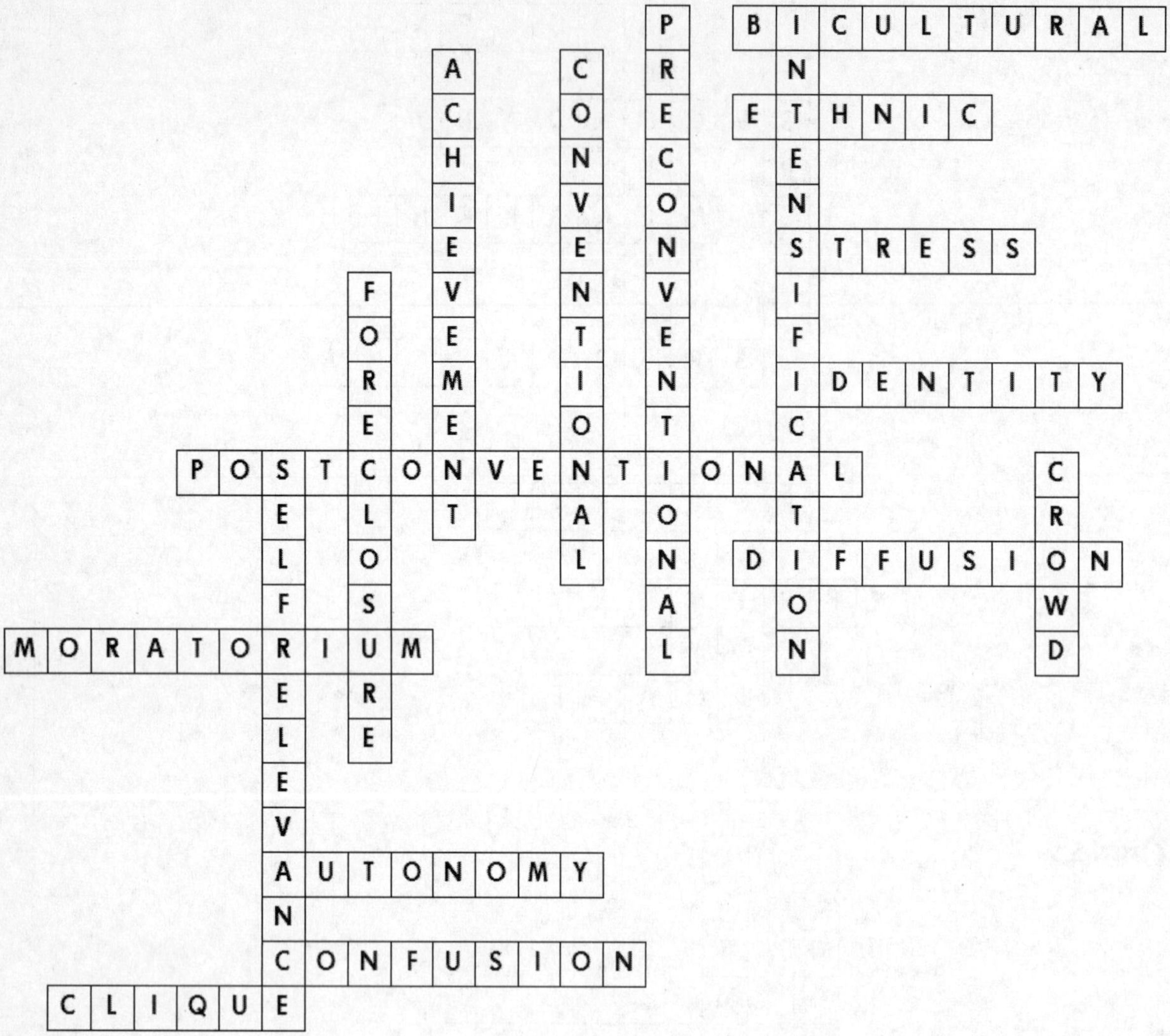

PUZZLE 17.1

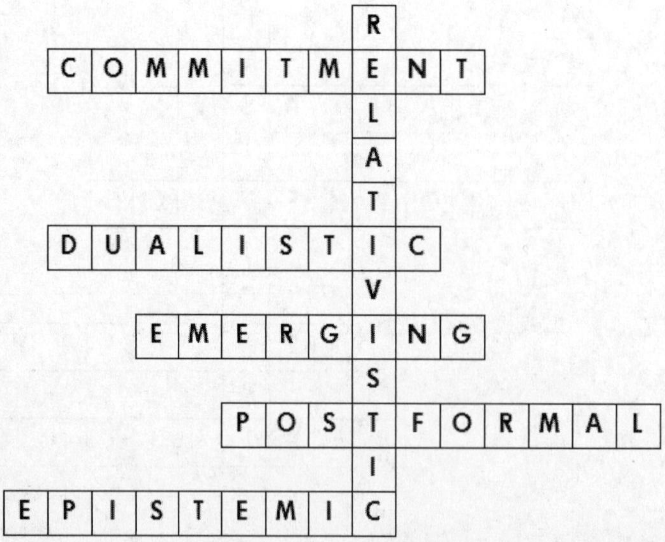

ANSWERS TO PRACTICE TESTS

CHAPTER 1

Practice Test #1

1. b	2. a	3. c	4. d	5. b
6. b	7. a	8. c	9. a	10. a
11. d	12. b	13. c	14. a	15. b
16. d	17. c	18. d	19. c	20. d
21. c	22. b	23. a	24. d	25. a
26. b	27. c	28. b	29. a	30. c

Practice Test #2

1. a	2. b	3. c	4. c	5. a
6. d	7. b	8. c	9. a	10. c
11. d	12. b	13. b	14. c	15. d
16. a	17. b	18. d	19. c	20. b
21. c	22. a	23. a	24. c	25. b
26. b	27. c	28. b	29. b	30. c

CHAPTER 2

Practice Test #1

1. a	2. b	3. c	4. b	5. b
6. b	7. b	8. c	9. a	10. c
11. d	12. a	13. d	14. c	15. b
16. c	17. d	18. c	19. a	20. d
21. b	22. a	23. a	24. d	25. b
26. c	27. a	28. a	29. d	30. a

Practice Test #2

1. c	2. b	3. a	4. d	5. c
6. a	7. a	8. c	9. b	10. d
11. a	12. b	13. a	14. b	15. d
16. b	17. c	18. a	19. b	20. d
21. a	22. b	23. c	24. d	25. b
26. a	27. c	28. c	29. b	30. b

CHAPTER 3

Practice Test #1

1. c	2. d	3. d	4. a	5. b
6. a	7. b	8. c	9. a	10. d
11. c	12. b	13. a	14. c	15. b
16. d	17. a	18. d	19. b	20. a
21. d	22. b	23. a	24. c	25. b
26. b	27. c	28. d	29. c	30. a

Practice Test #2

1. b	2. d	3. c	4. a	5. d
6. a	7. c	8. b	9. b	10. d
11. c	12. c	13. b	14. a	15. a
16. a	17. c	18. c	19. a	20. b
21. c	22. a	23. c	24. a	25. c
26. d	27. a	28. a	29. d	30. b

CHAPTER 4

Practice Test #1

1. a	2. c	3. b	4. a	5. d
6. c	7. b	8. c	9. d	10. a
11. c	12. a	13. c	14. b	15. c
16. c	17. c	18. b	19. b	20. c
21. d	22. a	23. b	24. c	25. b
26. d	27. a	28. c	29. a	30. b

Practice Test #2

1. d	2. a	3. b	4. c	5. d
6. d	7. a	8. c	9. d	10. b
11. c	12. d	13. a	14. a	15. c
16. c	17. c	18. b	19. c	20. b
21. c	22. a	23. c	24. d	25. b
26. c	27. b	28. b	29. b	30. c

CHAPTER 5

Practice Test #1

1. c	2. a	3. b	4. d	5. c
6. b	7. c	8. a	9. c	10. c
11. d	12. d	13. c	14. b	15. d
16. a	17. d	18. c	19. d	20. b
21. d	22. c	23. a	24. d	25. a
26. b	27. a	28. c	29. b	30. a

Practice Test #2

1. d	2. b	3. d	4. b	5. a
6. a	7. b	8. c	9. d	10. c
11. b	12. b	13. a	14. b	15. a
16. c	17. d	18. b	19. d	20. b
21. a	22. d	23. b	24. c	25. a
26. b	27. d	28. c	29. c	30. b

CHAPTER 6

Practice Test #1

1. b	2. b	3. c	4. b	5. b
6. c	7. b	8. a	9. b	10. a
11. b	12. d	13. a	14. c	15. c
16. a	17. c	18. a	19. b	20. d
21. b	22. b	23. b	24. c	25. d
26. b	27. b	28. b	29. a	30. a

Practice Test #2

1. c	2. b	3. d	4. d	5. c
6. a	7. a	8. d	9. a	10. d
11. d	12. a	13. c	14. a	15. d
16. c	17. c	18. a	19. b	20. c
21. d	22. c	23. c	24. b	25. b
26. c	27. a	28. a	29. a	30. c

CHAPTER 7

Practice Test #1

1. d	2. c	3. a	4. c	5. d
6. b	7. a	8. c	9. a	10. b
11. d	12. b	13. c	14. c	15. a
16. b	17. c	18. d	19. c	20. b
21. b	22. d	23. a	24. b	25. a
26. c	27. d	28. b	29. b	30. c

Practice Test #2

1. a	2. a	3. b	4. c	5. c
6. b	7. a	8. d	9. a	10. b
11. d	12. c	13. b	14. b	15. c
16. d	17. b	18. c	19. b	20. a
21. d	22. b	23. d	24. d	25. a
26. b	27. c	28. c	29. c	30. a

CHAPTER 8

Practice Test #1

1. b	2. b	3. c	4. a	5. d
6. c	7. d	8. c	9. a	10. b
11. d	12. c	13. c	14. a	15. a
16. b	17. c	18. a	19. b	20. d
21. a	22. c	23. b	24. d	25. d
26. d	27. b	28. a	29. c	30. b

Practice Test #2

1. b	2. a	3. c	4. d	5. b
6. a	7. d	8. c	9. a	10. d
11. b	12. a	13. c	14. d	15. b
16. d	17. b	18. d	19. a	20. b
21. d	22. b	23. d	24. a	25. b
26. d	27. c	28. d	29. c	30. d

CHAPTER 9

Practice Test #1

1. b	2. a	3. d	4. a	5. b
6. c	7. a	8. d	9. c	10. a
11. b	12. d	13. b	14. c	15. a
16. d	17. b	18. c	19. d	20. a
21. a	22. c	23. a	24. b	25. a
26. b	27. c	28. d	29. b	30. b

Practice Test #2

1. c	2. d	3. c	4. a	5. a
6. c	7. a	8. d	9. c	10. c
11. a	12. b	13. a	14. b	15. a
16. c	17. b	18. a	19. b	20. c
21. d	22. a	23. c	24. b	25. d
26. c	27. c	28. a	29. d	30. b

CHAPTER 10

Practice Test #1

1. b	2. a	3. b	4. a	5. c
6. d	7. b	8. c	9. d	10. b
11. c	12. a	13. d	14. c	15. c
16. a	17. d	18. b	19. c	20. b
21. c	22. d	23. c	24. b	25. a
26. b	27. d	28. c	29. a	30. b

Practice Test #2

1. c	2. a	3. d	4. a	5. c
6. b	7. d	8. a	9. c	10. c
11. d	12. b	13. a	14. d	15. b
16. a	17. c	18. b	19. b	20. c
21. b	22. a	23. a	24. c	25. b
26. d	27. c	28. d	29. b	30. d

CHAPTER 11

Practice Test #1

1. c	2. c	3. b	4. d	5. b
6. a	7. b	8. b	9. d	10. a
11. c	12. d	13. b	14. c	15. a
16. b	17. c	18. a	19. c	20. b
21. c	22. d	23. a	24. b	25. a
26. c	27. c	28. b	29. a	30. d

Practice Test #2

1. c	2. b	3. a	4. d	5. a
6. b	7. c	8. d	9. d	10. a
11. c	12. b	13. d	14. c	15. a
16. b	17. b	18. d	19. a	20. c
21. b	22. d	23. c	24. d	25. c
26. a	27. c	28. b	29. a	30. d

CHAPTER 12

Practice Test #1

1. c	2. b	3. d	4. a	5. c
6. a	7. c	8. a	9. b	10. a
11. d	12. c	13. a	14. b	15. c
16. d	17. c	18. a	19. b	20. c
21. a	22. b	23. a	24. c	25. b
26. d	27. c	28. c	29. a	30. d

Practice Test #2

1. a	2. c	3. d	4. b	5. a
6. b	7. d	8. c	9. d	10. b
11. a	12. c	13. d	14. a	15. b
16. b	17. a	18. c	19. d	20. b
21. a	22. d	23. b	24. a	25. c
26. b	27. c	28. c	29. a	30. b

CHAPTER 13

Practice Test #1

1. c	2. a	3. d	4. b	5. a
6. c	7. c	8. b	9. d	10. b
11. c	12. a	13. b	14. c	15. d
16. c	17. b	18. b	19. d	20. b
21. a	22. c	23. d	24. a	25. c
26. b	27. a	28. d	29. a	30. c

Practice Test #2

1. d	2. a	3. b	4. a	5. c
6. b	7. d	8. a	9. c	10. d
11. b	12. c	13. a	14. b	15. c
16. d	17. b	18. c	19. a	20. b
21. a	22. b	23. c	24. b	25. a
26. d	27. c	28. a	29. b	30. c

CHAPTER 14

Practice Test #1

1. b	2. c	3. c	4. a	5. a
6. d	7. b	8. d	9. a	10. b
11. c	12. a	13. d	14. b	15. c
16. a	17. c	18. b	19. d	20. d
21. a	22. b	23. c	24. a	25. b
26. d	27. d	28. a	29. c	30. b

Practice Test #2

1. d	2. d	3. b	4. b	5. a
6. c	7. a	8. c	9. b	10. d
11. a	12. c	13. c	14. b	15. c
16. a	17. a	18. a	19. b	20. d
21. b	22. c	23. c	24. a	25. a
26. b	27. d	28. c	29. b	30. d

CHAPTER 15

Practice Test #1

1. a	2. b	3. d	4. c	5. c
6. c	7. b	8. b	9. a	10. c
11. b	12. d	13. a	14. d	15. b
16. a	17. d	18. c	19. b	20. c
21. b	22. b	23. c	24. b	25. d
26. b	27. a	28. c	29. a	30. a

Practice Test #2

1. a	2. b	3. c	4. a	5. b
6. a	7. c	8. d	9. a	10. c
11. d	12. a	13. b	14. c	15. c
16. d	17. a	18. c	19. b	20. c
21. d	22. b	23. c	24. a	25. a
26. c	27. d	28. d	29. c	30. b

CHAPTER 16

Practice Test #1

1. d	2. a	3. b	4. b	5. d
6. a	7. c	8. a	9. b	10. c
11. d	12. a	13. b	14. b	15. d
16. b	17. c	18. a	19. b	20. d
21. b	22. a	23. c	24. a	25. a
26. c	27. d	28. d	29. a	30. c

Practice Test #2

1. c	2. b	3. c	4. a	5. d
6. c	7. a	8. a	9. c	10. b
11. b	12. d	13. a	14. b	15. a
16. b	17. c	18. c	19. c	20. a
21. d	22. b	23. c	24. b	25. d
26. c	27. a	28. b	29. c	30. c

CHAPTER 17

Practice Test #1

1. c	2. a	3. b	4. d	5. a
6. d	7. c	8. b	9. d	10. c
11. a	12. d	13. b	14. a	15. b
16. c	17. b	18. a	19. d	20. b
21. c	22. d	23. a	24. b	25. c
26. d	27. a	28. b	29. d	30. c

Practice Test #2

1. b	2. c	3. d	4. a	5. c
6. b	7. d	8. b	9. a	10. b
11. a	12. c	13. a	14. b	15. c
16. c	17. b	18. d	19. a	20. b
21. b	22. a	23. c	24. a	25. d
26. c	27. b	28. a	29. c	30. b

NOTES

NOTES

NOTES

NOTES

NOTES

NOTES

NOTES

NOTES